Shackleton's Dream

PRAISE FOR *SHACKLETON'S DREAM*

'Extraordinary. A story that will prove to anyone who doubts it, that courage, determination, danger and disaster remain as much a part of Antarctic exploration in the Modern Age as in the Heroic Era.'

SIR RANULPH FIENNES

'Thoroughly researched and engagingly written, *Shackleton's Dream* tells the in-depth story of the first crossing of the Antarctic continent, an expedition with more than its fair share of adventure, rivalry, ego, and controversy. Following in the footsteps of his biographies of Frank Bickerton and J.R. Stenhouse, this book further establishes Stephen Haddelsey as a key historian of Antarctic exploration.'

BEAU RIFFENBURGH, AUTHOR OF *NIMROD* AND *RACING WITH DEATH*

'The story of the most daring British polar expedition since Shackleton's and an important link between the heroic and modern eras of Antarctic exploration.'

NICHOLAS OWENS, DIRECTOR OF THE BRITISH ANTARCTIC SURVEY

'A superbly readable and well researched book on the trials and tribulations of the first successful crossing of Antarctica.'

KEN BLAIKLOCK, SURVEYOR AND DOG HANDLER ON THE COMMONWEALTH TRANS-ANTARCTIC EXPEDITION

'The first crossing of the Antarctic continent remains a benchmark in the exploration of our planet. Haddelsey's book provides an important insight into the achievements of Fuchs, Hillary and their companions.'

JULIAN DOWDESWELL, DIRECTOR OF THE SCOTT POLAR RESEARCH INSTITUTE

Shackleton's Dream

Fuchs, Hillary and the
Crossing of Antarctica

Stephen Haddelsey

For my son George Fitzwilliam Haddelsey as he
embarks upon the greatest adventure of them all.

Every reasonable effort has been made to trace copyright holders and to
obtain their permission for the use of copyrighted material. Any valid issues
that may arise will be corrected in subsequent editions.

First published 2012
This paperback edition first published 2022

The History Press
97 St George's Place, Cheltenham,
Gloucestershire, GL50 3QB
www.thehistorypress.co.uk

British Library Cataloguing in Publication Data.
A catalogue record for this book is available from the British Library.

ISBN 978 1 80399 166 5

Typesetting and origination by The History Press
Printed and bound in Great Britain by TJ Books Limited, Padstow, Cornwall.

MIX
Paper | Supporting
responsible forestry
FSC
www.fsc.org   FSC® C013056

Trees for LYfe

'A pity we contribute yet another soiled page to the already extensive book of polar intrigue.'

Hal Lister, glaciologist on the Commonweath Trans-Antarctic Expedition

'... to think only in terms of miles travelled is to include but a small part of the polar heritage that is ours.'

E. W. Kevin Walton, Two Years in the Antarctic

'A journey is like the life of a man. The labours of its birth are heavy, its youth is full of ideals and hopes, its main course leads swiftly to harsh reality and its end, whether of failure or success, is bitter.'

August Courtauld, Surveyor on Gino Watkins's British Arctic Air Route Expedition, 1930–31

Contents

Acknowledgements

I would like to express my admiration for all of the surviving veterans of the British Commonwealth Trans-Antarctic Expedition (TAE) and, in particular, I should like to thank Ken Blaiklock, Richard Brooke, John Claydon, Rainer Goldsmith, Roy Homard and the late Jon Stephenson, without whose support and encouragement this book could not have been written. In addition, I should like to acknowledge the immense patience of Ken Blaiklock who has not only answered a constant flow of questions on all aspects of the expedition but has also very kindly read the entire manuscript to ensure its historical accuracy. It has been a novel and rewarding experience to have my account of an Antarctic expedition commented upon by one of the leading participants. Despite their immense achievements, very few of the veterans have chosen to formally record their experiences. Regrettable though this decision will undoubtedly appear to future generations, it is typical of their modesty and inclination to self-effacement. If it achieves nothing else, therefore, I hope that this book will serve to preserve some of their memories and views regarding the remarkable exploits in which they played such a leading part. I would also like to thank Derek Williams, the BP cameraman who accompanied the Advance Party on the *Theron*, for his highly evocative descriptions of his journey to the Antarctic.

Although the events of the TAE took place in relatively recent times, the task of piecing together its full story has been rendered unusually difficult by the fact that very few contemporary documents, especially diaries and letters, have so far found their way into accessible public collections. I am therefore also enormously grateful to a host of individuals, usually the widows or descendants of the explorers, who have been immensely generous in permitting me to use documents in their possession and in assisting me to trace other previously unknown sources. In particular, I would like to thank: Peter and Ann Fuchs, for their hospitality and for granting me complete access to the papers and diaries of Sir Vivian Fuchs; Peter and Sarah Hillary for permitting use of the diary of Sir Edmund Hillary; Mary Lowe and Margaret Lister for allowing me to read and quote from the diaries of their husbands, George Lowe and Hal Lister; Jan Fullarton and Roger Miller, for granting me access to the diary of their father, Sir Holmes, or 'Bob', Miller; Lionel Stephens, Lindsey Hinks and David Stewart, for their help in piecing together the story of Tony Stewart; Paul and Colin Rogers for the TAE anecdotes of their father, Dr Allan Rogers; Sheila and Stephen Marsh for permitting use of the papers of Dr George Marsh and Rosemary Breen for facilitating access to those papers; John Cooper and Sydney Cullis for their assistance in tracing the TAE publications of Hannes La Grange; Derek Gunn for permitting me to quote from the memoir of his father, Bernie Gunn; and Eliane George for sharing her memories of working in the TAE office at 64, Victoria Street.

I would also like to express my appreciation to Anthea Arnold whose account of the TAE's Advance Party, *Eight Men in a Crate*, first inspired me to research the expedition; to Joanna Rae of the British Antarctic Survey for her assistance in tracing the TAE papers contained within the BAS archives; and to Andy Stevenson for producing such dynamic maps for the book. This list is not, indeed cannot, be comprehensive and I hope that those who have not been named individually will not think that their help is any the less appreciated. Every effort has been made to obtain the relevant permissions and I should like to crave the indulgence of any literary executors or copyright holders where these efforts have been unavailing. All photographs are reproduced by the kind permission of the explorers and their families, with particular thanks due to Peter Fuchs, George and Mary Lowe, David Stewart and Stephen and Sheila Marsh.

Above all, I should like to express my gratitude to my wife, Caroline, whose love and support have, as always, been unfailing, and to my son, George, for not hammering too loudly on my library door.

It should be noted that many of the diaries and letters quoted in this book were written in circumstances of extreme stress and hurry; inevitably, this resulted in an array of spelling mistakes and grammatical errors. For purposes of clarity and ease of reading, spelling has been corrected; punctuation has also been adjusted where absolutely necessary. Any words inserted by the author for clarity of meaning are identified by the addition of square brackets. All temperatures are given in degrees Fahrenheit and other measures in imperial as these were the most commonly used during the expedition.

Stephen Haddelsey
Halam, Nottinghamshire

Fahrenheit/Celsius conversion

-75	-59.4
-60	-51.1
-50	-45.5
-40	-40
-30	-34.4
-20	-28.8
-10	-23
0	-17.8
10	-12.2
20	-6.7
32	0
40	4.4
50	10
60	15.6
70	21.1

1

The Last Great Polar Journey

Somewhere on the floor of the Weddell Sea, at a point approximately 69° South, lies the twisted wreckage of the steam yacht *Endurance* – one of the most famous and yet also one of the most short-lived of all polar exploration vessels. On 21 November 1915, after a drift of more than 1000 miles among the grinding floes, Sir Ernest Shackleton and his party of 27 survivors had watched from the ice as the pack squeezed the life from their hapless vessel before finally letting her slip silently down to her last resting place. Caught in the chaos of splintered wood, buckled metalwork and tangled rigging lay Shackleton's dream of being the first man to complete the crossing of Antarctica: an exploit which he had described in his expedition prospectus as 'the last great polar journey that can be made.'

The events following the loss of the *Endurance* have made Shackleton's name a byword both for high adventure and for heroic failure – after all, his plan for a trans-continental journey ended even before he or any of his men had so much as set foot on the shelf ice of Antarctica. With his crew marooned on the disintegrating floes hundreds of miles from the nearest inhabited island and with only his ship's boats to rely upon, the rest of the grandly named Imperial Trans-Antarctic Expedition became, quite simply, a struggle for survival against seemingly overwhelming odds, with any thought of geographic exploration or scientific discovery long since abandoned. In real terms, therefore, for all his brilliance as a leader and as a polar explorer, Shackleton's only contribution to the idea of a continental crossing was to imbue it with an even greater weight of romance and expectation.

If events had turned out differently and the *Endurance* had survived to disgorge men, supplies and equipment at Vahsel Bay on the southern edge of the Weddell Sea, the odds stacked against Shackleton and the rest of his six-man crossing party would have been colossal. The continental crossing would involve a journey of roughly 2000 miles across the most demanding landscape on the face of the planet. Mean temperatures range between −40°F and −94°F during the long Antarctic winter while bitingly cold winds not only reduce visibility by hurling clouds of drift snow into the air but also, through the phenomenon known as 'wind chill', push the temperatures lower still, so that exposed flesh will freeze almost immediately and even teeth will split. On clear days, the power of the sun, combined with the thinness of the ozone layer and the reflective glare of the ice, will cause skin to burn and peel. On cloudy days, even in the middle of the summer, visibility can be reduced to nil or else massively distorted; in these conditions of 'whiteout', all contrast is lost and objects lying only a foot away can appear to be far distant, and vice versa.

Despite the presence of spectacular mountain ranges that soar to around 16,000 feet, only 2 per cent of Antarctica's landmass is free of ice and snow, while the rarefied atmosphere of the central Polar Plateau, rising to some 14,000 feet above sea level, inhibits the performance of men, dogs, motor vehicles and aircraft. Over large tracts, the wind has sculpted the surface ice into 'sastrugi', wave-like crests which can be up to 4 or 5 feet tall and as hard as iron. In other areas, less subject to the scouring action of the wind, soft snow collects in layers so deep that a man will sink to his thighs, making every step a struggle. Vast ice sheets flow down from the plateau buckling and splitting as they collide with rocky protuberances or with each other, to form deep crevasses capable of swallowing whole a man, a dog team, or an entire motor vehicle. Even worse, these fissures are often concealed by lids or bridges formed by the gradual accumulation of drift snow.

Sometimes these bridges will support a considerable weight and allow relatively easy passage; sometimes they will collapse at the very slightest pressure. But these were just the obstacles that Shackleton knew to exist on the side of the continent that he, Amundsen and Scott had done so much to explore. So far as the other side was concerned, he, along with everybody else, was almost totally ignorant.

A glance at the map of Antarctica will reveal, even to the least accomplished geographer, that the shortest crossing point lies between two deep indentations in the continent's coastline. These indentations are formed by opposing seas: the Weddell Sea, lying directly beneath the island of South Georgia and first navigated by the eponymous English sea captain, James Weddell, in 1823; and the Ross Sea, to the south of New Zealand, named after Captain James Clark Ross, who discovered it, as well as Ross Island, the volcanoes Erebus and Terror and the Great Barrier (later renamed the Ross Ice Shelf) during a remarkable voyage in 1841.

The two seas are very different in character. In the period following the discoveries of Weddell and Ross, a number of expeditions proved that, of the two, the Ross Sea is far easier to enter – though pack ice and icebergs remain an ever-present danger threatening the unwary. The Weddell Sea, on the other hand, has earned a fearsome reputation for trapping and destroying the vessels of even seasoned mariners. As a result, all assaults on the South Pole – the objective closest to most polar explorers' hearts in the early years of the twentieth century – had been launched from the Ross Sea, with the majority of expeditions over-wintering in huts erected on, or in ships tethered to, its shores. And the identification of the glacial highways up to the Polar Plateau, most notably the Beardmore Glacier discovered by Shackleton during his *Nimrod* Expedition of 1907–09, only served to reinforce this trend.

In contrast with the Ross Sea's well-mapped coastal hinterland, by 1914 that of the Weddell Sea remained largely unknown and only one expedition, led by the Swede Otto Nordenskjöld between 1902 and 1904, had over-wintered anywhere on its shores. Undertaking mostly geological investigations, Nordenskjöld's party had spent two winters on Snow Hill Island off the north-eastern side of the great Antarctic Peninsula, which juts out from the Weddell Sea's western flank. Despite the loss of its expedition ship, the *Antarctic* – destroyed by pack-ice 25 miles to the north of Paulet Island in February 1903 – the Swedish expedition achieved a great deal, proving in particular that Antarctica was essentially similar in geological makeup to the planet's more temperate continents. But the Swedes had managed to make only limited sledging journeys, the most extensive being made in October 1902, when Nordenskjöld and two companions covered 380 miles in 33 days, and their discoveries would be of limited value to anyone hoping to thrust deep into the continent's interior.

While Nordenskjöld focused his attention on the western edge of the Weddell Sea, during the summer season of 1903–04 William Bruce's Scottish National Antarctic Expedition explored its eastern limits. During this voyage the underrated Bruce made two important geographical discoveries. The first was a wall of giant ice cliffs on the sea's eastern flank. Having correctly surmised that these cliffs were an extension of Enderby Land, more than 1000 miles to the east, Bruce named his discovery Coats Land, after the Coats brothers of Paisley, who had in large part funded his expedition. His second discovery, which would prove vital for all future exploration of the Weddell Sea, was that, during the summer months, a coastal lead, or channel, opens down the sea's eastern edge in the shadow of the ice cliffs. Although, in February 1823, James Weddell had followed a much more westerly course and had reached 74°15'S with remarkably little difficulty, future navigators would discover Weddell's easy passage to be so unusual as to be practically unique. No route into the pack ice of the Weddell Sea could ever be considered safe – as Bruce himself discovered when his ship, the *Scotia*, became temporarily beset at 74°01'S – but the eastern lead, which is formed by the action of the wind plunging down from the cliffs above, is at least more reliable than any of the alternatives.

The southern reaches of the Weddell Sea were left to the German, Wilhelm Filchner, to explore during his *Deutschland* Expedition of 1911–12. Setting out from South Georgia in November 1911, Filchner hoped to benefit from Bruce's earlier discoveries by sailing down the edge of Coats Land. However, his ship quickly ran into dense pack ice and he was forced further west than originally planned, eventually following a course lying between those pursued by Weddell in 1823 and Bruce in 1904. Filchner first spotted land at the end of January 1912. This completely unknown coastal region, an extension of Coats Land, he named Prince Regent Luitpold Land (now the Luitpold Coast). Continuing south through the pack, the *Deutschland* eventually entered an ice-rimmed bay at the foot of an enormous floating ice shelf, later named in Filchner's honour by Kaiser Wilhelm II, while the bay itself was called Vahsel Bay, after the captain of the *Deutschland*.

Believing it to be securely cemented to the face of the ice shelf, Filchner decided to erect his winter quarters on a large tabular iceberg and construction work began on 9 February. Unfortunately, his confidence in the stability of the optimistically named Station Iceberg proved to be ill founded and in the early hours of 18 February the Germans' campsite echoed to a series of loud reports, which quickly grew in frequency and volume. Under the influence of the spring tide and a sudden drop in barometric pressure, the ice had begun to split in all directions with large areas of the ice shelf, some up to 18 miles in length, breaking off completely. In no time at all the Station berg itself was rotating freely, with the expedition hut, eight Manchurian ponies, the dog teams and all the expedition's equipment – not to mention many of the explorers themselves – turning with it. Realising that their position had become untenable, Filchner gave the order to abandon the berg – but not before the hut had been dismantled and carried back to the *Deutschland* along with the majority of the expedition's stores.

Enjoying a reputation for quite literally laughing in the face of danger, the burly Filchner was undeterred by this near-catastrophe. The ice conditions made another landing impracticable but with most of his stores and equipment salvaged, he decided to retreat to South Georgia for the winter before returning the following spring to continue with his planned programme of work. But it was not to be: by early March his ship was completely beset and for nine months she remained locked in the pack, unable to steer or free herself – a fate that would be shared by the *Endurance* just three years later. Unlike the *Endurance*, however, the *Deutschland* survived her months of helpless drifting and when the floes eventually began to break up she was able to limp back to South Georgia, which she reached on 19 December. Once again, the risks of navigation in the Weddell Sea had been amply demonstrated.

Given that the Weddell Sea was known to be so dangerous and that the 1000-mile wide expanse between Vahsel Bay and the South Pole remained, to all intents and purposes, *terra incognita*, why would any expedition intent upon prosecuting a cross-ing of the continent start from there instead of from the much better known Ross Sea? The answer, of course, lies in the fact that the Weddell Sea *was* known to be so difficult. Were a cross-ing party to start from the Ross Sea, it might find neither depots nor ship on the far side of the continent, because the pack ice of the Weddell Sea had either denied access to the rescue ship or, worse still, trapped or crushed it. With no means of evacuation and depleted rations and fuel, a successful crossing party would be doomed. Travelling in the opposite direction, even if their ship were delayed by unusually difficult ice conditions in the Ross Sea – as Scott's *Terra Nova* had been in December 1910 – a party could survive on the stores known to be cached on Ross Island by previous expeditions.

The nature of the terrain, where known, also needed to be considered – particularly when expedition plans included the use of motor vehicles. Any party travelling between the Pole and the Ross Sea must traverse the vast ring of the Trans-Antarctic Mountains. Rising to more than 14,000 feet, these mountains might prove to be an insurmountable obstacle to motor vehicles and it would be better to attempt their crossing as late as pos-sible in the journey, as precedent had shown that, in the event of vehicle failure, sledging parties could reach the coast from the mountains with dog teams or, if necessary, by man-hauling. Of course, this theory made no allowance for impassable mountain ranges on the Weddell Sea side of the continent, but the explorers had little option but to plan for the obstacles that they knew to exist.

Finally, the experiences of the pioneers, who had fought against the katabatic winds which sweep down the glaciers from the high Polar Plateau, had led some to believe, mistakenly, that the prevailing wind blew across the continent, from the Weddell Sea to the Ross Sea. If this were really the case, then it would be far less gruelling to travel with the wind rather than against it.

Although there is some evidence that Shackleton may have given at least passing consideration to a continental crossing as early as 1907, long before *Nimrod* reached McMurdo Sound at the beginning of his own attempt on the Pole,[1] he was not the first explorer to draw up and publish detailed plans for such an expedition. The primary objective of Filchner's 1911 expedition had been to attempt a crossing, with the specific aim of determining whether Antarctica was a continent or a great archipelago, with a frozen strait linking the opposing seas.

Filchner had first announced his plans in 1909. On 17 March of the following year, William Bruce placed his own proposals for a crossing before the Royal Scottish Geographical Society. According to his scheme, a party would be established in Coats Land, where it would be left to over-winter. In the meantime, the expedition ship would land a second party on the opposite side of the continent. During the second season, the Coats Land party would launch its attempt to cross the continent on foot. The Ross Sea party, meanwhile, would also push inland with the intention of meeting the crossing party and helping it to complete its journey.

Of course, none of these plans ever reached fruition. Filchner's expedition, like Shackleton's, foundered in the Weddell Sea. As for Bruce, his own prickly nature, coupled with the machinations of Sir Clements Markham – the erstwhile president of the Royal Geographical Society (RGS), who never forgave Bruce for

competing with his own beloved *Discovery* Expedition – meant
that he was never able to raise sufficient funds and his project
was stillborn. He did, however, exercise some influence over
future events by lending generous support to Shackleton. Despite
his urgent desire to do so, the embittered Bruce never returned
to the Antarctic after 1904. Filchner also turned away from the
frozen south, though with less reluctance. Originally famous for
his travels in Central Asia, after 1912 he confined his activities
to Nepal and Tibet. As for Shackleton, drained by the terrible
months on the ice; by the epic open-boat journeys to Elephant
Island and on to South Georgia; and by his battles with the establishment to secure the rescue of his men from Elephant Island
and McMurdo Sound, he did not live to make a second attempt
at the crossing.

Despite this sorry catalogue of aborted schemes and near-
fatal expeditions, the dream of an Antarctic crossing lived on and
explorers from later generations soon stepped forward hoping to
make it a reality. The first fresh aspirant was Gino Watkins, the
wunderkind of British Arctic exploration in the early thirties.
Following successful small-scale expeditions to Edge Island and
Labrador, in 1930 the 23-year-old Watkins led the British Arctic
Air Route Expedition to East Greenland, with the objective of
taking detailed weather observations to support a proposed air
route from England to North America. As well as collecting a
mass of meteorological and geological data, the expedition discovered the important Skaergaard intrusion, manned the first
all-winter meteorological station on the Greenland ice cap and
completed a daring 600-mile open boat journey around the
south of the island. Acclaimed a spectacular success, the expedition brought Watkins both international fame and the Founders'
Medal of the Royal Geographical Society – making him its
youngest-ever recipient.

Given this meteoric rise, it was not very surprising that influential figures in the RGS should seek to steer Watkins south. With
the exception of Shackleton's rather chaotic *Quest* Expedition
of 1921–22, no major British Antarctic expedition had been
launched since 1914 and many believed that, unless bolstered,

British influence in the sphere would rapidly decline. In contrast, American interest was clearly on the rise: Admiral Richard Byrd's Little America Expedition of 1928–30 had already made the first flight over the South Pole and Byrd and Lincoln Ellsworth were both rumoured to be planning further sorties. In this context, the handsome and charming but also surprisingly tough and experienced Watkins appeared to be the obvious successor to Scott and Shackleton.

Watkins was altogether less convinced. Having fallen deeply in love with Greenland, at first he pooh-poohed the idea of abandoning its people, its rich wildlife and its hunting in favour of the comparatively barren southern continent. The Antarctic, he said, did not appeal to him at all: 'there were no natives, and hunting was just a case of knocking fat and fearless animals on the head. The place was all ice, five million square miles of it, very cold and deadly dull.'[2] Despite these reservations, however, it did not take him long to realise that, although Amundsen had already claimed the Pole, the south still offered prizes greater than those to be found in Greenland. In particular, the question of whether the Antarctic constituted a single landmass or a series of two or more islands remained unanswered – and must remain so until someone crossed the continent. With the enthusiastic encouragement of Antarctic worthies like Hugh Robert Mill, the friend and biographer of Shackleton, James Wordie of the *Endurance* Expedition, and Frank Debenham, a veteran of the *Terra Nova* Expedition and now Director of the Scott Polar Research Institute (SPRI), after a tentative start Watkins's plans evolved swiftly. Debenham gave an outline of the proposed expedition at the Antarctic Club's annual dinner on 9 January 1932 and wider publication of the expedition's prospectus followed just days later.

From the outset, Watkins made no bones about the fact that he considered the crossing to be 'unfinished business' for the Empire and that he was deliberately stepping forward to assume the mantle of Shackleton. The primary objective of his expedition, he announced, was 'To cross the Antarctic from the Weddell Sea to the Ross Sea, thus carrying out Shackleton's plan for his 1914 Expedition "to secure for the British flag the honour of being

the first carried across the South Polar Continent".'[3] His expedition would land in the vicinity of Vahsel Bay in January 1933
and immediately commence laying depots 300 miles southwards.
The main journey would begin towards the end of October and
would last four and a half months at the most, with the crossing
party being picked up from the Ross Sea side of the continent no
later than the middle of March 1934. Eight men would make the
journey, including fellow Air Route Expedition veterans Freddie
Spencer Chapman, Quintin Riley and John Rymill, with eight
sledges and 120 dogs. This would be the first British Antarctic
expedition to rely so heavily upon dogs – but it would also be the
first with real knowledge of the capabilities and the limitations
of dog teams, as Watkins and his colleagues possessed considerable experience of dog-driving, having learned directly from
the Eskimos themselves. It would also be the first crossing plan
to include air support, with aeroplanes being used to undertake
reconnaissance for the depot-laying parties and to chart the unexplored Weddell Sea coast between Vahsel Bay and Graham Land.

Having announced his intentions, Watkins now faced the
unenviable task of raising the necessary funds and he soon found
himself in direct conflict with what Freddie Spencer Chapman
described as 'a cynical, damping world, peopled mainly with
business men, whose outlook was entirely different from our
own.'[4] Of course, the outlook Chapman so deplored had been
shaped by the impacts of the Wall Street Crash of September 1929
and Watkins's guileless enthusiasm and his tales of the great white
wastes to be conquered did little to impress Britain's bruised
financiers. While his ambitions might provide them with a happy
respite from more pressing worries, none had money to spare for
such romantic and essentially profitless pursuits.

By the middle of May 1932 the situation looked desperate and,
in a last ditch attempt to shame his countrymen into parting with
their cash, on the 16th Frank Debenham wrote an impassioned
letter to *The Times*. 'In another week or so', he asserted, 'it will be
too late to secure a ship for the expedition, and their plans will
have to be given up, their personnel dispersed, and the chance
lost forever ... It seems a thousand pities that for lack of a timely

£10,000 their [Scott's and Shackleton's] successors should be forced to give up their brave project, to abandon their hope of following in the footsteps of Scott and Wilson, "to strive, to seek, to find, and not to yield".'[5]

Debenham's letter brought in a few cheques but nothing substantial and on 20 June the same newspaper published another letter on the subject, this time from Watkins himself. 'May I claim a small space in your columns', he asked the editor, 'in which to announce with regret that my plans to cross the Antarctic this year have had to be abandoned for lack of financial support. A recent letter in *The Times* on the subject brought a great deal of moral encouragement and many good wishes, but it is clear that the financial crisis has prevented the more material assistance without which such an expedition cannot proceed.'[6] On the same day, at the annual general meeting of the RGS, Admiral Sir William Goodenough, the Society's president, told Watkins that he hoped 'that in the future you will be enabled to carry out that great project in the Antarctic which I know fills your mind.'[7] But it was not to be. By the middle of the following month Watkins was back in his beloved Arctic seeking to build upon his earlier air route surveys and by 20 August he was dead, drowned while seal hunting alone in Lake Fjord. He was 25.

Watkins's brief glance southwards did produce some results. The evening before his untimely death, he was still discussing with his companions the future potential for an Antarctic crossing and on their return from Greenland, Rymill and Riley joined other veterans of the original Air Route Expedition to launch the British Graham Land Expedition (BGLE) of 1934–37. Under Rymill's leadership, this expedition, which proved to be the last pre-war British expedition to Antarctica, was highly successful in its geographic and scientific investigations. In particular, using dog teams and a De Havilland Fox Moth aeroplane, it mapped most of the coast of Southern Graham Land and proved decisively that it was a peninsula and not an archipelago divided by one or more channels. In most people's eyes, this expedition formed the bridge between the Heroic Era and the modern age of properly equipped and funded expeditions – it did not, however, seek to push south from the Antarctic Peninsula. The BGLE was also significant because, sailing before the mast of its expedition ship, the *Penola*, was a 21-year-old volunteer who would eventually become one of the final contenders for the prize of completing the first Antarctic crossing; though it would be another two decades before Duncan Carse staked his claim.

During the war years, Britain limited its activities in the Antarctic to the establishment of three manned bases: on Deception Island in the South Shetland Islands and at Port Lockroy and Hope Bay on the Graham Land Peninsula. This Royal Navy-led exercise, known as Operation *Tabarin*, had two objectives: to deny these shelters to German U-boats and surface raiders and to reassert British territorial claims in response to incursions by pro-German Argentina and Chile. Although scientific and geographic investigations formed no part of the function of these bases, when they were ceded to the newly established Falkland Islands Dependencies Survey (FIDS) after the war they – and similar bases later established at Signy Island, Admiralty Bay, the Argentine Islands and Stonington Island – became the hub of further British exploration on and around the Antarctic Peninsula. Just as importantly, they became the training ground for a new generation of British Antarctic explorers and scientists.

Typical of this new breed of British polar explorers was Vivian Ernest Fuchs – or 'Bunny', as he had been known since his prep school days. Born at Freshwater on the Isle of Wight in 1908, to a German father and an English mother, Fuchs had been educated at Brighton College and at St John's College, Cambridge, where he read geology, zoology and botany. Handsome and athletic, with a shock of dark hair swept back from his forehead and a penchant for illicitly climbing the college roofs, at Cambridge Fuchs was a close contemporary of Gino Watkins, Peter Scott, son of Britain's foremost Antarctic hero, and of Launcelot Fleming, who would later serve on the BGLE. Most important of all, it was at Cambridge that Fuchs, like Watkins before him, fell under the spell of James Wordie, who would do more then any other to shape his future career as an explorer.

In 1926 Wordie, whom Fuchs described as 'a man of great reserve and few words, but with an unexpectedly pawky sense of humour',[8] had led a party of undergraduates on the Cambridge University East Greenland Expedition. He had planned a follow-up expedition in 1927, for which he recruited Watkins, but had been forced to postpone the trip until 1929, by which time Watkins had launched his own expedition to Labrador. Looking for replacements, at the end of the summer term Wordie asked Fuchs to join the party and the young geologist accepted with alacrity.

As well as making the first ascent of the 9623-foot Petermann Bjerg, then thought to be the highest peak in the Arctic, and completing a detailed programme of geological investigation, Wordie's 1929 expedition was important for giving the 21-year-old Fuchs his first taste of travel in the polar regions. Between 2 July and the beginning of September, he encountered pack ice, crevasses, glaciers and polar bears for the first time – and he relished every minute. 'I keep on feeling how impossible it is to realise my luck in being here to revel in and marvel at all these things', he enthused in his diary. '... I wish I had thought of wintering.'[9]

Although the expedition had been 'a memorable baptism of ice',[10] which gave Fuchs an abiding passion for travel in high latitudes, he spent most of the next two decades in rather warmer climes. In 1930 the Cambridge zoologist, Barton Worthington, launched a university expedition to East Africa, his primary objective being to study the biology of Lakes Baringo and Rudolf in the Eastern Rift and Lakes Edward and George in the Western Rift. But Worthington also wanted to study the geological history of the lakes and for this he needed a specialist. 'To my amazed delight,' recorded a grateful Fuchs, 'Wordie suggested my name.'[11]

Fuchs quickly proved as susceptible to the sights, sounds and atmosphere of Africa as he had been to those of Greenland. 'These early African years were to prove a revelation,' he later wrote. 'This great black brooding continent caught my imagination and interest as completely as the Arctic pack ice had done,'[12] and he spent most of the next nine years baking in temperatures which often topped 100°F, surrounded by dusty bush and acacia thorn trees, breathing the exotic scents of the tropics and listening to the trilling of cicadas and the calls of the larger beasts. Worthington's 1930–31 expedition was followed immediately by Louis Leakey's 1931 East African Archaeological Expedition and in 1934 by an expedition, which Fuchs led himself, to the Lake Rudolf Rift Valley, where he undertook surveys and geological investigations over an area of some 40,000 square miles. The material gathered during these expeditions enabled Fuchs to complete his doctoral thesis before launching his final African expedition to Lake Rukwa in Tanganyika (now Tanzania), where his small team worked from 1937 to 1938 on geology, surveying and palaeontology.

The years 1929–1938 were invaluable to Fuchs, honing his skills both as a field scientist and as an expedition leader as well as bringing him to the attention of influential figures in the world of exploration who would help to open further opportunities in future years. No less significant, though he probably didn't realise it at the time, was the experience he gained of travelling over long distances in extremely remote and sparsely inhabited regions of challenging terrain. 'Roads were either non-existent or indescribably bad,' he recalled, 'and all our work was done against a background of incessant punctures and a constant struggle to get our vehicles to the points we wished to investigate.'[13] With the exception of the punctures, he might easily have been describing his future travels in Antarctica.

In 1939, Fuchs was commissioned into the Cambridgeshire Regiment and, with a wide knowledge of the people, customs, languages and geography of East Africa it was almost inevitable that he should be posted to *West* Africa, about which he knew practically nothing. He spent 18 months in the West African Command Headquarters at Accra on the Gold Coast, kicking his heels and breeding chameleons for amusement, before returning to England in the autumn of 1943 for further training at Camberley Staff College. In June 1944, he landed in France as a member of the Army's Civil Affairs department, and at last he felt a part of the real war effort, moving in behind the combat troops to create some kind of order from the aftermath of the fighting and to set up a functional civil administration in towns, many reduced to rubble, which had only just been evacuated by the Germans.

Like many of the explorers of the Heroic Era, who had moved straight from expedition life to what Shackleton described as 'the red fields of France and Flanders',[14] on being demobilised in October 1946, with the rank of major and a mention in despatches to his credit, Fuchs found himself unemployed and doubtful about his future. His entire adult life had been spent on expeditions or in the army and finding employment commensurate with his peculiar experience and qualifications might well prove difficult. The answer to his quandary came from an unexpected source and in an entirely unexpected arena.

After Cambridge, Fuchs's friend and fellow geologist, Launcelot Fleming, had sailed south with John Rymill's BGLE, combining the functions of geologist and chaplain. On his return, Fleming had maintained a passion for the Antarctic, becoming a keen advocate of further exploration and, eventually, Director of SPRI. When he heard that Fuchs needed a job, the explorer-clergyman was ideally placed to help. In particular, he told Fuchs that FIDS needed scientists to man its newly acquired Antarctic bases. 'This perhaps was something I was competent to do,' wrote a relieved Fuchs, 'and I applied to the Colonial Office for a position as a geologist.'[15]

To his utter astonishment, instead of being offered the position he had applied for, immediately after his interview the selection board asked Fuchs if he would accept the post of Overall Field Commander of all seven Antarctic bases, with his headquarters at Base 'E' on Stonington Island. The appointment, however, would last for one year only, partly because the government remained uncertain regarding its long-term commitments in a period of post-war austerity and partly because FIDS itself was in a state bordering on chaos. Not only had the embryonic Survey recently been inherited from the Royal Navy by a distinctly reluctant Colonial Office, it also suffered from a divided command, its activities being overseen by a Polar Committee in London while

day to day management rested with Sir Miles Clifford, the bullish
and opinionated Governor of the Falkland Islands. Despite these
uncertainties, Fuchs accepted the post and immediately began to
read up on a region about which he was almost entirely ignorant.
His appointment dated from July 1947 and on 20 December he
set sail for the Antarctic on board the MV *John Biscoe*. 'I was given
no directive about the general programme, nor the work to be
undertaken', he wrote four decades later. 'It was indicated that
as much survey, geology and meteorology as possible should be
done, and to this end I began collecting and reading past scientific papers. The upshot was that we went into the field with
virtually a blank cheque to plan our own programme.'[16]

Arriving at Stonington Island, Marguerite Bay, on 22 February
1948, Fuchs immediately embarked on a crash course in Antarctic
survival, covering everything from construction work in sub-
zero temperatures to the handling of small boats in ice-choked
waters to dog-driving. The first important test of his newly
acquired 'ice-craft' came on 27 July, when he led a party of five
on a 220-mile depot-laying expedition to Alexander Island.
Whiteout, thick drift, high winds and an appalling surface made
the 110-mile outward journey gruelling for men and dogs but
these conditions did nothing to deter the 40-year-old novice
and, in September, he led a 940-mile geological reconnaissance
of George VI Sound to a point just south of Fossil Bluff. By the
time he regained Stonington Island on 19 January 1949, the bay
ice had begun to disintegrate with wide pools forming close to
the shore. Usually, this would be a precursor to a wider break up
of the sea ice but when Fuchs climbed the 3000-foot Roman IV
Mountain on 11 February, he could see that between the coastal
pools and the open sea there lay a vast, unbroken stretch of ice
some 40 miles wide, rendering Stonington Island completely
inaccessible to shipping. By 1 April, with ice conditions showing
no sign of improvement, he knew that the *John Biscoe* would not
be able to relieve Base 'E' before the end of the season. 'Our fate
was confirmed', he wrote, '– it would be another year before we
saw a new face.'[17]

Always on the lookout for compelling tales of derring-do, the British Press was not slow to pick up on the story of what it rather melodramatically insisted on calling the 'Lost Eleven'. In fact, though coal would have to be carefully husbanded, in all other respects the Stonington Island party was well equipped for another winter, though it would be very hard pressed if the *John Biscoe* failed to reach them the following year. To keep his men occupied and to prevent them dwelling on the exaggerated reports of their own plight, Fuchs inaugurated a programme of improvements to the cramped base hut and then started planning additional sledging journeys to be completed the following summer. Most important among these were a trip to study the emperor penguins at a newly discovered rookery on the Dion Islands and another extended geological survey along George VI Sound, the latter involving an epic journey of 1084 miles, which Fuchs and his sledging companion completed in 90 days. On 6 February 1950 relief arrived in the form of a De Havilland Norseman, despatched from the *John Biscoe*, and the long-awaited evacuation began at last.

On his return to England, any concerns that Fuchs may have harboured about his future employment were quickly allayed. Faced with an ever-increasing mass of scientific data flowing from its Antarctic bases, the Colonial Office had decided to create a new body dedicated to the collation, study and publication of this material. Having so recently returned from two highly productive years in the Antarctic, Fuchs was an obvious candidate to become the first director of the new FIDS Scientific Bureau and, on 19 June 1950, he took up his new post. Under his energetic direction, the Bureau's reputation and its responsibilities grew rapidly – largely because no other body existed which could answer an increasing number of enquiries on Antarctic matters. To their credit, the bureaucrats of the Colonial Office accepted that their creation had taken on a life of its own and, at the end of its initial 3-year term, they decided to extend the Bureau's life by another 3 years. 'We were in business', wrote Fuchs, '– and this time it was for keeps.'[18]

Despite his genuine interest in the work of the Bureau, Fuchs had spent most of the last 20 years in the field and it was probably inevitable that, as he sat at his desk in Queen Anne's Chambers in London, he should continue to mull over other possible expeditions. Foremost among these was a crossing of Antarctica. The idea seems to have occurred to him first in August 1948, during his depot-laying expedition to Alexander Island. On 15 August, a ferocious blizzard overtook the party, keeping them pinned down for four frustrating days. On the 16th Fuchs noted in his diary 'Tonight I have since 20.00hrs been round through the driving snow to visit the other tents to explain our position and perhaps cheer them up. Heaven knows I'm gloomy enough myself, though I hope I don't show it.'[19] It was during this round of morale-boosting visits that he first discussed the idea of a crossing with Ray Adie, the South African geologist who had taught him the rudiments of dog handling. 'So, in a snow storm,' Fuchs later wrote, 'originated the idea of crossing Antarctica, and that evening I set to with a stub of pencil to outline the concept of such a journey.'[20]

With the wind rasping round his tent, Fuchs noted that the objectives of such an expedition would be fourfold: '(a) Cross continent to find structural junction Ross Sea – Graham Land Peninsula; (b) Test cold weather equipment for services; (c) Give personnel experience; (d) [Assess] Weather conditions in centre of continent – fly party in.'[21] His team would be drawn from the Royal Navy, the RAF, the Army and FIDS and they would be equipped with two ships and six aircraft. The main motive power of the expedition, however, would be provided by twelve dog teams made up of 140 animals. Significantly, in this summary, scribbled on a single side of foolscap, Fuchs made no reference to mechanised transport – though this was hardly surprising given that he had absolutely no experience of motorised sledges.

Although the idea began as little more than an idle fancy designed to while away tedious hours of inactivity, it quickly grew into something more substantial. When the *John Biscoe* and the Lost Eleven stopped at Port Stanley on their way home to England, Fuchs took the opportunity to mention his embryonic

scheme to Miles Clifford. According to Fuchs's later account, the
Governor 'immediately grasped the idea that such a journey was
of potential scientific value and could add to British prestige.'[22]
Given Clifford's influence, this response was hugely gratifying.
Fuchs was rather less pleased, however, when the Governor dispatched the impressively named Lieutenant-Colonel Kenelm
Somerset Pierce-Butler, the previous commander of Base 'E' and
now secretary to FIDS, to ask him to hand over his plans on the
basis that such an expedition should be executed by FIDS. Much
to Clifford's irritation, Fuchs refused absolutely to divulge the
details of a scheme which he saw as his own property – though
the Governor's annoyance would probably have turned to
amusement had he known that Fuchs's jealously guarded 'plans'
consisted of just one scruffy sheet of pencil jottings.

For his part, Fuchs was 'flabbergasted by this attempted
poaching'.[23] What he may not have known, however, was that,
at more or less the same time that he had first committed his
ideas to paper, Pierce-Butler and Gordon Robin, physicist on
the Norwegian-British-Swedish Antarctic Expedition (NBSAE)
of 1949–52, had also been discussing the potential for a crossing. Although the idea had not been pursued, Pierce-Butler had
raised it with Clifford who, he told Robin, 'was very keen on
the outlined scheme I gave him'[24] and also responded positively
to the idea of its being managed by FIDS. This being the case,
Clifford probably saw Fuchs as the 'poacher' rather than vice
versa. Still smarting from his skirmish with the Governor, on
his arrival in England, Fuchs raised the matter with Wordie who,
as well as being 'wise in counsel and strong in support',[25] now
occupied a seat on the Colonial Office's Polar Committee, the
governing body of FIDS. As a member of Shackleton's *Endurance*
Expedition and an advocate of Watkins's 1932 plan, Wordie
was naturally interested in the scheme; but he told Fuchs that
his timing was poor. Instead of pursuing an idea which would
inevitably require an extended period of absence and substantial funds, for the time being he should focus on the work of
the new Scientific Bureau and trust Wordie to determine when
conditions were more propitious.

Of course, for Fuchs, the greatest risk in adopting this strategy was that Clifford – or the representatives of another country
altogether – would steal a march on him. Certainly, the Governor
had been swift to action and, shortly after his first talk with Fuchs,
he had approached James Griffiths, the Secretary of State for the
Colonies. 'It has been held,' he wrote on 24 March, alluding to the
geographical puzzle that Filchner first sought to unravel, 'that the
Antarctic continent may, in fact, be sub-divided by an ice-filled
depression linking the Weddell Sea and the Ross Sea; geographi-
cally this is entirely possible. My object then would be to form
a special expedition within FIDS to undertake the investigation
of this theory, using Stonington Island as the main base for it.'[26]
Completely side-lining his uncooperative junior, in a later letter
to Griffiths he also proposed that the expedition should be led by
Pierce-Butler on the basis that 'familiarity with the area, proved
sledging ability and leadership qualities are required and are combined in this officer.'[27] In another letter from the same period,
he went on to tell one Colonial Office official that Fuchs 'has
his points from a Bureau point of view but is likely to be tire-
some in other directions. He has an extremely high opinion of
Dr Fuchs.'[28] At this stage, there seemed little likelihood of Clifford
choosing to 'forgive and forget'.

Fortunately for Fuchs, Whitehall's response to Clifford's suggestion was typically non-committal: yes, the plan had its attractions
– but it would be costly and highly complicated. Undeterred, the
Governor continued to press for a more definitive answer, and on
12 December he received another prevaricating cable from the
Colonial Office telling him that the '... way is not yet clear for
decision [on] your proposals. In any event long period of preparation would be necessary. You therefore can assume that in any
case project could not be put in hand early enough to affect your
plans for season 1951–52.'[29] In July 1951, the irrepressible Clifford
raised the subject yet again – and this time the reply was much
less equivocal: 'It was agreed that the transcontinental expedition
from Graham Land to the Ross Sea was not a project suitable to
be undertaken by the Falkland Islands Dependencies Survey in
present circumstances, and should be left in abeyance.'[30] Clifford

might have taken some solace from the fact that the proposal was to be 'left in abeyance' rather than dismissed altogether, but clearly he would find no support in the short term.

Wordie had been much shrewder in reading the government's mood. Unlike Clifford, he had realised that in the immediate post-war period, with the future of FIDS itself uncertain, the debt-conscious mandarins of the civil service would view any costly and ambitious scheme with grave scepticism. However, with the death of King George VI in February 1952 and the accession of the 25-year-old Elizabeth II, Wordie believed that the mood in government had changed and that bold initiatives which might serve to underpin Britain's prestige would be viewed more sympathetically. Early in 1953, with preparations for the Queen's spectacular coronation well underway and the country being swept by a new feeling of optimism about its place in the post-war world, he began cautiously to put out feelers in the tight-knit polar community. Perhaps most importantly of all, rather than exclude Clifford, Wordie decided to recruit him to his cause. It proved an astute move and very soon the Governor would become one of the scheme's most ardent champions.

Primed by Wordie, Clifford raised the idea at the Polar Committee on 24 March and quickly demonstrated that past rebuffs had done nothing to diminish his enthusiasm. According to Launcelot Fleming, who also sat on the Committee, 'the Governor of the Falkland Islands was quite clear in his mind that he wanted to choose a leader and get a general plan under way before he returned to Port Stanley.'[31] It was probably during the ensuing discussion that Wordie again put his protégé's name forward as an obvious candidate for leadership. With the passage of 3 years and in the interests of presenting a unified front, Clifford was willing to let bygones be bygones and, on 28 March, he raised the subject directly with Fuchs. 'At a meeting of the Polar Committee on the 24th of March', he wrote, 'I explained my proposals for a trans-Antarctic journey combined with the delimitation of the Weddell coast, the main objects of the journey being exploration, seismo-glaciology and such geology as might be possible.'[32] Although by this point he must have been told by

Wordie of the Committee's deliberations and of his candidacy for leadership, Fuchs may well have been surprised when his old enemy then went on to request that 'On the assumption that if such an expedition is approved you will be invited to lead it, please prepare a paper for submission in the first instance to the Chairman of the FIDS Scientific Committee who will then pass it, with their comments to the Polar Committee.'[33]

Overall Fuchs must have been enormously relieved by the Governor's letter, as it indicated that his most powerful adversary had now switched sides. His relief, however, would have been tempered by two events which followed in quick succession and revealed that, for all the assurances of Wordie and Clifford, the competition for leadership of the trans-Antarctic expedition might not be a one-horse race after all. The first event was a conversation in 'The Feathers', a public house near Fuchs's office, and a popular FIDS watering-hole; the second was receipt of a draft proposal for a transcontinental journey. Fuchs's interlocutor in the pub and the author of the proposal were one and the same: Duncan Carse.

Since his return from the BGLE in August 1937, Carse's career had followed an unusual course for a man who would one day put himself forward as the prospective leader of a major Antarctic expedition. Except for wartime service with the Royal Navy, he had spent most of the period since leaving the *Penola* with the BBC. Initially acting as a general presenter and announcer, in 1949 he had beaten more than a thousand other applicants to succeed Noel Johnson as the eponymous hero of the hugely successful radio show 'Dick Barton, Special Agent'. But for all their popular appeal Carse found Barton's fictional escapades a poor substitute for real adventure and in 1950 he took the daring step of resigning from the show in order to lead the South Georgia Survey (SGS).

In spite of the most appalling weather, between 1 November 1951 and 18 April 1952, Carse and his six-man team had undertaken a detailed survey of the largely unmapped island, exploring the Allardyce mountain range and, in the manner of Scott and Shackleton, man-hauling their sledges over ice fields and glaciers to create an accurate map of the area between King Haakon Bay and Novosilski Bay. Despite the usefulness of this work, however, Carse seems to have viewed it as little more than a means to an end. According to his biographer and fellow SGS veteran, Alec Trendall, many of Carse's key career moves, including his service on the *Penola* as well as his ultimate leadership of the SGS, should be seen as 'a succession of decisions that Duncan made as part of a plan to be involved in Antarctic exploration.'[34] This dearly-held ambition had suffered a major setback in 1945 when a recruitment panel rejected Carse's application to join the newly-formed FIDS – ostensibly because of his lack of specialist skills, but perhaps also because of a well known impatience with authority. Despite this blow, aged only 31, Carse was far from ready to admit defeat. 'I have something to give to polar exploration' he told a friend after his rejection, '– I have always believed that and I always will.'[35] In this context, the role of Dick Barton was nothing more than a stopgap. As for the SGS, he saw it simply as a 'useful tuning-up job before tackling really big business.'[36]

When, on his return from South Georgia, Carse learned from his friends in the polar establishment that the idea of a trans-Antarctic crossing was once again being mooted, it seemed that his chance to tackle 'really big business' had arrived at last. In March 1953, he met with Wordie and with Colin Bertram, biologist with the BGLE and Director of SPRI from 1949, to discuss the project. Given that Wordie obviously favoured Fuchs and that he had previously refused to support the SGS, it might seem unlikely that he should invite Carse to work up plans for such a complex and demanding project as the crossing of Antarctica. But, at this stage, Wordie appears to have been casting his net wide. In February he had also spoken to Gordon Robin, asking him to further develop the outline sketch for a crossing that he had first drawn up with Ken Pierce-Butler. Whatever Wordie's motivation may have been, Carse immediately set to work and by 23 March – a day before the Polar Committee's meeting and five days before Clifford's formal invitation to Fuchs – he had completed an eleven-page proposal, presenting 'as briefly and clearly as possible, a practical solution to the problem of sledging across Antarctica.'[37]

Like his predecessors, Carse considered that treacherous ice
conditions made it more sensible to start the journey from the
Weddell Sea and to end it at the Ross Sea, thereby establishing the crossing as an east-to-west transit, with Marguerite Bay
and Vahsel Bay as the possible starting points. The expedition's
equipment and supplies would be towed by a combination of
dog-teams and 'Weasels', a form of motorised sledge designed
and built in America for use by the military. In terms of timing,
if fortune smiled on the expedition, then a crossing might be
launched during the summer season of 1955–56, though he
admitted that such a schedule was highly ambitious. 'Finally,' he
asserted, 'it must be realised that the first crossing of Antarctica by
sledge is going to be quite an assignment – a hard job for hard
men.'[38] It was a conclusion with which few experienced polar
travellers would disagree.

Having prepared his outline, Carse immediately asked for
Wordie's opinion. To his immense surprise and frustration,
instead of offering encouragement, Wordie replied with the suggestion that he should avoid circulating his proposal 'till matters
have gone a stage further.'[39] Even worse, wrote Carse, 'Wordie
now tells me that Sir Miles has asked Fuchs to plan and lead the
Expedition; he does not tell me that he, also, is backing Fuchs
… as a potential leader I'm not prepared to sit back and be confronted in due course by a fait accompli, possibly making use of
my plans.'[40] Irascible at the best of times, Carse was infuriated by
the realisation that there were other competitors in the field and,
spurning Wordie's advice, he immediately proceeded to distribute
additional copies of his proposal, each copy being accompanied by a letter in which he complained bitterly about what he
considered to be 'backstairs technique, intrigue, subterfuge and
dishonesty.'[41] The recipients of these letters included Fleming,
Bertram, Robin, Brian Roberts of SPRI – and Fuchs.

Why did Carse send a copy of his proposal to a man whom
he now knew to be a favoured contender for the role of expedition leader? Perhaps he felt that his own chances had been
effectively scotched and that he had nothing to lose; more probably, he intended to make it impossible for Fuchs to duplicate any

portion of his plan without opening himself up to accusations of plagiarism. Whatever Carse's objective may have been, given that he had not yet published his own proposal, Fuchs clearly felt uncomfortable. On 8 April, he replied to Carse, telling him that 'You will remember that when we last discussed matters in "The Feathers" I told you that "I reserved my position" in regard to the Trans-Continental. I also said that you ought to leave your plans with Roberts and Wordie and not with me. I refer to this as I do not want you to feel that I have been anything but open with you on this matter. This is particularly pertinent since a certain quarter has requested me to put forward proposals for a trans-Antarctic journey.'[42] Of course, the 'certain quarter' was Miles Clifford and it was to Clifford that Fuchs wrote on 7 July, again emphasising that Carse had shared his plans with him 'contrary to my request that he should not do so.'[43]

According to his biographer, Carse had always felt that his position as an outsider placed him at a considerable disadvantage when dealing with the polar establishment. Now, as well as being disgusted by what he saw as duplicity on Wordie's part, he clearly felt that Fuchs's greater Antarctic experience and his position as Director of the Scientific Bureau were bound to make him the preferred candidate in the eyes of others besides Wordie and Clifford – and he was not alone in thinking so. On 14 April, Colin Bertram, who had known Carse on the BGLE and was broadly sympathetic to his cause, told him that 'My judgement of the position is that if government funds should prove to be available then the leadership of the venture would really be a government choice. That choice I guess would not fall upon you.'[44] Just three days later, Carse more or less acknowledged that the game was up. 'I don't think I shall be doing the job myself',[45] he admitted to Gordon Robin, though this private admission of defeat did not prevent him from developing a more detailed plan, which he completed at the end of August.

In fact, one of the key factors counting against Carse was his decision to downplay the importance of science during the expedition. 'The Transcontinental Journey is a major expedition in itself,' he asserted, 'and while plans should be made for the carrying out of other useful work … all must be subordinated to the attainment of the main objective. For this reason, it is probably inadvisable to try to combine the Crossing with an elaborate scientific programme – the danger of falling between stools must be avoided at all costs.'[46] Although Heroic Era explorers like Shackleton and Amundsen would have sympathised with this view, it was hardly politic to state it so bluntly. After all, the expedition would probably be sponsored in large part by FIDS, with its emphasis on scientific rather than 'heroic' exploration, and to a lesser degree by bodies like the Royal Society, the RGS and SPRI.

Having studied Carse's proposal, Fuchs told Clifford that 'I cannot agree to much of his ideas … the journey *must* have scientific importance.'[47] His own proposal, which he issued, rather belatedly, in July, emphasised the need to complete a demanding programme of scientific study throughout the course of the expedition. In particular, in a statement which still resonates among climate change scientists today, he wrote:

> An important object of the journey will be seismic sounding of the ice from coast to coast. The profile so provided will reveal the nature of the polar ice sheet. The measurement of its depth and volume is pertinent to problems of world wide significance. These include climatic changes past and present; eustatic changes (world wide changes of sea level), isostatic movements (local elevation and depression of the earth's crust); and the relation between glaciation, sea temperature and the biological balance of the Southern Ocean.[48]

In addition, detailed gravimetric, geological and meteorological observations would be made. Overall, as might be expected of the head of the FIDS Scientific Bureau, Fuchs was at pains to communicate his conviction that the 'importance of the scientific results achieved must be sufficiently great to justify the combined Commonwealth effort involved … The journey will combine geographical exploration with scientific studies given special prominence.'[49]

Science, however, would not be the only potential benefi-
ciary of the expedition. Since the launch of Operation *Tabarin*
in 1943, Argentina had continued to hotly dispute Britain's claim
to its Antarctic and sub-Antarctic possessions and, as recently
as February 1952, armed Argentinian sailors had attempted
to prevent a FIDS party from landing stores at Hope Bay. The
Argentinians retreated after the arrival of the frigate HMS
Burghead Bay, dispatched from the Falklands by Clifford, but it was
clear that they would continue to challenge British sovereignty
whenever the opportunity arose. In the light of such aggression,
in a document marked 'SECRET' and prepared some time after
his main proposal, Fuchs outlined for the Polar Committee what
he saw as the potential political and territorial advantages of
launching a high profile expedition. 'It has been considered', he
wrote, 'that the Trans-Antarctic Expedition would have considerable prestige and political value for this country, particularly in
regard to the dispute with Argentina and Chile.'[50] He then went
on to explore a number of options for the future of the British
presence in Antarctica, ranging from a complete abandonment
of the FIDS bases to a significant expansion of FIDS activities in
the region. He thought this last option highly desirable but also
acknowledged that, because of the 'considerable annual outlay of
money ... it is perhaps unlikely that the government will be willing to make such a long term commitment.'[51] Overall, he believed
that the most pragmatic way forward would be for Britain to
expand its operations for a period of 5 years, during which time
it would be possible to establish the economic potential of the
continent. In the event of the government choosing this, or any
of the other options which involved a continued presence of
whatever duration, he asserted that 'the expedition itself will be
a powerful factor in supporting the United Kingdom [*sic*] claims
and those of the Commonwealth as a whole.'[52]

Although early sight of Carse's plans had placed Fuchs in a
difficult position, his own proposal actually bore a far closer
resemblance to Robin's than to anyone else's – a fact unlikely to
prove contentious since Robin had long since abandoned any
idea of leading such an expedition himself and, encouraged by

Wordie, the two men had willingly exchanged ideas. The key elements of Robin's plan were that a base should be established in
the southern reaches of the Weddell Sea, at a position roughly
77°S, 40°W and that a convoy of motor vehicles should make its
way from this base to the Bay of Whales or via the South Pole to
McMurdo Sound, carrying out a programme of surveying, geology and glaciology en route. 'While the Weddell Sea base was
being established,' Robin continued,

> ... a second expedition should establish headquarters in the
> Ross Sea for one year to provide support in the final stages
> of the journey. This support should consist of surface and air
> reconnaissance to select a safe route for [the] final stage of
> the trans-Antarctic journey ... This part of the expedition ...
> should be based on, and perhaps run by New Zealand.[53]

When writing to Robin on 19 February, Fuchs, too, had
emphasised that he 'envisaged a form of Combined Commonwealth Operation drawing on Britain, Australia, New Zealand
and Canada for finance, personnel and equipment'[54] and in
his detailed proposal he also recommended the establishment
of a 'Reception Base in the Ross Dependency'. The Ross Sea
base, he suggested, 'could be conveniently operated from New
Zealand, possibly by a joint New Zealand and Australian party
if those countries wish to take part.'[55] The role of this second
party would be 'to find a route to the inland ice via the Ferrar
Glacier and to establish a depot at Mount Albert Markham. They
will also assist the trans-continental party in their descent.' Key
elements of both proposals, therefore, were that they should
involve other Commonwealth nations and that bases should
be established on both sides of the continent. Of course, the
involvement of other Commonwealth nations might also serve
as an effective means by which to relieve the financial and
logistical burdens of the undertaking and as early as June, even
before he distributed his proposal, Fuchs obtained an interview
with the New Zealand and Australian Prime Ministers, who
were in London to attend the coronation. He received an

encouragingly sympathetic hearing but neither was willing to make any commitment before Fuchs could confirm the extent of the British government's involvement.

So far as routes were concerned, Carse and Robin suggested a number of alternatives and Fuchs, too, considered two options: one starting from Stonington Island and the other from Vahsel Bay. The primary disadvantage of the Stonington Island plan, however, was that it would increase the total distance to be travelled by some 700 miles and, since Fuchs now accepted that the journey must be made with motor vehicles with dogs serving only as backup, this would mean a substantial increase in the expedition's fuel requirements. The extra mileage would also place a significant additional strain on motor vehicles which, despite the improvements in reliability and endurance achieved since the Heroic Era, had never been tested over such huge distances. In addition, the need to travel so much farther would seriously limit the expedition's ability to undertake an extensive scientific programme; it would increase the risks; it would take much longer to complete; and it would be more expensive, with Fuchs estimating that the Stonington Island plan would cost £224,500 against the £144,200 required for the Vahsel Bay plan. Overall, he believed that the Vahsel Bay plan was 'simpler, safer, and more likely to succeed'.[56]

Of course, the Vahsel Bay plan was not without its own risks. Foremost among these were 'ignorance at this stage of a good landing place and doubts about the sea ice conditions which may prevail in the Weddell Sea in any particular year.'[57] So far as the establishment of a base on the Weddell Sea coast was concerned, Fuchs argued that both Filchner and Shackleton had been severely hampered by their reliance upon dog teams, which made it essential that they should minimise the distance to be travelled. In contrast, his own use of motor vehicles, with their greater load-carrying capacity and range, gave his expedition 'considerable latitude in the distance to be travelled' and therefore made it 'possible to use a landing place further north in Coats Land.'[58] As for the uncertainty over ice conditions, he emphasised that the *Deutschland* and the *Endurance* had been wooden-hulled sailing vessels with only auxiliary engines.'Just as tracked vehicles and aircraft now enable us to undertake a journey of the type proposed,' he concluded, 'so do high powered modern ships of better design and accumulated experience of ice navigation provide confidence in present day ability to sail down the east coast of the Weddell Sea.'[59] It was a bold assertion and one that would come back to haunt him.

In its essentials, Fuchs's plan did not evolve significantly in its passage from the drawing board to execution. One important development was the decision to spread the expedition over two full years, instead of just one. In the Antarctic summer of the first year, an Advance Party would land at Vahsel Bay to erect the expedition's Winter Quarters, which would be named 'Shackleton Base.'They would also commence the programme of meteorological observations and undertake preliminary surveys. The following January, the Ross Sea base would be established while, in the Weddell Sea, the Advance Party would be joined by the main Crossing Party, led by Fuchs. Any members of the Advance Party not included in the Crossing Party would return to England with the expedition ship. The primary advantage of this modified plan was that, on its arrival in Antarctica, the Crossing Party would be free to concentrate exclusively on preparing for the journey ahead rather than being distracted by construction work. The crossing itself would be launched in November and was expected to take approximately 100 days. All the men over-wintering during the second year would cross the continent and the base itself would be abandoned when they set off into the interior.

Another change related to the timing of the expedition. Before the idea of the Advance Party was developed, Fuchs had hoped that the expedition would land in Vahsel Bay early in 1955 and embark on the crossing sometime in November. Some interested parties, including Sir Lawrence Kirwan of the RGS, had expressed doubts as to whether a year was sufficient to organise such a major undertaking 'since polar expeditions have usually taken longer to launch than originally planned'[60] but it was not until Fuchs became embroiled in the problems of fundraising that he was eventually forced to push back his schedule by 12 months. Eventually, it was agreed that the Advance Party would land early in 1956, to be followed by the main Crossing Party a year later. This would mean that the journey would begin in November 1957 and be completed by early March 1958. Disappointing though this delay might be, it would mean that the expedition's scientific investigations would complement the work of the Antarctic bases being set up by various nations, including Britain, as part of the International Geophysical Year (IGY), also planned for 1957–58.

By the middle of 1953, the race for leadership of the expedition was all but over. Having studied Carse's initial proposal, Clifford told Wordie that 'I have examined the paper with some care and I am not impressed … I have no confidence whatever in Carse as a Leader; there is something lacking. He is too glib.'[61] Five months later, he finally quashed any idea of adopting Carse's scheme when he reported to the Secretary of State for the Colonies that 'I consider this to be a meretricious and over-ambitious plan resting on ill-founded assumptions, working to a highly improbable time-table, and without adequate safety margins.'[62] Though it would be some months before Carse finally admitted it to himself, like those of Filchner, Bruce, Shackleton and Watkins before, his plan for a trans-Antarctic crossing had been consigned to the ever-growing pile of 'might have beens.'

In stark contrast to his scathing commentary on Carse's submission, Clifford's assessment of Fuchs's proposal was almost fulsome in its praise:

I have read this paper with the very greatest interest and congratulate you on a very clear exposition of the intention and well-reasoned argument in support of your own proposal for carrying it out. I agree entirely with your conclusions … I hope that your proposals will commend themselves to the Pundits and that the necessary financial and departmental support will be forthcoming for I remain convinced that it is a project of the first importance, the successful completion of which would redound very greatly to our prestige.[63]

The Governor's one major suggestion related to the choice of aircraft: 'if funds run to it I would strongly recommend a Beaver which will take up to 1080lb, and with the emergency tank has a range of 815 miles ... There is a bigger version known as the "Otter" which might do very well indeed for the Ross Sea Party.'[64] It was a suggestion that Fuchs was happy to take up as it would substantially increase the expedition's ability to undertake aerial reconnaissance and eventually the expedition's air contingent swelled to include two Austers and one Otter for the Weddell Sea party and an Auster and a Beaver for the Ross Sea party. Ultimately, it would also lead to the last major development in Fuchs's plan: the decision to make the first trans-Antarctic flight by a single-engine aircraft, the flight to be undertaken by the RAF personnel after the departure of the main Crossing Party.

As early as July, Fuchs could report that 'There is a general atmosphere in favour of the project', [65] and by October he was able to tell Clifford, who had returned to Port Stanley, that the 'Polar Committee received the proposals quite well ... New Zealand seemed definitely in favour, South Africa interested, Australia sat on the fence and Canada kept quiet ... Colonial Office definitely supported it.'[66] Some highly vocal opposition had yet to be overcome, however: most notably that of Brian Roberts, a veteran of the BGLE and one of the originators of Operation *Tabarin*, who now divided his time between the Polar Desk of the Foreign Office and SPRI. Fuchs later wrote that, initially, he had been greatly puzzled by Roberts's objections to the expedition, which became so determined and oft-repeated that Wordie even went so far as to remark 'when faced with Brian at SPRI, "That's the enemy!"'[67] Only when it became apparent that Roberts thought, incorrectly as it turned out, that government funding of the expedition would militate against his own plans for an aerial survey of the Dependencies did his opposition begin to make any sense. Roberts was also a friend and supporter of Carse, but once the aerial survey work to be conducted by the expedition had been scoped to his satisfaction he was, in the words of Colin Bertram, 'able to take a somewhat different attitude.'[68]

Despite such skirmishes, the momentum behind the expedition was rapidly becoming irresistible. Having already obtained the support of the Polar Committee, at the beginning of 1954 Fuchs submitted his plans for further consideration and comment by the RGS. Given that the RGS Council chose Wordie to lead its analysis of the proposal, it was not very surprising that on 1 February his sub-committee of Antarctic experts should report that 'the plan of the proposed Trans-Antarctic journey is a reasonable one produced by an Antarctic explorer of considerable experience and one well worth attempting. The Sub-committee recommend that the project should be warmly encouraged by the Royal Geographical Society on grounds of geographical exploration apart from other considerations.'[69] In passing its findings to the Commonwealth Relations Office, the RGS also accepted that the plan was 'more likely to be carried out by Dr Fuchs than by anyone else. He is a Gold Medallist of the Royal Geographical Society and has the right to set up to lead and also take part in the scientific work of the expedition.'[70]

With this emphatic endorsement still ringing in his ears, Fuchs next set about forming the administrative bodies that would be essential in putting his plans into effect. Beneath a General Management Committee, chaired by Air Marshall Sir John Slessor and with Rear Admiral Cecil Parry as its secretary, a number of separate sub-committees were formed to deal with matters including finance, the scientific programme and personnel selection. The mountain of work facing the committees was formidable, as Parry observed: 'In short we had no accommodation, no men, other than the leader, no material, precious little ready cash and no precedent for an enterprise of such magnitude.'[71] Fuchs sat on, or reported to, every committee and with the demands on his time increasing daily, he obtained a temporary leave of absence from the Scientific Bureau, his sabbatical to last for the duration of the planning and execution of the expedition.

In common with practically every Heroic Era expedition,
perhaps the greatest challenge of all was fundraising – and as he
turned his attention to this uncongenial but essential task Fuchs
might well have sympathised with Bruce and Watkins, whose
trans-Antarctic dreams had come to nought because of their inability to obtain the necessary finance. Government approval of the
expedition, particularly when that approval was supported by a
grant, was seen to be absolutely vital and at the inaugural meeting
of the expedition's Management Committee in June 1954, Slessor
asserted that 'the main problems to be faced were not operational but financial, particularly as private support could not be
expected until financial support were given by the Government.'[72]
Although Slessor went on to state that a 'Government decision
on financial aid was hoped for at the end of July', it was not until
the last day of November that Fuchs could report that 'through
the Colonial Office, HM Treasury had been asked for a sum of
£100,000 towards the cost of the expedition'[73] and it took until
17 February 1955 for Winston Churchill, the Prime Minister, to
announce that the money would be forthcoming.

The credibility that this grant gave to the expedition in the
eyes of potential private donors was further reinforced when
the Queen agreed to become patron and Churchill's successor, Anthony Eden, launched the public appeal for funds. In his
speech, Eden paid tribute to the 'spirit of adventure' that under-
pinned the expedition, comparing Fuchs with the explorers of
the Elizabethan age. But he also took the opportunity to bolster Britain's claims in the region, telling his audience – and no
doubt trusting to the newspapers to ensure that his voice was also
heard in South America – that 'We – Her Majesty's Government
– have no wish to extend our influence beyond those areas which
have been recognised as ours. For that reason the route of the
Expedition, long though it is, crosses only Commonwealth territory; but we do intend to maintain the right to our wide areas
and to explore them.'[74]

So far as raising private finance was concerned, Fuchs had
an obvious model to follow. Unlike the brusque Bruce and the
guileless Watkins, in seeking backing for his *Nimrod* and *Endurance*

expeditions Shackleton had excelled at playing on the egos of wealthy backers such as James Caird and Janet Stancomb-Wills; at obtaining sponsorship from companies who saw the potential of advertising through association; at drumming up popular support through the shrewd manipulation of the press; and at coercing a reluctant establishment to cough up additional funds through methods little short of moral blackmail. Learning from the master, Fuchs employed all of these strategies, typically telling one potential backer that 'the expedition will contribute substantially to the newly arising "Commonwealth-Elizabethan Era". As I have explained, we shall be asking for substantial contributions from industry for which in fact there will be no return except prestige for this country and the Commonwealth as a whole.'[75] The style, and the cool assurance with which, in the same letter, he asked for £25,000, were pure Shackleton. And given that Fuchs's original estimate of £144,000 quickly proved to be woefully short of the mark, he needed to be ambitious.[76] Fortunately, his boldness paid off and, unlike every previous British expedition to Antarctica, the TAE was never seriously short of funds, with his successes ranging from the sponsorship of sledge dogs by British schools to British Petroleum's agreement to meet all of the expedition's colossal fuel needs, making it the expedition's single biggest corporate sponsor.

With his expedition's future now assured, Fuchs could at last turn his attention to selecting his men and, just like his fundraising, his approach to recruitment bore an uncanny resemblance to Shackleton's. Although willing to take expert advice in order to assess a candidate's professional competence, when it came to judging their character and overall fitness for expedition work, Shackleton relied exclusively upon his own shrewdness and insight. Indeed, so great was his conviction that he could gauge a man's abilities almost at a glance, applicants often found themselves appointed or rejected on the basis of interviews lasting no more than a few minutes. And to his credit, subsequent events had shown his self-confidence to be justified, with the team selected for the *Endurance* Expedition, in particular, remaining remarkably united despite the most appalling strain.

Like his illustrious predecessor, Fuchs eschewed any form of what we now call personality profiling and he even asserted that the 'idea of taking a psychiatrist on a polar expedition hardly bears thinking about.'[77] To some, including Rainer Goldsmith, the man recruited as the Advance Party's medical officer, this refusal to adopt more objective means of assessing character seemed both extraordinarily old-fashioned and short-sighted. According to Goldsmith, Fuchs 'took people, generally, who wanted to go and that was his only criterion. He didn't ask anything about whether you got on with people or whether you had schizophrenia or depressions ... We suggested to him that it might be a good idea to have some sort of psychological profile or something to help select people. But he was dead against this – dead against it! He knew exactly who to choose: "I know who to choose! If I like somebody then I'll choose him".'[78] Psychiatrists were not the only candidates likely to receive short shrift. In an unconscious echo of Shackleton's rejection of 'three sporty girls',[79] in a later lecture, Fuchs admitted that he too had 'steadfastly opposed the inclusion of women in an Antarctic team as liable to cause more trouble than they are worth.'[80] Despite these restrictions, however, there was no shortage of candidates, some experienced polar veterans, others complete novices whose applications were based on their expertise in other specialist fields.

Typical of the former were Ken Blaiklock and Roy Homard. Blaiklock, one of the first men to be appointed, was a professional surveyor who had originally served with Fuchs at Stonington Island in 1948. Hearing of Fuchs's plan while returning home from another FIDS expedition, he had sent a telegram saying 'Don't forget me!'[81] and had been rewarded with appointment to the leadership of the eight-man Advance Party, as well as membership of the twelve-man Crossing Party. Homard's desire to take part had been no less intense. A senior NCO with the Royal Electrical and Mechanical Engineers, he had been responsible for the maintenance of the vehicles on the British North Greenland Expedition (BNGE) of 1953–54 and, when standing before the Queen to receive the Polar Medal for his work in Greenland, in a spontaneous aside he had asked whether she, as patron of the expedition, would support his application![82] Although the sovereign had declined to exert her influence, Homard's experience guaranteed him a post as one of the Weddell Sea party's two engineers.

A key team member without previous polar experience was the expedition's senior engineer, David Pratt. Having served with a Royal Engineers tank squadron during the war, Pratt was very familiar with tracked vehicles but he had also taken an engineering tripos at Cambridge and was therefore able to approach engineering problems from a theoretical as well as a purely practical standpoint, planning complex vehicle recoveries long before he reached the Antarctic. According to Fuchs, he also had 'the happy knack of persuading unsuspecting people into doing far more than they intended when first confronted with a Pratt Scheme, and it was undoubtedly due to his untiring and relentless energy that the immense amount of work on our vehicles, in England, Norway and the Antarctic, was completed in the short periods of time available.'[83]

Of course, one of Pratt's first duties was to help in the final selection of the vehicles to be used on the crossing. Summing up the history of motor transport in the Antarctic, he wrote that its development 'has been slow. This may be due to the very nature of the continent and the ensuing practical economic reasons.'[84] Whatever its causes, this slow evolution meant that, in real terms, the British Commonwealth Trans-Antarctic Expedition (TAE), as the expedition was known from June 1954, had few alternatives from which to choose. Fuchs, Carse and Robin had all assumed that their expeditions' primary motive power would be provided by Weasels, though all acknowledged that it might well prove problematic to obtain sufficient numbers of a vehicle which was produced only in small quantities and was already in high demand as a result of increased polar activity on the part of the United States.

The Weasel also had a dubious reputation. It had been used by the Norwegians in Finnmark towards the end of the war and, according to John Giaever, leader of the NBSAE, 'they were a perpetual source of anxiety for the transport officers. The fan

belts broke and the tracks broke.'[85] The French Greenland
Expedition of 1949–51 had also discovered that they wore out an
endless supply of tracks; that they must be handled with extreme
caution; and that they could not be relied upon to pull more than
1.5 tons. Although the experiences of the NBSAE had been altogether more satisfactory, taken together, these limitations made
using the Weasel for a largely unsupported journey of more than
2000 miles, much of it across unmapped and unknown territory,
a distinctly risky proposition.

Of course, the Weasel had been designed not for the Antarctic
but for the Arctic and this was true, also, of a revolutionary new
vehicle which would eventually become the mainstay of the TAE:
the 'Sno-cat.' Designed and built by the American Tucker Sno-cat
Corporation, this vehicle was intended primarily to facilitate the
repair and maintenance of telephone lines in northern Canada
and Alaska. Powered by a 200hp Chrysler V8 petrol engine and
capable of 15mph, the Sno-cat's greatest advantage was its unique
traction system, designed to provide almost 100 per cent traction
even when turning in soft snow. The vehicle also possessed four
independent tracks, one for each of its four pontoons, located at
each of the vehicle's four corners in much the same manner as the
wheels of a standard car. When the front pontoons were turned
to the right, the rear pontoons automatically turned to the left, so
that the vehicle always turned on its own axis, thereby reducing
friction and preventing the Sno-cat from ploughing a trough for
itself when it turned – a common fault in more conventional
tracked vehicles like the Weasel. Taken in the round, these features
made the Sno-cat far more attractive than the alternatives, but
their high cost (£5000 per unit), their limited availability and the
fact that the expedition had 'few pounds and no dollars'[86] meant
that Fuchs would not be able to rely upon them only. In effect,
as Homard later wrote, 'we had to take what we could get'[87]
and, ultimately, this meant a combination of Sno-cats, Weasels, a
Canadian-built Muskeg tractor and even Ferguson farm tractors.

Fuchs had long since moved out of his Bureau office and
into a small suite of rooms at 64 Victoria Street in London, just a
stone's throw from where Scott had established his headquarters

for the *Terra Nova* Expedition. Describing the life of the office, Homard wrote that 'Months of high pressure work resulted in mounting numbers of files, trays, desks, telephones and cabinets filling the offices and even overflowing into adjacent rooms as new members "clocked in" and were given a chair and part of a desk. Everybody worked "flat out" in anticipation of field work to follow and the honour of having been chosen.' [88] Individual responsibilities ranged from estimating the number of thermometers likely to get broken, to determining how many spare pairs of socks, how many light bulbs and how many drive sprockets would be needed. The work went on well into the night, seven days a week, and grew so frenetic that, by the end of spring 1955, Parry believed that the TAE offices were generating 'the highest level of noise and bustle of any in London.' [89]

Despite the expedition's seemingly unstoppable momentum, one vital question remained unanswered almost until the last minute: who would take charge of the Ross Sea Party and become, in effect, Fuchs's overall second-in-command? Fuchs told Noel Odell, a veteran of both the 1924 and 1938 British Everest expeditions, that the 'leader at McMurdo Sound should no doubt be a New Zealander', [90] but who should that leader be? To many commentators there was only one obvious candidate: Sir Edmund Hillary. Hillary's conquest of Everest on 29 May 1953 had made him not only the most celebrated New Zealander of his day but also one of the most famous men alive; it was not unnatural, therefore, that once the idea of New Zealand participation had been mooted, people should begin to link his name with the project. One of the first to make the suggestion publicly had been the New Zealand *Morning Advertiser,* which, in January 1954, asserted that 'Sir Edmund Hillary, and his close friend, George Lowe, have both previously expressed eagerness to visit the regions in the south. This is not surprising for the trans-Antarctic trip, if ever made, would be one of the greatest exploration journeys ever undertaken by man.' [91]

Neither Hillary nor Lowe, who had served as cameraman on the Everest Expedition, had any experience of polar travel, but lack of expertise would be more than made up for by the huge benefits of what, in modern parlance, would be described as celebrity endorsement. By obtaining not only Hillary's support for the expedition, but also his active participation as leader of the Ross Sea Party, Fuchs would gain not only the financial and logistical backing of a previously hesitant New Zealand government but also a guaranteed place in the headlines of the world's newspapers. In official circles, too, the climber's name was soon being mentioned in connection with the expedition with a committee of experts established by the New Zealand government reporting that 'if a decision in principle to participate in the expedition should be made, a well-known person should be chosen to act as leader for the Ross Island party. Dr Marsden and Sir Edmund Hillary were mentioned as persons who could be associated with such an expedition.'[92]

Although Fuchs later wrote that the New Zealand government 'Rather naturally ... chose Sir Edmund Hillary to lead the New Zealand contingent',[93] he was playing down his own involvement in the selection process. In fact, in late 1953 it was he who had first sought a meeting with Hillary, asking George Lowe to act as intermediary. Like Watkins before him, however, whatever others might think about his fitness to lead a team to the Antarctic, Hillary was far from convinced. 'My ideas of the Antarctic were hazy in the extreme', he later wrote, 'and, if I thought about it at all, I imagined a sombre land of bitter cold and heroic suffering, of serious men dedicated to impossible ideals, and of lonely crosses out in the snowy wastes – not really my cup of tea at all.'[94] Nonetheless he had met with Fuchs on 18 November and later admitted to being 'immensely impressed by his forceful personality and his air of determination and confidence'.[95]

At the meeting Hillary expressed interest in the expedition and agreed to assist with publicity in New Zealand – but he was slow to commit himself to taking a more active role. As late as October 1954, Fuchs told Odell that 'I have talked to Hillary and George Lowe about the project and while I gained the impression that Hillary was not interested in the Antarctic, it seemed to me that Lowe might well be a suitable man.'[96] A month later, writing to L.B. Quartermain of the New Zealand Antarctic Society, he didn't mention Hillary's name at all:'I hope that it will be possible to have the Ross Island base under a New Zealand Commander (George Lowe?) and largely manned by your people.'[97] Despite his caution, however, Hillary's curiosity had been pricked and he not only watched Fuchs's progress from afar but also, in conjunction with the New Zealand Antarctic Society, began to press his government to take a greater interest in and responsibility for the Ross Dependency. Inevitably, his name became ever more closely associated with the expedition and when, in May 1955, the New Zealand government finally agreed not only to contribute £50,000 but also to take on responsibility for the establishment of what would come to be called 'Scott Base', it was almost inevitable that they should ask Hillary to take command of the Ross Sea Party. The request was made on 9 June and he accepted without hesitation.

When he heard the news, Fuchs was still in the throes of selecting equipment and supplies and ensuring that they were packed and labelled ready for loading onto the expedition ship, which was expected to sail on 14 November. There was still an enormous amount of work to be done and, according to Parry, as the time for the Advance Party's departure drew ever closer, 'pressure in the office was really rising and matters previously resting quietly in the background forced themselves aggressively to the fore.'[98] In these conditions, Fuchs had very little time to devote to consideration of events in New Zealand, but as he stood among the packing cases and straw with the pieces of his long-planned expedition finally slotting into place, Hillary's appointment must have seemed like his last and greatest public relations coup. Measured from the date of their first meeting, it had taken 18 months to persuade Hillary to accept the leadership of the Ross Sea Party, but the New Zealanders would not sail until December 1956, and Fuchs could therefore feel confident that there was still ample time for his expectations regarding publicity and funding to be fulfilled. Had he been able to foresee the repercussions of Hillary's appointment he would have felt altogether less jubilant. Over the coming months and years, the New Zealander's involvement would generate huge conflict within the TAE and would eventually come close to tearing the expedition apart in the most public manner possible. For Fuchs, at least, the appointment would become the most bitterly regretted decision of the entire Commonwealth Trans-Antarctic Expedition.

2

The Voyage of the *Theron*

After what Admiral Parry described as 'some hard bargaining, reminiscent of Oriental bazaars',[99] the ship selected to transport the Advance Party to the Weddell Sea was the 849-ton Motor Vessel *Theron*, a sealer and part-time Arctic research ship built by the James Lamont Company of Glasgow in 1950 and operated by Christensen Canadian Enterprises of Montreal. The *Theron* steamed into Millwall Docks on 3 November 1955 and, from the moment she tied up, she became the focus of intense, even frenetic, activity reminiscent of every Antarctic expedition since the time of Scott. Over the course of the next eleven days Fuchs and Captain Harald Marø supervised the process of loading the equipment required by the TAE's eight-man vanguard while the expeditionaries themselves assumed the role of stevedores – their individual expertise now far less important than their willingness to strain every muscle in order to bundle over 300 tons of supplies across the creaking gangplank.

'Since the ship was specially designed for ice conditions in the polar seas of the Canadian Arctic,' a correspondent of *The Times* remarked, 'she can be regarded as well suited for her forthcoming voyage to the Antarctic, though she has not yet sailed in those southern seas.'[100] In particular, the *Theron*'s design boasted three large insulated holds capable of storing up to 30,000 seal carcasses – though her capacity, as the same reporter facetiously observed, 'is, of course, measured in rather different terms by those who will load the ship with stores and equipment for the Trans-Antarctic Expedition.' Now these holds would be expected to accommodate hundreds of packing cases of food, clothing, books and tools; sacks of coal and drums of vehicle and aviation fuel; stacks of telegraph poles donated by the GPO to serve as a ramp from the ship to the base-site; an Auster aircraft, two Ferguson tractors and two Weasels; and, most important of all, the expedition hut. A second Auster and a Sno-cat would be secured on deck. Inevitably, given these volumes, the holds quickly reached capacity and then stores and equipment spilled out onto the decks, which soon took on the appearance of an obstacle course fiendishly designed to trip and snag the unwary. Even in the last hours before departure on 14 November deckhands and explorers continued to carry supplies aboard and Rainer Goldsmith, the Advance Party's cynical and detached young medical officer, quickly recognised that 'it was obvious that we would not sail at 12 or even at 2.'[101]

Educated at Charterhouse, Cambridge and Bart's Hospital, and with two years as an Army doctor under his belt, Goldsmith possessed both the intelligence and confidence to challenge received wisdom. His outspokenness would soon lead to a cooling of relations with the conservative Fuchs, who later described him, rather dismissively, as a 'large young man of 28 with a tendency to look for new ways of doing things.'[102] For the time being, however, the young medic was more preoccupied with unravelling the romantic ties which complicated his private life than with criticising the management of the expedition and, in his diary, he restricted his observations to the 'rather comic-tragic interlude of the multitude of goodbyes' and to the fact that, even as he said his farewells, he 'couldn't get any sense of importance for the occasion'.[103]

One contingent of the TAE, however – the 24 sledge-dogs – could harbour no doubts regarding either the significance of the *Theron's* departure, or the critical part they were expected to play in the expedition. All morning, as they sat in two vans a short distance from the waterside, the huskies had attracted the notice of the well-wishers and idlers gathered on the quays. Although attention was momentarily distracted by the complicated loading of the enormous crated Sno-cat, which could only be managed with the assistance of a floating crane, the dogs remained the clear favourite of the spectators. In the early afternoon, a party of dignitaries led by Lord Waverley, chairman of the Port of London Authority (PLA), descended to inspect them and shortly afterwards the clanging bell of the stevedores' electric truck warned the crowds to step aside as the dogs' embarkation commenced. The throng of sight-seers had become so dense that the PLA police were obliged to exert themselves to establish order, but the mood was good-humoured and applause and cheers erupted as the first two dogs filed across the gangplank, followed shortly afterwards by the remaining animals, who were swung aboard with rather less ceremony by the dockside derricks.

Later in the day Lord Waverley made a second appearance, this time on board the PLA's yacht, St Katherine, accompanied by other dignitaries including representatives of the governments of Australia, New Zealand and South Africa and by Wing Commander Eddie Shackleton, youngest son of the great explorer, whose presence added, in the words of one journalist, 'a special and intimate association with British Antarctic exploration'.[104] Then, at four o'clock, some four and a half hours later than her scheduled departure time, the indolent swirl of smoke from the Theron's single funnel at last gave place to an altogether more determined black plume that billowed in time to the pulse of her engine. The green, oily water at the ship's stern began to boil with the rotation of her propeller and, to everyone's relief, Captain Marø finally gave the long-anticipated order to cast off. The spectators hurrahed and, as the ship nosed out into the estuary, tugs and steamers sounded their horns in valediction. Puzzled by this unaccustomed display, it took the dour Marø a moment to appreciate what the commotion indicated, but once he realised, the Theron's hooter added its shrill note to the cacophony, mingling with the howling of the huskies. At last, after 7 years of planning and preparation, the TAE, the latest in a long line of aspirant trans-Antarctic expeditions was underway.

Unfortunately, feelings of bathos quickly superseded the fanfare of departure as the Theron, instead of plunging heroically southwards, merely ran down channel as far as Gravesend where she hove-to to embark explosives and one of the least glamorous, but nonetheless essential, items of expedition equipment: a

collection of stovepipes, which had mistakenly been sent to the
Royal Society's IGY vessel, the *Tottan*, at Southampton. Luckily,
this unscheduled stop provided an opportunity to weatherproof
the dogs' crates and to erect a temporary rail that would enable
passengers and crew to negotiate the crowded decks in heavy seas.
It also gave Goldsmith the chance to go ashore to purchase that
most vital of medical supplies, seasickness tablets, to supplement
those inadvertently buried in the depths of the hold. Having
bought the necessary medicines and enjoyed a surreptitious beer
in a local pub – an experience he likened to the last meal of a
condemned man – he rejoined the ship to assist in stowing the
all-important stovepipes. At 6.15pm the expedition was ready to
proceed on the first leg of its long voyage: to São Vicente in the
Cape Verde Islands.

Over the course of the next ten days, the expeditionaries
gradually became accustomed to shipboard life – and the *Theron*'s
eighteen-strong crew to the presence of sixteen more-or-less sea-
sick landlubbers lurching from their tiny cabins across the chaotic
decks to the rail and back again. Despite the masses of expedition
correspondence demanding his attention, Fuchs found it impossible to do anything but prop himself against the wheelhouse
window to watch the spray bursting over the forepeak, while a
prostrated George Lowe struggled to make even the briefest, but
nonetheless telling, entries in his diary: 'Nov. 17: Bay Biscay –
sick'; 'Nov. 20: Towards Canary Is. – sick'; 'Nov. 22: Rough sea
beyond Canary – sick.'[105] Squadron Leader John Claydon, the
senior pilot of the RNZAF contingent who was accompanying
the Advance Party as an observer, noted that 'the ship pitched
very badly in a head sea which was most uncomfortable. On such
occasions it was difficult to stand in the cabin and the journey
to and from the dining and smoke rooms was something of an
adventure, with the high sea coming over the bow and sides.'[106]
John Lewis, Claydon's RAF counterpart, summed up the *Theron*'s
sailing qualities more succinctly: 'She's a good sea boat,' he
acknowledged, 'but she'd roll on wet grass!'[107]

The routine of those members of the Advance Party who were
able to stagger to their feet focused almost exclusively on the care

of the dogs. Inevitably, with the animals confined to their roughly converted crates, subject to the elements and to variable seas which alternated between a glassy stillness and stomach churning turbulence, daily swabbing of kennels and the surrounding deck became necessary and disgusting in equal measure. Split into two working parties, the eight men sluiced and retched with such tedious monotony that the introduction of a new broom and dis-infectant made 21 November a red-letter day. It was the first test of the stoicism which would prove so vital in the months ahead.

The early days of the voyage also gave the expeditionaries an opportunity to size-up their companions, many of whom they had not met prior to embarkation, and to begin the process of forming friendships. For his part, Fuchs was lucky enough to find one confidant to whom he could speak with unaccustomed openness: the young filmmaker, Derek Williams. Having agreed to sponsor the expedition by meeting all of its massive fuel needs free-of-charge, British Petroleum of course hoped to obtain some return on its investment through publicity. In order to maximise the opportunity, the company had asked Fuchs to give a berth to Williams, who would make a short film about the *Theron*'s pas-sage through the ice and the establishment of the Advance Party's beachhead. In Williams's opinion,

> The fact that I wasn't a real member of the expedition ... allowed him in his mind to talk more freely to me than to his men ... And he spoke to me very frankly about many things – about his struggle to mount the expedition, for example; about the people he felt had been against him and the rivalries in what you might call the polar establishment ... He spoke to me very frankly about them.[108]

Perhaps it was inevitable, given Williams's unique status on board, that the two men should also discuss how Fuchs had chosen his team and on one memorable occasion the filmmaker observed an incident which served to emphasise Fuchs's methods of selection particularly well. One day, as he opened its kennel door, a dog ran out and bit Fuchs on the shin. Giving the animal a hearty kick,

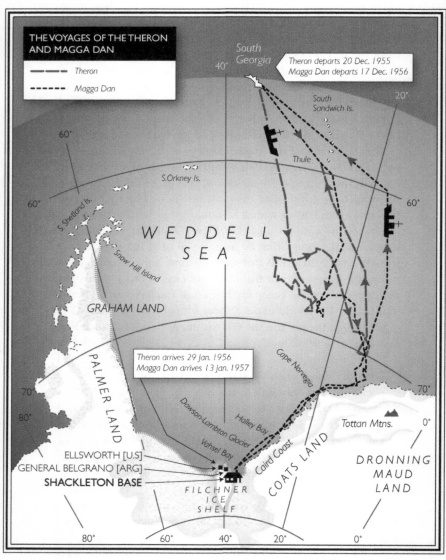

THE VOYAGES OF THE THERON AND MAGGA DAN

— — Theron
- - - Magga Dan

South Georgia

40°

Theron departs 20 Dec. 1955
Magga Dan departs 17 Dec. 1956

20°

South Sandwich Is.

60°

Thule

S.Orkney Is.

60°   60°

S. Shetland Is.

W E D D E L L

S E A

Snow Hill Island

GRAHAM LAND

Theron arrives 29 Jan. 1956
Magga Dan arrives 13 Jan. 1957

Cape Norvegia

PALMER LAND

70°   70°

80°

Dawson-Lambton Glacier

Halley Bay

Tottan Mtns.

0°

ELLSWORTH [U.S]
GENERAL BELGRANO [ARG]
SHACKLETON BASE

Vahsel Bay

Caird Coast

COATS LAND

DRONNING MAUD LAND

FILCHNER ICE SHELF

80°   60°   40°   20°   0°

Map created by Andrew Stevenson

the explorer manhandled it back into its crate and then turned to his companion. 'You see this dog, Ivik, has a narrow head,' he said. 'Now I've found that with huskies the ones with narrow heads are temperamental and less stable, more nervous. You must try and pick dogs with a broad forehead; they are more placid and equable in nature – and that goes for all dogs.'[109] 'I can hardly say that goes for all people, the forehead shape,' remembered Williams, 'but he sought to choose, and he told me this, calm equable people – people who were undramatic, phlegmatic and, it goes without saying, unimaginative and less critical – didn't think too much, didn't brood. And people who didn't brood were optimistic, cheerful and above all steady, stable people. So most of the expedition had that temperament: they were phlegmatic, optimistic and remained as cheerful as they could under the circumstances.'[110]

Fuchs hoped that the disparate members of his team would integrate as a result of the close proximity inseparable from shipboard life and, in the eyes of many, this strategy worked well. 'The Norwegian-speaking officers, the young Canadian crew and ourselves formed a happy crowd,' remembered Hannes La Grange, the South African meteorologist, 'and many an evening we gathered on the afterdeck or in the small reading room, where John Lewis ran a canteen, to sing songs to the accompaniment of an accordion played by Harold, the ship's radio operator.'[111] Goldsmith, on the other hand, found that familiarity could also breed, if not contempt, then disillusionment. 'It's amazing the low standard of conversation we were able to put up', he remarked after a rather desultory party arranged to mark the chief engineer's birthday. 'It consisted, mostly from the RAF of talk of remember this booze or that and always a talk of drink. Curiously even [Bunny] and [David Stratton] could only talk of their last expedition and what had happened at Stanley or Montevideo when last they were there. I felt perhaps that with these [*sic*] rather select band of men one might get away from this one topic talk that you can hear in every male society.'[112] Fortunately, the doctor ascribed his feelings of dissatisfaction to the uneasy motion of the *Theron* and, as the roughness of the sea gradually abated, he felt able to push his doubts to the back of his mind – for the time being at least.

The *Theron* reached the Cape Verde Islands early on 25 November in beautiful, calm weather and for a few short hours the expeditionaries enjoyed the sights and sounds of São Vicente without the infernal clanking and creaking of the ship drumming in their ears. But their stay was a brief one and that evening, with her fresh-water tanks replenished, the ship was again underway, bound for Montevideo. As they approached the equator, each morning the sun flooded the tiny cabins with light and heat. Poor ventilation rendered the dining and smoking saloons uninhabitable during the hottest part of the day and, with the cluttered decks polluted by the odour of the dogs, the ship became increasingly uncomfortable under the glare of the tropic sun. A few of the men threw off their clothes to be dowsed by the ship's hose – but the relief proved only temporary.

After lunch on 27 November, Fuchs broke the monotony, albeit temporarily, when he gathered his men together in the dining saloon and gave them their first full briefing. With the temperature standing at over 90°F, he kept the talk short and to the point, focusing on the division of the team into task groups responsible for various aspects of unloading and establishing the Advance Party's base. Deliberately practical and devoid of any attempt to strike an heroic pose, the talk left some members of the expedition feeling uninspired but overall, and despite the excessive heat and over-crowding, the mood on board remained predominantly one of excitement and anticipation, which increased with every nautical mile they made south. Pent-up energy found a welcome release on the 29th when the *Theron* 'crossed the line' and, conforming with ages old maritime tradition, those members of the expedition who had not previously crossed the equator were dragged before Neptune, represented by Ralph Lenton, the Advance Party's carpenter and deputy leader, to answer for their crimes. Having heard the charges, the pantomime monarch of the seas invariably found the prisoners 'guilty' and sentenced each to be dunked in a tarpaulin bath and then ritually shaved by the gleeful third mate.

On 8 December, after a day of rough seas on which she bounced 'like a rubber ball'[113] the *Theron* entered the mouth of the River Plate and by 9 o'clock the following morning she was riding peacefully at anchor off Montevideo; she had been at sea for 23 days. Almost as soon as she came to rest, a troop of Uruguayan officials boarded the ship – as determined and vocal as a horde of pirates, but all waving forms requiring immediate signature, rather than cutlasses and belaying pins. Then came a posse of enthusiastic journalists and photographers, scribbling and clicking incessantly and, finally, Ed Hillary and his second-in-command, Bob Miller.

Like Claydon, Hillary and Miller hoped to use the voyage to gain some much needed Antarctic experience. To make their rendezvous, they had left New Zealand on 1 December, flown across the Pacific to Vancouver and then on, via Mexico, Peru, Bolivia and Argentina, finally arriving in Montevideo just two days before the *Theron*. Swinging himself over the rail, the 6 foot 2 inch Hillary immediately made a favourable impression on the rest of the explorers. Disarmingly informal, his first words were 'Call me Ed!' – removing at a single stroke any awkwardness that his recently conferred knighthood might have engendered. Hillary particularly impressed Derek Williams, who found him 'Very easy-going, seemingly, and very pleasant to get along with. Pleasant to everyone; slow drawling speech; a fine looking man, of course; terrific quiet charisma. Everybody loved him.'[114] Only on closer acquaintance, did doubts begin to surface, when it became apparent that, for all his *bonhomie*, Hillary did not carry his achievements quite so lightly as it had at first seemed. Goldsmith, while fully acknowledging the mountaineer's personal charm, also found him 'very self-important – terribly self-important. I mean unbelievably self-important! "I'm the great climber of Everest!" He never said that, but…'[115] For the time being, however, the cracks remained well concealed.

Leaving the crew to replenish the *Theron*'s oil tanks, the members of the land party spent the rest of the day investigating the narrow cobbled streets of Montevideo. They met for dinner and drinks at the English club and then one member of the expedition at least, only too well aware of the celibate days ahead, slipped away to seek out and enjoy more fleshly pleasures – the

last such experience for many months to come. Having sated
themselves with all the good things that the city and its residents
had to offer, the explorers regrouped the following morning for
a last drink ashore and then made their way back to the waiting
ship. By 2.00pm on 10 December they were once again underway, with Montevideo sinking rapidly in their wake.

The *Theron* headed out into the roaring forties bound for
South Georgia. 'About three days later,' Williams recorded, 'heading south, I woke up and there was a completely different feeling
in the air – the ship was cold. I went onto the deck and there was
a rush of cold air – the raw breath of the south.'[116] The sea, too,
took on an ominous appearance, its deep swell a lustreless grey-
ish green, and yet, when sitting in the lee of the crates stacked
on deck, the expeditionaries still found the sun almost too hot
to bear. It seemed as though the *Theron* was floating between
two worlds: the one epitomised by the bustling, intensely human
Montevideo, its atmosphere rich with the scents and colours
of innumerable flowers and ripening fruit, and the other the
Antarctic, hostile and barren – but still exerting an irresistible pull
on Fuchs and his men.

On 15 December, the first penguins appeared, darting around
below the surface of the sea like miniature black torpedoes and
the next day, after a passage lasting just under a week, the expedition reached South Georgia, the last inhabited landfall before
crossing the Antarctic Circle. Jutting from the turbulent waters of
the South Atlantic like a shattered jawbone, at first sight the island
stirred very different feelings among Fuchs's men. Williams and
Lowe, sharing the cameraman's eye for contrast and drama, found
it hugely impressive, with its iron-grey mountains thrusting
into the sky, their sides slashed with snowdrifts. But Goldsmith
thought it inhospitable and oppressive: 'It was snowing: the first
snow we had seen; the mountains were blanketed in woolly
clouds. The few huts on the point were cheerless and the oily
water unfriendly. It was cold and wet.'[117]

At the time of the expedition's arrival, South Georgia still
formed the hub of the southern whaling industry with every
member of its tiny population, except for a kernel of British

administrators, engaged in the hunting and exploitation of the leviathan. From the moment that the whaling fleets had moved south from the depleted waters of the Arctic towards the end of the nineteenth century, all efforts had been focused upon turning the island into one enormous factory designed exclusively for slaughter on a massive scale. The equipment and by-products of the industry could be seen everywhere: the flensing platforms onto which the giant carcasses were winched for dismemberment; behind them, the great gaunt redbrick factory with its vats for boiling the whales' blubber down to oil; and, in the foreground, piles of ships' chandlery, ready to service the needs of the swift whale-catchers. Whale bones lay all around: enormous ribs, collapsed in on themselves like the roofs of abandoned houses, myriad skulls and colossal vertebrae, all picked clean by seagulls that flocked to this charnel house from far and wide. Most horrible of all, the clean, crisp air of the South Atlantic was laden with the stench of boiled blubber. Alister Hardy, who had visited South Georgia on the RRS *Discovery* in 1926, had described it as 'being like a mixture of the smell of a tanning factory and that of fish meal and manure works together with a sickly and almost overpowering odour of meat extract.'[118]

To the men of the TAE, the island was probably most famous for its close association with Shackleton. On 9 May 1916, after an epic 750-mile open-boat journey which had become the stuff of Antarctic legend, Shackleton and five companions had landed at King Haakon Bay, 30 miles overland from Stromness whaling station. Shackleton, Frank Worsley and Tom Crean had then become the first men to cross the mountainous interior of the island to announce the plight of their fellows marooned on Elephant Island after the destruction of the *Endurance*. Six years later, after his death during the early stages of the *Quest* Expedition, Shackleton had been buried in a small cemetery overlooking Cumberland Bay. Over the course of the next few days, all the members of Fuchs's team made their way up to the small cemetery to pay their respects to the great explorer and, perhaps, to wonder whether they could succeed where he had so spectacularly, but so heroically, failed.

The expeditionaries next turned their attention to more practical matters, foremost among which was the assembly and testing
of one of the two Auster aeroplanes so that it would be ready
for ice reconnaissance when the *Theron* entered the Weddell Sea.
During the voyage south, the fuselage of the Auster had been
secured in a special float cradle mounted on top of the central
hatch, while the wings had been removed and sealed in plastic
and canvas covers and carried in a crate on deck. Fortunately,
despite the rough passage, all the components remained undamaged and Peter Weston, the RAF Flight Sergeant responsible,
took a day to complete their reassembly, assisted by the pilots. As
a spectator, Goldsmith was unimpressed; he thought the exercise
involved 'rather a lot of messing about' and wondered whether
some of the RAF contingent had been well chosen, no matter
what their previous experience. '[Lewis] doesn't seem to be the
ideal leader for such a party,' he wrote in his diary after watching
proceedings, '– too slap-dash and at the same time not allowing
anyone to tell him anything. [Weston] isn't easy either, he is difficult to get to know and while he has been feeling unwell it has
been exceedingly difficult to get anything out of him.'[119]

Subsequent events seemed to justify the doctor's doubts. The
small aeroplane, painted bright orange and with the cockades of
the RAF blazoned on its wings, was swung out from the ship's
side and lowered gently onto the water. Lewis took the controls
and throttling-up sent the machine careering across Cumberland
Bay, its small engine racing. Unfortunately, as it gathered speed,
the floats, instead of leaving the water cleanly, began to bounce
dangerously, jarring the entire machine. Anxious to avoid damage
that might prove irreparable in this far-flung outpost of empire,
Lewis decided to abort the run and to wait for the waters to
settle before trying again. He succeeded on his second attempt
and the explorers, gathered at the *Theron*'s rail and on the quayside, cheered as the Auster rose into the leaden sky, looking like
some gaudy tropical bird against the bleak, snow-clad mountain
scenery. Gordon Haslop, the third pilot, wasn't so lucky. During
his first take-off later that day, the aircraft fell back heavily on
the water, and the Auster was left with an undercarriage so badly

buckled that immediate repairs were required. Happily, Grytviken included a burly Norwegian blacksmith among its residents and the RAF contingent breathed a collective sigh of relief when this colossus 'indicated by sign language and a series of grunts that he could do the job.'[120] After this somewhat embarrassing episode, Lewis and Claydon made a series of further flights, partly, perhaps, to regain lost face and partly to test the Auster's radio transmitter. The machine was then swung back aboard ready for departure.

The inhabitants of South Georgia had proved so hospitable that when the time came for the *Theron* to depart on 20 December – refuelled, her tanks filled with fresh drinking water and her rails festooned with chunks of whale-meat to feed the dogs – even the sceptical Goldsmith had been converted, describing it as 'this delightful island'. So far as the islanders themselves were concerned, they had forged another link in a chain of association with Antarctic exploration stretching back to the days of Captain Cook. On this occasion, however, as Fuchs himself readily admitted, 'Though they were far too polite to say so it was perfectly obvious that they thought it would be purely a matter of luck should we ever reach our destination with all that we were attempting to carry.'[121] The *Theron* sailed at 8.00am with flocks of seabirds wheeling and screeching overhead and, at last, the expedition had embarked on the last leg of its long voyage.

Heading south-eastwards along the coast of South Georgia, Harald Marø steered his ship round Cape Disappointment and then headed due south. Almost immediately, as if to mark the occasion, the first iceberg hove into view and hearing the cry of 'ice!' the explorers abandoned whatever they were doing and rushed to the rail to admire the great craggy berg as it floated serenely by, its wave-worn indentations glistening eerily blue and green. Over the next two days, as the ship approached the boundary of the Weddell Sea, more and more ice drifted past and by 5 o'clock on 22 December the *Theron* was in the pack. 'There was a stir of excitement in the ship,' Williams remembered, 'everybody was looking over the bow to see the pieces of ice – and we smashed through them, brushed them aside effortlessly! We thought "This is wonderful – wonderful progress!"'[122]

Like his father before him, Captain Marø had spent much of his career navigating Hudson Bay and feeling his way along the coasts of Labrador and Belle Isle Strait in the pursuit of seals. His knowledge of ice navigation was, therefore, extensive – but now his mettle would be tested to the utmost. The *Theron* must push through the pack, land the Advance Party and all its equipment and stores and then beat a hasty retreat – either that or risk sharing the fates of Filchner's *Deutschland* in 1912 and Shackleton's *Endurance* in 1915.

As the pack began to thicken, the small chunks being interspersed at shorter intervals with larger flat-topped bergs, Marø took to the crow's nest and directed the ship's course from there, trying to locate the path of least resistance. Working on their kit, sewing sledging harnesses and making alterations to their clothing, every few minutes the explorers felt their ship shiver as she collided with a bigger piece of the floe, which then scraped noisily down her side before being left to bob and roll in her wake. Every now and then, to avoid too hard an impact, the captain gave the order to stop engines and the *Theron* glided silently forward until she stopped with a shudder against the ice-face. With the light now so constant that day and night could be distinguished only by reference to a bulkhead clock, the ship remained underway 24 hours a day, with the continual stopping and starting, the clanging of bells, the churning of the propeller and the noise of the ice making sleep all but impossible.

Time and time again the ship halted as Marø, straining his eyes to see through the snow squalls, waited for a lead to open. On Christmas Eve, the *Theron* crossed the Antarctic Circle – but the distance travelled in the previous 24 hours had been limited to a mere 75 miles. Despite this painfully slow progress, however, the mood on board remained almost excessively optimistic – the good humour of the less seasoned sailors being given an additional fillip by the millpond-like smoothness of the sea. 'Gone were the hot, moist days in the tropics when I lay panting on my bunk;' wrote a delighted La Grange, 'gone were the miserable days of terrible seasickness.'[123] So great was the sang-froid of some, indeed, that Williams, perhaps imbued with a greater degree of objectivity by his limited role in the expedition, thought his shipmates were showing a tendency to be 'emotional and "heroic" and unduly optimistic'.[124] Certainly there were no signs of doubt or pessimism as the Christmas festivities commenced later that day. 'The jollities of the evening began at about 6.00pm in the captain's cabin,' Goldsmith recorded. 'Everyone was in good form. The captain himself is always better for a few drinks, his hard exterior which amounts almost to rudeness is softened by a little alcohol ... From then on the evening went swimmingly, singing, laughing until I was taken to bed having dispensed aspirins to all and sundry. Felt very giddy in bed and rather sick and the ship rolled drunkenly.'[125]

The following day George Lowe noted that 'Most looked the worse for wear after celebrating'[126] but, despite the hangovers, the expedition made unusually good progress, bumping and smashing its way through loose pack, closely watched by apparently fearless seals and penguins. From time to time, great leads would open in the ice, so straight and wide that they looked like manmade canals. Even more promisingly, dark blotches in the sky apparently indicated that large patches of open water lay not too far ahead. But these signs proved illusory, as Fuchs later confirmed:

It was on 26th December that our troubles really began. First the promise of the wide pools of open water through which we had been passing ended when we reached an area of large and old hummocked floes through which it became increasingly difficult to penetrate. The day itself was, for the first time since we entered the ice, one of clear visibility and bright sun. How exasperating therefore, when we became immovably held at midday. It took four hours to free the ship from the accumulation of up-ended pieces of ice, three feet thick and twelve to fifteen feet across, which had been forced alongside and beneath her. There they stood, jammed by the pressure of the floes and cemented by a mush of broken fragments and slushy snow, holding the ship in a vice.[127]

In choosing to head almost due south from South Georgia, Fuchs and Marø had taken a calculated risk. The Weddell Sea had first been penetrated in 1823 by the *Jane*, a sealing vessel commanded by Captain James Weddell. The conditions which Weddell had experienced had been miraculously benign, allowing him to reach a latitude of 74° South almost unhindered. But this remarkably trouble-free passage had never been repeated. Every subsequent ship venturing into these waters had encountered thick and often impenetrable pack ice. In his account of the *Deutschland* Expedition, *Zum Sechsten Erdteil (To the Sixth Continent)*, Wilhelm Filchner had advised those explorers following in his wake to shape a course bearing south-east rather than due south, and to follow the strip of open water discovered by William Bruce in 1904 and subsequently called the 'coastal lead'. During the summer months, this coastal lead offers the best chance to avoid the worst of the floes – its disadvantage for Fuchs, however, was that it meant measuring two sides of a triangle to reach Vahsel Bay rather than the one side that a direct southerly route would require.

In the Antarctic summer of 1954–55 the Argentinian ice-breaker, the *General San Martin*, had come closer than any other ship to duplicating Weddell's remarkably easy voyage south – and the Argentinian ship had sailed even farther west than the *Theron's* present course. Fuchs knew of this feat and believed that if, by taking the shorter but more risky direct route, he could emulate Weddell's astonishing voyage, or even enjoy the more limited success of the Argentinians, then the landing of the Advance Party might be accomplished in record time – and a route identified which could then be followed the following year when he led the main Crossing Party south. Early in December, even before he reached Montevideo, he had received a telegram from FIDS advising him that the ice had been reported as being well to the south; he accepted this message as 'another good augury'[128] and it may well have increased the temptation to try the experiment. Not long after the expedition, Hillary asserted that Fuchs, perhaps at the suggestion of James Wordie, was actually attempting to prove that the currents of the Weddell Sea formed two neighbouring vortexes, with a safe, but narrow, passage in between. If this were the case, Fuchs made no public acknowledgement of the fact and in his diary he asserted 'I purposely entered the ice as far west as 30°W to allow diversion to the east but there has been a general control of our movement in a southerly direction',[129] indicating that his course was dictated almost as much by accident as by design. Whatever the cause, however, in Derek Williams's words, the result was that 'we went into the heart of the pack ice and we got what we deserved: we got a five weeks' delay in which the whole expedition was in total jeopardy ... We certainly didn't discover anything, we just discovered that it was a big mistake.'[130]

With conditions worsening, at 4.45pm on Boxing Day, the RAF contingent launched the Auster in an attempt to find a route through the thickening pack. 'A little more organisation,' Goldsmith opined, 'and the launching and recovery would take half the time. At the moment there seems to be altogether too much mucking around.'[131] Despite these problems, the flight appeared to have been well worth the effort when Lewis returned to report that he had sighted promising leads to the south. If the *Theron* could barge her way through to these then she might be able to make rapid progress. Unfortunately, as Bob Miller later recorded, 'This encouragement led to the party's undoing'[132] because Lewis's optimistic report resulted in the *Theron* being sucked farther and farther towards a dead-end from which retreat would become increasingly difficult. The ship struggled on but it proved either impossible to break through to the open leads spotted from the Auster or, when the *Theron* did reach the point indicated, the leads had once again closed up, leaving nothing but a few hummocks to show they had ever existed.

These were conditions almost exactly replicating those that had resulted in the *Endurance* being caught and ultimately destroyed four decades earlier – a fact not lost on the increasingly gloomy expeditionaries. As Williams later recalled, 'This was a time when the entire expedition looked as if it was going to founder because if that ship had been lost, it wasn't our ship, it was a hired ship, every week that passed cost thousands of pounds. If we'd lost it, it would have been a calamity, the expedition couldn't continue. What would have happened to us, God knows. And it was a time of increasing seriousness. Everyone was saying "God knows what Bunny is feeling. God knows what he's thinking".'[133]

Despite his long experience and what Hillary called his 'brilliant ferocity', Marø seemed more depressed than any by the expedition's poor progress and by 31 December a clear difference of opinion could be observed between the captain and Fuchs. 'Bunny thinks we should have kept further east and Captain thinks we should have followed lead further to south', Lowe noted in his diary.[134] Listening to the opposing arguments, Hillary noted 'Personally I favour the South theory although I may be wrong. I have never felt particularly happy about this route anyway and would have been happier following the old route to the East of the *San Martin*'s route.'[135] So great are the risks of ice navigation, and so immense the strains imposed upon those engaged in it, that partnerships of much greater strength and longer duration than that of Marø and Fuchs have suffered as a result – perhaps, most famously, in the breakdown of the previously close friendship between Sir Douglas Mawson and Captain John King Davis during the British, Australian, New Zealand Antarctic Research Expedition (BANZARE) of 1929–31. Although Miller believed that 'On Fuchs alone rested the decision as to which route would be chosen,'[136] as the man responsible for the safety of the ship and her crew, Marø's opinion on the course must have been sought. Now, both men laboured under the realisation that, whether as a result of individual or joint decision-making, the expedition teetered on the very brink of disaster.

'It is difficult' Fuchs wrote on 2 January 1956, 'to describe the sense of complete frustration which assails one at various times during the day as we sit here unable to move by our own volition and drifting hither and thither in a compact mass of ice which stretches to the horizon.'[137] The following day, spurred on by the news that the *Tottan*, the Royal Society's ship, was making splendid progress just a few miles to the east, and by the London Committee's instruction that, if the expedition failed to break through before the end of January it must return home, the TAE resorted to desperate measures. In scenes reminiscent of Shackleton's attempts to release the stricken *Endurance*, Fuchs and his men clambered down the ship's side and began the back-breaking work of digging the *Theron* free. Over the next two days, an exhausted Lowe noted that they had 'prised ice clear and rafted it to stern; all worked extremely hard and made great clearance ... *Theron* is doing her best – she's a stout ship, but this very thick, deep ice (10 feet) and slushy concrete-like snow is terribly hard.'[138]

With the men risking total exhaustion in order to move only a mile or two each day, more extreme methods were now adopted, in the form of explosives. First they experimented with light charges but when these proved ineffective, they risked larger quantities placed near the ship's bows. Although Goldsmith thought the explosions produced nothing more beneficial than 'small holes and a large amount of flying snow', Claydon believed them to have been 'quite successful'. Successful or not, however, the strain on the ship, caused perhaps by the use of dynamite and certainly by the constant ramming of the ice, was enormous. As Fuchs noted in his diary: 'the ship jars, twists and shudders till one feels she will fall apart. The most frightening noises are when the propeller strikes the ice and a thundering hammering shakes us from stem to stern, or when going astern the rudder butts a heavy floe and the hydraulic release valve screeches in apparent agony.'[139]

Despite these efforts, some of which had the ring of 'kill or cure' about them, progress remained so pitifully slow and the ship's position so precarious that Hillary compared her to 'a nut in a nutcracker'. With the expedition in real peril of failing almost before it had begun, and with the time available for the establishment of Shackleton Base now severely restricted, Fuchs – looking 'a little grey and crestfallen at times'[140] – had no choice but to fundamentally revise his strategy. With his chosen path to the south blocked, with the ice beginning to bunch up into distinct pressure ridges and with the pack's drift already taking on a north-westerly trend, the only viable course was for the TAE to retreat northwards and attempt a different route. This plan, which he had been revolving in his own mind since the end of December, finally crystallised on 15 January, when the *Theron*

made radio contact with HMS *Protector*, a Royal Navy ice-patrol
ship currently in the vicinity of Port Lockroy in West Graham
Land. Fuchs and Captain Wilkinson of the *Protector* agreed that if
their two ships could rendezvous at the northern ice edge, then
the Royal Navy would use its Westland Whirlwind helicopters
to reconnoitre a passage through the floes. Since the helicopters
were launched straight from the *Protector's* flight deck and did not
require a lead or large pond to take off, much time might be
saved and the TAE given a helping hand to reach its destination
before the entire expedition was fatally compromised. But, just
when it seemed that they might have found a solution to their
plight, an unfortunate accident nearly brought the expedition to
an ignominious end.

On the 18th, as the *Theron* sought to rendezvous with the
Protector, she rammed two floes, each with a depth of about 15 feet
below the waterline. Watching these manoeuvres from a vantage
point on the pack, Goldsmith thought it 'most impressive to see
the ship charging the ice … it looks like some huge monster rearing out of the water only to fall back again, beaten by the thickness
of the ice.'[141] As the floes crumbled before the ship's onslaught, it
became necessary to haul some of the larger fragments away from
the bows by using the vessel's stern winch. During the process, a
slab of ice broke free with unexpected ease, causing the 3-inch
steel cable to suddenly slacken and its loose coils to become entan-
gled in the rapidly spinning propeller. Looking down through the
clear water at the fouled propeller shaft, Marø summarised their
situation in stark terms: 'Either the shaft will wear through the
rope and we'll come to no harm or the rope will wear through the
shaft and the propeller will drop off.'[142] In the latter eventuality the
ship would be entirely disabled and the expedition would be at
an end. When the tough nickel-steel propeller was once again set
in motion, a 12-foot length of severed steel wire thrashed in the
water like a hooked eel, striking the keel with a resounding crash
at every rotation. That night a lugubrious Lowe noted that the
incident left 'gloom everywhere'. Worse was to follow.

On 19 January, with the severed cable showing no immediate
signs of crippling the ship, despite the noise, the *Theron* began

painstakingly to negotiate a narrow and jagged lead which had opened between the floes. So narrow was the lead and so acute its twists, that they obliged the chief officer to issue a stream of orders to the engine room, ahead one moment and astern the next, as he sought to manoeuvre the ship round each dogleg. Inevitably, during this process the ship's rudder struck the ice wall and when Marø took over the following day he found that the vessel answered to only six degrees of port helm, rendering her nearly impossible to steer in open water. With his ship seriously handicapped, the captain had little choice but to take extreme measures. Putting the rudder hard over to port, he deliberately backed his ship into the ice – seeking to remedy with a deliberate collision damage that had been wrought by an accidental one. The first two attempts failed and then, in Lowe's words, the captain 'took courage – or was it anger – and forced the ship hard astern into relatively thin ice.'[143] Despite its brutality and the very real risk of fracturing the rudder beyond repair, the plan worked. The force of the impact was so great that it actually over-corrected the rudder to starboard but to the relief of everyone on board – and to none more than to Marø himself – the ship had regained her manoeuvrability. 'Looking back,' a grateful Fuchs wrote, 'one realises that this was one of the occasions when the fate of the whole expedition must have hung in the balance. Certainly his only alternative to taking this risk was to move almost helplessly about in the ice hoping only that we should come clear before the freeze up, but with no chance of establishing our base.'[144]

As if to reward the captain's courage, almost as soon as the vibrations of the impact died away, the *Theron* entered the largest pool that she had encountered for some time – large enough for the Auster to be launched. This time the New Zealander, John Claydon, took the controls and after a hair-raising take-off in which he used every inch of the available 350 yards of water, he spent three hours in the air, flying in all directions in an attempt to find an escape route for the ship. From his vantage point 5000 feet above the jigsaw-like floes, Claydon could see that the *Theron* 'was trapped in an enormous area, stretching to the horizon, of solid ice with tremendous icebergs scattered all over it.'[145] So far as he could judge, however, if the ship could be nursed through about 2 miles of thick ice to the west, and then through close pack for a further 18 miles to the north-west, before finally turning north for another 30 miles through fairly open pack, she might reach open water. If she managed to get that far she would then be able to proceed eastwards at normal speed prior to making what would have to be her final attempt to reach Vahsel Bay. Hearing Claydon's fairly upbeat assessment of their chances of escape, the relief among the expeditionaries was palpable; 'broad smiles appeared on the faces of all those around,' Goldsmith observed. 'There were as usual some sceptics ... But [Claydon] I feel would give a far more accurate picture of the ice than did [Lewis] whose rosy accounts have ended up in three weeks in the ice.'[146]

With the Auster secured, the *Theron* got underway. Following the course surveyed from the air, as Claydon had predicted, the ship broke free of the heavy floes into an area of thinner ice, only 2 feet thick. In normal conditions, the reinforced bows of the *Theron* would have made light work of this obstacle, but the ice was under such enormous and sustained pressure that she found it impossible to break through. The tried and tested methods of breaking the ice by hand and dynamiting were employed but with frustratingly little success as the ice proved too thin to work easily by hand while the explosives tended merely to blast circular holes instead of causing the crust to split into leads. By 3.30am on 21 January the concerted efforts of all on board had succeeded in clearing one side of the ship's hull but then, with a sudden and seemingly malicious heave, perhaps precipitated by the ill-timed detonation of an explosive charge by Gordon Haslop, the floes instantly pressed forward to close the gap which it had taken so long to create. 'Nine hours work wasted,' a doleful and exhausted Lowe noted when he staggered back to his cabin in the early hours. Behind the *Theron*, the track which she had made through the ice closed and even the pool from which the aeroplane had been launched the day before disappeared altogether. Even more disturbing, as they stood on deck, the men could see that the ice was climbing the ship's sides, forced 3–4 feet upwards by the immense pressure of the pack. It seemed as though they might never be released.

Then, the next day, just as suddenly and inexplicably, the pressure relaxed allowing the ship to surge forward. Throughout the course of the afternoon she ploughed onwards towards her rendezvous with HMS *Protector* and, by 10pm, a jubilant Lowe could record that 'we are going steadily ahead – making perhaps 3 knots through heavyish but opening pack. Hooray! … Captain working like a wild man, determined as hell!'[147] Every hour the *Theron*'s radio operator switched on the ship's beacon to guide the *Protector* and on the morning of the 23rd, after a brief exchange of radio messages, one of the Royal Navy's helicopters came into view. '[We] saw him,' Goldsmith wrote, 'a tiny dot between two icebergs; rapidly he came nearer, an orange and black dragonfly, out of its cabin the pilot waved, took our portrait, circled once or twice and was off again.'[148] Approximately 40 miles still separated the *Theron* from the ice edge but she continued to push through the open pack with relative ease and at 8.00pm she at last joined the *Protector*, wallowing in a heavy swell about a mile north of the ice edge. Ungainly though she might be, with her grey paint streaked with rust, her lines spoiled by the large helicopter hangar on her afterdeck and her rails lined with bearded ruffians, the Royal Navy vessel was a sight for sore eyes.

Captain Wilkinson immediately despatched a whaler to bring Fuchs and a small party of expeditionaries aboard and then treated them to a slap-up meal – somewhat to the chagrin of those left behind. Having discussed the condition of the pack with Wilkinson, by midnight the TAE was once again on its way, with the *Theron* heading east through the outer fringes of the pack. Fuchs now intended to follow the ice edge eastwards until they located the open water through which the *Tottan* had sailed with so little trouble a month earlier. The *Theron* maintained a steady 12 knots while, just a few hundred yards to the south, the floes at the ice edge could be seen and heard jostling against each other in the gentle swell. Given the weeks that had been wasted, Fuchs and Marø were reluctant to enter the pack until they were confident that the route was sufficiently free to allow them an

unfettered passage south: discretion had become the better part
of valour.

At last, on 25 January, having sailed some hundreds of miles from
the point at which she had emerged from the pack, the *Theron*
turned east-south-east towards Cape Norvegia where Fuchs
expected his men to catch their first glimpse of the great Antarctic
continent. Sailing conditions remained excellent with, at times, no
pack at all visible and the ice restricted to a few isolated bergs and
much smaller growlers. From Cape Norvegia, a chastened Fuchs
intended to follow the coastal lead he had rejected so disastrously
a month earlier. Hoping for landfall the following morning, he
announced his intention of making an aerial survey in the direction of Maudheim, where the NBSAE had made its base in 1949.
To an increasingly impatient Hillary, this plan seemed to be both a
waste of valuable time and an unnecessary risk: 'If anything should
happen on this trip', he scrawled angrily, 'it will be the second
major boob he has made … his route into the Weddell Sea being
the first whopper. However I won't say anything as I'm already
rather in disfavour I fear due to my comments earlier when we
were making our way out of the ice.'[149]

In the event, the next day visibility rapidly deteriorated, Cape
Norvegia remained shrouded in snow squalls and largely hidden
from view, and the flight was cancelled. For ten days overcast skies
had rendered it impossible to take a sun shot and, as a result, the
Theron's exact position could only be estimated, with a margin
of error as wide as 30 or 40 miles. 'In spite of all modern aids to
navigation,' Goldsmith observed, 'no one has any real idea exactly
where we are. The first land was sighted through the mist and
snow at about 4.30 but it was anyone's guess and most people had
a guess.'[150] This hardly constituted the dramatic first view of the
continent that the expeditionaries had hoped for, but by the 27th
weather conditions had improved and, at last, a delighted Derek
Williams could begin to film the kind of scenes that he – and his
sponsors – had hoped for. '[When] we broke free from the ice,' he
later enthused, 'suddenly the weather changed completely and we
steamed down the coast, down to Vahsel Bay in beautiful slanting
sunlight, with the icebergs and the cliffs well lit and everybody

on deck. Not perhaps an important or dramatic moment in the expedition but very good for photography.'[151]

Sailing round icebergs which Fuchs identified as the shattered remnants of the great Stancomb-Wills Ice Promontory, discovered and named by Shackleton in 1915 but now reduced to frozen rubble, the *Theron* reached the Royal Society's IGY base at Halley Bay during the evening of the 27th. In the event of the *Theron* being unable to reach the Filchner Ice Shelf at the head of the Weddell Sea, it might prove necessary to land the Advance Party at Halley Bay. This possibility made it imperative to determine whether a successful crossing – albeit a crossing some 200 miles longer than planned – could be launched from here.

With an ice anchor securing the ship to the ice edge, the crew swung out the Auster and placed it gently on the waters of the bay. Unwilling to rely upon a second hand account of surface conditions which could make or break the most important element of his enterprise, and perhaps also remembering Lewis's unduly optimistic description of ice conditions on Boxing Day, on this occasion Fuchs joined him in the cockpit. The aerial survey proved decisive: flying at only 800–1000 feet towards the Dawson Lambton Glacier, which fell into the sea to the south of Halley Bay, the aeroplane's shadow was soon dancing across heavily ridged *sastrugi* and crevasses which would render the area completely impassable to vehicles. Even more crevasses could be discerned to the east along the margin of the ice shelf. Fuchs very quickly realised that 'to establish our base here might prejudice the trans-continental journey at the very beginning. I therefore decided, while still in the air, that only in the very last resort would Shackleton Base be set up at Halley Bay.'[152]

'Everybody,' Lowe noted in his diary, 'wants to set the Base further south' and at 2.00pm on 28 January the members of the TAE waved farewell to the IGY party and embarked on what had to be the expedition's last throw of the dice. Sailing through waters which remained so free of sea ice that Fuchs compared their passage to 'a Mediterranean cruise with unusual scenery' the expedition plotted a course adjacent to the vast walls of coastal ice, which, for many miles, continued to be far too heavily

crevassed and broken to permit landing. South of the Dawson
Lambton Glacier the *Theron* began to encounter more and more
icebergs, sculpted into a thousand fantastic shapes by the action
of wind and sea, but by working out further from the coast, she
was able to continue her steady progress south.

The floes gradually became more tightly packed but still
a single lead, 3 miles wide, remained open. The ice to either
side stretched as far as the eye could see, its heavily ridged and
hummocked appearance providing everyone on board with an
unpleasant reminder of the tortured ice-scape through which
they had passed during the previous weeks. 'Never had I seen
such thick or such universally crumpled ice,' Fuchs remembered,
'impassable to a ship, impossible to cross with any form of transport ... Had the wind and current which forced the ice apart
allowed it to close again not even the stout build of the *Theron*
could have withstood the pressure.'[153] For all on board, it seemed
that the pages of Shackleton's epic *South* had sprung to vivid and
terrifying life before their eyes – an impression made all the more
poignant and troubling by the realisation that their ship now lay
within just a few short miles of the position where the *Endurance*
had become fatally trapped.

As the lead gradually dwindled in width, it seemed for a while
that circumstances were once again conspiring to frustrate Fuchs's
plans, but when the explorers awoke the following morning conditions had once again miraculously changed for the better. By
5.00am on the 29th, the *Theron* was pushing confidently through
light floes from which the menace had receded with the night. To
the south, various potential landing points could be seen where
the previously precipitous ice cliffs descended in comparatively
easy sweeps down towards the coast. 'Everyone most heartened
by the progress,' a relieved Goldsmith wrote, 'after weeks of disappointment it looks as if we shall get to our destination after
all.'[154] But not everyone shared in the general satisfaction. Fuchs's
relationship with Hillary had continued to deteriorate and now
the New Zealander admitted to feeling 'rather peeved for the
last few days at the way I have been completely ignored on the
planning and information side. I have had less information on

what is going on than Bob Miller or John Claydon and I feel each time I make a suggestion that it just isn't wanted.'[155] Perhaps Fuchs considered that, as a newcomer to the Antarctic and with no meaningful part to play on this element of the expedition, Hillary's presence at planning meetings was simply unnecessary. Perhaps, too, he found Hillary's self-confidence and willingness to voice his opinions more than a little irritating. Whatever his motivations, however, by bruising Hillary's ego in this manner, he was storing up trouble for the future.

Marø believed that the *Theron* must now be very close to Vahsel Bay, but to pinpoint the ship's exact position, Claydon and the captain took to the air. 'The vast ice cap of the Continent could be seen rising gradually in the distance towards the Pole,' Claydon reported, 'but the most significant sight was a few isolated patches of black rock sticking through the ice some distance to the south. These were obviously the Bertrab Nunataks of Vahsel Bay.'[156] It was an historic moment: after a passage of some two and a half months, and despite weeks of delay during which it seemed that the expedition might fail altogether, the Advance Party of the TAE had at last reached its destination. Now all that remained was to select the best spot for a landing.

With Vahsel Bay so near, Marø brought the *Theron* close into shore to prospect for a suitable base site. Initially, the snow slopes appeared too steep and too deeply crevassed to allow easy access for the vehicles and so the ship continued to inch its way south towards the bay itself. Taking to the air once more, this time with Haslop at the controls, Fuchs flew west along the face of the Filchner Ice Shelf and then back again, probing all the time for a suitable landing point. This survey led him to believe that the expedition's best plan would be to moor the *Theron* against the sea ice; here the stores and equipment could be offloaded ready for the tractors to drag them half a mile across the sea ice and then up the 150-feet incline to the floating ice shelf where the Advance Party's tents could be pitched and the main hut built. Once established, Shackleton Base would then become the launching point for the continental crossing the following year. Having outlined his decision to the members of the expedition,

Fuchs ordered the *Theron* to continue her progress along the ice edge until she reached a point he had identified from the air, approximately 20 miles from Vahsel Bay.

Once they reached the spot selected, David Stratton, the FIDS surveyor whom Fuchs had chosen as second-in-command of the Crossing Party, undertook a reconnaissance inland to test the surface of the old sea ice. Ken Blaiklock, meanwhile, whose home this would be in the months ahead, flew inland with Claydon to obtain some impression of the terrain over which he would sledge during the following spring. Both returned with satisfactory reports – yes, the sea ice and the interior of the ice shelf were crevassed but, unlike those observed in the vicinity of the Dawson Lambton Glacier, the obstacles did not appear insuperable. Besides, time was now, more than ever, of the essence. The original plan as sketched out in London had been to land the Advance Party and spend some weeks in helping its members to establish the base. Now, after so many weeks of delay and with the weather closing in, there would be little enough time to fling the supplies and equipment onto the sea ice before the *Theron* beat a hasty retreat to avoid the floes snapping shut behind her.

To Blaiklock's men, at this point the amended plan, forced upon them by the delays encountered in the pack, seemed of little significance. The expedition had reached its objective and the mood was one of excitement and enthusiasm. Even Goldsmith, whose experiences to date had led him to question some aspects of the expedition's planning and execution, was carried along by the prevailing spirit: 'The sky was friendly and the sun shone,' he wrote on the eve of disembarkation. 'It was certainly quite friendly ... A gently rolling snow slope with sea ice in the foreground, in the distance a view of some rocks ... It doesn't look a too unfriendly place to spend the winter.'[157] He could not have been more mistaken.

3

Oh, What Chaos!

On the morning of 30 January, with the *Theron* secured by a 'dead man' to the edge of the sea ice, Fuchs and David Stratton set off up the snow slope to reconnoitre a suitable location for the main hut. In looking for a site, Fuchs was only too well aware that in February 1912 Filchner's *Deutschland* Expedition had been brought to the very brink of destruction when the iceberg upon which the expedition had built its hut broke free of the bay ice and began an inexorable drift northwards. Only by a miracle had Filchner been able to salvage the bulk of his stores and save the lives of every member of his expedition, bar that of one wilful husky who refused to be coaxed back onto the ship. With the German explorer's disaster in the forefront of his mind, Fuchs's requirements for the TAE's base site were clear: 'A firm foundation in an area free of crevasses and in a position from which certain distant and recognisable features would be visible.'[158] After a careful survey of the surface, the position he now decided upon was at an elevation of about 150 feet above sea level and a little over three-quarters of a mile from the edge of the ice shelf. 'From our position on the inward curve of the ice front,' he wrote later that day, 'because of the appearance of the ice, because of the relation of crevasses to waves in the shelf and from the distance from the active area of movement in the vicinity of Vahsel Bay, I am confident that there is no chance of this part of the ice shelf breaking off as it did with Filchner.'[159] Despite these protestations, however, the decision remained a calculated risk.

Having completed their survey, the two men returned to the ship – and to a scene of what many of the participants considered to be near total chaos. From the moment the *Theron* had slipped down river from Millwall Docks, it had been obvious that, whether as a result of poor planning, the constraints of the ship itself, or simply because of the rush, supplies and equipment had been packed seemingly at random, with insufficient consideration of what might be needed and when. Realisation that the seasickness tablets had been buried deep in the hold might have appeared fairly comical in Gravesend, but when the ship entered the ice and skis and other useful equipment were found to be completely inaccessible, the confusion seemed altogether less amusing. Now, with the scheduled weeks of unloading compressed to just a few days, such an apparently slapdash approach had the potential to become life-threatening for the eight men who would be marooned at Shackleton Base. 'It is a pity,' wrote Goldsmith, 'that so much has been left to chance and to individuals who are not quite capable. Incisive leadership would raise morale considerably but instead we go blundering on without real direction so that by no means the maximum of work is done.'[160] For his part, Hillary simply observed, 'I did a good day's work but really prefer jobs where there aren't so many people milling about giving orders.'[161]

Worst of all, except for the Sno-cat, all the vehicles upon which the expedition relied to cart the hut and stores from the landing point to the base site had been stowed in the depths of the hold, where they remained totally unreachable and useless until tons of material had first been shifted and dumped onto the sea ice. Very quickly, as Bob Miller recorded, the 'immediately surrounding bay ice became a litter of all that had been the top hamper of the ship – dogs, dog crates, sledges, wire matting, lumber of all descriptions.'[162] Claydon considered the process of clearing the decks and the upper portions of the holds a 'wretched task', and the realisation that perfect flying weather was being squandered while skilled pilots sweated like navvies did nothing to improve his mood. 'Although an attempt was made to work around the clock,' he noted ruefully, 'this was found to be impossible as everybody was completely worn out.'[163] Even Hillary, whose physical prowess none could dispute, thought the process of manhandling the heavy crates 'hard work for our soft hands and unaccustomed muscles.'[164]

Perhaps the only member of the expedition who felt truly happy during the unloading was Derek Williams. When he had been offered the chance to film the launch of the TAE, the young cameraman had leaped at the chance, believing it to be a scoop that could set him firmly on the road to fame and fortune. But the blank, overcast seascape of the Weddell Sea had been a huge disappointment to one whose art depended upon light and contrast. 'It was heartbreaking for the photographer,' he remembered, '... Not what I'd expected and far beyond my wildest nightmares. Very, very poor conditions to shoot – the worst conditions in my subsequent forty years of filmmaking.'[165] And if he, on the ground itself, found the scenery dull and uninspiring, how could he hope to thrill a cinema audience with his images? But now, with the sun shining, and the sea ice a hive of activity, with the prospect of brightly coloured vehicles dashing to-and-fro, with the presence of the dogs lending something of the Heroic Era to the scene and with the men themselves looking as intrepid as any of their predecessors, he began to believe that some part of his dreams of glory might be salvaged after all.

In spite of their grumbling, Lowe considered that all the members of the TAE 'worked like blacks'[166] and by 11.00pm on the 30th the disburdened *Theron* floated a foot higher in the water. But, for those expeditionaries with energy enough to dream that night, a grim spectre lay at the back of their minds, ready to shock them into wakefulness. During their examination of the mooring area, the explorers had discovered a vicious-looking tidal crack less than half a mile from the ship – a reminder, were any needed, of the inherent instability of sea ice. Any combination of changes in temperature, wind direction or tides might cause the ice to rupture catastrophically, sending the vulnerable stores either out into the bay, like Filchner's, or straight down to the seabed. If that happened, the Advance Party would have no choice but to return to England with the *Theron*. 'We have to hope,' wrote Goldsmith, summing up all their fears, 'that nothing breaks off the bay ice and swims away.'[167]

Fortunately, luck seemed to be on the TAE's side and the next morning both ice and stores remained where they had been left the night before. Now, at last, work could begin on unloading the Weasels and Ferguson tractors. When the vehicles reached the light of day, however, their condition caused dismay among some of the explorers. The Weasels, in particular, were not new, but well-used hand-me-downs from the Canadians, whose focus on IGY work meant that they had neither funds nor manpower to donate to what they considered an expedition of secondary importance. So limited had been the Canadians' interest, indeed, that they hadn't even bothered to wash the machines, which now stood on the Antarctic sea ice still caked with the mud of the Arctic tundra. Even worse, it quickly became apparent that, as well as being dirty, the Weasels were little better than derelicts at the end of their natural lives. The Sno-cat, unloaded the previous day, had started almost immediately – but the clutch of the first Ferguson tractor was found to be frozen solid and the inevitable difficulty in locating batteries and spare parts meant that hours passed before Homard and David Pratt could get the rest of the machines operational. Finally, around lunchtime, the hoarse roar and acrid exhaust fumes of the tractors and Weasels began to fill the crisp air of the Antarctic and the laborious process of hauling the Advance Party's equipment inland could commence. 'I suppose everything will go more smoothly now that we have at last got more towing vehicles going,' asserted a nervous Goldsmith. 'I hope so.'[168]

Whatever Fuchs's aspirations regarding a site free of crevasses, he knew that locating the base close to the edge of the ice shelf made this criterion impossible to meet. As soon as the first tractor began to climb the snow slope towing two sledges loaded with a generator, timber and tools, as well as Lowe, Pratt, Stratton, Miller, Haslop and Fuchs himself, the machine began to labour in the soft snow and the sledge bearing the generator quickly had

to be abandoned. Then, near the top of the slope, as it negotiated a number of fairly small crevasses, the tractor began to break
through; it crossed safely, but the edges of the crevasses collapsed
leaving what Fuchs described as 'unpleasant looking blue holes
into the depths.' 'Though it was unlikely that a tractor would go
down these apparently small crevasses,' he wrote that evening,
'there was certainly some risk'[169] and the threat to men on foot
would be even greater. With these sobering thoughts to keep them
focused, he and his companions marked out the base site with let-
tered flags and then made their way cautiously down the slopes,
placing stakes along the route to guide drivers in poor visibility
and watching anxiously as crevasse bridges crumbled beneath the
Ferguson's weight. So frequent were the collapses that, once he
regained the ship, Fuchs ordered a number of his men to follow
his tracks up the slope and to construct wooden bridges over the
crevasses. These, he hoped, would help to make what looked like
an increasingly perilous – but unavoidable – route serviceable.

That evening, Fuchs and Captain Marø discussed the schedule for unloading. Although the long delays in the pack meant
that their stay would be shorter than planned, they agreed that
it should still be possible to remain until 14 February. This gave
them two weeks in which to unload the ship, transport the stores
from the sea ice to the base camp and see the Advance Party
well established. As they both acknowledged, this plan would be
subject to the vagaries of the weather. If changes in the wind
direction and a drop in temperature brought the risk of the
Theron becoming trapped, then they would have to retreat immediately. It was therefore essential that the unloading should be
expedited. In the meantime, regular flights in the Auster would
enable them to keep an eye on the movements of the pack –
though such reconnaissance would also be dependent upon
weather conditions. Unfortunately, the events of the following
day would demonstrate not only that the Antarctic weather could
not be relied upon – but that it would, if treated with compla-
cency, threaten not only the explorers' plans but their very lives.

The morning of 1 February began well, with the temperature
standing at a positively balmy 26°F – a full 19 degrees warmer

than at any point since the *Theron* had come to rest against the ice edge. But the unaccustomed warmth did nothing to reduce the confusion of unloading. After his experiences in the Ferguson, Fuchs had decided to limit the tractors' role to dragging the loaded sledges to the inland edge of the sea ice; here the sledges, with their 2-ton cargoes, would be coupled to the Weasels, whose superior traction would enable them to make better headway up the snow slopes. Unfortunately, while on paper this scheme seemed eminently sensible, utilising as it did the different vehicles to their best advantage, the decrepitude of the Weasels meant that the plan rapidly unravelled. Despite the unremitting efforts of the two engineers, the Weasels repeatedly ground to a halt suffering from an assortment of ailments and the desperate effort to locate spare parts in the hold contributed to the piles of stores on the sea ice. 'Difficulties with synchronising ship unloading with haulage up to site,' a disgruntled Lowe noted. 'Ship can be unloaded faster than haulage can be effected. Too many people milling around ship.'[170] Characteristically, Goldsmith's appraisal was even more forthright: 'Oh what chaos,' he exclaimed. 'The lack of organisation is almost too much to believe. [Fuchs] seems to be too mild a man to get any control of the events. Consequently plans change every minute and no one knows what is going on.'[171]

By 1.00pm the temperate conditions of the morning were giving way to strong winds from the north and the *Theron* began to move uneasily at her moorings. But still the unloading continued, with apparently no regard for the possible consequences. 'We were warned by the IGY of the dangers of landing and leaving stores on bay ice,' wrote Goldsmith, 'but in spite of that by 3 p.m. when it began to snow and the wind blew harder from the north there were great piles of stores lying not 25 yards from the ship.'[172]

Buffeted by an increasingly ferocious gale, the *Theron* began to bounce and jar against the ice and more and more water slopped onto the surface; puddles became streams and streams turned to rivers which then flowed inexorably towards the stock-piled provisions. It was not until 4.00pm, with the stores now in imminent peril of being completely engulfed, that realisation dawned. 'When it became clear that the flood was steadily increasing,' Fuchs recorded, 'I started an all-out effort to move everything back to the tide-crack about ¼ mile away.' To the other men involved, the decision appeared extraordinarily late and the ensuing action altogether less deliberate. 'Now suddenly there was panic,' scribbled an enraged Goldsmith, 'and cases were thrown onto sledges and taken away to a safer place for at this time it looked as if the ice would break away and swim out to sea. The snow became thicker and visibility almost nil. The tractors bogged down in unseen hollows and the water became deeper and deeper, conditions rapidly deteriorated.'[173] David Pratt set off up the snow slope in a Weasel to warn the men working at the base site to return to the ship, while the rest wallowed about, working like madmen in the freezing slush, hurling vital stores away from the encroaching water and shouting warnings and instructions to one another. All to no avail – as Fuchs himself admitted: 'All our efforts, however, still lost the battle and some boxes were floating and others completely submerged ... Though I salvaged them I cannot think they will survive.'[174]

Meanwhile, as the blizzard grew in intensity and the explorers dashed dementedly to-and-fro, the *Theron* continued to plunge against the ice edge, her two aft cables slackening and then tautening with such violence that they flung the rime encrusting them high into the air. Finally, at 5.15pm, with the cables screeching under the strain, the ice to which they were secured parted with a crack like gunfire. The ship's stern immediately swung away, increasing the tension on the forward cables until it became insupportable and then they too broke away, flinging the *Theron* out into the bay.

In markedly similar circumstances, on 6 May 1915, the SY *Aurora* had been torn away from the ice edge in the Ross Sea during the *Endurance* Expedition and she had then spent ten months adrift, entirely helpless and in imminent danger of being crushed by the pack. Fortunately, however, while the *Aurora*'s boilers had been blown down, ready for the ship to winter in McMurdo Sound, Fuchs and Marø had always intended that the *Theron* should sail north before the onset of winter. As a result, the vessel had been resting against the ice rather than being encased within it and her engine had been kept warm in case of such an eventuality.

Now the captain, shouting through a megaphone above the scream of the wind, told Fuchs and his companions on the ice that he would return for them as soon as the weather conditions allowed. 'My chief concern,' Fuchs later wrote, 'was, of course, the wet state of all of us and the possibility of being isolated for some time in low temperatures without change of clothing. As it was, the temperature was only 26°F but had it dropped much we could have been in trouble.'[175]

For the time being, the men ashore had little choice but to keep working – trying desperately to nurture the hope that the intrepid captain would be able to bring the ship back to her moorings. If he failed, their plight would be a very sorry one indeed. Half an hour later they breathed a collective sigh of relief as the *Theron*'s bows and foremast suddenly loomed above them like a wraith, the sound of her engine completely lost in the gale. The churning sea made it impossible for the ship to moor, so instead the crew began to fling ropes and rope ladders down her sides in the hope that the explorers would be able to reach them as she lurched past. Gordon Haslop immediately leaped forward and grasped a rope swinging from the forepeak but the overhang of the bows made it impossible for him to reach safety and he quickly found himself in imminent danger of falling between the ice edge and the ship's rusty plates. If he fell, his chances of surviving the cold and the grinding of the *Theron*'s side against the ice would be practically nil. Fortunately, Fuchs and the others managed to grab his wildly flailing legs and pull him back, with a bump, onto the ice. Homard, too, was caught in a precarious position, dangling from a rope which left him clawing at the sheer side of the aeroplane crate until his cries attracted the attention of the crew; but everyone else managed to swarm up the ship's sides without incident. Thanks to Marø's brilliant seamanship, all of the men who had been on the sea ice had made it onto the ship with only minor abrasions. But David Pratt, Bob Miller, David Stratton, Ralph Lenton and Peter Jeffries, the latter one of the Advance Party's three meteorologists, were nowhere to be seen.

As soon as Pratt had delivered his warning about the dangers developing at the ice edge a few hours earlier, all five men had clambered into the Weasel and started their descent. But the blizzard was no less intense at 150 feet above sea level and, with near-zero visibility, they repeatedly missed the carefully placed marker poles that should have guided them down the slope. With the constant risk of plunging over the edge of the shelf, the party soon had no choice but to stop. Besides, given the urgency of Pratt's original summons, it seemed improbable that they could now reach the ship before she abandoned her position.

For nearly eight hours the five men huddled in the Weasel, teetering, for all they knew, on the very edge of the precipice. Only when the drift began to settle could they discern their route and complete their journey. As they expected, the *Theron* was nowhere to be seen and her absence made the abandoned and waterlogged boxes look all the more forlorn. As Miller later reported, only now did the five castaways realise the seriousness of their predicament:

> They were ashore with some food; among the unloaded mate-rials they knew there were some tents somewhere. They had no spare or dry clothing, no heating for cooking or means of heating, no cooking or eating utensils, but worst of all the bay ice at which the ship had been docked, instead of being bor-dered by open water to the horizon, was packed by broken hummocky ice as far as they could see ... While those on shore never doubted for a moment that the *Theron* would return, it seemed obvious that she would never be able to approach the former spot by many miles.[176]

Whether they knew it or not, the thoughts now running through their minds were exactly the same as those of the marooned men of Shackleton's Ross Sea Party when they awoke on 7 May 1915 to find nothing of the *Aurora* but the severed cables that had secured her to the ice.

Anxious to prevent what could now become life-saving equip-ment from becoming frozen solid in the 18 inches of sludge,

Stratton immediately commenced a salvage operation, dragging as many of the abandoned boxes as possible to a more secure spot away from the ice edge. They worked until about 3.30am and then made their way, now bitterly cold and exhausted, back up the slope to the base site. Here they ate a scratch meal of tinned ham and sugar, erected a makeshift shelter from hut panels and then rolled themselves in fibreglass insulation in the hope of being able to sleep for a few hours. They breakfasted on icy sardines, tomatoes, margarine and dried milk and then, in a rather belated but nonetheless welcome *eureka* moment, Jeffries remembered that the cockpit of the Auster, which had been tethered on the sea ice, contained an emergency primus stove and fuel. With a hot drink thawing their chilled innards, they looked with a sudden surge of optimism at the bay: miraculously, a southwest wind was beginning to blow the pack ice away from the shore – perhaps the *Theron* would reach them after all.

The evening before, the flying snow had become so thick that those on board the ship had been forced to gather round the flickering radar screen on the bridge to obtain any view of the deserted landing point. 'All those on the ship were utterly miserable with the cold,' Claydon reported, 'but were mainly concerned about the fate of the others who had been left behind.'[177] Hillary admitted to being 'very subdued' but Fuchs, keen to keep up morale, presented an optimistic front: 'Though I knew the men ashore would have an uncomfortable time I was not unduly worried about them,' he wrote that night, 'because they had plenty of tents or vehicles to shelter in and plenty of food ... As there was nothing more that we could do, I encouraged everyone to get a meal and go straight to bed, which they were glad to do.'[178]

During the night, with the ice closing in from the north, he and Marø agreed that they should head west into an area where a strong swell gave them at least some confidence that open water lay ahead. For much of the following day the north wind kept the *Theron* alternately drifting and running 'half-ahead' to keep off the coast but at 3.00pm the wind swung round by 180° and, at last, she could head back towards the landing point. In an unaccustomed outpouring of emotion, Fuchs acknowledged:

With what anxiety we have thought of what could happen
to the sea ice carrying stores, hut parts, dogs and aeroplane!
How relieved we were when approaching the landing we
could see figures moving about, the vehicles, dogs and stores
all present![179]

With the ship once again anchored to the ice and the castaways
back on board, the sense of relief was immense – but short-lived.
In particular, the events of the last two days – the sudden, unpredictable shifts in the wind, the southward movement of the pack,
and the now obvious risks of unloading onto sea ice – all con-
spired to rob Fuchs of his earlier confidence:

> Yesterday before we left I had very carefully examined the
> cracks in the ice and none of them were 'working'. I had
> therefore thought all would be well but during the night and
> today with only the radar to watch, its pictures confused by
> the accumulating ice floes, nasty doubts began to come in my
> mind. True, the ice was at least 12ft thick and along the edge
> we had seen it was 20 to 25ft but even such old stuff can be
> broken by such an on-shore swell and gale.[180]

Hillary, too, noted that 'a very jittery atmosphere reigned on board
the ship'[181] and the inevitable result of this growing nervousness
was an exhortation to work harder and faster. Stratton and the
others had made significant inroads on the waterlogged depot,
but more needed to be done and now the Weasels and tractors
began to drag the drums and crates away from the slushy morass
and onto the dry snow where they could be loaded onto sledges
and pulled to the bottom of the ice slope. The inundation of the
seawater had made everything heavier and much more difficult
to handle, but despite cold fingers and wet feet, the expeditionaries made good progress.

By the evening of Saturday 4 February, Number 2 hold was
almost empty, with a significant proportion of both Number 1
and Number 3 holds also cleared. The same day, the explorers
hauled the first two sides of the dismantled Sno-cat crate up

to the base site, the intention being to use the 3.5-ton box as a workshop while the Advance Party completed work on the construction of the main hut. At last, after the trials and tribulations of the preceding days, the process of unloading and transporting the stores had reached such a state of efficiency and order that even Goldsmith felt compelled to admit that 'Work today went fairly well with a well regulated shuttle service from ship to dump.' Although he also added, rather grudgingly, 'It's certainly very much better to feel that we are at last achieving something though not very much.'[182]

Despite the progress, Marø remained tense. The immediate danger had passed and the radar showed that a wide lead remained open all the way to Vahsel Bay; but the pack maintained a southward trend. The captain's anxiety steadily increased during the course of 5 February and, at 6.00pm, he interrupted the evening meal with the startling announcement that the *Theron* might be forced to leave within the hour. 'Panic everywhere,' wrote Lowe, 'especially Bunny … Chaotic state; I felt the decision was rather a wild, bleak prospect for Advance Party. Began working at mad pace.'[183]

Abandoning their unfinished meal, the explorers immediately started heaving the remaining hut timbers over the side in a desperate attempt to reach the essential coal which lay at the very bottom of the hold. 'We were suddenly told to pack our bags and be ready to leave in an instant,' Goldsmith recorded. 'Last minute preparations were made in a terrible hurry … We all busily wrote letters and made recordings for the people at home … This seemed to be it. I felt nothing except an anger with the complete lack of preparations which had been made for this contingency.'[184] As the eight men of the Advance Party raced to find essentials such as lavatory paper and toothpicks, the remainder of the explorers at last reached the coal and began to heave it overboard, ton after ton. Soon pilots, meteorologists and mountaineers were as black as chimney sweeps but by 2.00am all but the last 10 tons had been heaped on the ice, where it made a great black, dusty stain. And then, as the exhausted men surveyed their handiwork, the wind, with a contrariness all its own, veered away from the north and the ship was again safe.

The following day, the stress and tension of the previous evening seemed to have evaporated entirely; unloading was completed in a fairly desultory fashion and the explorers transported only a tiny portion of the 300 tons of stores up the hill. The men working at the hut site completed the reassembly of the Sno-cat crate, however, and to formally mark possession by the TAE they unfurled the Union and Commonwealth flags. Goldsmith climbed the incline for the first time to watch the ceremony but, as he reached the crest of the slope, his heart sank within him: 'How bleak it is,' he groaned, 'only a few flags fluttering in the breeze and a few crates standing about in an apparently abandoned fashion. Not very much here to comfort anyone.'[185] But, whatever his feelings, many of his companions appeared to be enjoying a holiday atmosphere, with a number of them taking to the air in the Auster, ostensibly to take photographs and to survey the general area, but also simply for pleasure. Even Marø had relaxed to such a degree that he declined an aerial survey of the pack and, when asked by Fuchs how quickly he would like to sail, casually replied that he would not hear of leaving and thought it wrong to do so if they could stay and assist the Advance Party. 'This is in fact perfectly true,' observed an understandably nettled Fuchs, 'but I have to take into account the necessity that we get out this year in order not to prejudice next year's programme. I told him that we want to stay for some days yet and that I rely on him to say when he considers we must move because of the ice.'[186]

During the evening, Fuchs also made an exploratory flight to the east of Vahsel Bay with John Lewis as pilot – and his discoveries filled him with excitement and satisfaction at an hypothesis proven. 'I have always had the idea,' he wrote that night, 'as I was preaching in London before leaving, that the mountain area of Queen Maud Land swings round to the south and that the nunataks [rock outcrops] found by Filchner might be the local expression of that feature in this area.'[187] Now, as the Auster reached a point some 30 miles to the southeast of Vahsel Bay and 60 miles from Shackleton Base, Fuchs swept the landscape with his binoculars and, just where he had expected it to be, a mountain range came into view, taking the form of an escarpment with the ice of the polar glaciers pouring through its fissures. Both men wanted to explore further, but with the long-range fuel tank only part-full and radio communications with the *Theron* becoming intermittent, they were forced to head for home. 'Back at the ship after about 3 hours in the air,' Fuchs enthused, 'we discussed this most interesting find, which not only gives an object to surveyors and geologists but presents us with an additional problem for the journey next year.' He decided to name the TAE's first major geographical discovery the Theron Mountains 'in honour of this ship and indeed her crew who have worked so well for us under most difficult circumstances.'[188]

Still brimming with excitement over his new discovery, on 7 February Fuchs sent Blaiklock aloft so that he might use his expertise as a surveyor to assess the range's height and to gather details for a general sketch map. Even as the little orange aeroplane dwindled to a speck in the distance, however, wind and ice were conspiring to bring this happy, relaxed period to a dramatic end. In the days since she returned to the landing point, new sea ice had been forming around the *Theron*, but the ice had remained thin and fragile and had presented no immediate cause for concern. Now the wind switched to the northeast bringing in more ice, which began to push up against the ship and then, forced forward by the wind, to over-raft and crumple against both the ship and the older sea ice. With the temperature standing at a steady −3°F, the new ice and the old began the inexorable process of knitting together − while farther around the bay the heavy floes could also be seen closing in. Watching these rapidly unfolding developments, Marø's airy confidence of the previous day quickly turned to apprehension, and he announced his intention of departing as soon as the Auster could be swung aboard.

Working in his tiny darkroom, oblivious to the growing threat to the ship and to the consternation now infecting his companions, Williams felt the *Theron* tremble; then, a few seconds later, something bumped and grazed against her side. Stepping out onto the deck to see what was happening, he found that the atmosphere on board had changed completely:

It was hectic and it was alarmist ... Bunny came running round the deck and bumped into me nearly and shouted 'Come with me, come with me to the stern.' So I went with him to the stern, lugging my equipment and he said 'Photograph this – film this! I want them to be sure in London of what's happening'... When we got to the stern and I looked over the back there was a funny sight: thin ice, like paper, comes up against the stern of the ship and then stops, then breaks and snaps; and then the ice from behind comes over and snaps again; and the next bit comes over – and you can see it happening. It was moving under the wind – the wind was rising and was coming from behind – and he said 'The wind has changed and it's rising – and this is how sea ice forms ... As soon as it gets a bit colder in the next hours it will harden and build and build.' Even if it remains slushy, of course, I knew from our experience in the Weddell Sea that it's difficult to navigate through: the propellers can't turn well. 'I think we'll have to go soon,' he said to me, 'I want you to photograph this as evidence of what's happening ... We'll have to go, we'll have to go!'[189]

All around them men bustled, the members of the Advance Party gathering their personal effects while those returning with the *Theron* made her ready for imminent departure. Blaiklock and Haslop landed at 1.45pm and made a hurried report of their observations, which included the sighting of another mountain range seen in the distance to the south of the newly discovered Therons. Then, as Blaiklock swallowed a hurried lunch, the crew lifted the Auster aboard and strapped it down.

By 3.30pm the time had arrived for the last goodbyes. As the Advance Party lined up to shake hands, their appearance struck Williams with a kind of horror. Each man had shaved thoroughly – not just beard, but head as well:

Suddenly there appeared eight men among us ... who were bald, bald as coots – they looked horrible! All our hair had grown on the journey down through the tropics and some had beards – suddenly white heads, bald as coots, and this really pointed the finger of condemnation at them: 'You are the ones who will stay!'[190]

With an astonishingly poor sense of timing, Fuchs also chose this moment, as the party stood on the sea ice next to the ship, to deliver to the eight men not a rousing speech but a lecture: 'I harangued the Advance Party for about one minute,' he noted complacently, 'emphasising that all the newcomers to Antarctica should not set themselves up as experts until they had had experience, (there has been such a tendency with some), when their opinions might be of value.'[191] For a leader capable of attracting the loyalty of men like Blaiklock, it was a curious blunder, leaving some of the eight feeling more like naughty schoolboys than intrepid explorers on the brink of a great adventure. Fortunately, the pace of events left them little time to dwell on the gaffe: within moments of shaking hands, the two parties had separated; the capstans turned; the mooring cables slithered across the ice and back through their hawseholes; black smoke billowed from the funnel – and the *Theron* put to sea.

As the distance between the vessel and the edge of the sea ice widened, Williams's 35mm camera whirred in his hands, capturing the scene for posterity. For all the bravado and light-hearted badinage at parting, he thought the distress of the Advance Party unmistakable:

They were all looking at my camera and they were waving and they had, I'm afraid, very forced smiles: they were obviously upset and perhaps frightened. They were thinking, I believe, 'I'm not looking at Williams and his camera, and I'm not looking at Bunny and David Pratt and David Stratton, I'm looking at my wife through that lens – I'm looking at my mother and father through that lens – I'm looking at my girlfriend through that lens: they are the ones who will see me left here and I'm trying to force a smile and wave goodbye to them.' I'm sure that's what they were thinking.[192]

As the *Theron* slid slowly away from the ice edge and turned in a wide sweep onto an easterly course, she gave three long valedictory blasts on her siren and the eight men standing on the ice waved and cheered. And then, as the distance grew, they shed their individuality, becoming anonymous black specs against a white background; soon they were invisible. A quarter of an hour later the edge of the sea ice had merged with the fast-moving pack and the base site had been lost to view.

That night, with the ship once again juddering as her bow met the floes, Fuchs thought back to the men he had left behind at the beachhead. 'I'm afraid', he admitted, 'they have an enormous task ahead of them.'[193] Williams put it rather more forcefully: in his opinion, the Advance Party 'would have a shocking bloody winter'.[194]

4

A Shocking Bloody Winter

The Advance Party had good cause to be anxious. The delays encountered in the pack ice of the Weddell Sea meant that only a fraction of the planned work had been completed prior to the *Theron*'s departure. Everyone had expected that the framework of the main hut would have been erected, but instead it lay amid the deepening drift as a kit of parts. Even worse, a huge quantity of essential stores and equipment still rested on the sea ice – vulnerable to tides and wind. Finally, the location of the stores meant that the vehicles – one Sno-cat, two Weasels and two Ferguson tractors – would now be absolutely essential to the completion of the Advance Party's objectives and yet all the trials to date had shown that they were anything but reliable. In the face of these challenges, the eight men of the Advance Party – almost entirely ignorant of each other's characters and peccadilloes – would have to bind themselves together as a team in order to face a common enemy. Any call upon outside aid, if heard at all, would not be answered for months. Boredom and discomfort would try tempers and fray nerves and intense cold and poor visibility would render their work difficult at the best of times and, at the worst, impossible. Theirs was not, by any standards, a prospect to be envied.

Of the eight men standing on the ice, only two had previously set foot on the continent: Ken Blaiklock, the leader, and Ralph

Lenton, his deputy. Blaiklock, whom one member of the expedition would later describe as 'a quiet, cool, tolerant gentleman',[195] had spent four winters in the Antarctic – two at Stonington Island and two at Hope Bay – while Lenton had spent five at various bases. Homard, too, brought invaluable expertise, having only recently returned from the Arctic, where he had maintained the Weasels of the British North Greenland Expedition. All three were recipients of the Polar Medal. The remaining five men benefited from varying levels of experience – but none of it polar. Two of the three meteorologists, Tony Stewart and Peter Jeffries, had served on Atlantic weather ships and Stewart had also taken part in the British Schools Exploring Society's expeditions to Iceland and British Columbia. The third met man, the South African Hannes La Grange, had previously been posted to the South African meteorological station on the sub-Antarctic Marion Island. All three therefore knew what it was like to work in small, isolated communities in difficult conditions. Only 'Taffy' Williams, the RAF radio operator, and Goldsmith, lacked any comparable experience.

A month earlier, after an exhausting day attempting to dig the ship free from the ice, Goldsmith had remarked that it was perhaps the men's ability to keep laughing that had led to their being chosen for the expedition. Now their stoicism and humour would be tested to its limits. 'We had,' the doctor acknowledged, 'no shelter and no home and a prospect of moving 300 tons of stores up the hill – a task which would take at least a month, building a hut another two months and then getting down to our work proper.'[196] Fortunately, however, although Blaiklock admitted to 'some slight feeling of trepidation',[197] and despite the naturally emotional reaction to the *Theron*'s hurried departure, morale remained remarkably high. Even Goldsmith, the man who, more than any other, had looked upon the unloading with a mixture of disbelief and despair, asserted, 'I can't say that I felt the slightest bit overawed or frightened.'[198] Certainly the immediate circumstances would not allow anyone the luxury of moping. With autumn just around the corner, with the temperature dropping and no shelter but the Sno-cat crate and their tents available to them, no one could afford to stand for long looking wistfully at the retreating ship.

Having motored back up the slope from the sea ice in the Sno-cat, the eight men set to work. Goldsmith and Jeffries pitched the four two-man tents and the others unrolled their sleeping bags, collected their personal effects and began filling the all-important primus stoves. A short time later they gathered in the crate for a meal. Until such time as the main expedition hut had been built, this timber box, measuring 21 feet by 9 feet by 8 feet and now christened the 'Sno-house', would remain the only shelter where the party could congregate. Serving as mess-room, kitchen and workshop and crowded with workbenches, mess table, stoves and radio equipment, the crate would, however, be too small to act as a dormitory. Instead, each night the explorers would be obliged to retreat to their tents: Blaiklock sharing with Lenton; Goldsmith with Stewart; La Grange with Homard; and Williams with Jeffries. After a dinner of bacon, tomatoes and cocoa, Williams attempted to make radio contact with the *Theron*, which they had last seen about a mile from the ice edge and already battling with the fast moving floes, but they heard nothing but the crackle of static in reply. Finally, at 12.30am, exhausted after a day of hard labour and mixed emotions, the eight explorers retired to their tents, to write diaries, to mull over the day's events and their uncertain future, and to sleep.

Over the course of the next few days, the enormity of the task facing them began to sink home. Day after day, they worked flat out, making their laborious way down to the tidal crack where the stores had been dumped, loading the sledges to capacity before dragging them up the slope behind the Sno-cat or a Weasel, unloading the cargo and then repeating the monotonous process over and over again. With each load weighing approximately 1 ton and with a maximum of only fifteen trips possible each day, this meant that even on a good day only 5 per cent of the total stockpile could be shifted. Nonetheless, by the tenth day, all the food had been brought to the base site, plus the timbers of the main hut, a substantial quantity of general and scientific stores and 50 drums of petrol and paraffin. At the same time, Lenton, who doubled as carpenter as well as deputy leader, worked on making the Sno-house more habitable by laying a floor, cutting a door and windows and putting up shelves. He also began a long-running battle with that plague of all Antarctic expeditions, the incursion of drift snow, which, in the words of Homard, 'will stream through a pin hole like a steam jet'[199] to then melt and soak everything it touches.

Homard, of course, faced his own demons – in the form of the vehicles. 'Mechanical troubles and breakdowns came fast and furious,'[200] wrote Blaiklock and, as the only qualified engineer in the party, the responsibility for maintenance and repairs fell squarely on Homard's shoulders. In the very first days, he had little choice but to condemn one Weasel and use it as a donor vehicle, in the hope that its components might keep its twin operational. The Sno-cat, by far the most versatile machine, also suffered from a range of problems, while the Ferguson tractors, though generally reliable, simply could not cope with the soft surface of the snow slope. During his interview for the expedition, Goldsmith had been puzzled when the panel asked if he – a candidate for the post of medical officer and surgeon – possessed any mechanical aptitude. Now he began to understand why the question had been posed. Any help which Homard might be able to call upon, even that of a gifted amateur, would not only relieve some of his burden but also make a direct contribution to the speed with which the stores could be moved. But Homard, perhaps impatient of dilettantes, preferred to work alone. 'Roy continues under the most dreadful difficulties to try to get the Sno-cat working,' observed a mildly frustrated but admiring Goldsmith. 'All tasks are difficult down here but the vehicles we have are so constructed that it is difficult to get at any part. He works alone all day long and this too must make his task more difficult.'[201]

Now that the materials for the main hut had been brought to the building site, work began on its construction – with the inevitable result that, with fewer men available, the transportation of the remaining stores began to stall. By the end of February, most of the petrol and paraffin still lay on the sea ice, along with the timbers for the garage, the anthracite for the Aga stove, the sledging rations, and the seal meat for the dogs. The dog-teams, too, remained picketed on the ice until the beginning of March when, in 'Operation Dogspan', they were brought to the camp site strung out between two vehicles. On the positive side, the work on the hut, led by Lenton, progressed well and already the foundations had been laid. The next task was to complete the half trusses that would form the main framework supporting the roof. 'The first eight were erected on the north side of the hut,' wrote Blaiklock, 'with a little more difficulty and effort than the designers had shown in their sketch, and the row looked somewhat like a line of the Queen's beasts. Once the other halves were in position and bolted together it was beginning to look more like a hut.'[202]

The design of the hut made the work far from easy. In choosing the pattern, Fuchs had been influenced by the experiences of the NBSAE. After only a year of service, the NBSAE hut had begun to buckle and leak under the huge weight of snow that had accumulated during the first winter. In order to avoid similar problems, Fuchs had decided that his main hut should be enormously strong – but with added strength came added difficulties: 'It was over complicated,' Blaiklock later acknowledged:

> We had perhaps four bits of timber all with holes in and of course when you came to fit it and the thing was slightly warped you couldn't get the bolt through. It was over strong … But if it had been done the other way and the hut collapsed after a year we might not have been very pleased! It's so easy to be wise after the event![203]

Goldsmith was altogether less forgiving: 'The man who conceived this hut and those who accepted his design … should all be shot,' he opined bitterly.[204]

Throughout the first half of March, the explorers struggled on, doing their best to complete as many outdoor jobs as possible and to ignore the falling temperatures, the flying drift-snow and the increasingly frequent whiteouts. And then, on 20 March, they found themselves imprisoned. Blaiklock:

During the morning we all had been digging out the big panel boxes and they were dragged close to the hut ready for starting on the roof and walls. With increasing wind and drift, we packed up in the afternoon and retired to the hut. And there we stayed for the next seven days with the blizzard raging outside.[205]

This was the onset of the first severe blizzard of the season and the day upon which the carefully laid plans of the Advance Party began seriously to unravel.

With temperatures plunging to -45°F and wind speeds rising to a howling 50 knots, day after day the eight men huddled inside their makeshift home, listening to the creaking of the wooden walls and jumping occasionally as the wind hurled a jerry can or piece of timber against their shelter. Gradually, though, as the crate became cocooned in the deepening drift snow, the roar of the gale grew more muffled and life assumed a new routine, albeit in a very limited sphere of operations. At one end of the single room a kitchen bench supported the three primus stoves used for cooking and, at the other, close to the entrance, stood a workbench and Williams's radio equipment. For most of the day the explorers sat at the long mess table that ran down the crate's length – there was simply too little room for them to do much else. The interior, lit by Tilley lamps, remained murky and, since the men opened the door only when calls of nature became imperative, the atmosphere became so stuffy that matches guttered as soon as they were struck. More immediately irritating, though, was the condensation that collected on the ceiling and walls and then dripped down incessantly, forcing the men to sit at the table with their hoods up, like a band of medieval monks. So far as they could, they remained productive, sewing rents in their clothing or writing up notes and diaries; but they also passed the time in conversation and by playing scrabble, 'battleships' and card games. Cooking was undertaken on a four-day rota, with each of the men practising his culinary skills with varying degrees of enthusiasm and confidence. Whatever the level of his success, however, the duty cook always enjoyed the privilege of sleeping indoors. The mess table might not be the most comfortable couch, but at least the crate remained comparatively warm and dry. Overall, the explorers found life uncomfortable but bearable. Besides, the Sno-house was intended as temporary accommodation only: once they had completed work on its construction, they would be able to move out of their tents and the crate and into the altogether more commodious surroundings of the new hut. Or so they thought.

Although the mood had remained fairly positive up to now, inevitably, as the days passed without any sign of the conditions relenting, tensions and anxieties began to surface. Goldsmith wrote on 24 March:

> We all joke about our situation which I suppose is pretty tough now but with shelter, warmth and food we can ask for little else. Scrabble is still the favourite game, with bridge today. No one wanted to leave tonight to go to bed; everyone fearing their own particular *bête noire*.[206]

For some, that *bête noire* was the discomfort and claustrophobia of their tents. Each night, as they retired to rest, the men had to break open their frozen sleeping bags before they could climb in. Once settled for the night, their body heat melted the ice both inside and beneath the bags, so that they were seldom dry and found that, night after night, their bags sank deeper into slushy trenches. According to Homard, 'we spent most nights being curled tensely into balls like dormice, but not sleeping like them, for we would be either awake and cold and trying to make ourselves into even tighter balls, or at best, slipping into a fitful doze.'[207]

The tents also shrank: the canvas walls pressed inwards by the weight of drift snow. And, since the nights brought no diminution of wind or drift, on most days at least some of the men had to call for their companions to dig them free, sometimes having to wait until the late morning before their turn came to be released. Goldsmith, among others, came to doubt his ability to tolerate these conditions indefinitely: 'I twice today got that nightmare feeling of panic, of just not being able to go on any further.'[208]

Men like Homard and Lenton also felt fear – but fear of a different order. They considered themselves to be polar professionals, employed so that they might complete their allotted tasks efficiently and with the minimum of fuss. Now, Homard knew that the already temperamental vehicles might be rendered completely useless by the prevailing conditions. Lenton, meanwhile, tasked with building the main hut as expeditiously as possible, realised that the onset of the blizzard – which might conceivably be the precursor of even worse and more prolonged storms – could delay his progress by weeks or even months. It seemed to these skilled technicians that the wind and snow were conspiring to render all their efforts nugatory. Lenton's frustration finally erupted at breakfast on 27 March. 'Ralph gave vent to his bad mood,' Goldsmith recorded, 'complaining of the lack of second course at breakfast and the appalling way we were living … He attacked poor Ken about the organisation which does leave much to be desired but Ralph I should say was the worst offender. Anyway the attack left its scar, breakfast was even more gloomy than usual.'[209]

Ironically, the day when tensions finally boiled over also turned out to be the day when the blizzard began to die away. Freedom from the confines of the crate came as a relief but a brief survey of the base site soon confirmed the men's worst fears. The skeletal hut, in particular, had been left in a sorry state, as La Grange described:

> The trusses of the framework had acted as a wind-break and almost the whole structure was filled with snow. A drift … had formed on the leeward side covering the panels which lay sorted out on the north.[210]

Even the stoical Blaiklock could not conceal his concern: 'It was an amazing sight – the drift was some 15 feet high, almost as high as the top of the hut trusses and already 50 yards long. All but one of the panel boxes had completely disappeared.'[211] The bitter cold also left the compacted snow as hard as ice and digging out the interior of the hut and the components for its ongoing construction would take weeks.

The vehicles, too, had suffered severely. Densely packed snow filled the Weasel's cabin and a great block of ice encased its engine and prop-shaft – but at least the Weasel was in one piece and, by a miracle, Homard managed to get its heater going to begin a thaw. The Sno-cat's engine, however, had been left partly disassembled when the blizzard set in. The tarpaulin protecting it had been torn to fluttering rags and the engine parts were either buried in the snow or dispersed over a wide area by the violence of the gale. 'Poor Roy,' wrote a sympathetic Goldsmith that night, 'I wonder whether he will ever get it going.' The discovery that the appalling cold had also killed one of the huskies seemed to fill the Advance Party's cup of woe – but the following day would bring news of a disaster so colossal as to make the events of the 27th pale into insignificance.

After a cold night, during which the temperature fell to −23°F, most of the explorers began the thankless task of digging out the hut and gathering the scattered stores. Blaiklock and Stewart, meanwhile, set out in the defrosted Weasel to collect some dog pemmican and more stores from the sea ice depot. Poor steering gear and the need to control speed by using the throttle mechanism inside the engine-bay meant that most of the men's attention was focused on driving the Weasel but, as they made their uncertain way down the slope, they were not too preoccupied to notice that the recent storm had wrought considerable changes across the face of the bay. Most disturbing of all, they could see a thick frost-smoke rising close to the site of the depot. This smoke indicated the presence of open water, as Blaiklock recounted:

As we approached the dump site we could see that more ice had gone out than we had at first supposed. Coming down the last rise we saw that the ice which had looked so solid two weeks earlier had broken right through the various piles of stores. Gone were three hundred drums of fuel, a tractor, all our coal, the many tons of timber for the workshop and many other engineering stores. All that was left was the dog pemmican for which we had come, the sledging ration boxes, a box of detonators, and a few drums of cement – one of them literally balanced on the edge of the ice.[212]

There could be no doubt that the violent storm and a rising tide had combined to snap off the portion of sea ice on which the stores had been stockpiled. Now, a Ferguson tractor and all those precious supplies lay either on the sea floor or on a sheet of ice currently floating northwards. After a few moments of horror-struck immobility, the two men had little choice but to load the pemmican into the Weasel and make their way back up the slope. 'Obviously, sea ice does go out,' Blaiklock would state in years to come, 'it's happened many times in FIDS – but you can't do anything about it. You know, if you do one thing you abandon something else.'[213] For the time being, however, as he bounced and jolted his way up the hill, he could only wonder how his companions would react to this appalling loss.

Arriving at the hut site, he told everyone to stop work and join him in the crate. Here he outlined the nature of the calamity which had overtaken them and then, when his bewildered audience had absorbed the news, launched into a discussion on the various economies that they must implement with immediate effect. Fortunately, no food had been lost and all the materials for the main expedition hut had been brought to the construction site: this meant that the objectives of the Advance Party had not been absolutely compromised by the disaster. But they would be chronically short of fuel since all the anthracite for the Aga stove and much of the paraffin now lay at the bottom of Vahsel Bay. This left them with only three gallons of paraffin per day for the rest of the year – and this must serve for all the cooking as well as heating the Sno-house and the tents. The probable impact upon the planned programme of work was also immense: the loss of vital equipment meant that Jeffries' upper-air observations would now be impossible; the dogs would go hungry because all the seal carcasses had floated away; and only very limited reconnaissance and depot laying would be feasible in the spring. Overall, if the eight men had endured discomfort before, this new and unfore-seen catastrophe rendered their very survival uncertain. For the time being, however, the mood remained largely optimistic – so optimistic, indeed, that Goldsmith thought it tinged with denial:

> The news was taken well by everyone. Tony seemed to believe that very little will change, but my feeling is that this shock will affect our work etc; might make it so that the hut will not get finished, then we would really be in the soup … Still, we shall see what we shall see.[214]

It was, he acknowledged, 'A memorable day that I shall long remember.'

The first practical response to the Advance Party's new circumstances was made by Lenton. Recognising that the crate would in all probability remain their home for the foreseeable future, he immediately rendered it more habitable by insulating it with fibreglass. This simple expedient reduced the condensation, effectively put an end to the indoor rain which had been such a blight and allowed the explorers to hang drying clothes from the ceiling. Next, he turned his attention to the main hut, completion of which remained the expedition's primary objective. Assisted by Williams, he began to fasten the purlins on its roof and then started work on fixing the roof panels – a distinctly disagreeable task in such an exposed position.

Throughout April, with the hours of daylight rapidly dwindling, the rest of the men concentrated their efforts on tunnelling to locate the buried panel crates, occasionally varying the routine by undertaking seal hunts to replace the 35 carcasses they had lost. When successful, these trips not only helped to replenish the supply of dog food but also provided the explorers with fresh seal liver – a welcome change from their usual menu. Homard, meanwhile, concentrated on rebuilding the Sno-cat, constructing a makeshift garage from the discarded panel crates and erecting a wind-charger which generated sufficient electricity to light the gloomy interior of the Sno-house. In another feat of mechanical genius, he manufactured a bread oven from a 5-gallon oil drum, which he insulated with fibreglass and heated with one of the primuses. Over the coming months, he would return repeatedly to the design, making a range of modifications to improve its effectiveness; but from the very outset, this remarkable invention meant that the explorers could enjoy fresh bread, cakes and pastry – adding significantly to their meagre comforts.

Towards the end of April, the sun finally sank beneath the horizon, shrouding the Antarctic landscape in darkness and leaving the eight marooned explorers quite literally benighted. But the loss of daylight could not be allowed to interfere with the completion of the expedition's vital tasks. 'It was work, work, work the whole time,' remembered Stewart. 'We worked on when our world became twilight, and on when day became black as night, with only the stars and the moon and the contrast of the snow to aid us.'[215] For the next four months the tunnellers and panel-fixers would labour by the light of their Tilley lamps and by the unpredictable illumination offered by the ethereal beauty of the aurora australis, a phenomenon caused by solar winds bringing high energy particles into contact with the Earth's upper atmosphere, where they are converted into ribbons of flickering light. 'One at the end of April was magnificent,' Blaiklock enthused, 'multi-coloured curtains and streamers, continually moving and changing colour. However with the temperature at minus 40 and a fresh breeze it was too cold to stand and stare for too long.'[216] Such distractions notwithstanding, by the end of the month, all the panel boxes had been excavated and the tunnels became a home for the puppies born during the expedition. The adult dogs, too, began to feel the effects of the cold and wind, so Goldsmith spent the next month enlarging the tunnel network and cutting alcoves so that all the animals could be accommodated.

In May the raging blizzards returned, trapping the weary men inside their crate for half the month. Outside tasks were limited to meteorological observations, bringing in food and snow for melting, and feeding the dogs – a task which involved sawing the frozen seal carcasses into 'logs' which could then be split with an axe. For the rest of the long, dreary days the explorers could do little but read, play games and write diaries, though the monotony of their existence left them with little to record.

The only bright moment in the whole of the month came when the Advance Party at last managed to make contact with the outside world. At 7.00pm on 7 May, as he sat at the radio transmitter idly playing with its controls, Lenton suddenly realised that he could hear voices. Leaping to his feet he yelled 'I've got through, I'm through!' and immediately, with his companions crowding round him, he began to broadcast the message that they had been hoping to send for the last three months. It turned out that he had accidentally broken into the radio schedule of the FIDS Research Base 'Y' on Horseshoe Island in Marguerite Bay, but the exchange was extremely brief. 'Unfortunately the line went dead before we got any official message out,' Goldsmith wrote that night, 'but at least we got through that we are all well.' In fact, after a brief moment of euphoria, this unexpected but curtailed contact with the outside world only served to impress upon the eight men the full extent of their isolation. 'How different to everything that had been planned,' Goldsmith continued:

> Where are the air-letters and other messages that we were promised? Nearly everything that could have gone wrong down here has gone wrong and now this enforced sitting in this hut while all the time it gets darker and darker and the hut does not grow; only the drifts around it get higher and higher.[217]

Inactivity and the complete lack of privacy began to prey on the men and incompatibilities in personality and outlook became increasingly difficult to reconcile. Homard, in Goldsmith's opinion, was almost perversely argumentative, 'sticking like a puppy to a slipper to the wrong end of the stick' and liable to flare into violent disagreement at the slightest provocation. But he was also industrious and inventive and his skills as an engineer and 'fixer' did much to improve the conditions of the party. At the other end of the spectrum, Jeffries, whose taciturnity had been marked even in the London office, seemed to have been rendered almost mute by the Advance Party's plight and, in particular, by the loss of the upper-air equipment which made his own planned meteorological programme impossible. At times the mercurial Goldsmith found the meteorologist 'who sits sullenly reading, never really cheerful and only entering a conversation to say how futile it is'[218] almost intolerable. Even Blaiklock, whose temper was not easily ruffled, found him irritating:

> He was obviously very disappointed. He was very quiet, he didn't say very much; he didn't interact with people discussing any subject under the sun. I think he was disappointed and saddened that he wasn't down there doing what he wanted to do. But nor was I ... and that's just tough![219]

Stewart, too, though conscientious, revealed a schoolmaster-ish superiority and an annoying inclination to criticise others through oblique remarks addressed to no one in particular, rather than by direct challenge – a habit which tended to make him an object of mockery. On 16 May, the receipt of a radio telegram from Fuchs did little to improve the atmosphere.

> Greatest sympathy to all for inevitable difficulties. Can you give general assessment stores lost? ... Expect to fly Otter to you from IGY early January ... All of you now elected members of Antarctic Club, am bringing ties.[220]

Despite Fuchs's obvious concern for the plight of the Advance Party and his attempt to cheer and encourage his men with the humorous reference to the club ties, Goldsmith's reaction was acerbic: 'Cold comfort', he growled, 'for having waited for so long for the first news from home.'[221]

Panelling the walls of the main hut began in mid-May, with the men working in brilliant moonlight and temperatures of -35°F. Blaiklock felt that 'By now we were very much more acclimatised to the cold and wind and what we had previously considered to be too bad to work in, were now the warm and good days.'[222] But not everyone shared his views. 'The idea of working in this cold, or going to bed or, in fact, of all our life, without comfort or real warmth is rapidly becoming a nightmare,' complained

a depressed Goldsmith.[223] Completion of the hut remained a
colossal challenge and the constant accumulation of drift snow
made it feel as though the explorers were fighting a losing battle.
Homard wrote:

> The cry was always 'Who's pinched my shovel?' No imple-
> ment is so necessary, so much in demand, so coveted or so
> frequently lost and broken as the shovel. Any expedition going
> to the polar regions should take at least twice as many shovels
> as it expects to use at any one time, and spares for all of them.[224]

As they dug out the tons of hard, compacted snow, the explorers found it incredibly dispiriting to discover that progress on
the construction actually made the problem worse rather than
better. As La Grange oberved, 'The more panels we put in the
more drift formed inside and this had to be dug out again.'[225]
According to Lenton, the entire site 'looked like a gravediggers'
tea shop. Everybody had a little Tilley lantern and shovel and
they walked off across the snow to their own grave from which
they were searching for stores. All around the camp we could see
lamps on the snow and a shovel flashing now and then.'[226] By the
end of the month, the roof, the south wall and the gable ends had
all been completed, but a five-day gale brought work to a halt.
When the explorers surfaced again they found that the landscape
had undergone a bewildering transformation, the drift forming
new hillocks and slopes that rendered their surroundings nearly
unrecognisable. Even worse, the hut had been filled to the ceiling
with around 8000 cubic feet of snow. And so the back breaking
process of excavation started all over again.

By the time Mid-Winter's Day arrived everyone felt that they
had more than earned a holiday – their first since the departure
of the *Theron*. Ever since the Heroic Era, every over-wintering
party in the Antarctic has celebrated 21 June – the day that marks
the sun's furthest declension – with a party, and the TAE was no
exception. For once, the weather seemed to be in tune with the
men's mood: the snow floated down in large flakes, its vertical fall
hardly disturbed by a breath of wind, and the whole scene was

bathed in glorious moonlight. If calm conditions outside cloaked the explorers' battleground with the tranquillity of a Christmas card, inside, too, a transformation had been wrought. The mess-table, normally littered with books, pieces of equipment and clothing, now looked resplendent, covered with a white sheet for a tablecloth and bedecked with crackers, paper napkins, and candles. Twinkling foil angels revolved slowly in the heat of the candles and a brightly wrapped present was at every place setting, each gift carefully hoarded for the last six months. Finally, in the centre of the table lay a large cake, baked by Lenton and decorated with a tiny clockwork train, the gift of Hal Lister, the Crossing Party's glaciologist.

Fortunately, the expedition's alcohol had not been lost with the other stores and, to mark this special occasion, everyone indulged – even the usually staid Tony Stewart. 'I am normally almost tee-total,' he recalled, 'but on this occasion, with the better weather to look forward to, I confess I celebrated in something stronger!'[227] With the aid of such lubricants, and despite the recent tensions, the party developed into an immense and increasingly boisterous success, as Goldsmith described:

> At dinner we opened Hal Lister's and Scott Polar Research Institute's parcel, containing musical instruments and all sorts of mad and intelligent things. We lingered over lunch, with white wine (KB's) – very good – beer, Arctic Ale, excellent in these climes, Cointreau, coffee, cigars – just as it should be … After lunch we just sat and talked and drank and then had more to eat. The party went on with much noise and hilarity – Roy, being especially tiddly, addressing a papier mâché mask for at least 10 minutes. Taffy playing the clarinet in the style of Benny Goodman was quite something. Very late Roy walked down to the beach somewhat the worse for wear, carrying a rifle and pursued by imaginary leopard seals … 2.30 a.m.: bed and a very good night.[228]

The celebration was amply justified. Despite the most appalling conditions, the Advance Party had made considerable progress on the hut – but, even more important, from this day, the sun would begin its long, slow climb back above the horizon. Spring might still be a long way off but, at last, the explorers could turn their minds to whatever elements of their original survey programme still seemed feasible – and, ultimately, to their relief by Fuchs and the Crossing Party.

By the beginning of July, the met-room, porch, darkroom, food store and kitchen walls had all been erected. Other non-construction activities also increased, such as the measurement of snow accumulation, a more detailed programme of meteorological observations, and survey work, which included the taking of an astro-sight to confirm the exact position of Shackleton and a series of levels to establish the height of the base above sea level. Goldsmith also continued to measure and record the men's fat deposits, although this programme, as Blaiklock recounted, tended to plunge the explorers into a state bordering on chaos: 'Pandemonium would reign with individuals undressing and dressing, clambering over each other and you were lucky if you got your own clothes again.'[229] Certainly no-one could be blamed for wanting to dress quickly; despite the passing of Mid-Winter's Day, the ferocity of the weather showed few signs of abating and 2 August proved to be the coldest day of the whole year, the temperature plunging to -63°F. 'In the tents at night,' wrote Blaiklock, 'I was sleeping with two terylene blankets as well as the double lined sleeping bag and went to bed fully clothed with down trousers [and] all my duffels and still was waking up during the night from the cold.'[230] Not surprising, given that the cold was now intense enough to turn paraffin to jelly.

The expedition reached another important milestone when, on 7 August, exactly six months after the *Theron*'s departure, Blaiklock and Goldsmith moved into the main hut. Initially, most of the men resisted the idea of occupying the partly completed building, believing that their tents would be much easier to heat than the larger two-man bunk rooms. And they were right: 'The primus had little effect in warming the place up,' Goldsmith admitted after a distinctly chilly night, 'in spite of the fact that we put a blanket over the door. Six months to the day in tents and I am not sorry to get out of it.'[231]

Over the next few weeks, the meteorological team set up their recording instruments, mattresses were unpacked and the Aga stove, installed by Homard, began to take the chill out of the air – an event so momentous to the eight castaways that they all ran outside to watch the smoke rise from the chimney. With these improvements, it was not long before the rest of the party took up residence. 'At last', wrote Blaiklock, 'we were in the main hut. We moved all the stores and equipment over from the crate, unpacked the crockery, chairs and tables and it felt very strange to sit down properly to a meal in a room at least very bright if not so warm.'[232] Strange, too, to abandon the Sno-house which had been their only refuge from the severity of an Antarctic winter. 'In a few hours the crate, for so long our home, became a desolate, dirty, empty box,' Goldsmith wrote on 20 September. 'Only the empty shelves and the radio reminded me of our former occupation.'[233] They had expected to use the crate for a few weeks; by the time they all moved out, it had been their home for more than seven and a half months.

With a gradual rise in temperatures and an increase in the number of daylight hours, preparations began for the spring sledging journeys to be made by Blaiklock and Goldsmith. First they built the sledges, then, as the temperature rose, Blaiklock decided that the time had come to bring the dogs from the tunnels and picket them outside, where they would acclimatise. Shortly afterwards, they took the two teams out on some training runs, with the inevitable chaos ensuing. 'We released the rope and we were off,' Goldsmith wrote on 25 September, 'but after a few yards the first dog fight began; having separated them we were off again, only to capsize a few yards further down again. This is how it went all day, the dogs fighting less and less as they got more and more tired.'[234]

Their first real test came on 29 September, when the two men set out for Vahsel Bay in an attempt to replenish the rapidly dwindling stock of seal meat. 'In worsening weather,' Blaiklock reported, 'we made only seven miles that first day and continued on the following days in high winds and low temperatures.' As they closed on Vahsel Bay, the weather began to clear and it was not long before they spotted their first seal, quickly followed by eight more. With only a few weeks' supply of seal meat and the remains of the dog pemmican left at the hut, this discovery came as a great relief as, without more meat, the planned survey expeditions would have been seriously jeopardised. Now they knew that, very soon, the whole of the Bay would be alive with seals, sunbathing, barking and fighting – and they need no longer count shortages of dog food among their problems. 'This was encouraging,' a relieved Blaiklock acknowledged, 'and we killed one for the dogs and had liver ourselves that night.'[235] The following day they loaded as much meat as they could carry onto the sledge and started for home.

In the ten days that the sledgers had been absent, back at the hut site all of the snow had now been dug out and Lenton had built the majority of the interior partitions. Preparations to install the generators and main radio transmitter were also well advanced and if completed to schedule this installation would enable the explorers to take part in a BBC broadcast planned for the end of the month. Outside, Williams had been labouring doggedly at the erection of the four main aerial masts – a difficult enough job without the cold and strong winds that made frost-bite an ever-present danger – and Jeffries had nearly completed the dexion meteorological mast. For this final achievement, in Goldsmith's view, Jeffries deserved all the credit: 'the other two met men have hardly lifted a finger to help him,' he observed in disgust on 9 October.

Homard's efforts, too, were to be tested by another trip to Vahsel Bay, this time in that most temperamental of all vehicles, the Weasel. As the engineer could not afford to leave the base until the generators had been installed and fully tested, it was not until 29 October that he and La Grange set out, supported by Blaiklock and his dog team. 'In bright sunshine we made good going along the sea ice,' Blaiklock reported, 'and ran the thirty-one miles to the Vahsel Bay area in 8½ hours.' Despite the executions carried out by Blaiklock and Goldsmith a month before, the seals seemed none the wiser and the following morning the three men had little difficulty in killing enough to fill the Maudheim sledge towed behind the Weasel. At 2.30pm, they began their return journey and arrived back at Shackleton the same evening. Although Blaiklock admitted to feeling 'rather tired after our two full days' and despite the fact that the route to Vahsel Bay had previously been surveyed during the earlier dog sledge journey, this remarkably rapid passage seemed to bode well for the forthcoming continental crossing. It also served to turn the men's minds towards that journey and to the preliminary surveys that would do so much to help the trans-continental party on its way. 'Now the next thing,' Goldsmith wrote that night after welcoming his colleagues home, 'is the journey to the south.'

Just before the Weasel party completed its journey, the five men at Shackleton had enjoyed the excitement of a prolonged conversation with the BBC, in readiness for a proper broadcast scheduled for 1 November. That night a jubilant Goldsmith noted:

> A great day for Shackleton today, in the afternoon we got through to the BBC first shot on the big transmitter – they came through as clearly as if they were next door – there we were chatting to London as if they were next door! They were clear and we could hear all the asides.[236]

Over the next couple of days, further contacts were made and Donald Milner, the BBC reporter, recorded a full interview with Blaiklock. As well as providing the BBC's listeners with an account of the trials and tribulations of the TAE's Advance Party, the contact enabled the expeditionaries to exchange messages with their loved ones at home and to learn something of events in the civilised world. And yet this contact also served to remind the explorers just how far removed they were from the concerns of that world. After the broadcast, a slightly dejected Goldsmith observed: 'They have very little understanding of the sort of things that we might be interested in.'[237] Blaiklock, too, would later acknowledge that, in their isolation, explorers become '... very parochial ... five minutes after the outbreak of the Vietnam War, for example, you're discussing have we got enough dog meat? You're very self-centred shall we say? You're concerned with your own problems – the whole base's problems, not the world's.'[238]

For Blaiklock, the problems now dominating his mind to the exclusion of all outside matters were those relating to the forthcoming sledging expedition, which he would make with Goldsmith. Sledging in a two-man party undoubtedly had its risks but, as Blaiklock described, this approach also brought significant advantages:

> There were only two of us, and if one had an accident it virtually meant the death of the other one. Well, I should think ninety per cent of sledging is done with two people. I mean you know the risks, you know that if somebody falls down a crevasse it's very difficult for one person to get him up – it has been done, but it's jolly difficult – but you weigh that with the advantages. Two people and two dogs is a very strong team so far as logistics go – you're carrying the minimum amount of equipment, tents and sledging gear, you only need one ice axe, and one ice spear and one tent, one stove and you've got two sledges with all the rest: dog food and man food, so you've got tremendous range ... my view was the risks were minimal.[239]

After two short preliminary journeys, during which they flagged part of the route and laid a depot, the two men launched their main expedition on 7 December. Their objective was the Theron Mountains, the discovery of which had so excited Fuchs ten months earlier.

'We made good going the first two days,' reported Blaiklock, 'and covered 45 miles. Turning due south we picked up our previously laid depot and travelled southwards over the flat, monotonous ice shelf.'[240] Although the two men and their dog teams passed through a series of crevasses as they traversed the Filchner Ice Shelf, they encountered no serious delays and, at 79°12'S they caught their first glimpse of the Therons, in the form of a peak which they named Mount Faraway. Estimating that the mountain was some 85 miles distant, they now turned east and headed directly towards it. After the rigours of the winter, the weather felt remarkably balmy and, with the temperatures hovering in the twenties, they decided to switch to night travel. Although the sun never dipped below the horizon now, at night it sank lower in the sky, reducing the temperatures and making the surface less sticky. The dogs performed well after their long period of inactivity and the party made a very respectable 15 or 16 miles per day, pausing every third day to relay its position to Shackleton Base by radio.

As they closed on Mount Faraway, the explorers could see that, as expected, the peak actually formed part of a long range, intersected by steep glaciers and marking the point at which the Filchner Ice Shelf joins the continental landmass. 'But it seemed to take a long time to reach the mountain wall that we were heading for,' remembered Blaiklock. 'On the 17th December we thought that we would reach them but plodding on for mile after mile we had to give up that night with the rock walls apparently only a short distance away.'[241] Frustratingly, the next day they found their way barred by a wide stream of melt-water that rushed down into a lake which had formed on the ice a few miles away to the south. Eventually, they found their way across a narrow stretch and established camp close to the rock wall. Above them small melt-water falls bubbled from the rock face but, as the sun sank in the sky, the temperatures plummeted and the spouts and rushing torrents froze solid or dwindled to puny streams gurgling beneath the scree. High up the mountainside, the two explorers could see hosts of snowy petrels wheeling across the sky and nesting in the rocky fissures, nearly 200 miles from their feeding grounds, while below them, dark skua gulls lurked, hardly visible until they darted forth to raid the petrels' nests.

Examining the cliffs, Blaiklock and Goldsmith collected rock samples, which revealed that the mountains contained strata of sandstone, limestone and anthracite, and Blaiklock took a series of sun observations so that he could accurately chart their position.

We could not stay long however in these mountains, as we were a small party and had to get back to our depot 120 miles away, with only eight days food left on the sledge. The weather had been very fine up to now but we could never tell how long it would last.[242]

Reluctant to leave scenes that offered such a welcome contrast to Vahsel Bay, the catalyst for departure came in the form of an avalanche, which hurtled down the mountainside one evening as the two men soaked up the last of the sun's rays, wearing nothing but their vests and long johns. Hearing a roar far above their heads, they ran from their tent to see a great mass of rock and ice come rolling and skittering to a halt a few hundred yards from their camp. They needed no second hint and the next day they turned their sledge around and began the long retreat towards Shackleton, which they reached without further incident at 9.00am on 27 December. They had covered 360 miles in 21 days.

The Advance Party's isolation was drawing rapidly to a close. Nightly radio schedules had been established with the Royal Society base and, from these, the eight men learned that two American ships intended to visit the TAE base. The news of a visit from the outside world, their first since 7 February, sent the suddenly house-proud explorers into a flurry of activity. On 30 December, the expected day of arrival, Goldsmith reported:

The kitchen had been scrubbed and tidied as it had never been tidied before; all the horrors, the dustbin, puppy bowl, water tin and washing up box have been taken out and the place made to look respectable. Even the clothes drying over the fire have all been removed.[243]

In the early hours of New Year's Eve, the two ships hove into view: the 14,000-ton US Navy cargo ship *Wyandot* and the 6000-ton icebreaker, *Staten Island* – both servicing the American Antarctic research expedition, known as Operation Deep Freeze. At about 4.30am the first helicopter took off and the explorers could see it circle the ships before it headed towards them to land close to the hut. Out of it, according to Goldsmith, 'stepped a Martian wearing a red helmet and a green suit with a yellow life jacket'; this turned out to be Captain Edwin A. McDonald, in command of the two vessels. Then a second helicopter arrived, carrying another Martian: Captain Finn Ronne, who would be in charge of the American base. A third machine brought Colonel Herbert Nicholl, a US Army officer who also, rather incongruously, worked as a correspondent for the *Christian Science Monitor*. The Colonel asked the members of the Advance Party a few questions about their experiences and aspirations and then the group toured the hut. It didn't take long, though the examination wasn't so cursory as to prevent the Americans noting the gulf that separated the fairly primitive Heroic Era conditions of the TAE from the altogether more high-tech approach of their own operation. Looking at the wooden hut, with its Spartan furnishings and traditional Aga stove, McDonald summed up their views with a telling remark: 'How quaint,' he said, donning his bright red crash helmet. The visit was over, seemingly, almost as soon as it commenced and in a matter of minutes the helicopters had buzzed their way back to their flight deck. McDonald immediately set his course and the two ships rapidly disappeared behind the overhang of the ice cliff, en route to establish Ellsworth Station at Gould Bay.

If this end to their solitude seemed somehow anticlimactic, the Advance Party did not have long to brood. On 4 January 1957, the Royal Society base reported the arrival of the *Theron's* replacement, the *Magga Dan*, and, by the 11th, the TAE's Otter aircraft had been unloaded and tested, ready for a flight to Vahsel Bay the following day. The men at Shackleton possessed no red carpet to roll out, but they did manage to lay the linoleum on the living room floor ready for Fuchs's arrival. The 12th dawned cold and bright with just a faint breeze – perfect flying weather. A short time later John Lewis's well-known voice crackled over the radio announcing his imminent arrival and all the castaways except Williams, who stayed by his radio, trooped outside to watch for the aeroplane. Blaiklock:

There it was to the east growing larger until it was overhead and circling the base. It was bigger than most of us had imagined and looked a wonderful sight – a bright orange glinting in the clear sunshine. It circled over the base a few times and then gracefully landed on our airstrip and taxied towards the base. Out jumped Bunny, George [Lowe], John Lewis and Donald [Milner] from the BBC. Handshakes all round … After picketing the plane down we all returned to the hut and had a noisy and happy lunchtime after which we all grabbed our sacks of mail and each retired to his own corner to read those long awaited letters. Before long the living room floor was knee deep in waster paper.[244]

After more than eleven gruelling months, the Advance Party's ordeal was over. Now it was up to Fuchs to ensure that the story of their sacrifices was not consigned to the dustbin of history, a little-known adjunct to yet another failed attempt to cross the continent.

5

To the Ross Sea

In August 1956, some 4000 miles from the Advance Party's still unfinished hut, two figures might have been spotted on the moraine at the foot of the Tasman Glacier in New Zealand. All around them, the great snow-capped mountains of the Southern Alps rose into a crisp, clear blue sky, their sides streaked with blue ice and black rock and their lower slopes scored and furrowed by innumerable avalanches. As one member of the TAE later commented, it was 'a magnificent setting to begin any adventure,'[245] but the two Alpinists seemed perfectly at home in the dramatic landscape. The first, dressed in a faded khaki anorak and with a clean-shaven, sunburnt face, was Lieutenant Richard Brooke RN, a 29-year-old veteran of D-Day and the British North Greenland Expedition; erstwhile third officer of the MV *John Biscoe*; and an experienced mountaineer, now appointed as surveyor to the TAE's Ross Sea Party. The second, clad in a Norwegian ski sweater, with thinning curly hair and a pipe permanently clenched between his teeth, was Dr George Marsh, the expedition's popular and urbane dog expert. Like Brooke, Marsh was already an experienced polar veteran, having formerly served as leader and medical officer to the FIDS base in Hope Bay between 1952 and 1953. Fuchs had recommended both men and they formed the British contingent within Hillary's team.

With their dog teams, Brooke and Marsh had descended from
Malte Brun Hut, where Hillary had established his training camp,
and were waiting to meet and guide two more team members,
Bernie Gunn and Guy Warren. The two geologists, both gradu-
ates of Canterbury University in Christchurch, arrived on skis
from Ball Hut, where they had been dropped by bus. After a short
but cordial greeting the party began its 10-mile sledge journey
up the glacier. Gunn later wrote that the pace set by the two
experienced dog-handlers with their light Nansen sledges 'was
absolutely tumultuous and I clung to the handlebars in an effort
to remain upright on ski while being towed at an alarming rate
up hill and down dale, or rather, over hummock and hollow.'[246]
After a helter-skelter couple of hours, the teams drew to a halt
below Malte Brun Hut and, having secured the eighteen dogs to
wire lines in the snow, the four explorers completed their journey with a 1000-foot climb up the snow slope to the hut itself.
Perched on the mountainside at an altitude of 5700 feet and originally built in 1898 as a shelter for climbers, for the next month
this small timber building would be their home. Their classroom
would be the Tasman Glacier itself.

The decision to bring his team together in the Southern Alps
constituted just one part of Hillary's carefully considered plan. In
February of the same year, while unloading the *Theron*, a despairing Rainer Goldsmith had commented: 'Ed must get a pretty
poor idea of what really cooks on this expedition … but he will
be able to learn from the chaos he sees here.'[247] In fact, Hillary
had very quickly demonstrated that he would take every lesson to
heart. Even as the *Theron* fought her way back through the closing pack of the Weddell Sea and out into the Atlantic, he had held
continual discussions with his fellow New Zealanders, Miller and
Claydon, regarding the improvements they might implement to
ensure that the establishment of Scott Base repeated none of the
mistakes witnessed at Vahsel Bay. Hillary had written in his diary:

> It is better to delay sailing from the loading point for several
> days and have things correctly stowed than arrive at your des-
> tination with immediate necessities at the bottom of the hold

... Any equipment unloaded on to the sea ice must be dragged
away immediately and never left at the mercy of bad weather
... All expedition members should be taught how to drive the
various vehicles before they are shipped south.[248]

With less than nine months left before his own element of the
expedition sailed, he had begun to put some of the lessons into
effect immediately upon his arrival back in England on 23 March.

Perhaps most crucial of all was the consideration given to the
motor vehicles. When outlining the probable objectives of the
Ross Sea Party early in 1955, Fuchs had opined that 'It is unlikely
that mechanical transport could be effective except in the vicinity of the base and the route finding will have to be done by
means of air recce and dog sledges on the ground.'[249] Hillary,
however, clearly had other ideas. In their official account of the
expedition, Bob Miller and Arthur Helm, a member of the New
Zealand Antarctic Society who acted as the expedition's Postal
and Liaison Officer, later asserted that their leader 'even at this
stage was fostering plans for the wider use of tractors than that
required by the immediate domestic and necessary local demands
of base maintenance and ship unloading.'[250] But whatever their
ultimate use, the high cost of specialist vehicles like the Sno-
cat made it probable that Hillary would be forced to rely upon
the cheaper and more readily available Ferguson tractors. These
machines had proved to be the most reliable of those taken south
by the Advance Party – but they had also been incapable, at least
when towing heavily laden sledges, of negotiating the soft snow
of the slope up to the base site. Unless this flaw could be overcome, their usefulness would be extremely limited.

Like most British vehicle manufacturers, the Ferguson company had taken to heart Sir Stafford Cripps' post-war injunction
to 'export or die' and a number of its vehicles had been shipped
to Norway where the engineers of Eikmaskin Ltd, Ferguson's
Norwegian agent, had conducted a range of experiments with
regard to their conversion for use on snow and ice. Both Scott
and Shackleton had trialled their motorised sledges in Norway
and now Hillary, Miller and David Pratt followed suit, spending

a week at Elvesetter in Jotunheimen testing various combina-
tions of tracks and skis. The most successful proved to be the
'full track', whereby the tractor's front wheels were locked and
a caterpillar-type track passed around them and the large drive
wheels. This modification rendered the steering wheel obsolete and made it necessary to steer by braking the left and right
tracks independently. The solution placed addition strain on the
engine but, overall, it proved simple and effective. For Hillary,
these experiments 'confirmed my view that the Ferguson was a
rugged, reliable, and highly adaptable vehicle.' Unfortunately, the
trials also tended to underpin the conclusion that in soft snow, it
could never compete with machines which had been specially
designed for such conditions. Despite this important reservation,
Hillary admitted to 'developing the conviction that we would get
the Ferguson a long way towards the South Pole.'[251]

Returning to New Zealand in mid-April, and leaving Miller
in London to deal with the multiple headaches associated with
the procurement of essential stores, Hillary had turned his attention to that *bête noire* of most Heroic Era expeditions, fundraising.
Although the Ross Dependency had been transferred from
Britain to New Zealand immediately after its establishment in
the summer of 1923, in reality the New Zealand government
viewed its jurisdiction in the area as more of an embarrassment
than an opportunity. Whatever the people of New Zealand might
think – and Hillary believed them to be largely supportive of
a more active participation in Antarctic exploration – those in
authority saw the region as a veritable Pandora's Box, the opening of which could generate a huge drain on their country's
limited resources. For 30 years, they had resisted all suggestions
that New Zealand should in any way seek to exercise the authority which had been foisted upon her – but now their opponents
had succeeded in enlisting a highly popular and influential figurehead to champion their cause. When Hillary joined his voice
to that of the New Zealand Antarctic Society, the government
at last bowed to the inevitable and three decades of stonewalling
came to an abrupt end. On 14 May 1955, the Minister of External
Affairs, T.L. Macdonald, announced that the government had

decided to grant £50,000 to the expedition – equivalent to 50 per cent of the total sum donated by the British government. Then, on 26 May, Macdonald made a further statement to the effect that the government would set up a Ross Sea Committee, which would assume responsibility for organising New Zealand's participation in the TAE.

Despite these significant developments, additional funds still needed to be raised – in fact, Hillary and the newly formed Committee estimated that another £100,000 would be required to ensure that the Ross Sea Party would be entirely self-sufficient in stores and equipment. This money would have to be sought through public subscriptions. In seeking financial backing for his own trans-Antarctic expedition four decades earlier, Shackleton had brazenly played upon the patriotic feeling of the general public, boldly asserting in *The Times* his conviction that 'our kinsmen in all the lands under the Union Jack will be willing to assist towards the carrying out of the full programme of exploration to which my comrades and myself are pledged.'[252] Learning from the master, the Ross Sea Committee resorted to equally barefaced nationalistic arm-twisting, stating in its pamphlets that 'Those New Zealanders who have volunteered and been chosen to take part in the arduous tasks of exploration have the right to expect their countrymen to support them.'[253] But, just as in 1913, the call alone was not quite enough. The New Zealand public responded generously to the appeal – but that generosity had to be milked through personal appearances and, of course, there could be no better fundraiser than the world-famous Hillary. As a result, both before and after his voyage on the *Theron*, and despite finding the process 'a somewhat distasteful business', the Ross Sea Party's leader had little choice but to criss-cross the country making speeches and attending functions in an attempt to charm the pounds, shillings and pence from the pockets of his countrymen. After three months of such uncongenial labour, the rough and tumble of training on the Tasman Glacier came as a considerable relief.

The men now collected at Malte Brun Hut were, in many ways, an extremely disparate group, consisting of mountaineers and guides; pilots and engineers; naval officers and scientists. 'Our expedition seemed to consist of an odd assortment of people,' wrote Gunn, 'in fact had the entire psychological talent of the country combined, I doubt 20 more dissimilar men could have been banded together for any purpose whatever.'[254] The first to arrive had been Marsh and Harry Ayres, a highly experienced mountain guide and long-time associate of Hillary's. Together these two had set about training the dogs – a process they had begun at Mount Cook by hitching the animals to a derelict vehicle chassis and racing them along the local roads. When Brooke and other members of the Ross Sea Party appeared, the training programme expanded to cover skiing, navigation and ice climbing. Two Ferguson tractors were also brought up onto the glacier and every member of the team was expected to achieve proficiency in driving them in a variety of conditions. At the same time, Peter Mulgrew and Ted Gawn, the two radio operators, installed a field set at the hut and thereafter maintained a regular schedule with Wellington, 300 miles away. Finally, the distance of the camp from civilisation meant that the expedition's pilots would have every opportunity to test their skills in flying in to and out of mountainous and snow-clad terrain using radio compass homing and in dropping supplies to sledge teams – skills that would prove vital when depot-laying and supporting the survey teams in the Antarctic. Perhaps most bizarre of all, in order to ensure that the dogs remained well fed, the expedition's Beaver aircraft was fitted with bomb racks from which sheep carcasses could be strung. This system gave the aircraft's wings the appearance of a butcher's stall and, as Marsh recorded, 'Some consternation was caused to the skiers on the slopes beneath by the remarkable sight of an aircraft flying over Ball Hut with either five mutton carcasses or a leg of horse dangling under each wing.'[255]

These flights also provided the RNZAF contingent with an unplanned and distinctly unwelcome opportunity to practise their crash-landing and aircraft recovery procedures. The Auster Aircraft Company had been asked by the expedition to develop an undercarriage that combined wheels and skis to enable the two-seater to land in a variety of conditions. Unfortunately, the tight timescales meant that the company had no opportunity to test their design prior to Claydon attempting to land the Auster on the glacier. The results were very nearly catastrophic. Having been alerted to the aeroplane's imminent arrival by radio, the members of the expedition gathered on the glacier to watch the landing. Soon, they heard the Auster's 145bhp Gypsy Major engine, its whirr magnified by the sides of the glacial valley, and then the tiny, brightly painted machine came into view, the sun glinting from its wings and canopy. 'Claydon touched the skis on the snow and lifted off again, three or four times,' Gunn reported. 'On each occasion the plane swerved violently as the wheels dug into the snow, which did not look good.'[256] Finally, taking the bit between his teeth, Claydon came in with tail low and put her down. As he did so, the two skis threw up a cloud of snow and ice particles as the protruding wheels ploughed into the surface; then, while the explorers watched in horrified silence, the aeroplane's nose dipped and its tailplane described a lazy upwards arc until, with a resounding crash, it fell forward and splintered against the glacier.

A similar incident in October 1911 had brought an abrupt end to Lieutenant Hugh Watkins's hope of being the first man to make a powered flight in the Antarctic during Douglas Mawson's Australasian Expedition. Although his Vickers REP had been broken beyond repair, Watkins had been lucky to escape with nothing more serious than a cracked sternum. Now the members of the Ross Sea Party sprinted across the ice fearing that Claydon might have been less fortunate. They needn't have worried: as the breathless explorers reached the wreckage, Claydon undid his harness and slid out onto the ice. 'Alright?' he asked in a tone of mild surprise, 'Of course I'm all right. Got some mail for you chaps here somewhere!'[257] Suspicious of the modifications made to the Auster's undercarriage, with great prescience Claydon had decided to remove the battery, radio and any loose gear from the cockpit and he had flown with the minimum of fuel – had he done otherwise the consequences might have been fatal. As it was, the Auster had sustained considerable damage: the tailplane had crumpled on impact, the propeller and canopy had been smashed and the wings had also been badly damaged. 'The upshot of this test,' Claydon reported with his usual understatement, 'proved that the wheel/ski combination on the Auster was obviously unsuitable. However, valuable experience was gained by the Expedition in the resulting repair, which was carried out in the field.'[258]

Training continued off the glacier as well. Selwyn Bucknell, the expedition cook, spent a number of weeks at the Army Cookery School; Marsh undertook an intensive course in dentistry; and Mulgrew and Gawn learned the rudiments of aeroplane maintenance so that they could support the RNZAF contingent in keeping the aircraft operational. The onerous task of procuring and sorting stores and equipment also continued uninterrupted – causing endless headaches for the conscientious Miller. 'Planning the stores for an Antarctic Expedition had literally to cover the procurement of everything from a needle to an anchor,' he recalled. 'Organising an expedition was similar to undertaking all at once the stocking of a department store, a garage, a hospital, a carpenter's and engineering workshop, a radio station and an hotel.'[259] Ably assisted by the members of the Committee and, in particular, by Helm, Miller ensured that nothing was left to chance and, despite the expedition's uncertain finances, he never allowed quality to be sacrificed to price. The government's decision that Scott Base should also house New Zealand's five-strong IGY party, led by Dr Trevor Hatherton, and that the IGY and TAE parties should work together, also meant that some expenses, particularly those relating to the hut, would be shared by the IGY Committee, thereby relieving some of the strain on the TAE's budget.

Finally, as the day of departure approached, consideration must be given to the loading of the expedition ship, the erstwhile *John Biscoe*. Originally built as a net-layer under the Lend-Lease Agreement, after service with the Home Fleet and with FIDS, in 1955 the wooden-hulled ship had become surplus when FIDS purchased a purpose-built steel replacement. It was at this moment that she had come to the notice of the Ross Sea Committee. With a proven track record as an Antarctic supply vessel, as well as meeting most of the Committee's requirements, she had the enormous advantage of being cheap. Once acquired, she was immediately renamed HMNZS *Endeavour* in honour of Captain James Cook's ship of the same name and the post of captain was offered to and accepted by her previous commander, Captain Harry Kirkwood, OBE, DSC, on secondment from the Royal Navy. On seeing the ship for the first time, Gunn was very unimpressed: 'One could easily swing a leg over her rail,' he observed, 'step on the rubbing strake and step down onto the ice, if she happened to be alongside ice, without bothering about a ladder ... "Bet a foot of ice stops her dead!" was my reaction.'[260] Whatever reservations Gunn or any of his fellows might entertain regarding the *Endeavour*'s suitability, however – and the discovery that a leaking hold had ruined a large portion of the supplies brought from England could have done nothing to reassure them – the decision was irreversible. When she arrived in Wellington in late October the process of stowing the vast array of boxes, crates, drums and parcels began immediately.

One of the most important lessons that Hillary, Miller and Claydon had learned when they accompanied the *Theron* was the need for a carefully considered loading schedule. At Vahsel Bay, huge amounts of time had been lost in trying to reach such fundamental items as the vehicles and the resulting chaos had done much to hinder the establishment of Shackleton Base. All were determined that the building of Scott Base would suffer from no such defects in planning or execution. This meant, as Miller explained, that 'it was necessary to ensure that the various portions were loaded in the exact reverse order in which they would be required once the base site was reached.'[261] So those items of equipment and stores that would be needed immediately upon arrival in the Antarctic should be stowed at the very top of the holds. The process was long and painstaking but, once the last item had been lashed down, the men of the Ross Sea Party could have confidence that when, in the teeth of an Antarctic gale, they called for a hammer, a hammer would come to hand.

At last, the months of preparation came to an end and on 15 December 1956 Kirkwood declared that the *Endeavour* was ready to put to sea. To the frustration of some, however, there now followed a long progress down the east coast of New Zealand as Hillary and his team attended farewell functions, made valedictory speeches and shook the expedition's collection box one last time. An official farewell ceremony was held in Wellington Town Hall, attended by the Governor General and other dignitaries; prayers for the success of the expedition were offered up at Christchurch Cathedral; Hillary laid a wreath at the Scott Memorial; and, finally, on the evening of 17 December, the Duke of Edinburgh wined and dined the explorers on board the Royal Yacht *Britannia* at Lyttelton.

Despite all the professionalism and attention to detail, the departure from Port Lyttelton on the night of the royal send-off demonstrated that no such venture could ever be entirely free of accidents and miscalculations. Of the expedition's two aircraft, the larger Beaver, which would be used primarily for depot laying, had been partly dismantled and stored in a crate on deck. The newly repaired Auster, on the other hand, with its skis replaced by floats, had been strapped into a cradle on the *Endeavour's* stern with its wing tips protruding either side of the hull. From this position the aeroplane could be lowered into the water at short notice, ready to undertake reconnaissance flights. When the order to cast off was given, instead of moving in a straight line towards the mouth of the harbour, the *Endeavour* began to yaw crazily to starboard, towards a large freighter named the *Huntingdon*. Through a moment's inattention on the part of one of the crew, a spring between the ship and the quayside had been left in place – with disastrous consequences. 'In spite of the shouts from onlookers on the wharf,' Claydon reported, 'the stern swung right around and with a sickening crunch, the starboard wing of the Auster crashed into the other ship.'[262] For the second time, the Auster's fragile wings had sustained serious damage, with a splintered main spar, a twisted aileron, smashed aileron hinges and numerous broken ribs. The only good news, as a wry Claydon commented, was that by 'acting as an effective fender, the Auster prevented any damage to the *Endeavour*.' Though this fact did little to lessen Hillary's ire.

After the first accident on the Tasman Glacier in August, Wally Tarr, the expedition's air mechanic, had shown that he could function as a one-man maintenance team, combining the skills of rigger, engineer and fitter – but the damage caused by this incident proved to be beyond even his skill to repair and subsequent inspection by an RNZAF team at Taieri revealed that a whole new wing would be required. Over the next few hours, frantic efforts were made to find a spare in both New Zealand and Australia, but to no avail. Eventually, after wasting two days, and with reports from American shipping indicating that good leads had been seen running through the pack ice on the fringes of the Ross Sea, Hillary and the Committee decided that the *Endeavour* should proceed south without further delay. A new wing would be sourced and then sent to Scott Base via an American transport ship. A simple, foolish oversight meant that the Ross Sea Party had been denied air reconnaissance to ease the *Endeavour*'s passage through the pack, the opportunity to reconnoitre McMurdo Sound to locate a suitable site for off-loading, and the ability to undertake an aerial survey of the Ferrar Glacier to identify a sledge route onto the Polar Plateau. Not surprisingly, as Miller observed, the incident 'had a dampening effect on the members' spirits' and it was a suitably chastened Ross Sea Party that finally set sail from Bluff at 11.30pm on 21 December, bound for the Antarctic.

The *Endeavour* nosed out into the South Pacific beneath overcast skies and into a grey, choppy sea. 'Some seasickness among Expedition members,' Miller noted in his diary on the 22nd, 'but really the general spirit is a happy one.'[263] In later years, Richard Brooke would assert that Miller, as Hillary's second-in-command, was 'a prime organiser of the details of the expedition'[264] and just as in New Zealand he had filled the role of quartermaster-general, Miller now saw to the minutiae of sorting the explorers into working parties. With the ship pitching and rolling, between their trips to the rail the landsmen began to perform all the usual duties of an expedition at sea: cleaning the wardroom, peeling potatoes, serving meals and washing up, feeding the dogs and, most unpleasant of all, swabbing out their kennels. The only incident worthy of note on that first day occurred late in the afternoon when two vessels loomed out of the mist like ghost ships and took up stations either side of the *Endeavour*. These were the Royal New Zealand Navy frigates *Hawea* and *Pukaki*, which had been shepherding the *Britannia* on the first leg of her voyage to the Chatham Islands. Having seen the Duke of Edinburgh safely on his way, as a gesture of goodwill they had now been detailed to escort the Ross Sea Party to the edge of the pack ice.

If many of the expeditionaries had read with trepidation accounts of the stormy seas between New Zealand and the Antarctic, for the time being at least the great Southern Ocean seemed inclined to treat them with incredible tenderness. After the first dull day, the explorers woke to beautiful sunshine and seas so smooth that they found it almost impossible to believe that they had entered the notorious 'screaming fifties'. 'This day even more glorious than yesterday,' Miller enthused on Christmas Eve. 'At noon 56°30'S yet so much warmth in the sun that crew and others out sunbathing. Seas moderate to calm. Almost unbelievable for these latitudes.'[265] No doubt buoyed by these benign conditions, the mood on board remained one of light-hearted camaraderie and co-operation, with the crew and expedition members working together remarkably well. Of course, these conditions could not last and on the morning of 26 December, a dense wall of fog surrounded the ship, reducing visibility to a quarter of a mile. Noticeably cooler temperatures reminded everyone of the proximity of the pack and Captain Kirkwood ordered the lookouts to keep their wits about them. They spotted the first ice at 11.30pm. Small chunks and larger bergs became commonplace and at noon the next day the *Endeavour* crossed the Antarctic Circle. Soon afterwards she entered lightly scattered pack. As the small growlers and bergy bits grew in number, the frigates moved astern and followed in the *Endeavour*'s wake. Then, at 4.30pm, the *Pukaki* again drew alongside. Her crew lined the bows and filled the air with three loud hurrahs; the *Hawea* sounded her foghorn in accompaniment and then the two vessels sheered away and were quickly lost in the fog. With the pack thickening around her, the *Endeavour* was on her own.

The descent of the fog and the appearance of ice had persuaded the captain to reduce the *Endeavour*'s speed, initially to

8 knots and sometimes to as little as 3 knots. Now, although the scattered floes did little to impede her progress and her bows, sheathed in green-heart oak, seemed immune to the 3-foot-thick ice, Kirkwood's caution increased. He stopped engines at 7.30 on the evening of the 28th and the ship remained motionless for eleven hours, floating in a kaleidoscope of colour with the white, green and turquoise of the icebergs contrasting with the blues of sky and water. She made good progress the following morning but at noon the clatter of the engines ceased so that the expedition and crew could enjoy a belated and boisterous Christmas dinner. 'Vessel stopped at midday,' Miller wrote later that day, 'but continued during afternoon to stop early evening – Goodness knows why. Expedition members irked by delays in very easy pack.'[266] The next day the explorers discovered to their disgust that they had lost more in drift than they had made in ice navigation and frustration at the repeated delays began to bubble to the surface. 'Captain appears reluctant to batter and nudge,'[267] wrote a disgruntled Miller and even Brooke, who had volunteered to take a watch and possessed far more knowledge of ice navigation than any of the other explorers, thought Kirkwood 'incredibly cautious in the early stages.'[268]

Of course, with his first-hand experience of the damage that unforeseen delays could do to an expedition's carefully laid plans, no one felt more galled than Hillary. 'When I think about the work to be done I grudge every wasted hour,' he had written on the 28th, though for the time being he had continued to give Kirkwood the benefit of the doubt. But when the next 48 hours produced no discernible quickening of the ship's funereal pace, his patience began to run out. 'Harry thinks the ice is too tough and the ship can't take it,' he grumbled in his diary. 'I think there's either something radically wrong with Harry or the ship – probably Harry.'[269] At last, aware of the discontented mutterings of his men, and unable to bear any further delays, he decided to challenge the captain – and a stormy confrontation quickly ensued.

As captain of the RRS *Discovery II* in the 1930s, Kirkwood had completed an arduous programme of oceanographical research, including a full circumnavigation of the Antarctic, and he was not used to being challenged – particularly by amateurs, however gifted. Opinionated, brusque and incapable of suffering fools gladly, Brooke later summed him up as 'a difficult man ... his opinion of what he would have [described as] the "so-called scientists" going down to join FIDS in 1948, '49, '50 really was rock bottom; he hadn't any time for them and I think that attitude carried on with the way he looked at our expedition members – quite unfairly.'[270] Such a character was hardly likely to respond kindly to criticism from Hillary and the exchange between the two was brisk: 'He completely lost his temper', Hillary wrote that night, 'but I'm pleased to say I don't think I lost mine. However I did get in a few solid home truths. Harry departed for the bridge in high dudgeon but I guess he'll recover.'[271] To his delight, Hillary soon discovered not only that Kirkwood had recovered but that his challenge had produced just the required result, with the captain now attacking the ice with quite uncharacteristic aggression. 'Well, what a change!' he enthused. 'For the last two hours we've been going like the proverbial bomb – through everything. We've made more progress than we have for days. Harry can certainly do it when he wants to and I feel I must have got him on the raw. Good show!'[272]

Other members of the expedition felt rather less pleased at an exhibition which at times seemed little short of suicidal. '*Endeavour* took some fearful blows as we struck hard ice about 4 feet thick head-on', Gunn recalled, 'and we expected at any moment to have the diesel engines tear out of their beds and crash through the engine-room bulkhead and into the ward room.'[273] Brooke, too, admitted that 'Kirkwood handled the ship extremely roughly, no question – but I'm glad to say the ship stood up to it.'[274] She stood up to it – but not unscathed. Gunn later noticed a mass of planking floating in the ship's wake and subsequent examination revealed that the captain's maniacal assault on the floes had stripped much of the green-heart sheathing from the *Endeavour*'s bows. Very soon, however, the captain's brutal handling of his vessel would pale into insignificance when compared with the violence of the sea itself.

For most of the last nine days the explorers had benefited from unusually balmy weather and calm seas: now they would discover why these latitudes enjoy such a fearsome reputation. The glass had been falling rapidly throughout 30 December and on the 31st a howling gale struck the *Endeavour* from the south-west, driving snow flurries before it. At first, to everyone's relief, the surrounding pack served to dampen the effects of the growing swell: the ice heaved and undulated, its edges emitting groans and sharp cracks as they rubbed against each other, but most of the landsmen remained on their feet. This all changed at 6.30am on New Year's Day, when the ship at last broke free from the belt of pack ice and into a violently tossing sea. The *Endeavour*'s keelless construction gave her a tendency to roll at the best of times, and now this propensity became wildly exaggerated, as Gunn described:

> The wind was blowing sixty knots and the sea was streaked white with the crests half a mile apart. The *Endeavour* would dip her bows under and the sea would wash along the deck until only the bridge was clear above the water and the ship would wallow and stagger drunkenly like a surfacing submarine. Then the Jackstaff on the bow would appear above the seas, then the top of the Beaver crate lashed on the foredeck, and finally hundreds of tons of water would cascade through the freeing ports and over the bulwarks and finally we would emerge...[275]

The storm lasted for three days, the grey sea constantly crashing over the *Endeavour*'s bows. Walls of foaming seawater rolled men into the scuppers, smashed crates, and left chaos in their wake. Dog kennels disintegrated into matchwood and Brooke, Marsh and Gunn floundered from rail to rail flinging themselves at bedraggled huskies and bundling them into cabins and down companionways, until the whole interior of the ship echoed to the yelping of the frightened animals. Since none of the dogs had been lost overboard, however, the fate of the expedition's Beaver aircraft gave more immediate cause for concern. At the height of the storm an immense wave smashed the end of the aircraft crate, and soaked the machine inside. Despite the violence of the wind, Tarr and the pilots managed to rig a tarpaulin over the hole in the planking but it would be some time before they could properly examine the aeroplane and ascertain the extent of the damage. With the Auster already rendered *hors de combat*, it was a casualty that the expedition could ill afford.

Tired, wet and cold, the members of the Ross Sea Party had been subjected to a tumultuous welcome by the Antarctic but their spirits lifted when, at 1.15pm on 3 January, the storm began to abate and the twin volcanoes, Mounts Erebus and Terror, came into view. A great plume of smoke rose impressively from the squat white cone of Erebus, but as the *Endeavour* approached Ross Island, the explorers marvelled too at the lower crest of the unclimbed Terror, dark and jagged as a broken molar. Reports of diminishing seas and milder weather tempted a number of the groggy explorers out of their noisome cabins and into the fresh air and now, their seasickness forgotten, they lined the ship's rails staring excitedly at this still largely unexplored continent. Clear blue skies with just a few hazy clouds on the far horizon gave the scene a startling beauty, while the presence of sleek, well-fed penguins and a pod of whales, lazily surfacing and spouting, gave the picture an added vivacity. Less welcome was the sight of a heavy belt of pack ice as the *Endeavour* steamed towards Beaufort Island to the south-west.

The next morning, the explorers awoke to find their ship beset. 'I wasn't on watch on that particular night,' Brooke recalled, 'but in the morning when I went out there we were stuck in heavy ice just off McMurdo Sound. I cannot imagine how that happened!'[276] All on board blamed Kirkwood who, apparently still smarting from the recent accusations of tardiness, had attempted to barge his way through the thickest portions of the pack instead of taking his time to find a more navigable route. 'Morning absolutely glorious,' fumed Miller, '– but here we are stupidly locked in ice beyond Beaufort Island. Just too silly for words.'[277] Time and again, Kirkwood launched his ship at the 8-foot-thick ice causing her to jar and shudder with the impacts, but without success. Eventually the pack might give way before the repeated attacks but the expedition was losing valuable time and with the engine straining and the ship's timbers groaning with each assault, a sullen Kirkwood was forced to admit defeat. Trapped at a point about 4 miles from Beaufort Island, he radioed Rear-Admiral George Dufek, commander of the United States' Operation Deep Freeze, to ask for assistance. Then, thoroughly humiliated, he waited for the world's largest icebreaker, USS *Glacier*, to release his ship. Just after 11.30am, the 8000-ton *Glacier* hove into view, her heavily reinforced bows and ten powerful engines enabling her to smash effortlessly through the pack that had brought the *Endeavour*'s progress to such an ignominious end. 'She looked splendid as she came up,' recorded a relieved Miller, 'with an icy spray from her bows heralding the approach.'[278] Perhaps, too, some on board felt a certain satisfaction that Kirkwood's pride had been so effectively and publicly humbled.

Having reached the *Endeavour*, the icebreaker forged ahead at an amazing 12 knots, with the tiny expedition vessel following in her wake. Within an hour, they had reached clear water and the pair proceeded together for 50 miles up McMurdo Sound in glorious sunshine. The whole western expanse of Ross Island now lay before the explorers' eyes and across the sound the Western Mountains of Victoria Land could be seen jutting into the frigid air. In the late afternoon, the two ships came to rest against the ice edge, approximately 8 miles east of Butter Point, where the expedition hoped to establish its base.

More than three years had passed since the idea of the trans-Antarctic crossing had first been expounded to Hillary. In that time, Fuchs's original conception of the part to be played by the Ross Sea Party had expanded radically, though Hillary still kept some aspects of that expansion close to his chest. Now, as he prepared to disembark, he knew that, once again, the eyes of the world rested upon him. If he faltered in the completion of his planned programme of work, the trans-continental journey would not be the only casualty. His own dearly held ambition of New Zealand adopting a leading role in the ongoing exploration of Antarctica would also be stillborn. The next few weeks of surveying and construction work would be critical in establishing the viability of his whole enterprise.

Fortunately, Hillary was far from ignorant regarding his surroundings. In December 1955, as part of the preparations for the

establishment of Scott Base, Bernie Gunn, Trevor Hatherton and
Bill Smith had undertaken a reconnaissance mission to the Ross
Sea. Relying upon the co-operation of the Americans engaged
in Operation Deep Freeze, their objectives had been to identify
possible base sites; to study the accessibility of these sites from
the sea; and to survey, by air and sledge, routes up onto the Polar
Plateau. Finally, they were expected to form an opinion regarding
the feasibility of aircraft landing and taking-off in this terrain as
part of the scheme for depot laying. Most important to the subsequent development of Hillary's plans, in January 1956 the three
men had undertaken a 12-day man-hauled sledging journey up
the 35-mile long Ferrar Glacier, which flows from the Victoria
Land plateau down to New Harbour in McMurdo Sound – a
route first pioneered by members of Scott's *Discovery* Expedition
over half a century earlier. Despite surface conditions that ranged
from soft sticky snow to hard blue ice, the presence of crevasses
40 feet wide and half-a-mile long, and the prevalence of katabatic winds that scoured the glacier from top to bottom, the New
Zealand Advance Party had reported back to the Committee that
the route seemed viable. They had also suggested that if for some
reason the Ferrar proved impassable, then the Skelton Glacier
offered an alternative. It was this report which had resulted in
Hillary's decision to select Butter Point as the spot for his base,
offering – on paper at least – the best approach by sea and relatively easy access to the mouth of the Ferrar Glacier.

During the evening of 4 January, Hillary dined with Admiral
Dufek and the *Glacier*'s captain, Commander Gerald L. Ketchum,
and the three men discussed the Ross Sea Party's plans. To
Hillary's consternation, Dufek expressed his firm opinion that
the prevailing ice conditions would make it extremely difficult, if
not absolutely impossible, for the expedition's heavily laden tractors to reach Butter Point from the ice edge. 'This was bad news,'
Hillary acknowledged, 'but I kept hoping that things wouldn't
prove too difficult.'[279] Obviously, a detailed reconnaissance
should be undertaken as soon as possible and Hillary gratefully
accepted Dufek's offer of a helicopter flight to Butter Point. At
9.15 that night, he, Miller and Kirkwood clambered into one of

the *Glacier*'s choppers and set off to examine the sea ice. 'The farther we went and the more I saw of the route over the ice,' Hillary later wrote, 'the more my spirits dropped. The whole area was broken up into great triangular segments which had frozen together in rough pressure ridges.'[280] They landed on the shingle beach 3 miles to the west of Butter Point and Hillary and Miller immediately began an inspection of the site which, up until a few minutes before, they had confidently expected to make their home for the next year. Of itself, the site was unexceptionable, offering ample room for the expedition's buildings and equipment. But the routes to it were little short of atrocious. As well as the jumbled chaos of the sea ice, a great melt pool blocked the approach from the glacier side, meaning that it could only be reached via the Bowers Piedmont Glacier with its steep ice slopes. For all their rugged reliability, the Fergusons would have little hope of overcoming such obstacles.

Having spent about an hour at the site, Hillary, Kirkwood and Miller returned to the *Glacier* for another conference with Dufek. Hillary, in particular, was feeling unusually deflated: 'We are going to require great determination and adaptability to get the base establishment operating efficiently,' he wrote that evening. 'I returned to the *Endeavour* a little overwhelmed at the magnitude of our tasks. Pray God I am capable of meeting them and overcoming them.'[281] Despite his anxiety he decided that he would not give up without a fight. First, he asked Dufek to use the *Glacier* to cut a channel from the ice edge to a point as close to Butter Point as possible. Then, as the huge icebreaker began to slice its way through the sea ice, he, along with Gunn, Miller, Roy Carlyon, one of the expedition's surveyors, and Jim Bates, the diesel mechanic, worked through the night preparing two of the Ferguson tractors for unloading. Using these vehicles along with the dog teams, he would thoroughly test the routes to his preferred base site. Only after all the options had been exhausted would he consider an alternative location for the Ross Sea Party's winter quarters.

Two days later, on the evening of 6 January, a highly satisfied Miller could note in his diary that the process of unloading the equipment and vehicles for the reconnaissance had gone like clockwork: 'Everything has come to hand exactly as planned,' he enthused. 'The 'tween decks of the *Endeavour* is almost empty and all is loaded on seven sledges ready for our getaway at 11.30.'[282] During the previous 36 hours, Hillary, Helm, Mulgrew and Ron Balham, the expedition's meteorologist, had assumed the role of pathfinders, testing the first portion of the route to Butter Point in a half-track Ferguson. Their survey had done nothing to disprove Dufek's assertion that the heavily laden tractors would struggle to cross the sea ice. One moment the party's single tractor was lurching over tall pressure ridges, the next it was floundering through pools of saltwater, which had risen to the surface through open cracks in the ice. 'It was a blazing hot morning and the surface of the bay ice was like a morass or a swamp,' wrote Hillary. 'It was heartbreaking trying to establish a feasible route.'[283] After three hours, and having managed to travel only a mile and a half, the four men had decided to return to the *Endeavour*, determined to try night travel instead, when the lower temperatures should produce an improved surface. Later that evening they set off again, this time with two tractors, and had found the surface much improved – but still difficult, with the innumerable diversions around melt pools and other obstacles practically doubling the distance to be travelled. Nonetheless, they had managed to survey a portion of the route and to mark it with flags to guide their successors.

The full reconnaissance party of three dog teams and four tractors towing seven laden sledges set off at midnight on the 6th. Over the course of the next two days, the party crawled with depressing slowness towards Butter Point, the tractors frequently sinking up to their axles in the pools, sometimes having to be hauled out by their companions and at others shedding their tracks, so that a series of running repairs became necessary. In the worst places, the sledges had to be relayed, one at a time, to prevent their becoming irrecoverably bogged down. Exhausted after four and a half hours spent splashing around in the icy water and slush, and with Butter Point still little more than a dark smear in the distance, the team finally came to a halt in the early hours of 7 January, ready for a meal and a few hours of much needed rest. 'We finally camped on a large slab of dirty ice, relatively free of open water', Bernie Gunn recorded. 'We threw up our dark blue pyramid tent and brewed up an odd meal of soup, sausage and potatoes. Unlike the clean conditions in the fresh cold snow of the previous year, we were covered in grease, dirt and rust and wet to boot. Bates seemed to thrive on it, I supposed having been covered in grease and rust for much of his adult life.'[284]

Bates was perhaps the only member of the party still enjoying himself. Given their experiences so far, his companions were beginning to feel increasingly despondent at their prospects and Gunn even felt that he had begun to detect 'a distinct lack of drive in some quarters.'[285] Fortunately, when they recommenced their survey at 2.00pm the following afternoon, the quality of the surface improved significantly, slushy puddles now giving way to smooth floes interspersed with shallow pressure ridges. But these conditions didn't last for long: as the explorers closed on the projected base site just to the west of Butter Point, their progress came to an abrupt halt. Miller, Gunn and Bates, who had been delayed when their tractor shed a track, arrived on the scene to find their companions looking disconsolately at a 6-foot-wide tide crack which split the sea-ice from the old bay ice, effectively cutting the party off from their objective. Faced with yet another obstacle, tempers began to fray with Gunn, the only member of the 1956 advance reconnaissance party present, becoming an obvious target. 'Mulgrew,' he remembered, 'began making sarcastic noises about people who recommended bases cut off by rivers.'[286]

Eventually the party managed to force a crossing, but the surface rapidly deteriorated into a series of streams, pools and tide cracks and progress slowed to a snail's pace. Hoping that he might be able to identify a more viable route, Hillary now detached Miller from the main party to lead a small contingent onto the Piedmont Glacier to test the feasibility of using the glacier as a highway to the base site. The rest of the reconnaissance party, meanwhile, continued to search for a route that would lead them off the sea ice and up towards the shingle beach. To their consternation they found that the ridges and hummocks became more and more pronounced. Two miles from the base site, Hillary was at last forced to admit defeat. At this juncture, Miller returned with the welcome news that although the ice slopes from the glacier to the base site were steep and the surface of the glacier rough, he believed that it might be possible for the Fergusons to pass that way.

Hillary decided to trial the route using two unladen tractors and it was not long before he discovered that Miller's assessment had been distinctly over-optimistic.

> We soon found that the surface was exceptionally rough as it had been thawing freely under the hot sun. We crawled over the glacier, clambering over icy bumps and grinding through fresh water pools. After half a mile of this I decided we had proved our point – it was possible to cross it but it certainly couldn't be called a good sledging route.[287]

As they made camp on the sea ice that night, the reconnaissance party had little choice but to accept that the Ross Sea Party's plans to establish their winter quarters at Butter Point had ended in abject failure. If the weather remained benign, the tractors might be able to force their way the 18 miles from the ship and to unload the expedition's stores and equipment; but the route was so strewn with obstacles that progress would be tortuously slow. Even worse, if a storm blew up while the tractors were en route, all might be lost if the sea ice broke up beneath them. The site itself was, in many ways, perfect – but only for static operations and observations. As the hub for an extended programme of exploration involving sledging journeys in all directions – and most importantly, up onto the Polar Plateau – it was fundamentally useless. As he climbed into his sleeping bag that night, Hillary knew that he faced a restless night. 'I couldn't get out of my mind,' he wrote, 'the logistic problem of dragging our supplies 18 miles or so from the shore to our base and the last few miles from the bay ice to the hut site over the Piedmont would be frightful.'[288] For all his confident assertion that there would be no repetition of the debacle he had witnessed at Vahsel Bay a year earlier, he now knew that his own expedition had fallen at the very first hurdle.

6

Shackleton Base

Looking around Shackleton Base as the members of the Advance Party devoured their letters from home, Fuchs was under no illusions regarding the appalling conditions his men had endured: '...more severe than anyone should expect to endure, even in the polar regions.'[289] Theirs had been the first expedition to spend a winter in tents at such high latitudes, they had survived temperatures as low as −63°F without effective heating, and they had lost a huge portion of the stores which most expedition leaders would have considered essential to survival. Despite this, they had built the main hut which would serve as the launch pad for the continental crossing and they had even managed to undertake a ground survey of the first part of the route that the Crossing Party would follow. That night, Fuchs wrote that 'it has been a remarkable feat to do so much under the conditions in which they have had to work.'[290] George Lowe, who would represent New Zealand on the crossing, was even more impressed:

> Their cheerfulness and spirit was grand and as they told us of their experiences during the year I was brought up sharply and was really aghast with the conditions that they endured ... They all had frostbite of the nose or face or ears but were able to keep their hands and feet warm. Their clothing is covered with great patches of canvas or odd dress material as they

found the wind proofs too light to stand the strains of building and sleeping in them. Tony Stewart even slept in his foot gear … When we arrived the inside of the hut was very cold but they thought it warm. The year they have spent could easily be the subject of a whole film – but building the hut in the dark and the cold is perhaps the most hair-raising part.[291]

Perhaps Hal Lister, the newly-arrived glaciologist, best summed up the feelings of the rest of the explorers when he wrote that 'Those men really were quite outstanding. Without their courage and dogged purpose, their pioneer team of the Trans-Antarctic Expedition would have collapsed … Those eight men really were heroes.'[292]

At 4.30pm the next day, 13 January, the *Theron*'s replacement, the 1850-ton MV *Magga Dan*, arrived alongside the ice edge. Unloading commenced at 5.30am the following morning and Fuchs, in particular, quickly demonstrated that he was as keen as Hillary to learn from the mistakes that had been made when unloading the *Theron* a year before. Although the temperatures led Jon Stephenson, the Crossing Party's Australian geologist, to marvel at 'the magical crackle of my exhaled breath freezing in the air',[293] the work progressed well, with the crew and expeditionaries ably supported by ten men from the Royal Society's Advance Party at Halley Bay. Having completed their tour of duty, these men were naturally anxious to start their homeward voyage as quickly as possible and now they set to with a will. First, a Canadian-built Muskeg tractor and three Sno-cats were swung out onto the ice, followed by the huge crates containing the stores and equipment of the RAF contingent and finally the Maudheim sledges and all of the remaining deck lumber. 'As usual the first day went rather slowly,' Fuchs noted that evening, 'as people had to work into the new system of dumps, the route and the vehicles, but a reasonably satisfactory start has been made.'[294]

The pace accelerated the following day and a relieved Lowe could report that 'Today we have shifted nearly 100 tons of stuff, which is about 5 times better than our best day last year … the

unloading is much easier and quicker.'[295] Even Goldsmith, who
had been appalled at the chaotic scenes the previous year, felt
compelled to admit that while the process had begun 'in a somewhat uncertain way' it had very soon 'gathered momentum'.[296]

Not everyone was satisfied. Like Goldsmith the year before,
Lister — who had served with Homard on the British North
Greenland Expedition — was becoming increasingly concerned
at what he perceived to be a lack of clear and decisive leadership. Unlike Goldsmith, however, for the time being at least, he
was willing to give Fuchs the benefit of the doubt: 'Perhaps now
there will be one plan of action and not only a broad system of
quiet evolution,' he observed hopefully. 'We all have our preferred
methods and so long as we get on with it and are not vociferous
about it we will be OK.'[297]

Over the next few days, the explorers used the newly arrived
vehicles to drag some 800 drums of vehicle fuel to the base site,
where neat rows of 100 drums each were formed. They also
hauled up the crates in which the vehicles had been transported,
two of them becoming workshops for the RAF and motor-
transport teams. A third crate, stocked with a wireless set, rations
and clothing, would serve as an emergency refuge in the event
of fire destroying the main hut — a risk that had materialised
tragically in November 1948, when two members of the FIDS
team at Hope Bay had died in just such an accident. John Lewis,
Gordon Haslop and Peter Weston replaced the Auster's floats
with skis and Fuchs then used the Muskeg to tow the aeroplane
out onto the sea ice, some 200 yards from the *Magga Dan*.
Attention also turned to the completion of the main hut. 'Shelves
in the kitchen, all the fires, the water tanks, the bath, the wiring,
the porch seemed to go up in no time at all,' wrote a slightly
dazed Goldsmith, 'and everywhere men like gnomes were busy
about their own job, hammering here, sawing there, heaving and
shoving until in a fortnight the hut was practically finished.'[298]

It was inevitable, perhaps, that Goldsmith should find himself
playing the role of detached spectator as the base grew around
him. Of the eight members of the Advance Party, only he and
Tony Stewart would be returning to England with the *Magga*

Dan. Peter Jeffries had accepted a post as meteorologist at Halley
Bay and the remaining five would stay at Shackleton to take
part in or support the trans-continental journey the following
summer. These five could now throw themselves into the hurly-
burly of preparing and planning, and the forming, or re-forming,
of relationships with the eleven men who had arrived on the ship.
But Goldsmith, Stewart and Jeffries found themselves reduced
to the status of supernumeraries. Despite the tensions, fears and
frustrations which had been a part of their everyday experience
for so long, the members of the Advance Party had welded themselves together into an effective team – now the bonds which had
held them together were beginning to dissolve. In such circumstances, it was not very surprising that Goldsmith should begin to
feel nostalgic and inclined to view the new arrivals as interlopers.
'As soon as the ship came in the hut and the base lost all its inti-
macy. All that had so long been ours exclusively suddenly became
transformed and was no longer home; intruders first slowly then
with ever increasing pace took over and moved in.'[299]

For his part, Fuchs was altogether too busy and too tired to
register the mixed emotions of his men. Having worked his team
for fourteen hours a day since their arrival at Halley Bay and
having shifted 75 tons of material every day since they docked at
Shackleton, on Saturday 19 January, he could report that, 'Today
all the unloading was completed and the ship rides high out of
the water.'[300] Work had progressed rapidly, helped, perhaps, by the
fact that poor flying conditions had limited the opportunities
to become distracted from the main task of unloading and base
construction. With its new subsidiary huts and the long lines of
stores and fuel drums, Shackleton Base had been transformed: it
was no longer what Homard jokingly described as a 'Toescrape
on Antarctica',[301] characterised by a giant crate and a skeletal hut,
but a substantial polar station, measuring 800 yards from east
to west and 400 yards from north to south. Now Fuchs could
turn his attention to the next major objective of the expedition:
establishing a forward base, some 300 miles south of Shackleton.
As well as contributing to the expedition's scientific programme
by providing a centre for meteorological and glaciological

observations during the course of the second winter, this station would eventually serve as the first staging post during the crossing.

Over the course of the next few days, Fuchs and other members of the expedition made a series of flights in the Otter, intending to identify a suitable location for 'Depot 300' and to undertake an initial survey of the route the Crossing Party would eventually take to reach the Polar Plateau. Three long-distance flights were made between 20 and 30 January and gradually Fuchs built up a picture of the landscape through which he and his companions would have to feel their way in the early stages of their 2000-mile journey. It was clear from the start that none of the options would be easy.

On the first flight, on 20 January, Haslop, Fuchs, Blaiklock and Lowe flew over a portion of the route which Blaiklock and Goldsmith had sledged a month earlier, before diverting to the south of the Theron Mountains. Their primary objective was to explore in the vicinity of the larger peaks first spotted from the air by Haslop and Blaiklock on 7 February 1956 and since called the Shackleton Range. During their traverse of the Filchner Ice Shelf, Blaiklock and Goldsmith had encountered a field of crevasses, but nothing that had hindered their progress unduly. Now, from the air, Fuchs could see that the area to the south of their sledge tracks, where the Recovery Glacier spilled out onto the ice shelf, was very heavily crevassed and presented a formidable obstacle. Only at the very foot of the mountains could he discern a route which might, just might, be passable to his vehicles.

Climbing to 6200 feet above sea level, but only 1500 feet above the snow surface, Haslop now followed a deep glacial valley into the very heart of the Shackleton Range. On the ground, any party taking the same route would have to wind slowly upward between crevasses and, in those areas where the angle of the surface exposed it to the wind, over large patches of polished blue ice. However, if the vehicles could get this far, Fuchs thought he saw a stretch of easier travelling: 'We observed two crevassed areas which almost met, but between them lay an apparently clear zone. It was impossible to tell from the altitude but it may be that the gap represents an ice-shed with glaciers flowing away to E and W

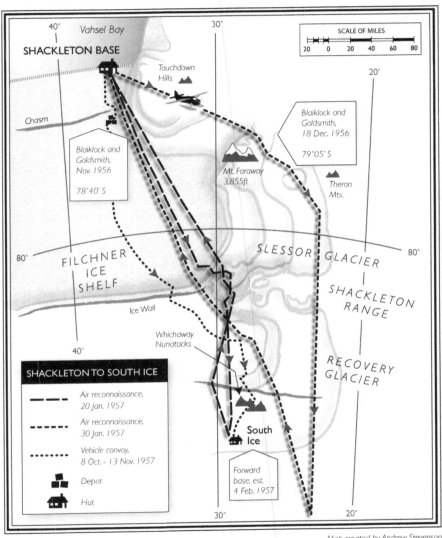

40° Vahsel Bay
SHACKLETON BASE

Touchdown Hills

Chasm

SCALE OF MILES
20 0 20 40 60 80

20°

Blaiklock and
Goldsmith,
18 Dec. 1956

79°05′ S

Blaiklock and
Goldsmith,
Nov. 1956

78°40′ S

Mt. Faraway
3,855ft

Theron
Mts.

80°

FILCHNER
ICE
SHELF

SLESSOR GLACIER

80°

SHACKLETON
RANGE

Ice Wall

40°

Whichaway
Nunatacks

RECOVERY
GLACIER

SHACKLETON TO SOUTH ICE

— — — Air reconnaissance,
20 Jan. 1957

— — — Air reconnaissance,
30 Jan. 1957

········ Vehicle convoy,
8 Oct. - 13 Nov. 1957

▪ Depot

🏠 Hut

South
Ice

Forward
base, est.
4 Feb. 1957

30°

20°

Map created by Andrew Stevenson

... Pushing on past these hills yet another snowfield could be seen undulating into the distance.'[302] Perilous though the approach might be, he believed that this last snowfield might prove an ideal location for his Depot 300. As well as providing what appeared to be a suitable surface for aircraft landings, it was punctuated here and there by pyramids of exposed black rock called, in the language of the Inuit, 'nunataks'. Varying in height from 50 feet to 1000 feet above the snow, these nunataks would provide excellent landmarks for both pilots and sledgers. Although the site was only 270 miles from Shackleton, rather than the hoped-for 300, the presence of the rocks would prove a decisive factor. As Lowe noted on his return to base, 'It's easier to find an isolated rock in a snow sheet than find a tiny dump of stores which will certainly become drifted over and covered before long.'[303]

'Before turning back,' Fuchs wrote, 'we gazed south with the binoculars and imagined we could still see rising and undulating snowfields extending into the distance. Here and there a white gleam seemed to indicate a crevassed area but no further mountains could be seen.'[304] Despite the almost beguiling appeal of that gently rising and falling snowfield, the chaos of the crevasse belt and the tortuous climb into the mountains made Fuchs more intent than ever on exploring all possible alternative routes to the South Pole. 'It's easy to be thrilled by the excitement of crossing and seeing new land for the first time,' Lowe admitted the next day, 'and to have reached 81°S is something – but Bunny is not satisfied that one recce is enough to base a decision on ... This is, of course, very sound. I feel that the way we saw yesterday can be crossed – but if there is an easier way we should try and find it.'[305]

In theory, one alternative route lay to the east of the Therons. Such a wide diversion from the more direct southerly course would entail travelling much farther, but if there were fewer crevasses it might still prove to be quicker. On 22 January, as he flew up a large glacial valley through the mountains, Fuchs was excited to see that, apart from localised areas of disturbance, the surface appeared smooth and unbroken with a gentle gradient rising to the snowfield above. 'Clearly this was a far superior route from a travelling point of view and I felt delighted at the prospect of a safe and relatively easy passage in this direction.'[306] But his satisfaction proved premature. Within a few miles it became apparent that the smooth surface was, in fact, a 'snow dome' and only a short distance farther on a complex tracery of crevasses formed an impassable barrier to any party on the ground. The Therons might offer other, more navigable routes, but the first to be surveyed had proved a dead end.

Any further flights were delayed by poor visibility and by the departure of the *Magga Dan*. On 24 January, the three men returning with the ship occupied their cabins while the members of the land party took possession of their bunks in the hut. For both parties it was a momentous event: for Goldsmith, Stewart and Jeffries it marked the severance of all but their very last ties with the expedition; for the rest, it heralded the beginning of their historic bid to be the first men to cross the frozen continent. The explorers spent the next few days shooting seals to supplement the dogs' food supply and writing letters home. 'I'll be back in just over a year,' Lister wrote to his pregnant wife, Anne. 'I hope then with results of value, with a grand story to tell of all of us safely across. To all at home I wish all the patience and as happy a waiting as possible.'[307] Parties were also thrown, one in the hut and one on board the ship, ostensibly to thank everyone for their efforts and to celebrate the beginning of the expedition proper – but also, no doubt, to provide some release for the emotions inseparable from the parting of the ways.

After a stay of a little over a fortnight, the *Magga Dan* sailed at 0815 on 28 January, taking with her the trio from the Advance Party and the men of the IGY, who had done so much to aid the TAE's preparations. Watched by the sixteen men of the transcontinental party, Captain Petersen backed his ship out of the little dock he had cut with his ship's high raking bows, and then turned to follow the ice edge before plunging into the thickening pack. 'In our case perhaps,' Fuchs later wrote, 'that much misused word "marooned" could have been applied, for, as in the days of the buccaneers, we had been purposely set down on a desolate coast and no ship would return to pick us up again. Our way out was not even along an inhospitable coast, but two thousand miles across a continent.'[308] For his part, Jon Stephenson, at 26 the youngest member of the expedition, felt nothing but exhilaration: 'It simply did not occur to me', he wrote more than fifty years later, 'that our proposed Antarctic crossing might prove to be impossible, dangerous or disastrous.'[309]

Two days later, with his companions settling down to their new duties, Fuchs at last felt able to complete his programme of reconnaissance flights. His objectives were twofold: first, he planned to make a long-range survey linking the routes which he had already traced through the Theron and Shackleton ranges; and, second, he wanted to make a southward dash to a point as far south as 82°15', or about 465 miles from the Pole. In clear skies, Fuchs, Haslop and Blaiklock flew towards the Therons and then pursued the route up the glacial valley towards the snow-dome. This time, by diverting east-south-east and then south-east of the route first flown on the 22nd, Fuchs believed that he had succeeded in discovering a potentially navigable route. 'As I expected, there is an undulating snowfield which falls away to the glacier. Although the area is heavily crevassed it is almost certain that we could pick our way slowly across, and then up steep snow slopes to pass between the rocky range which bounds the southern flank of the glacier as a series of nunataks.'[310] Beyond the rocky outcrops the snow surface continued to rise in what appeared to be a series of enormous steps. Although the slopes were scored with innumerable crevasses, it might just be possible to force the vehicles through the region – but, as Fuchs admitted, 'it was certainly not an attractive proposition.'

As Fuchs considered their discoveries, Haslop turned the Otter onto a direct southerly course and away from the mountains. As far as the eye could see, the snowfield continued to rise towards the Pole in a series of broad slopes, their surfaces pitted with crevasses which the bright sunlight rendered clearly visible from the air, and with one or two ice streams flowing westwards. In terms of a general route survey, this portion of the flight revealed nothing of particular significance: the surface appeared challenging but passable to vehicles and in line with the overall scheme for supply operations, the ground teams would be able to select the best places for the Otter to land. The suitability of the surface for landings became an altogether more pressing concern, however, when without warning the Otter's engine – a 600bhp Pratt & Whitney Wasp – spluttered and stopped. Frowning at his instruments, Haslop immediately switched to the reserve fuel tank but again, after a momentary burst of life, the engine stalled. He switched back – with precisely the same result. After the fifth failure, the Otter's shadow was becoming disconcertingly large as it skimmed and flopped its way across the contours. While Haslop continued to jab at his controls, Blaiklock and Fuchs searched the slopes and crevasses for a place to land. Then, as the Otter glided into its final descent, Haslop suddenly identified the problem: to enable it to undertake the long-range reconnaissance flights, the aeroplane had been fitted with an auxiliary tank. As the primary tank drained, the complicated method of connecting the long-range tank now meant that the fuel pump was sucking air instead of fuel. Haslop shouted to Fuchs to close the main cock from the extra tank and immediately the fuel began to flow back into the engine. The effect was instantaneous: the engine's nine pistons leapt into motion and the aeroplane pulled up and away, its shadow shrinking once again to more reassuring proportions.

Although enough fuel remained for a short continuation of the southward flight, by mutual consent, and no doubt shaken by the unplanned glide, they now turned back towards Shackleton. Having reached a point well to the south of the potential site for Depot 300 that he had observed on 20 January, and suspicious of the viability of the passage just plotted through the Therons, Fuchs decided to fly back via the Shackleton Range, but by a route slightly different from that taken on the first flight. It proved to be a momentous decision, as he recorded in his diary:

> This time, instead of flying over the glacier we had followed through the mountains, we kept to the south of the whole mountain block and observed an easier surface route that way if it should prove possible to turn the most southerly point of the mountain massif. After close examination we believe this to be possible ... As a result of this flight it had become

apparent that the difficulties of travelling more or less due south or going around the head of the glacier are much the same. Indeed, it would seem that once we are off the ice shelf, it is likely that we shall have fewer problems on the southern route together with an apparently smoother run beyond the proposed depot site.[311]

It seemed that, at last, Fuchs had found his route onto the Polar Plateau.

Having completed the surveys and selected a location for the forward depot, the primary task now was to establish the depot before the weather closed in and rendered further flights impossible. At Shackleton everyone became involved in the process of sorting, weighing and packaging the required supplies and equipment to ensure that the Otter's load-bearing capacity was not exceeded and that the delivery of each payload was timed to guarantee that the party establishing the base received the necessary materials in the correct order to facilitate efficient construction.

The party selected to man the depot consisted of Blaiklock, Lister and Stephenson though, to the surprise of some – and to none more than Lister himself – it was he rather than Blaiklock whom Fuchs chose as base leader. 'Because he has had 5 years down here and was leader at Base last year,' Lister wrote, 'I suggested to Bunny that Ken be made leader ... I didn't mind and I could see that to catechise such a man into my way of doing things would be impossible.'[312] Fuchs disagreed and instead told Lister that 'it was my job and I had the experience and ability to run this place effectively.' Inevitably, Fuchs prevailed. Fortunately, and as Fuchs no doubt anticipated, Blaiklock bore no grudge. Indeed, he was the first to acknowledge that Depot 300, with its focus on glaciological research, '... was Hal's project – not only for concept but in planning, hut design, scientific work programme, etc ... Hal actually did not want it and argued strongly with Bunny ... but I think it was the right decision of Bunny to pressure him in accepting it.'[313]

The first flight out to the depot site was made on 4 February, the Otter carrying the three men of the depot party accompanied by Lowe, who would assist with the construction work. 'I've made many take off runs in aircraft,' wrote the cameraman, 'and always find the experience exciting':

> ... At the starting point John Lewis, who is pilot, checked his dials, altered the engine revolutions, set the wing flaps – all with special care and attention as our next landing is to be at 6000 feet – 300 miles inland on unknown surface in unknown wind direction. With the checks done he opened the throttle and the plane came unstuck from its frozen position and moved forward a yard or two – John eased back the throttle, turned to [we] three who were lying on the piles of skis, sleeping bags, food, survey theodolites, shovels, wireless and tents which fill the aircraft; he turned, gave a questioning thumbs up signal to ask if we were set – we gave a thumbs up; he turned, opened the throttle and we lurched forward faster and faster into our take off run. The petrol dump flashed by with all the boys standing on them waving as we became airborne. It was here that I felt the tremendous thrill, a mixture of many feelings as we made our departure on the first move across the continent. The sea smoking with vapour from the air temperature changes was covered with strips of dull lustred new ice. Elsewhere it was blue – as blue as the Mediterranean – and Jon Stephenson and Hal Lister who won't see it again until we reach the other side of the continent looked back with some feeling as we turned our course inland.[314]

Six and a half hours later, Lewis arrived back to report that the party, along with their camping equipment and 30 days' worth of food and fuel, had been landed safely – although, to their disappointment, they had discovered that their planned base site, some 30 miles to the south of the nunataks, was in the midst of a completely barren snowfield, the lie of the land rendering the black pyramids of rock completely invisible. With no landmark whatsoever to break the monotony of the scenery, it would be a desolate spot indeed to spend the next nine months.

Despite this disappointment, Lister and his team worked
swiftly to establish their new home in the snowy waste, their
efforts supported by repeated flights made by Lewis and Haslop,
bringing in hut material, tools, furniture, generators, scientific equipment, food and fuel. 'We are progressing steadily and
I think quickly with the hut,' Stephenson reported to Fuchs
on 9 February. 'I never dreamt we would stand any chance of
keeping up, or almost so, with the aircraft's loads. It looks a solid
little hut. Everyone keeps fine spirits and we live pretty comfortably ... Hoping you will be up again before long yourself
(– come up for a weekend sometime!).'[315] In the privacy of
the snowfield, however, comments made upon the hut's complexity – the instructions for its erection covered six sheets of
foolscap, supported by more than 60 diagrams – were somewhat
less complimentary. Its obvious strength, too, attracted some wry
remarks as the four men struggled with its innumerable compo-
nent parts. 'The hut was designed by a bridge architect and the
strength of the design is fantastic,' wrote Lowe, 'Hal also glumly
said as we fixed the 600 bolts – "We could have built the thing
in Shackleton and free dropped it from the aircraft and I'm sure
nothing would break".'[316]

Unlike the main base hut, that for Depot 300 was based upon
an aluminium frame which bolted together, making its construction far less prone to the frustrations caused by warped timbers. It
would also sit in a pit 5 feet deep, allowing it to be quickly buried
by the drift. This plan had both its advocates and its detractors,
as Lister recounted: 'Ken, leader of last year's advance party, was
very sceptical and because of his experience ... both Jon and
George thought he may be right ... Somehow there is a lack
of appreciation of snow and how it is better to live *in* it than
on it.'[317] In reality, the plan had advantages and disadvantages:
the insulation provided by the drift snow would help to keep
the interior much warmer than a hut exposed to the elements,
but the risks of fire and asphyxiation would be much greater. A
buried hut also necessitates constant work to keep the exits clear
and snow-covered windows would render it as a dark as a tomb.
Tomblike or not, however, the tiny hut would be home to Lister,

Blaiklock and Stephenson and to personalise it, they now gave
it a new name. During the British North Greenland Expedition
of 1952–54, Lister had served at the expedition's central station,
some 250 miles from the main base in Dronning Louise Land.
That three-man station had been known as 'North Ice'. 'It was a
reasonably obvious succession when I went south,' Lister recalled,
'that the tiny advanced station inland from our main base in from
the Weddell Sea, became "South Ice".'[318] Besides, given that the
station was only 270 miles from Shackleton, 'Depot 300' had
become something of a misnomer.

Whatever their reservations regarding the hut's design, construction work progressed so rapidly that the four men at South
Ice found that their demand for materials constantly outstripped
supply – resulting in repeated and increasingly aggravating halts.
'Today we have waited and waited for the aircraft to bring us
hut supplies,' complained Lowe on 11 February. 'The framework stands there stark and bare and we are working constantly
with tarpaulin wind deflectors to keep the hut site free of
drift.'[319] Continual interruptions to radio communications with
Shackleton made the situation worse, often leaving Lister and his
companions wondering why the pilots were failing to take advantage of what appeared to be ideal conditions. On one particularly
frustrating day their transmission to Shackleton read quite simply
'No wind, no cloud, no aircraft'[320] – a galling message for Lewis
and Haslop to receive when, 270 miles from South Ice, they had
been pinned down by a furious blizzard. Contrariwise, sometimes
the pilots would set out from Shackleton in perfect weather, only
to discover that further inland, high winds and clouds of drift
forced them to abort their flight. 'Bad wireless communications
are a curse,' wrote an exasperated Lowe after yet another unex-
plained delay, '– worse than no radio at all.'[321]

With the onset of worsening weather during the middle of
February, and with only six flights having been completed out
of the required eighteen, it began to seem that the establishment of South Ice might have to be abandoned altogether. 'If
this weather continues much longer,' Lowe wrote on the 18th,
'I can't see how they can make enough flights to consolidate

this position for the winter. We have only 25 days supplies left
now.'[322] After a near-suicidal landing on the same afternoon
– an admiring Lowe recorded that Haslop 'could not see the
ground and merely flew in, cut the motor and guessed – and
guessed rightly' – miraculously, the blustery weather receded to
be replaced by much calmer conditions. Flight after flight was
completed and the hut grew so swiftly that, on the 20th, Fuchs
felt able to order Lowe back to Shackleton, believing that the
three permanent residents of South Ice would be able to complete their base without further aid. Two days later, the depot
party abandoned their tents and moved into their new home.
'They are now safe enough in the matter of shelter, food and
fuel for the winter if anything should happen to the aircraft,'
wrote a relieved Fuchs. 'This has been something of an anxiety
to me the whole time since we put them up there, as it is not
yet certain that we can reach them quickly on the ground.'[323]
The discoveries of the following spring would make Fuchs very
grateful indeed that a ground-based rescue operation never
became necessary.

The establishment of South Ice emboldened Lister to make a
special request. Fuchs had already decided that, before the onset
of winter, the men of the forward base should be given an opportunity to return to Shackleton to collect their chattels and to say
goodbye to their companions. Now Lister asked if Fuchs would
also consider acceding to Stephenson's urgent request to undertake a brief survey of the rock formations to the north. Such an
opportunity, he believed, would serve to bolster morale during
the long months of isolation. In particular, he thought that an
opportunity to geologise would 'give Jon a terrific boost for the
winter.'[324] Having been given the go-ahead to explore the newly
named Whichaway Nunataks, however, Stephenson revealed no
signs of fatigue, either mental or physical. Instead, he turned as
giddy as a schoolboy, bombarding Fuchs with suggestions and
questions pertaining to his forthcoming expedition. 'The weather
has faired up here', he enthused, 'and I hope it lasts to allow Ken
and I a decent look at Whichaway. I hope we can get a good 24 or
48 hours there.'[325]

In line with the agreed plan, on 3 March Lewis landed David Stratton at South Ice to support Lister in his ongoing observations and then dropped Blaiklock and Stephenson about a mile from the largest of the rock formations. They had with them a fully loaded 6-foot Nansen sledge, a radio receiver and fuel and rations to last ten days – 'We planned to have no more than 4–6 hours at the Whichaway Nunataks,' Blaiklock recalled, 'but as is normal on any trip, you try to plan for some unplanned eventuality.'[326] If poor weather or other events prevented the aeroplane reaching the two men, then the 30 miles to South Ice should not present too much of a challenge to Blaiklock, a highly competent navigator whom Lister described as 'quicker than anyone I have seen'.[327] Stephenson was altogether less experienced, but Blaiklock entertained no concerns regarding his companion's abilities: 'He was a tough, stocky Aussie who had had ice climbing experience in Switzerland and he learnt very quickly how to cope with the conditions.'[328]

Once they had waved farewell to Lewis, the pair's first task was to erect their pyramid tent. Standard practice among veteran sledgers was to leave the four 7-foot bamboo poles laced to the tent's covers so that it might be unfurled like a giant umbrella – but this process was far from easy in a stiff wind. The tightly woven cotton flapped and snapped like a torn sail but, after a vigorous struggle, they managed to restrain the tent's wayward motions and piled blocks of snow onto its skirts to prevent it blowing away. They took a brief rest to catch their breath and then turned towards the nunataks to embark upon their separate tasks. Blaiklock climbed the nearest with his theodolite to undertake some survey work, while Stephenson began to examine the geology of the rock formations, his excitement at the discovery of 500-million-year-old coral-like fossils helping to make up for the pain caused when he broke a tooth biting into frozen chocolate.

On the morning of the second day, expecting the aeroplane to arrive at any moment, they kept close to their camp. With still no sign of the Otter by the afternoon, however, Stephenson felt able to further explore the nunataks, fossicking about among the loose debris until he discovered some plant fossils similar to those that had been discovered in the Therons. It was during their second night under canvas that the sledgers' plans really began to go awry. When considering Stephenson's proposal, Fuchs had warned the geologist that, so late in the season, the weather might close in at any time. Now his warning became prophecy. On the third day, the fine weather retreated before a strong wind, heavy with drift and so loud that it made normal conversation practically impossible. With visibility reduced to 50 yards and with no chance of the Otter being able to reach them, Blaiklock decided to go onto half rations and to conserve fuel. 'Lying in a tent on that routine is no great problem', he observed, 'although by the seventh day we were getting a bit hungry and had minor frostbite at times on our extremities.'[329] Stephenson, meanwhile, in spite of his frost-nipped cheeks and nose, had lived up to Blaiklock's expectations and was actually enjoying himself: 'I was pleased,' he wrote, 'that my Antarctic adventure had really begun!'[330]

Back at Shackleton, Fuchs was feeling altogether less exuberant. 'I am now becoming slightly concerned about Ken Blaiklock and Jon Stephenson who are still out at the Whichaway Nunataks,' he recorded on 9 March, after poor weather had forced him to abort his third attempt at collecting them.

> As from the evening meal today they have four days rations … manhauling a 6-foot Nansen with tent etc in the low temperatures, (below -40°F) and with the high winds of 15 to 35 knots which have been prevailing at South Ice, will not be a pleasant experience.[331]

He also recognised that, even for a man as experienced as Blaiklock, the thick drift would make navigation so problematic that the two men might pass within 50 yards of their hut and never see it. 'For this reason I am proposing to tell South Ice to put up a recognition signal at a regular time each night. As the Whichaway party can hear our radio, they will know to watch for this light which will give them a bearing above the drift.'

In fact, Blaiklock and Stephenson began their trek not one, but two days later. '[Fuchs] had worked out', Blaiklock recorded,

... (as I did) that at 7–8 miles per day, it would take 4 days man-hauling to South Ice. We did in fact leave on 11th March with 4 days full rations and 2 days very basic emergency food. Very luckily I had taken a compass bearing to the Whichaways from a rise close to South Ice so I knew the course to take back. What did worry me more was finding the hut itself as it was in a shallow dip and the nunataks could not be seen from the hut. My attitude was 'Worry about that when we get very near!'[332]

The trek was gruelling. Wearing moccasins, which were warm but provided very little grip, and with only one pair of crampons between them, the two men floundered across the wind-blown ice, frequently losing their footing so that their bodies were soon covered in bruises. As their distance from the mountains increased, the nature of the surface changed, the polished ice giving way to soft snow. Now, instead of skittering from side to side, the sledge became more difficult to drag forward as its runners clogged with the sticky snow. Every time it ground to a halt, the two tired men would have to jerk it back into motion, straining at their harnesses to do so.

As they struggled on, day after day, with no improvement in the weather and with no chance of the aeroplane relieving them, even the experienced Blaiklock began to find the going tough and, with no sledge-meter to record the distances travelled, he began to doubt that they were travelling as quickly as they should:

I thought on leaving we could achieve the daily distances planned. However I sensed that we were not going as far as we would have liked. The weather was pretty horrid, temperatures down to the high -40s and wind 20 knots-plus. During our walk the only time we were comfortably warm was when we were man-hauling.[333]

Stephenson, too, despite his enthusiasm and his gritty determination found himself suffering from the intense cold and reduced rations:

We woke regularly and rolled over to combat the cold, which nags at different places – hips, feet. Heads are also a problem, muffled in a woollen balaclava, and I felt annoyed about losing the precious warmth of my breath. But breathing into a sleeping bag only forms more ice.[334]

Fuchs had also been getting increasingly uncomfortable about the plight of his men. On the 11th, the day that Blaiklock and Stephenson had finally broken camp, the weather reports from South Ice indicated that it might be possible to land there. Haslop and Fuchs bundled two bags of rations and fuel into the Otter and then took off, praying that the weather might hold off at least long enough for them to drop their bags of supplies to the sledgers.

The weather did not hold off. By the time they reached the point at which the Recovery Glacier descended from the Shackletons to smash into the ice shelf, conditions looked very far from promising. Fuchs:

> We saw the drift pouring down the slope in great streamers which merged into a sheet where they reached the level surface. Flying on over the glacier towards the Whichaway Nunataks the whole surface was a snaking, writhing mass of drift which somehow had a stealthy evil look.[335]

They circled the nunataks but could see no sign of the field party, then, flying in a zigzag pattern to maximise the area covered, they proceeded on to South Ice.

> From above the station was clearly visible, but as we ran in to land the surface disappeared and suddenly everything was blotted out and we were descending through a driving white mist till suddenly the skis touched and we bounded gently over the sastrugi to a standstill.[336]

By this point, conditions on the ground had deteriorated to such a degree that the South Ice hut was completely invisible and only by following the sound of the aeroplane's engine could Lister find the Otter and exchange a few brief words with Fuchs. Then, having handed over a pair of frozen chickens, Fuchs and Haslop took off to make their return flight. Of Blaiklock and Stephenson they saw no trace. 'Everyone is upset that we could not find the two wanderers,' Fuchs wrote that night, 'and we are now faced with the necessity of an all out effort to get food and fuel to them or pick them up.' Though neither party knew it, the Otter had probably passed within 50 feet of the men on the ground, its orange fuselage rendered invisible by the thick drift and the roar of its engine lost in the howling gale.

By 13 March, the sledgers' food and fuel had dwindled almost to nothing. Both men knew that unless they reached South Ice or were either rescued or re-supplied by aeroplane, in temperatures of nearly -50°F and wind speeds in excess of 30 knots, their chances of surviving for more than two or three days were extremely slim. The hard physical labour of hauling their sledge, when coupled with reduced food intake and the need to conserve their precious fuel, also meant that they were beginning to weaken. Exhausted and underfed, their movements became slow and clumsy, with the inevitable result that they both became prey to frostbite. 'Nights in the tent were often painful,' Blaiklock recalled. 'I can remember one night when my frost-bitten toes had thawed out, I was in some pain and put my feet out of my sleeping bag to chill them down.'[337] Stephenson, meanwhile, suffered from welts around his wrists and blistered fingertips after he had fumbled putting on his gloves. Despite these painful distractions, Blaiklock continued to amaze his companion with the accuracy of his navigation, which he based upon the bearing taken prior to leaving South Ice, the wind-direction and the outlines and shadows of the nunataks behind them. At this stage, any failure in navigation could prove fatal as it would not only prolong their journey but also take them off the course along which the aeroplane would search. What had started as little more than a jaunt to the Whichaways had now become a race with death.

The same day, at Shackleton George Lowe wrote 'it was expected that the Whichaway party's food and fuel would finish. If this were so they could only last a day or two without either ... Most terrible conditions.'[338] Fortunately, Blaiklock's early decision to conserve supplies meant that the sledgers had one extra day's leeway. On the 14th, conditions for the two men took a turn for the better when the wind finally died away, allowing the drift to settle: 'The weather began to brighten and enabled us to see some distance ahead,' wrote Stephenson. 'The scene was one of endless, featureless snow – quite beautiful … We hauled on, wonderfully encouraged to see where we were heading.'[339] After a better day, the night proved to be one of the worst they had experienced, the cold took on what Stephenson described as a 'razor-like intensity' and, at -50°F, became so extreme that it froze the moisture in their nostrils and numbed the backs of their throats. The living space inside the tent would normally have been approximately 6 feet wide by 7 feet long and 5 feet 6 inches high, but two days earlier, one of the four tent poles had broken before the wind and now the two men huddled in a much reduced area, one side of the tent sagging in towards them. Mulling over their position, their growing weakness and depleted supplies, they came to a stark resolution. 'We decided', Blaiklock wrote, 'that if there was no plane the next morning, we would finish up the last of the food, abandon the tent and sledge, and walk on, carrying only our sleeping bags.'[340] Without the weight of the sledge, with its tent and equipment, the men might make more rapid progress. Long experience, however, had shown that sledges could also be lifesavers, often acting like a brake if a man travelling on foot fell into an unseen crevasse. With no shelter, no food and no fuel, if prolonged poor weather overtook them or one or other of the men sustained an injury before they reached South Ice, they would die.

They slept fitfully that night, with cold, hunger and the prospect of a do-or-die trek the next day all conspiring to rob them of their much needed rest. The following morning they breakfasted on the last of their supplies, a tin of bacon, a few biscuits and some cocoa. 'The bacon was nauseatingly rich and greasy,' Stephenson remembered, 'and we had just started to drink our cocoa when Ken stiffened.'[341] The wind had fallen away almost completely and now, cutting through the crisp, cold air, they could hear an alien but intensely welcome sound: the whirr of an aeroplane engine. Fuchs, Lewis and Haslop were on board and, having already landed at the sledgers' original campsite and located a note left by Blaiklock on 11 March, they were now flying along his intended course, scanning the landscape for any sign of life, as Fuchs recorded:

> This time, when ten to twelve miles from South Ice, I suddenly saw through binoculars about a mile from us, a tiny black triangle set against the vast white expanse of snow. This could only be their tent and in a moment we were swinging east towards it. It was the tent all right but there was no sign of activity and I had unpleasant visions of them being incapacitated by frostbite or worse … Soon we were bounding over the snow and came to rest about 15 yards from the tent … When we came to rest I lost no time in bounding out of the plane and sticking my head into the tent, where I found them both well and drinking a cup of cocoa which they wanted to finish before coming outside. Not surprising perhaps as the temperature was -35°F.[342]

Despite their seemingly casual response to the arrival of the aeroplane, the reunion was an emotional one, with Stephenson admitting to tears of relief and gratitude.

Everyone knew that the rescue had come not a moment too soon. Having discussed Blaiklock's desperate determination to make a last dash for South Ice, Fuchs considered that their chances of success had been very limited: 'I very much doubt,' he observed that night, 'if they would have reached it as the distance was still 10–12 miles, and they had not done better than six miles a day previously.'[343] 'They were practically out of food,' Lowe noted. 'The primuses had only one fill left. They were in fact found only just in time.'[344] But the last word must surely go to Ken Blaiklock:

> It was only some years later that I realised it was a 'damned close thing' and probably the nearest thing I had experienced in my years down South which might have ended in our death. Still the Gods look favourably on the foolish.[345]

7

Ross Sea Reconnaissance

On board the *Endeavour* the mood was grim. Unpopular though he might be, Harry Kirkwood's oft repeated criticisms of the Butter Point site possessed a resonance which the reconnaissance party's long absence and its interrupted radio transmissions had done nothing to deaden. Claydon and Helm grew more anxious with every passing hour and by the morning of 8 January they had decided that they could wait no longer – they must obtain more accurate information regarding Hillary's situation. To do that they would have to fly to Butter Point, but with the Auster still awaiting the delivery of its replacement wing and the Beaver not yet reassembled, inevitably this meant a further request for American aid. Fortunately, the source of that aid now lay much closer to hand as the previous day the *Endeavour* had moved up McMurdo Sound to anchor off Ross Island, opposite the US base at Hut Point.

According to Vern Gerard, the IGY physicist, Butter Point had originally been chosen as the Ross Sea Party's base site because 'It was thought desirable for us to be some distance from the Americans, who were already established on Ross Island, so that we would not be completely overwhelmed by them.'[346] Now, with the US base spread before them, for the first time the New Zealanders could appreciate the full extent of that risk. The facility had been established during the Antarctic summer of 1955–56 when, as part of Operation Deep Freeze I, four long-range US Navy aircraft had flown the 2200 miles from Christchurch to make a hazardous landing on the bay ice of McMurdo Sound. Initially, two bases had been established: one close to Captain Scott's old headquarters at Hut Point and the other, known as Little America V, at the eastern extremity of the Ross Ice Shelf, some 450 miles around the coast of the Sound. As part of the United States' ambitious IGY programme, tractors from Little America had then pushed into the interior of Marie Byrd Land to establish Byrd Station late in 1956. The base at Hut Point, meanwhile, had served as a launch pad for the airlift of men, vehicles, equipment and building materials to the most important of America's planned IGY bases: the Amundsen–Scott South Pole Station, where construction had commenced in October.

By the standards of any other nation, the Hut Point base was colossal, boasting not one, but two airstrips – one for the enormous four-engined Globemaster transport aircraft, which ferried most of the equipment to the South Pole, and a second for the (relatively) smaller aeroplanes, such as the DC3s, which were used for lighter payloads and for Admiral Dufek's tours of inspection. An entire airport had been constructed on the sea ice, with every fixture, including the control tower, on wheels or tracks to facilitate a hasty retreat in the event of the ice breaking up. The base itself stood on solid rock and in all its essentials, save the bright orange colour of the huts, it resembled the kind of temporary installation that might be found in any number of military outposts across the world. The rattle of tracked vehicles echoed across the Sound and everywhere the pristine white snow had been ploughed into grey, slushy troughs. To anyone familiar only with the tiny scale of the Heroic Era expeditions, this ugly shantytown of huts and fuel dumps, set in one of the most beautiful and dramatic landscapes on the planet, came as a nasty shock. Richard Brooke would later sum up the feelings of many: 'I wasn't very enchanted with … the close proximity of the American base, which is so big and, in my view, so out of keeping with the polar regions, or the magic of the polar regions. It's a pity.'[347]

Despite the Ross Sea Party's concerns about being over-whelmed by the sheer weight of the American presence, at no point during the planning and execution of the expedition had these reservations manifested themselves as a reluctance to take full advantage of the Americans' resources. In response to Claydon's latest request for air-support, as on every other occasion, the United States Navy showed itself willing to render any service requested of it. A helicopter was quickly made available and by 1.30pm on 8 January Claydon, Helm and Commander Ketchum of the *Glacier* were standing on the sea ice below Butter Point, discussing their options with Hillary. Claydon, in particular, argued strongly for the abandonment of Butter Point and proposed instead that the Ross Sea Party should accept the Americans' suggestion of a site at Pram Point, a rocky spur on Ross Island, about 2 miles southeast of their own base. In order to reinforce his case, he reminded Hillary that the imminent break up of the sea ice and the honeycombed and rotten surface of the Piedmont Glacier would make it impossible to operate air-craft from Butter Point – though, in Gunn's opinion, 'John was more concerned with keeping his aircraft operational year round, than in any other consideration.'[348] Having listened to Claydon's arguments and to Ketchum's assurances regarding continued American co-operation, Hillary finally agreed that he and Miller would undertake a survey of the proposed site. In his absence, the dog-sledge teams under Marsh's command would attempt to blaze a trail up the Ferrar Glacier and onto the Polar Plateau while Hatherton tested the feasibility of driving the tractors up the glacier's steep inclines.

That evening, after dining with Dufek at Hut Point, the two New Zealanders clambered into yet another helicopter to make the short flight to Pram Point. After only a brief survey of the site, which Scott had named after his Norwegian dinghy, Hillary felt that a huge weight had been lifted from his shoulders:

As soon as we started walking around my excitement rose. It was a very pleasant spot with magnificent views. To the north of us were the great volcanoes Erebus and Terror; to the south stretched the Ross Ice Shelf and to the east were the lovely mountains of Victoria Land. It had all the advantages of close proximity to the Americans and yet was fresh and untouched. A series of easy terraces were readily accessible off the bay ice and the smooth snow out in front seemed to offer admirable opportunities for our airstrip. There was no doubt that we had no protection from the easterly and southerly winds but I felt that there were other compensations. Bob seemed as impressed as I and we decided on the spot forthwith.[349]

He had good cause to be relieved. After a disappointment which had brought the expedition's entire plan into question, it now seemed that he had located (or had pointed out to him) a near-perfect base site. It provided a reasonably level area approximately 50 feet above sea level and solid rock foundations for the huts and radio masts; a nearby Weddell Seal colony would furnish food for the dogs and a suitable landing strip was located only a quarter of a mile away. Finally, the hub for all Antarctic flights to and from New Zealand lay on the expedition's doorstep, providing excellent communications with the outside world.

So far as Miller and Hillary could see, Pram Point suffered from only two flaws. First, the sledging parties would be forced to travel an additional 30 miles in order to access the Ferrar Glacier and, second, they estimated that it would take more than three hours for a fully laden tractor to cover the 9 miles from the ship to the base site – a far from ideal journey time, but one which would lessen as the edge of the sea ice melted, allowing the *Endeavour* to move progressively closer. Miller thought 'Everyone delighted with site,'[350] but, in reality, some members of the IGY party were far from convinced. From a scientific point of view, Gerard, in particular, believed it to be 'one hell of a place for a geo-magnetic observatory being on the lower slopes of Mt. Erebus, an active volcano and thus the source of strong magnetic anomalies.'[351] But, as the physicist admitted, 'Of course there was no option, so that was where it was put.' Not for the last time, and not unreasonably in the circumstances, scientific needs were placed a very definite second to the exigencies of exploration.

Having reached his decision, Hillary ordered the *Endeavour* to collect Hatherton's tractor party from Butter Point, leaving the dog teams to continue their exploration of the Ferrar Glacier. With the arrival of the Fergusons, the process of unloading the ship and hauling stores and equipment to Pram Point could begin in earnest, the teams being divided into two shifts so that the work could continue around the clock. Despite Hillary's insistence that all members of his team should learn how to drive the tractors before the expedition sailed, the process was far from trouble free: 'Only Bates and I really had the experience to keep farm tractors rolling,' Gunn remembered, 'our other Expedition members ranging from fair drivers to relentless destroyers of anything mechanical.'[352] Breakdowns and accidental damage were commonplace and the actual travel-time from ship to base ranged from 1¾ to 9 hours. Nor was the work free from danger. One moment a vehicle might be splashing its way confidently through a melt pool, the next it could be disappearing altogether – as the Americans discovered on 13 January, when a Weasel carrying cargo to Hut Point broke through the sea ice and plunged to the seabed carrying the unfortunate driver with it. 'It behoves us,' reflected Miller, 'to be very careful. Our own tractors still operating. Fortunately no drivers have lost heart.'[353]

An innovation which proved more immediately effective than the training of the tractor drivers was Hillary's decision to include in his team a dedicated eight-man construction party. This contingent, led by a foreman named Randal Heke, would remain in the Antarctic only for as long as it took to build the base and would return to New Zealand with the onset of winter. In theory, its presence would ensure not only that the construction work was completed expeditiously but also that surveyors and scientists could concentrate on the specialist tasks for which they had been employed; in practice, things turned out somewhat differently. 'Scientific work proper, of course, could not start until the huts were erected,' Gerard later wrote, 'so the scientists served their Antarctic apprenticeship living in tents and helping Randal about 26 hours a day!'[354]

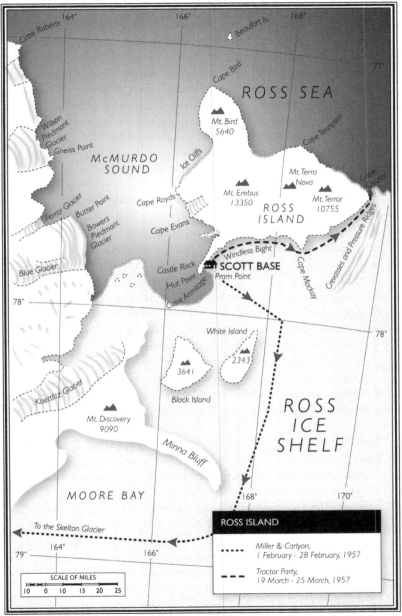

ROSS SEA

McMURDO SOUND

Cape Roberts
164°
166°
168°
Beaufort Is.
77°
Cape Bird
Mt. Bird
5640
Wilson Piedmont Glacier
Gneiss Point
Ice Cliffs
Cape Tennyson
Mt. Terra Nova
Mt. Erebus 13350
ROSS ISLAND
Mt. Terror 10755
Cape Crozier
Ferrar Glacier
Butter Point
Cape Royds
Bowers Piedmont Glacier
Cape Evans
Crevasses and Pressure Ridges
Blue Glacier
Castle Rock
Windless Bight
SCOTT BASE
Pram Point
Cape Mackay
Hut Point
Cape Armitage
78°
78°
White Island
3641
2343
Koettlitz Glacier
Black Island
ROSS ICE SHELF
Mt. Discovery 9090
Minna Bluff
MOORE BAY
168°
170°
To the Skelton Glacier
164°
166°
79°

ROSS ISLAND

········· Miller & Carlyon, 1 February – 28 February, 1957

– – – – Tractor Party, 19 March – 25 March, 1957

SCALE OF MILES
10 0 10 15 20 25

Map created by Andrew Stevenson

As well as the assistance, voluntary or otherwise, rendered by the scientists, the tradesmen benefited enormously from the Ross Sea Committee's early decision to abandon the traditional type of hut used at Vahsel Bay and to instead adopt a design based upon large insulated panels that bolted together. Perhaps the most important feature of this design was the fact that the panels were interchangeable, removing at a stroke much of the complexity of the wooden huts so favoured by FIDS while at the same time allowing the final building design to be adjusted to meet local conditions. Not that the design was without its faults. In construction terms, the chief of these was the weight of the separate panels, which caused the usually stoical Miller to complain of the 'frightfully heavy work unpacking the floor and roof panels. We feel as if we are pulled apart.'[355] But perhaps the greatest disadvantage overall was the cost. A FIDS-type hut large enough to accommodate the entire expedition could be bought for about £9000. In stark contrast, the six huts of the new design required to house the Ross Sea Party cost in excess of £36,000 – a revelation which had drawn a horrified outburst from Hillary during the planning stages of the expedition. 'Fuchs and self appalled at increased cost and luxury of new hut plan,' he had written to Arthur Helm on 29 March 1956. '... We cannot afford and do not require American hotel comfort and sleeping area or elaborate safety precautions. If we cannot produce our module plans at reasonable cost we would be well advised to either purchase a FIDS type hut in England or get one made in New Zealand.'[356] Fortunately for the Ross Sea Party, however, the Committee remained true to its conviction that the expedition should have the best possible equipment, no matter how expensive, and the new style huts were duly ordered. After hearing of the enormous problems encountered by the Advance Party, and despite his initial shock at the cost, even Hillary would later admit to being 'very thankful that we had chosen differently.'[357]

Over the course of the next few days, the work at Pram Point progressed rapidly. The Americans – whom Miller described as 'most generous and big-hearted'[358] – lent yet more aid in the form of a 35-ton bulldozer to level the new site and, by 14 January, a delighted Miller could claim:

> A highlight today. Hut A is completed – apart from the titivating and heating installations. A long day's work sees this whole job done – a great credit to Randal Heke and his seven off-siders ... Thanks to the careful work we did on the levels of the foundations yesterday everything just slid into place. Not a thing was missing or fitted badly.[359]

Ken Blaiklock and his team would have been quite astonished by the New Zealanders' rate of progress.

While the huts rose at Pram Point, Claydon, Wally Tarr and Bill Cranfield, the expedition's luxuriantly moustachioed second pilot, began the process of reassembling the Beaver. First they swung the machine from its broken crate and fitted the undercarriage; then they hosed off the accumulations of salt and installed the elevators, rudder, radio gear and aerials. On the same day that the Ross Sea Party celebrated the erection of its first hut, Tarr declared the Beaver ready for final assembly on the ice. Watched by an anxious Claydon, the derrick mounted on the *Endeavour*'s deck was used to lower the fuselage gingerly over the side. Then, with the help of expeditionaries standing on fuel drums, Tarr reconnected the wings and after many more hours of work in a bitterly cold wind, linking controls and attaching fairings, the aircraft was finally ready for test in the early hours of 15 January. As Claydon reported, 'of course no lighting problems exist during the 24 hours of summer daylight in the Antarctic and the aircraft was test flown in brilliant sunshine at 0200 hours.'[360] The expedition had regained a degree of independence – but the first results of this new-found freedom of action struck yet another blow at the heart of Hillary's plans.

As Tarr made the final touches to the Beaver, Hillary received a disturbing radio signal from George Marsh, still camped among the melt pools and streams of Butter Point. In Marsh's opinion, the badly broken surface of the Ferrar Glacier rendered it quite impassable as a route up on to the Polar Plateau. Richard Brooke fully supported this analysis, later asserting that 'in our view, it simply wasn't on, as either a dog sledge route or as a vehicle route.'[361] An ardent and highly experienced exponent of dog-sledging, no-one could seriously doubt the accuracy of Marsh's assessment, while, in Gunn's opinion, Brooke's 'judgement in the field was impeccable.'[362] Nonetheless, Hillary was so reluctant to accept their gloomy report that he ordered Claydon to fly him to Butter Point so that he could interview the sledgers personally and then make a flight up the glacier to assess its challenges for himself. But the flight left him no room for doubt, as he himself admitted: 'We flew back and forwards across the lower Ferrar Glacier seeking a chink in the defences, but in the end I had to admit defeat. The glacier was a continual succession of melt pools and ice pinnacles, and it was split by great ice trenches which carried turbulent streams down to the sea.'[363] Even more worryingly, as Brooke observed, 'from the air ... it was pretty obvious that one good blow from the west and the whole lot would go out to sea.'[364] Faced with such unassailable evidence a crestfallen Hillary immediately ordered the withdrawal of the dog teams and sent a signal to Kirkwood requesting that the *Endeavour* evacuate them to Pram Point. 'Of course,' Claydon commented, rubbing salt into the wound, 'had the Auster wing not been damaged, reconnaissance flights could have been carried out in this area a week previously and much valuable Expedition time could have been saved.'[365]

Convinced that his most pressing concern must be the iden-tification of an alternative route onto the Polar Plateau, Hillary now focused his attention almost exclusively on survey work. One option, in particular, still needed to be explored. After their reconnaissance of the previous year, Hatherton, Gunn and Smith had firmly recommended the Ferrar Glacier. This route had now been comprehensively explored and rejected. At the time of the 1956 reconnaissance, however, Gunn had also suggested that the Skelton Glacier might be worth considering as an alterna-tive. Although, as Gunn himself recognised, 'My mana was at an all time low because of the Butter Point fiasco,'[366] Hillary knew that he now had little choice but to test Gunn's suggestion. If the

Skelton proved as impassable as the Ferrar then the whole expedition would be in jeopardy.

Early on 18 January Cranfield, with Hillary, Miller, Brooke and Marsh as passengers, flew from the *Endeavour*, across a zone of crevasses around Minna Bluff and then out, over the Ross Ice Shelf. 'Flew direct to Skelton Inlet,' Miller wrote that evening, 'and finding it a beautifully smooth glacier, flew up it to the névé at about 6000–7000 feet and seeing possible route to plateau returned down Skelton picking depot point, then along to point 20 miles off Minna Bluff skirting crevassed areas round White Island and back to ship.'[367] Two hours later they made a second flight, with the same passengers but with Claydon as pilot. This time the Beaver flew straight up the Koettlitz Glacier to its divide with the Skelton, passing beneath the unclimbed 12,200-feet Mount Huggins, and on to the furthest extent of the morning's expedition. Swinging north-west across the compacted surface of the snowfield, the party then followed the Skelton, carefully tracing a route between crevasses, before exiting onto the plateau via a pass just south of the Lashly Mountains. 'We crossed the pass and found it perfectly easy,' wrote an excited Hillary that night, 'and out beyond it the Polar Plateau swept away unbroken to the horizon. What a thrill!'[368] Finally, they turned due east to skim across the heavily crevassed Upper Mulock Glacier before again reaching the coast just to the south of the Skelton Inlet.

Combined, the two flights had taken an exhausting ten hours to complete – but the tiredness of the aerial survey team was more than made up for by its discoveries. 'They came back brimming with enthusiasm,' reported a vindicated Gunn, 'they had discovered the way up to the Icecap!'[369] Inevitably the route identified was far from free of crevasses but, from the air, it appeared to be so eminently navigable that Hillary believed 'We have found the easiest way to the Polar Plateau yet discovered.'[370] To prove this, the next step must be to send the dog teams across the Ross Ice Shelf and then up the glacier to undertake a detailed ground survey in the manner of that so recently aborted on the Ferrar. On the evening of the 19th, Marsh and Brooke left the base, accompanied by Harry Ayres and Peter Mulgrew, who wanted to

test the field radio sets, which had so far proved extremely unreliable. The party set off at a great pace, their plan being to strike
out across the localised pressure ridges and onto the ice shelf,
heading beyond White Island and on towards the Skelton Inlet.
They would then lay a depot and rendezvous with the Beaver
at a point some 70 miles south at Minna Bluff, where Murray
Ellis, the second engineer, would replace Mulgrew before the
attempted ascent of the glacier. 'They were going great guns,'
wrote a delighted Miller, who also clearly enjoyed a spectacular
capsize by Brooke's team. 'It is remarkable,' he marvelled, 'what
the sledges will take.'[371]

At the end of the party's first day on the ice, Hillary was
pleased to hear that they had managed to cover a very respectable 16 miles and hopes were high that the combined experience
of Marsh and Brooke might enable the survey team to make
up for much of the valuable time lost on the earlier reconnaissance trips. These hopes were quickly dashed when, in the early
hours of 22 January, Miller awoke 'to hear Richard's unmistakable "Now Boys" away out across the Barrier. I could not believe
it. Thought I was dreaming. But heard it again and got up and
reached dog lines just as he and Peter Mulgrew drew up.'[372] The
sledgers' story was quickly told. Soon after leaving Pram Point,
Marsh had begun to complain of feeling unwell; he had insisted
on pressing ahead but his discomfort had increased and shortly
after passing White Island, some 32 miles from Scott Base, he had
finally admitted that he could go no further. Anxious for their
companion, but also hoping that this development would not
cause them to abort their journey, Mulgrew had tried to call for
air support – only to discover that, as on so many other occasions,
the temperamental field radio had malfunctioned. This failure left
Brooke with no choice: leaving the prostrated Marsh with Ayres,
he and Mulgrew had harnessed the huskies and made a dash back
to base. In a helter-skelter journey, they covered the distance in
just under seven hours – 'wonderful going' in Miller's opinion.

Weather conditions remained benign and early the following
morning the Beaver took to the air, ready to make the expedition's first landing away from base. The aeroplane carried John

Findlay, the expedition's second doctor, who was relieved to find Marsh somewhat improved and able to make the return flight to Hut Point, before being transferred to the USS *Curtiss* for further observation and treatment. Marsh's illness gave rise to much speculation with diagnoses ranging from severe gripe to appendicitis to toxic tonsillitis, but it was eventually identified as diphtheria which, while it did not necessitate his evacuation to New Zealand, would preclude the genial Shropshireman from undertaking any further field work until the winter. 'Bad luck for Geo', wrote a sympathetic Miller, 'who had planned so much and so well and for us who needed his experience. But all will be well.'[373]

In the face of such repeated blows to their survey programme, to some members of the expedition Miller's upbeat assessment must have seemed a trifle optimistic – and to none more than Hillary. 'I realised that this setback had wasted a great deal of time – time that we could ill spare so late in the season – and decided on a drastic alteration in plans.'[374] Up to this juncture, Hillary had always intended to safeguard the Beaver by only allowing it to land on surfaces which had been inspected by parties on the ground. As well as preventing the invaluable aircraft from sustaining damage when landing on unsuitable surfaces, this practice would also minimise the chance of its crew sustaining injury or becoming marooned at any point too far distant from the ground teams. Now, however, he determined to adopt a more risky strategy. Instead of undertaking the route survey as one sequential journey, it would be split into two journeys, to be undertaken simultaneously. One team would test the first portion of the sledge route to the Skelton Inlet, following a route similar to that pioneered by Scott, Wilson and Shackleton in 1902 during the *Discovery* Expedition. The second team would be flown direct to the inlet, there to begin the all-important reconnaissance of the route over the Skelton Glacier and up on to the Polar Plateau. This would mean landing the Beaver on an untested surface, but Hillary believed he had no choice if he were to entertain any hope of making up for lost time and completing the vital route survey work before the onset of winter.

At midday on 25 January, he, Claydon and Brooke – who would now replace the stricken Marsh as survey leader – flew out in the Beaver to perform the experiment. The spot they chose to attempt their landing was a patch of apparently smooth snow, adjacent to a strip of moraine that stretched out from a great rock bluff some 20 miles up the glacier. Unfortunately, as had been demonstrated so often before, surfaces which appeared to be as level as bowling greens from above frequently proved to be extremely rough on closer examination. As the Beaver glided down into its final descent, Hillary was appalled to observe that sastrugi littered the surface – but it was too late to take evasive action. The next moment, the skis struck the first of the rock-hard crests with a violent concussion and snow and ice particles rattled against the windows as the aeroplane lurched forwards to crash through another ridge. 'It really seemed as if we were for it!' Hillary recalled, but fortunately Claydon's long experience now paid dividends:

> John had seen the danger and reacted immediately. He swept the throttle open and tried to lift the plane off once more. The propeller clawed at the air, there were a couple more resounding crashes, and then, to our immense relief, we floated up to safety. John looked fairly calm, but Richard and I were decidedly white about the gills and agreed it had been a little too close for comfort. I was surprised to see we had any skis left after the treatment they had received, but nothing appeared to be damaged.[375]

Four days later and 2000 miles across the continent, Fuchs would also come worryingly close to a crash-landing hundreds of miles from his base at Shackleton. Within a single week, the TAE came within a hairsbreadth of losing both of its long-range aeroplanes and its two leaders. Whatever his feelings at the time, however, in later life, and at a safe distance, Brooke would be able to make light of the near miss: 'When you're young and enthusiastic, you're prepared to take the risk without too many worries!'[376]

Rather than make a second attempt to land on this wind-sculpted surface, the three men now decided to try an alternative site close to the glacier's mouth, opposite Teall Island. The landing could hardly have been more different from the first attempt with Claydon bringing the Beaver down so gently that, for a moment, it hardly seemed that they had landed. A quick survey convinced Hillary and Claydon that the site, 175 miles from Scott Base, would be ideal for the first depot to be laid by the expedition, and the last that would be picked up by Fuchs's Crossing Party. The position also seemed perfect as the starting point for the detailed survey that Brooke would now lead. All in all, as a much-relieved Hillary quickly recognised, 'This was an important day for the expedition.'[377]

Anxious to make up for lost time, Brooke returned to Scott and having collected Ellis, the first team of dogs and their camping equipment, flew back to the depot site the same evening. Two days later they were joined by Harry Ayres and Murray Douglas, another mountaineer whom Hillary had recruited as assistant dog-handler and tractor driver. 'The Beaver roared in and out all day,' wrote a jealous Gunn, 'carrying dogs and supplies with sledges and tents in the bomb racks ... I seethed some more, having enough conceit to take it for granted that I should be somewhere closer to all this action!'[378] These flights would continue even after the sledgers had left, with Claydon and Cranfield completing nineteen trips to and from the embryo depot, gradually stockpiling the 44-gallon drums of fuel and lubricants that would enable Fuchs to make his last push to the finish line.

The two teams under Brooke began their 8000-foot climb up the Skelton and towards the plateau on 28 January. After the numerous disappointments and setbacks of the last few weeks, the bold decision to 'leapfrog' the sledging party over the Ross Ice Shelf meant that the expedition was now a full three days ahead of schedule and all were keen to maintain the momentum. Initially, despite their enthusiasm, they found the going extremely tough. At first the windswept ice made crampons essential in order to avoid repeated and bruising tumbles – but at least the dogs pulled well. When they left the last of the ice behind them on 3 February, however, a much softer snow surface left the dogs floundering and made it necessary for Ellis to travel ahead on skis to encourage them along. Eventually, with loads of 1000lb each, the struggle became too much and they decided to relay their sledges before recruiting their strength for the attack on the steep stepped portion of the glacier, which they named the Upper Staircase.

By the end of its eighth day on the glacier, and having travelled an average of 12 miles per day, the party had reached the top of the Staircase and they were relieved to see that only comparatively gentle slopes lay before them. They now stood in the midst of spectacular scenery, bounded on all sides by mostly unclimbed mountains – presenting a sore temptation to mountaineers like Brooke, Ayres and Douglas. Their primary focus, however, continued to be the jumble of peaks and nunataks that marked the edge of the plateau and in particular, a wide gap they named the Portal, between Portal Mountain and the Lashly Mountains. This was their gateway onto the plateau itself – the ultimate objective of their reconnaissance.

The following morning, 6 February, they woke to find visibility much reduced; but remembering that the flights of 18 January had revealed no major obstacles in their path and with the Lashly Mountains looming through the gloom, Brooke decided to press on. More immediately troubling than the poor visibility was the plunge in temperatures, from +10°F to -10°F, and the realisation that some of their clothing left much to be desired. Having endured the rigours of an Antarctic winter under canvas, Rainer Goldsmith had proclaimed that the TAE's 'clothes were awful. I mean the clothes that we wore for so-called everyday work were so delicate that as soon as you snagged them on something you got a tear – and if you got a tear it was bloody cold! We spent our lifetimes sewing these wretched things up.'[379] Now Brooke and his companions discovered that, among other faults, their gloves fitted too closely, making them difficult and slow to put on, while their anorak hoods did not fit closely enough, allowing both wind and drift to find an entrance. Brooke, perhaps, suffered the worst. In Greenland in 1952, an accident with a petrol Primus had set fire to his tent; although he had escaped from the inferno, he suffered burns to his face. 'Because of that,' he later observed, 'my nose which, of course, is a bit long anyway, has always been very susceptible to frostbite … I found on several occasions, just the mere act of putting my face close to a cold lump of metal, I could feel my nose click – one of the first signs of frostbite.'[380] This proved a significant disadvantage for a man who, as the party's navigator and surveyor, had to regularly handle a theodolite to complete his observations.

With the sky so overcast and the light so uncertain, however, his observations had become largely pointless and by the close of the day Brooke was forced to admit that he could not pinpoint the party's exact position. Nonetheless, a good firm snow surface had considerably aided their progress, giving the dogs a much better grip than hitherto, and the sledge-meter, a simple bicycle wheel trailing behind the sledge, confirmed that they had travelled a very respectable 18 miles. In fact, though it was difficult for them to appreciate it, that night they camped in the Portal itself, on the very edge of the Polar Plateau.

The next day visibility remained poor, with a fierce wind and sporadic drift, but Brooke persuaded the others to continue. Soon they found themselves ascending a series of slopes and they agreed that, given the distances travelled, they must be climbing up to the lip of the plateau. Now they must decide whether to stand still or push on. According to the somewhat tentative plan sketched out before they left Scott Base, they were free to establish the next depot at whichever point they deemed most appropriate. But they could also assume that, weather permitting, the aeroplane would be searching for them and they might reasonably expect to rendezvous with it at any time. After some discussion, they agreed that their tents would be easier to spot if they remained fairly close to the Portal rather than debouching onto the plateau, which would be so much more difficult to search. Even before they could climb into their tents, however, an aeroplane flew directly overhead, obviously being severely tossed about by the strong wind. It was the Auster, finally restored after its collision with the *Huntingdon* the previous December, and in

it were Cranfield and Hillary. Unfortunately, the radio sets once
again lived up to their dire reputation. While Hillary could hear
Ellis on his walkie-talkie, they found it impossible to establish
two-way communication. Uncertain whether they could be
heard, the ground team sent repeated transmissions to the effect
that the local surface was crevassed and unsuitable for a landing
and, from his vantage point above them, and with his experiences
of 25 January still fresh in his mind, Hillary could only agree.
'After circling around for a while we were getting short of fuel so
wiggled our wings at them and headed for home.'[381]

The following morning, in spite of appalling weather, the
ground party moved on, intent on finding a site more suitable for
landings and comfortable in the knowledge that the pilots would
now know where to look for them. Finally, they breasted the last
of the slopes and found themselves standing on the plateau itself.
As if to reward them for their tenacity, almost immediately the
strong wind died away to little more than a light breeze. They
trudged on across sticky snow for another 12 miles, both dogs
and men feeling thoroughly exhausted and desperate now to be
airlifted back to the comparative luxury of Scott Base. With no
sign of the aeroplanes that evening, Brooke decided not to break
camp the next day but to stay still and await their arrival. On
9 February, as the four men finished the last of their late lunch,
once again they heard the welcome buzz of an aeroplane engine.
They dashed outside to see the Beaver in the distance, obviously
looking for their camp. Eventually, they managed to attract the
pilot's attention by using a helio mirror and at 3.00pm the Beaver
circled the tents and came in to land. 'This was an historic occasion for the NZ Expedition,' wrote John Claydon, 'as it marked
the successful traverse of the Skelton Glacier by the ground party
as well as the establishment of the first depot on the Plateau, also
the suitability of the aircraft operating from these high altitude
landing fields was proved.'[382]

Over the course of the next four days both the landing strip
and the aeroplane were tested to extremes, as the Beaver flew in
and out no fewer than ten times, carrying 1400lb of cargo on
each occasion, the greater portion being made up of fuel and

lubricants for the Crossing Party. In Claydon's view, 'One of the main advantages of Antarctic summer flying, when the weather is fine, [is that] flying can be continuous day and night.'[383] Brooke and his party might have disagreed, however, as they now assumed the roles of ground crew and freight-handlers, expected to leave their tents at any time of day or night to unload the aeroplane's cargo hold and unfasten the various impedimenta strung from the bomb-racks beneath its wings. Much of this work was completed in poor weather, with high winds, plentiful drift and temperatures plunging to as low as -30°F bringing the constant risk of frostbite.

At last, on 13 February, the backbreaking work was completed and the members of the sledging party – minus Ellis who had already flown back to Scott – could finally turn their backs on the windswept Plateau Depot and embark on the first stage of their 290-mile journey to winter quarters. En route, they surveyed the various rock outcrops and nunataks strewn around the head of the Skelton névé. Then, having been instructed by Hillary to rendezvous with the second sledging party at the Skelton Depot no later than the 24th, so that they might all be evacuated by air, Brooke, Douglas and Ayres began their descent of the glacier on 18 February. For much of the way the dogs bounded downhill, seemingly aware that their work for the season was nearly done, while the drivers rode on the leaping sledges – a far cry from their uphill slog a fortnight earlier. When they reached the lower depot on the 20th, however, the only sign of the second reconnaissance party was a solitary, empty tent, pitched close to the huge pile of fuel drums and boxes, the legacy of the repeated flights made by Claydon and Cranfield. With its sides sagging inwards under the pressure of the accumulated drift and various items of hastily discarded equipment lying strewn around, the site had a peculiarly desolate appearance. Of the second reconnaissance party there was no trace.

When asked by Hillary to lead the expedition across the Ross Ice Shelf to the newly established Skelton depot, Miller's response had been enthusiastic. 'Much as I will be disappointed at not seeing the Base completed board by board,' he wrote on 29 January, 'I am thrilled at having this early opportunity of getting down to the real job. I accepted with alacrity – no more heaving and hauling – my back and shoulders feel better already.'[384] And no one could begrudge him a respite from construction work: as well as being a superb quartermaster, in the two weeks since the expedition's adoption of Pram Point as its winter quarters, the 36-year-old ex-commando had become the lynchpin in the establishment of Scott Base, overseeing the laying out of the site, the erection of the first three huts and radio masts and the transportation of most of the stores and equipment from Hut Point.

So omnipresent had he become, indeed, that many now saw Miller as the *de facto* leader of the expedition: the man to whom they turned for both instructions and advice. 'I think he adopted the role of Edward Wilson,' Brooke opined, 'of being the person that people go to if they've got problems.'[385] For his part, Gerard believed that 'Miller hardly slept for a few weeks, because he always seemed to be up and around, doing something whenever one emerged from one's tent in the perpetual daylight.'[386] Hillary, meanwhile, had become a remote figure, spending most nights on board the *Endeavour* and content to abandon to his able lieutenant much of the routine drudgery of establishing the base while he focused instead upon the expedition's broader objectives. Essential though the planning and execution of the route surveys might be, it left some members of the expedition feeling sour about the division of labour. 'At this time,' wrote a disgruntled Gerard, 'most people who could find an excuse like exploring, or flying an aeroplane ... disappeared because hut erection was not compatible with mountain climbing, which, in retrospect, I think a lot of them thought was their *real* job.'[387]

As he considered the task before him, Miller knew that substantial portions of the route from Ross Island to Skelton Inlet had been surveyed twice before: by Scott, Wilson and Shackleton in the spring of 1902 and by George Mulock and Michael Barne, also of the *Discovery* Expedition, a year later. Together, these two surveys meant that this portion of the coastline of Victoria Land was probably the best understood and mapped of any – but data regarding the entrances to the Skelton Inlet remained scant and neither party had gathered any material on the surface conditions between Minna Bluff and the inlet or on the glacier itself. Besides, the information they had collated would now be half a century out-of-date and surface conditions considered suitable for a man-hauled sledge might be anything but for the 3370lb Fergusons. The job of Miller's team, therefore, was to establish a viable vehicle route across the ice shelf to the newly established depot at the foot of the Skelton Glacier. If they succeeded in reaching the depot, they would then undertake further field surveys in the immediate area prior to being picked up by aeroplane.

With Marsh's team of eleven huskies, Miller and Roy Carlyon left Scott Base at 11.30 on the evening of 1 February, carrying enough rations for 21 days. 'Lord how I envy them', recorded Hillary, 'but I seem destined to become a base camp hero. There are so many decisions to make and I feel sure that if I go off old Harry Kirkwood will panic and head for NZ with our construction party.'[388] Neither Miller nor Carlyon had handled a dog team before and they shouted themselves hoarse in the early stages of the journey – but, overall, the team pulled extremely well, despite the significant distraction caused by its one bitch, Tutluk, coming into season. On 4 February, they struck a field of crevasses, caused by the collision of the ice sheet with White Island, but these were easily circumnavigated by diverting east for half a mile before resuming their southerly course. The following day a 30-knot wind and thick drift forced them to lie-up – an event cursed by most sledgers but welcomed by the overworked Miller, who thought it 'The most restful day in two months'[389] – and even this delay was made up for on the 6th, when a clear run of 20 miles allowed them to make camp 17 miles to the east of Minna Bluff, at latitude 78° 37'S.

'All day new country has been opening up and McMurdo Sound disappearing,' Miller recorded on the 8th. 'Erebus now just visible, Black Island gone and White going. Away ahead 100 miles distant is our goal, the Worcester Range ... Each day will bring an unfolding panorama.'[390] The entire south side of Minna Bluff also became fully visible, with its gigantic snow-

slope – the accumulation of centuries of drift – trailing behind
like the tail of a petrified comet. Despite a series of nights disturbed by the howling and fighting of the sex-crazed dogs, by the
evening of 11 February, the party had only an estimated 27 miles
to travel and Miller calculated that they had crossed five merid-
ians of longitude in four days – a wonderful rate of progress for
any sledge team. The Bluff had dropped into the distance behind
them, while to their front, Teall Island reared up at the entrance to
the inlet, forming an easily identifiable landmark.

'Roy wished me many happy returns first thing this morning,'
wrote a delighted Miller on 12 February, 'reminding me it was
my birthday ... Day began gloriously in lovely sunshine. Temp
about 0°F mid-afternoon, wind was springing up from west and
sky clouding in [east]. We had been approaching on our starboard
beam the northern cape of Skelton Inlet. Immediately we came
abreast of this the full force of westerly hit. We struggled through
last six miles in whirling drift and camped after five marches totalling 17.3 miles at 5.30.'[391] The two men now found themselves in
a mixed zone of crevasses and sastrugi, forged by a combination
of the fierce winds being funnelled down from the Polar Plateau
and the impact of the glacier against the Ross Ice Shelf. Surface
conditions were the worst that they had encountered since leaving Pram Point, but even here they managed to navigate a route
which the heavily laden tractors should be able to follow and
their only real disappointment was their inability to spot the piled
fuel drums and boxes of the Skelton Depot. 'We had topped a rise
and looked down into the basin of the Skelton,' Miller recorded
that night after an epic struggle with their wind-blown tent, 'but
could see no sign of depot. We should be able to see it from here
but not in this blizzard – we must be within 9–12 miles of it. We
are here in this camp until weather improves. No use moving
until we can see.'[392]

The blizzard blew itself out during the morning and by midday
Miller and Carlyon were underway. Here, at the confluence of
the glacier and the shelf, the ice sheet lay in great folds at intervals of about a mile. As they crested each slope the two explorers
pulled out their binoculars to sweep the landscape, fearful only

that the depot might have disappeared under a shroud of drift snow. They need not have worried: at 3.15 that afternoon they spotted it, a mile away on their port bow and almost exactly nine miles from their last camp. In just twelve days, they had covered 175 miles, achieving an impressive daily average of 14.6 miles. 'So here we stay,' wrote Miller that night, 'until the plane comes to take me back to Base if that plan still holds or someone comes down from up the glacier.'[393]

The 'someone' turned out to be not Brooke's survey team but a three-man geological party led by Gunn, which had been air-lifted to the foot of the Skelton shortly after the departure of Miller and Carlyon from Scott. Gunn's team arrived at 1.00am on 17 February, after Miller and Carlyon had spent a very frustrating few days confined to their tent by a relentless blizzard. Miller wrote:

This morning when wind was lashing madly, dogs awoke me with excited yells. Not three minutes later a voice yells 'Anybody home' and [I] replied 'Come on in Bernie,' so until nearly 3 a.m. we drank cocoa and swapped experiences.[394]

Although Gunn expressed his doubt that 'any group had ever before set forth so casually and with so little planning',[395] and despite the fact that the absence of any available dogs had forced them to man-haul, the geological party had achieved a great deal more than might have been expected. In the manner of Scott and Shackleton, they had dragged their heavily loaded sledges a full 60 miles – an experience which Gunn thought 'can only be compared to a stretch at the oar in the galleys'[396] – and, from a geologist's point of view, made the exciting discovery of the telltale folds, quartz lenses and shining micas of greywacke on Teall Island, where none was thought to exist. Of much greater significance to those of a non-scientific bent was the fact that they had made the very first ascent of the 9090 feet Mount Harmsworth, the highest mountain on mainland Antarctica climbed to date. Together, the ascent and descent had taken a marathon 29 hours to complete, 'no great feat when you are under thirty years of age,' opined Gunn modestly, 'but it leaves one aweary.'[397]

The day after the geologists' arrival the blizzard continued uninterrupted, trapping all five men in their tents, the parties separated by a vortex of whirling, hissing drift, which left exposed skin raw and threatened the unwary with complete disorientation. This time, Miller found the experience altogether less restful than he had done on his journey across the ice shelf. Full of energy and anxious to complete the local survey work, he lay confined in his sleeping bag for long hours, listening to the roar of the wind and watching as the deepening drift gradually caused the tent's walls to bulge inwards. He and Carlyon, who had now been trapped for days, even began to worry about the risk of bedsores and, outside, the huskies curled themselves into tight balls, covering their noses with their tails and gradually taking on the appearance of just so many hummocks in the snowy landscape. The only interruption came in the early evening when, in a sudden break in the weather, the Auster appeared, piloted by Cranfield and carrying Peter Mulgrew, who had been working on the wireless at the Plateau Depot. Arnold Heine, a member of Gunn's party, was expected to return to New Zealand with the *Endeavour* on 22 February, so in a flurry of activity he packed his gear, shook the hands of the men remaining on the Skelton and scrambled into the cramped cabin of the tiny aeroplane. In a matter of minutes, he was gone.

On 19 February, a lull in the weather encouraged Miller and Carlyon to embark upon a survey around the bluff on the northwest side of the glacier while Gunn and Guyon Warren waited to be air-lifted back to Scott Base. The first part of their journey they completed in the face of chill winds and stinging drift, but as soon as they rounded the bluff the wind died away allowing them to relax in their tent with the sun streaming in through the open flap. 'The psychological effect of being a few hundred feet up is amazing,' wrote Miller, 'after weeks of Barrier travel.'[398] The following day, the two men left the dogs on their spans outside their tent and undertook a 1000-foot climb up the bluff, scrambling alternately over slippery, wind-polished ice and coarse granite to complete a round of observations of all the visible features.

Then, for the next two days, they found themselves once again tent-bound, their world circumscribed by an impenetrable wall of fog-like drift. During the evening of 21 February, with the tent flapping around his ears, a frustrated Miller described the slow passage of time:

> Sleep most of day as did not sleep too well last night. Played Roy at smashing Nazi navy – he won by a pocket battleship – anything to kill time. Dogs appear happy enough although very exposed to wind here with little drift. Read a little – early night wind crashing about us. Tiring of this lying up. Either activity or back to base – but there is nothing wrong with us that a bath, a change of clothes and a warm bed wouldn't put right. Pemmican again tonight after living out of tins for a week.[399]

With the exception of the tinned food, which would have been considered a rare and unnecessarily heavy luxury on any Heroic Era expedition, Miller might have been describing the conditions encountered during any sledging expedition of the previous 50 years.

On 23 February, with their rations dwindling, the two sledgers decided to take advantage of a lull in the blizzard to make a dash for the depot. 'Dogs off down slope and through plugged crevasses at a great rate. Visibility decreasing with onset [of] light snow as we proceed ... Roy and I running alongside – frightfully hot and perspiring for temp is at +20°F.'[400] Aided by the downward gradient and with the dogs full of energy after their enforced rest, the party made swift progress, covering the 10.8 miles to the Skelton Depot in just two hours. As they approached the depot at breakneck speed, Miller was surprised to see two tents where he had expected just one: 'Must be [the] boys from up Glacier ... Sure enough Richard comes out to meet us. Harry and Murray D. make the most wonderful cup of tea I have ever had. Three cups straight off.'[401] During their absence, and before the arrival of Brooke's team, Gunn and Warren had been evacuated by the Beaver, leaving in their hurry to vacate the campsite the disorder that had greeted Brooke and his companions. 'Bernie G. and Guy W. apparently hied off [in]

the plane three days ago,' noted the fastidious Miller, 'leaving
their tent up and quite a mess around.'[402]

Now the five sledgers remaining at the Skelton Depot must
await their own rescue – but again the weather closed in, with
40-knot winds blowing great masses of drift snow down the glacier. Miller, Brooke and the others attempted to pass their time
usefully by undertaking local surveys, but conditions made their
task almost impossible. At times, visibility was reduced to less than
100 feet at ground level and to absolute zero overhead, making
any attempt at landing an aircraft little short of suicidal. With
no immediate prospect of a rescue flight and with the certain
knowledge that conditions would deteriorate still further as the
season advanced, the sledgers soon felt compelled to consider the
option of making their own way home across the ice shelf – an
unpleasant proposition as the temperatures plummeted and the
wind continued to hurl the drift about in opaque clouds. '[With]
this continued bad weather it is madness to delay here until
10th March as Ed's instruction,' wrote Miller, referring to a note
left at the depot when Gunn and Warren had been collected.
'There has not been an hour in last seven days when a plane
could have come in and with sun now setting at midnight, temps
will drop and we must allow at least 3 weeks for the journey. One
does not want to be sledging here in April!!!!'[403]

On 27 February the hopes of the sledgers soared when
during a momentary lull in the blizzard they saw an aeroplane
passing high overhead and some distance to the north. This at
least proved that flying continued to be possible, though, high
above, Claydon could see nothing but a swirling mass of cloud
obscuring the depot. The problem, as always, was that, in the
absence of effective radio communications, the men at the
Skelton Depot and those at Scott Base remained in complete
ignorance regarding the weather conditions being experienced
by the other party – a situation nearly as worrying for the
men at Scott as for those at the depot. 'Hillary by this time
was also becoming rather anxious,'[404] recorded Claydon and,
when the weather at Scott Base cleared again around midnight
on the 28th, he decided to seize what might well be the last

opportunity to recover the sledging party before the onset of winter brought an end to flying.

'At 3 a.m. on 28 February,' wrote Miller in the official account, 'out of the roar of the same incessant wind came another roar, the Beaver. It circled once and landed, with Claydon, the pilot, as eager to get away out of that place as anyone else.'[405] Claydon's anxiety was entirely justified: to transport all five men, their dog teams and the majority of their equipment, three flights were necessary and each time the Beaver settled on the glacier, it rocked so violently before the onslaught of the wind that an overturn seemed almost unavoidable. First, Ayres and his eight dogs were bundled on board; then, at 8.20am, the aeroplane reappeared with Cranfield at the controls. In a quick turnaround, Miller, nine dogs and an assortment of supplies were crammed in before the Beaver again whirled away in a cloud of drift. Desperate to complete the airlift before the weather closed in again, Cranfield took a short cut between Mounts Discovery and Morning, cutting down to just one hour a journey that had taken Miller and Carlyon twelve days to accomplish. The time saved meant that Claydon had just enough time to make one last flight to pick up Brooke, Douglas, Carlyon and the eleven remaining dogs, though they were forced to leave behind them a tent full of equipment, which would have to be recovered at a later date.

Hillary's relief was enormous. Despite all its detailed preparations, the early days of his expedition had ended in almost complete disarray, with both his intended base site at Butter Point and his route onto the Polar Plateau via the Ferrar Glacier abandoned. But now, as he was quick to recognise,

> We had an established route all the way from Scott Base to the Polar Plateau – and a particularly good route, at that. Along this route we had two well stocked depots – the Skelton Depot which was 180 miles [*sic*] from Scott Base, and the Plateau Depot which was 290 miles away. These would serve as an effective springboard for our operations after the winter.[406]

Against all the odds, it seemed that the Ross Sea Party might just have snatched victory from the jaws of defeat.

8

The Basement Flat

Life at Shackleton had been far from dull during the establishment of South Ice. Those not involved in loading and servicing
the Otter for its supply flights to the forward depot spent most
of their time adding the final touches to the main hut and on
preparing themselves, the dogs and the vehicles for the onset of
winter. Throughout much of February, high winds and flying
snow meant not only that the pilots found themselves repeatedly grounded but also that the building and anything left outside
became buried ever more deeply in drifts which could change
the whole landscape in a matter of hours. 'Our steps to the surface from the west door were completely filled,' Fuchs wrote on
11 February after a severe blizzard from the northeast, 'and our
only exit was through the small meteorologists' porch at the east
end. Even that was becoming difficult and we had some difficulty in disposing of the "gash" and waste water.'[407] The same day
Fuchs celebrated his 49th birthday but the conditions allowed
no break from the intense physical activity and he and Stratton
spent the day laboriously digging a long, sloping trench to the
hut's door. By roofing the trench with boards they created an
entrance tunnel that could be accessed through a hatch set far
enough from the lee of the hut to remain largely clear of drift. Or
so they hoped. In fact, within a few days of completing the tunnel
a strong easterly wind brought such dense clouds of drift that the

following morning the trapdoor had disappeared beneath 3 feet of snow.

Despite the weather conditions, on 18 February Fuchs recorded that he had been able to conduct 'a loud and clear conversation with Ed Hillary for half an hour or more'.[408] During the conversation Hillary studiously avoided making any reference to his rapidly evolving plans for extended tractor journeys and instead focused on the successful Skelton Glacier reconnaissance, led by Miller and Brooke. The two leaders also discussed the positioning of the final depots to be picked up by Fuchs's Crossing Party and agreed that, subject to atmospheric conditions and the vagaries of the radio equipment, they would attempt to keep a weekly radio schedule in order to keep each other fully informed as to their respective progress. 'Our reception was so good,' observed a delighted Fuchs, 'that we were able to make a recording; let us hope that this contact will remain so good in the future.'[409] It would prove a vain hope.

Perhaps spurred on by the news of the Ross Sea Party's successful reconnaissance, Fuchs now called a meeting of the entire expedition to outline his own plans for a trial journey using one Sno-cat and two Weasels. He would lead the expedition, accompanied by Stratton, David Pratt and Geoff Pratt, the expedition's geophysicist. Lenton, meanwhile, would take charge at the base. The journey would serve four purposes: to reconnoitre the ground route; to carry out the seismic and gravity traverses for the first 150 miles, thereby removing the need to complete this work on the main journey in the spring; to establish a small fuel depot; and to test the vehicles and give their drivers some much needed experience in their handling. 'If the project comes off,' Fuchs wrote in his diary on 22 February, 'it will be a somewhat unpleasant journey because the weather is deteriorating daily. On the other hand that will not be a bad thing so far as gaining experience with the vehicles is concerned.[410]

Although Fuchs routinely called the members of the expedition together to discuss his plans, among the explorers opinion was divided as to whether their views were really being sought or whether they were simply being told the details of what had already been decided. The new medical officer, Allan Rogers, who admired Fuchs's 'enormous experience and remarkable personality', would later assert that 'all important decisions (except in utmost emergency) were made after full discussion amongst the whole party and were joint decisions.'[411] But Blaiklock, who knew Fuchs better than anyone, thought differently. In his opinion, Fuchs's attempts to obtain consensus were little more than token efforts:

> He was, I can see now, I won't say dictatorial, that's too strong a word, but if there was a decision to be made, shall we say, he would listen to people's comments – but he didn't really discuss it in great detail. He decided what he thought was best and that was it. He was a little authoritarian maybe.[412]

Others, like Lister and Lowe, thought Fuchs both unnecessarily secretive and sometimes indecisive. What was beyond doubt, was that few in the expedition felt entirely satisfied with the means by which key decisions were made or communicated and this seed of dissatisfaction would only grow as the pressures upon the expedition increased.

So far as Fuchs's latest plan was concerned, the biggest obstacle to its fulfilment was a shortage of manpower. As well as the constant physical labour required to keep the entrances clear, the explorers must dig tunnels to house the dogs, hunt seals to supplement the supplies of dog food, saw the frozen carcasses into manageable chunks and build the vehicle workshop, which was still little more than a half-buried kit of parts. Understandably, they were also anxious to benefit from what little daylight remained to them before the long Antarctic night descended like a photographer's hood. This meant digging down to the hut's windows and covering the vertical shafts with translucent hatches, which, Fuchs noted, 'keep out the drift and allow light to filter down into our "basement flat"!'[413] Clearing these hatches became the latest in the long list of essential maintenance jobs, all of which must take precedence over the initial ground reconnaissance.

Erecting the vehicle workshop proved to be particularly onerous and time-consuming. Its design duplicated that of the main
hut, albeit on a much smaller scale, and Fuchs and his companions quickly came to experience first-hand the difficulties
encountered by the Advance Party – in particular the need to
handle a complicated set of timbers and heavy iron bolts with
the wind constantly nipping at fingers and faces. 'A great deal of
our effort is expended on searching for vital timbers in the 3 feet
of snow which covers the site,' [414] grumbled Lowe but at least the
construction party benefited from the expertise of Lenton, who
had already been through the process once before. And unlike
the Advance Party, when the work became too uncomfortable
they could retreat into the warmth of the hut instead of into a
dank, cold vehicle crate or half-buried tents. Nonetheless, progress remained painfully slow and no one felt very surprised
when, towards the end of March, Fuchs announced his decision
to cancel his intended reconnaissance owing to the lateness of the
season and the need to prioritise other activities.

Despite such frustrations, overall the men had begun to settle
down well into their day-to-day existence. They maintained a
strict 24-hour routine, emphasised by the diesel generators which
thundered all day from breakfast to lights out, and everyone sat
down to their meals at set times: breakfast between 8 and 9.00am;
morning coffee from 11–11.15am; lunch at 1.00pm; afternoon tea
from 4–4.30pm; and dinner at 7.00pm. According to Rogers,

> Usually everybody worked all day until dinner and many
> relaxed over books or other occupations after dinner, but there
> were always a few working right up to lights out at about
> 11.30 p.m., at which time five or six people often had a hot
> drink and a quiet chat in the kitchen. [415]

Remarking on the atmosphere, Rogers went on to state that
'Morale was consistently high and there were none of the quarrels
that have so commonly occurred in small groups of men isolated
for long periods in difficult conditions.' [416] The doctor ascribed
this general air of contentment to the fact that his companions

'were all volunteers and specialists with a specific task they wanted to do'[417] and now, with the base fully established, everyone could begin to focus on his particular area of expertise. Geoff Pratt started to prepare his seismic sounding apparatus which, in the first instance, would enable the expedition to determine the thickness of the Filchner Ice Shelf. In Lister's absence, he also took on responsibility for testing the ice-core drills, which would contibute to the glaciological analysis of both ice temperatures and ice-crystals. Lowe continued the process of recording the expedition for posterity while Homard and David Pratt spent long hours trying to coax the Advance Party's derelict second Weasel back to life. Stratton, acting as quartermaster, unpacked boxes and stored their contents in the attic and La Grange, the only meteorologist left at Shackleton, maintained his programme of three-hourly observations. 'Everyone indeed is very busy,' Fuchs observed, 'and it is difficult to find anyone at all for casual labour purposes.'[418]

The industry of some of the explorers may have been motivated partly by their anxiety to avoid the eye of the new doctor who, according to Homard, 'was with us not so much to ensure that we kept fit, as to find out how fit we were keeping.'[419] A 38-year-old academic from the University of Bristol, Rogers had devised an ambitious programme of physiological experiments to be conducted during the winter and throughout the transcontinental journey. Unfortunately, this programme relied very heavily not only upon an array of delicate and temperamental instruments, which Rogers spent hours calibrating and adjusting, but also upon the co-operation, willing or otherwise, of his companions – some of whom approached the role of 'guinea pig' with less enthusiasm than Rogers might have liked. Even Fuchs observed privately that 'we'll probably be pathological cases by the end of it.'[420]

One particularly unpopular experiment involved the use of Rogers's Integrating Motor Pneumotachographs, a form of apparatus designed to measure the energy expenditure of men at work and at rest. From the point at which Rogers finally persuaded his instruments to function, those who had volunteered, been bribed or press-ganged into taking part might have been seen around the base undertaking their daily chores, reading, writing and even sleeping while wearing a rubber mask over nose and mouth and with a small knapsack-like pack strapped to their backs. Perhaps spurred on by his own scientific curiosity, Geoff Pratt went further than most and actually volunteered to wear the equipment for an entire week, removing it only to eat and drink. He quickly learned to regret his decision as the experience proved acutely uncomfortable: 'Having continuously to breathe through the mouth leads to unpleasant dryness,' he complained, 'and outside in the cold the front teeth become "edgy". You never, for a single moment, escape from a suffocating feeling and a very conscious effort in breathing.'[421] The experiment turned out to be only marginally less miserable for Rogers, as he needed to maintain a constant check on the equipment and to regularly change the recording cylinders. But, as Fuchs recognised, 'whereas Allan has a satisfactory piece of work completed, Geoff can only look back on a period of irritation and waste of time. I have told both of them not to discuss the subject until some time has elapsed and the "full fresh horror" is over!'[422]

So far as the more routine elements of hut life were concerned, Rogers acknowledged that there were 'no special privileges, conditions were the same for everyone and everyone in turn shared the less pleasant chores.'[423] On a day-to-day basis, many of the more mundane tasks fell to the 'gashman' – a role described by Lowe as the 'cook's chief washer-upper and, in addition, sweeper and cleaner as well as feeder of dogs'[424] – but, like all the other unskilled and laborious jobs, this was shared equally. Modern innovations like an electric washing machine made some tasks much easier than they would once have been ('blessings on the Hoover electric washer which does sheets and all', wrote a grateful Fuchs)[425] but others, like feeding the dogs, had changed very little since the Heroic Era. Another job that could only be viewed as a necessary evil was the changing of the 40-gallon latrine barrel: 'quite a business getting it down the tunnel, up the steps, and onto the surface,' Fuchs recorded. 'This task arises about once in three weeks and the filled barrel is carried by sledge far to the east beyond our emergency hut. As the barrels are deposited there they form useful visibility markers for the meteorological observations.'[426]

Cooking was shared by all on a strictly enforced rota with only one man exempted – 'not because he was unwilling to do his share,' Rogers confided, 'but because the others were unwilling to share the results.'[427] Some, like Weston and Lenton, revelled in their skills in the kitchen and constantly vied to generate the most imaginative and appetising meals. Others approached their turn with something akin to dread. 'It's the most hectic and frightening task as meals come round so quickly,'[428] observed Lowe, while Stratton admitted that, at the end of four days of cook duty, 'the feeling of escape and relief has to be experienced to be believed.'[429] Afternoon tea, served on Sundays, became a particular challenge for the novices as they strove to meet a seem-ingly insatiable demand for fancy confectionary – and any chef who failed to live up to expectations could expect a barrage of caustic observations on his shortcomings. Inevitably, failures and mishaps in the kitchen also provided much needed comic relief, as when the accident-prone Gordon Haslop left an unpierced tin of tomatoes in the oven to warm, with explosive results. The neglected tin, Fuchs noted, 'suddenly blew up and showered hot tomatoes over the entire scene. In doing so it blew two oven doors wide open, chipped the metal catch off one and also nearly broke the hinges away!'[430]

The menu itself consisted mainly of tinned food, such as meat, vegetables and butter, and dehydrated foods including egg, milk and potatoes, although these could be supplemented with seal and penguin meat, penguin eggs and the occasional crop of mustard and cress grown on trays in the loft. Fresh bread and cakes were baked several times a week – the task made immeasurably easier now that the expedition no longer relied solely upon Homard's ingenious home-made bread oven – and each man also swallowed a daily capsule containing the prescribed dietary supplements. Overall, the food was both reasonably nutritious and plentiful, so plentiful indeed that some of the explorers later discovered that they had put on weight during their Antarctic winter.

On 25 March, Haslop and Taffy Williams made the last flight of the season to South Ice. The trip gave Williams an opportunity to install the large RAF receiver that had been sent up two days earlier, but a last-minute search for useful equipment left at Shackleton also resulted in a final delivery which included 1900lb of paraffin, three mapping nibs, a bottle of ink, a bottle of photographic developer and a 12-inch wooden ruler. After a visit lasting a mere 30 minutes, the Otter once again roared down the temporary runway, throwing up clouds of ice particles, before climbing into a clear, windless sky. Having watched the aeroplane dwindle to nothing, Lister, Blaiklock and Stephenson turned back to their hut, now so deeply buried that only its aluminium roof panels and chimneys showed above the surface. For the next seven months this tiny building, measuring just 16 feet by 16 feet, would be the centre of their universe. Very soon the TAE's aircraft would be earthbound for the winter and, with no dogs or tractors of their own, and no proven surface route in any direction, in a winter emergency theirs would be a very sorry plight indeed.

With the men of South Ice left to their lonely vigil, at Shackleton the last days of March were spent in completing essential outdoor activities before the coming of winter. The dogs, in particular, urgently needed to be properly housed. As the temperatures dropped, the animals curled themselves into tight balls, shielding their noses with their tails and allowing themselves to be buried by the drift. But their body heat melted the snow beneath them and when the slush froze again, the wretched animals became welded to the surface. Their new home was constructed by digging a trench 140 feet long, 8 feet deep and 4 feet wide and by using the displaced snow to form walls either side. A roof made of thin boards and tarred paper was added and this rapidly disappeared under the accumulating snow, providing additional insulation. Finally, the engineers strung electric lights along the tunnels and for 12 hours every day the animals benefited from light that they would otherwise have been denied throughout the winter. 'The dogs certainly seem to appreciate it,' Fuchs noted on 30 March after installing the first of the animals, 'and already "Joe" and the others brought in yesterday are behaving in a happier manner.'[431] Finishing the tunnels also made life marginally more comfortable for the men tasked with feeding the dogs, as now they could saw up the frozen seal carcasses under cover and in temperatures generally hovering a few degrees above freezing.

The second major task was to prepare the two aeroplanes. The small Auster could easily be turned to face into the wind and Weston had only to lock its ailerons, rudder and elevators with wooden clamps. Decommissioning the Otter proved altogether more complex. To prevent it being buffeted by every gust of wind, Weston first of all removed the rudder and then protected the engine by fitting a canvas and wood cover. Next he and Lewis used the Ferguson's high lift loader to gouge out a 4-foot-deep pit in the snow before pulling the aeroplane into it so that the wings were level with the snow surface, thereby reducing the lift generated by the strong southerly gales. Finally, they placed windbreaks in front of the nose and behind the tail. These would help to protect the Otter from the full force of the southerlies and prevent it being completely buried by the drift.

A few days later, a sudden and, to those less experienced among the explorers, distinctly freakish change in the weather confirmed that the work had been completed only just in time. For many days, the temperature had refused to rise above -30°F, with a steady wind from the south; but then, as Lowe recorded on 4 April:

Last night at 11 p.m. the wind died away in half an hour to a light breeze and Hannes predicted a sudden northerly swing. In fifteen seconds as we watched the recording instruments the wind direction indicator swung to north and a great front of wind hit the hut and roared on inland leaving us in swirling drift with winds from 40 to 50 miles an hour. The temperature rose from minus 6 to +24°F in fifteen minutes with the 'warm' air blowing off the sea. With this we settled down for the night.[432]

The following morning they woke to find the trapdoor jammed with drift but once they had forced it open the change outside was remarkable. Snow continued to billow around, but now the climate seemed almost temperate. 'A wind only a few degrees below freezing is like a warm, balmy summer breeze after minus 30°F', wrote an astonished Lowe. 'I collected snow and moved around outside dressed in only a light woollen vest with a shirt and windproof. It's too hot to have the hood up and bare hands easily handle the shovel and snow and the sledges.'[433] The veterans recognised the violent northerly blizzard as a feature of the winter weather in the Weddell Sea area – and no matter how welcome it might be now, by the time it died away in the late spring everyone would be glad to see the back of it.

So far, the weather had not prevented the continuation of work outdoors –although, on occasion, it could be distinctly uncomfortable, as Stratton, Lowe and Geoff Pratt discovered on 13 April, when they embarked on a seismic survey of the ice shelf. When they set out at midday, the sun rested only a few degrees above the horizon, turning the hummocks of snow a reddish-pink while the blustery wind hurled the loose flakes across the surface. Looking at the landscape as he climbed into the Sno-cat, Lowe thought the effect 'eerie and memorable ... It reminded me strongly of the effect created in films to show a "dream" sequence when a pinky light shines on blowing cloud and people flow and walk through it – seen from the waist upwards.'[434] The experience was made even more surreal by the fact that, with the thermometer reading -25°F and with a 25-knot wind beating against the vehicle's sides, the Sno-cat's heater made very little impression on the ice encrusting the double-glazed windscreen, forcing Pratt to drive completely blind for nearly half a mile.

Having reached the row of crevasses and hummocks at the top of the snow slope, he turned the Sno-cat to face inland and stopped. Once they climbed out of the cab, any inclination to loiter to appreciate the view very quickly evaporated. 'The wind was cruel and my nose froze and turned white,' observed Lowe. 'I leapt back into the cab and thawed it with my hands but all day it pained me and kept freezing stiff.'[435] With the wind lashing them, the three men struggled to unload the cables, geophones, explosives, detonators, ice-auger, marking stakes and other oddments of

equipment essential to reflection seismology. Pratt then surveyed
a line running due south from the coast and laid 320 metres of
cable along it before connecting 48 geophones. These geophones
would be used to monitor the energy waves generated by con-
trolled explosions and reflected by the subsurface geology and,
in a manner similar to echolocation, enable him to calculate the
thickness of the ice. Next, they drilled a 10-foot-deep hole with
the auger, into which they lowered a four-ounce charge of dynamite. 'The drifting snow caused such a lot of static electricity that
the handling of the detonators seemed dangerous,' Lowe noted
nervously, 'but I was assured that it was not so.'[436]

After a short break for lunch the party started work again at
2.00pm, just as the sun began to set. Half an hour later, with the
full moon bathing the clouds of swirling drift and the Vahsel Bay
hills in its silvery light, Pratt detonated the charges and studied
the readings on the monitor in the back of the Sno-cat. They then
moved the vehicle and drilled and fired again. With the exercise
complete, the three men dug the geophones and the cable from
snow now nearly 2 feet deep and, at 5.30pm, they staggered back
into the hut, exhausted and slightly frostbitten. But, as so often in
the Antarctic, it had all been for nothing. When Pratt developed
the results, he discovered that the drift had caused so much static
interference that the readings were confused and meaningless.
The entire day's effort had been wasted.

With the disappearance of the sun on 23 April, the Antarctic
winter finally clamped down on Shackleton and, with temperatures regularly falling well below -50°F, most outdoor work
became all but impossible. Some tasks, however, could not be
postponed – in particular, the completion of the vehicle workshop. Towards the end of March Lowe had written that: 'We must,
I feel, get the roof and walls covered in this week or the weather
will become so impossible as to stop us completely'[437] but it was
not until 7 June that he could record that 'the garage is now finished and David, Ralph and Gordon are installing lathes, drill
presses and welding plants.'[438] The completion of the workshop,
which the explorers christened 'The Chapel' because of the steep
pitch of its roof, constituted a major milestone and significantly

contributed to the comfort of Homard and David Pratt as they prepared the vehicles for their 2000-mile marathon. Up to now, the engineers had been obliged to work in the somewhat novel surroundings of a temporary inflatable garage, which offered very little protection from the worsening conditions. Moreover, as Fuchs later described, the rubber building 'had one curious and uncanny characteristic. When the sun was high its warmth heated the air within and the structure stood up firm and rigid, but as the sun sank it shrank and slowly collapsed, enveloping, as in a shroud, any vehicle it contained.'[439]

The one slight, but unavoidable, disadvantage of the garage's completion was that the engineers could now operate their machinery with much greater regularity, placing a considerable additional strain on the diesel generators. Aside from the engineers, perhaps the heaviest user of the available 30 amps was Taffy Williams, as he struggled to maintain his regular radio schedules not only with South Ice and Scott Base, but also with Port Stanley in the Falklands, with the GPO in London and with the British and American Antarctic bases at Halley Bay, Ellsworth and the South Pole. Assisted by Lenton and La Grange, he transmitted a seemingly endless series of messages, ranging from formal reports to personal greetings. Sometimes, too, the operators spent hours sending technical data, a particularly arduous job, as Hal Lister acknowledged: 'Hannes and Taff are always very patient and bright,' he wrote at South Ice. 'Today they kindly sent us a Vapour Pressure table we asked for. This type of signal is very tedious to the sender (and receiver too, but he uses it later so doesn't mind, we hope), but [it] is a very valuable contribution that the radio makes.'[440]

As well as enabling the transfer of essential information, the radio also provided the explorers with a very welcome link with the outside world and messages giving news of events like the birth of Weston's son and the engagement of Fuchs's daughter not only gave cause for celebration but also reduced the explorers' feelings of isolation. The BBC's 'Calling Antarctica' programmes also served to let the explorers know that they had not been forgotten and their enthusiasm swelled still further when the programmes included personal messages – often broadcast in person – from friends and family at home, more than 10,000 miles away. Inevitably, the frequent interruptions caused by atmospheric conditions resulted in considerable frustration for both transmitters and receivers. In particular, as one of only two New Zealanders in the Weddell Sea party, Lowe found the disruptions to service not only galling but also potentially divisive: 'This lack of contact, I feel, is a great pity and does more and more to keep the two ends of the expedition apart,' he complained after yet another of the schedules with Scott Base was reduced to the hiss of static.[441] On the other side of the continent, Hillary, who perhaps made insufficient allowance for the problems being encountered at Vahsel Bay, simply remarked that 'their radio set up seems extremely inefficient.'[442]

Except for the engineers, the men now spent the majority of their time confined within the hut, preparing equipment for the crossing and conducting whatever scientific work remained feasible, such as Stratton's indoor climate observations. Warmed by solid-fuel-burning stoves and insulated by the deep banks of snow piled against its exterior walls, he discovered that the hut maintained an average air temperature of 57°F at head height and more than 70°F at the apex of the roof, where clothing could be aired. But at floor level it seldom rose above freezing point and those responsible for scrubbing the linoleum always found it necessary to adopt the hazardous expedient of using a blowtorch to melt the accumulations of ice.

La Grange, meanwhile, continued to conduct his meteorological observations with all the conscientiousness of a zealot. His work necessitated regular forays outdoors to check the meteorological screens; even worse, these visits had to be continued throughout the night, as Fuchs described:

As [the] hour approaches [the] observer dresses appropriately for outside conditions and attempts to glide stealthily from living room to avoid waking irate light sleepers ... Once outside [his] route leads over hard snow crust surface above [the] sounding board roof which vibrates to every crunching footstep. Happily unconscious of this and, striving to find a way through driving drifts, [he] falls down six foot drift slope finally arriving at the screen which is certainly full of snow. Clears it sufficiently to read instruments – crunches way back over roof, trips over aerial mast stay, falls up six foot slope and regains tunnel entrances. Now frozen and covered in snow – compromises with seven doors by leaving most of them open. In Met office [he] records and codes observations then back to recline on bunk till repeat performance 3 a.m.[443]

To ensure the programme's absolute integrity and comprehensiveness, this ritual was to be completed twice every single night of the entire expedition, making the lot of the meteorological officer and his assistants particularly unenviable. But, then, as La Grange explained, 'It's like a religion, either you believe in it, or you don't.'[444]

Inevitably, the explorers watched eagerly for any lull in the weather and, when they occurred, they sallied outdoors on any pretext. On one occasion, Homard and David Pratt constructed a fish trap of wire netting which they lowered through a hole cut in the sea ice, but their efforts were rewarded with little success and the only seafood addition to the winter menu was a dish of pink shrimp-like crustaceans, prepared for Stratton's birthday. Despite the care devoted to its cooking, the meal was not a success. 'Manfully he tackled the delicate pink pile,' Fuchs recorded, 'only to find that each multi-legged corpse contained no more than a few drops of pink oil.'[445]

Fortunately, an entrée of pink skeletons did little to spoil Stratton's birthday party and the TAE, like most polar expeditions before and since, continued to relish any event that provided an excuse to let off steam. Most important of all in the almanac was the much anticipated Midwinter's Day, which gave rise to what Stratton described as 'many more or less secretive preparations'.[446] As if to mark this important watershed, when the men emerged from the hut on the morning of 21 June, they could discern a red glow to the north: the sun's reflection on very high cirrus clouds. This unexpectedly beautiful and delicate colouration in the usually dark sky provided an excellent start to a day which, except for the completion of vital routine tasks, like the bringing in of ice for drinking water and coal for the stoves, was traditionally dedicated to pleasure. The workshop, the object of so much backbreaking labour over the previous months, now came into its own as the venue for a cocktail party, hosted by Pratt and Homard. 'They with prescience,' wrote an appreciative Stratton, 'had lit a flare path down the track as an aid to navigation, and inside a transformed workshop we found benches gratefully carrying bowls of champagne cocktails and plates of snacks instead of the work-a-day clutter of spanners and spare parts.'[447] As each man entered, the enthusiastic hosts thrust brimming glasses into each hand and the party was soon in full swing with Irish folk music blaring in the background and a roaring coal fire raising the temperature to an unusually balmy +35°F. 'When one remembers that we have spent many months together with only our own society,' observed Fuchs, 'it was remarkable that there was still the atmosphere of a sherry party, with new arrivals being acclaimed and merging with this or that discussion group.'[448]

Given Haslop's reputation with explosives – during the voyage of the *Theron* his ill-controlled detonations had blown holes in the Auster's wings and closed up a gap in the ice which had taken hours to dig – his companions might have been forgiven for anticipating the 'Haslop Firework Display' with some trepidation. And their anxiety would not have been allayed by the sight of the pilot stumbling among the fuses with a beer mug in his hand. Fortunately, however, the 12-minute extravaganza, consisting of flares and rockets and beginning with a series of detonations spelling out 'TAE' in Morse code, went off without a hitch and everyone, including 'a singed Gordon gallantly complete with pewter mug'[449] filed back into the hut unscathed. Before they could sit down to enjoy their dinner at tables festooned with paper hats, crackers and toys, South Ice came through on the radio, delaying the meal while greetings were exchanged and Williams transmitted congratulatory telegrams from home to Blaiklock, Stephenson and Lister. Finally, at 3.00pm, the party sat down to green turtle soup, roast turkey, roast potatoes (frozen under the ice since the departure of the *Magga Dan*), plum pudding, champagne and liqueurs. 'Everyone went quickly to sleep after this,' Lowe noted, 'and the extensive buffet which Ralph and John L had prepared was almost untouched. The Party spirit carried through until Saturday night and on Sunday the hut was cleaned out and we all rested.'[450]

With everyone keen to make the most of the celebration, Midwinter's Day had been an unqualified success. Importantly, the event provided each of the men with a very welcome psychological fillip and, as Lowe observed, over the course of the following days there was 'a quickening in the activities of everybody. There is an involuntary surge of excitement at the nearness of spring and the journeys to be made.'[451] On 3 July, at +1°F the warmest day since the sun set in April, Fuchs at last felt able to confirm the details of those journeys. At the beginning of September he, accompanied by David and Geoff Pratt and Homard would trial a Sno-cat and a Weasel on a four- or five-day journey to the 50-mile depot established by Blaiklock and Goldsmith at the end of 1956, where they would cache more fuel. Immediately upon the return of this party, Lewis would fly Fuchs, Lowe and Geoff Pratt on a relief mission to South Ice, returning with Stephenson and Blaiklock and leaving Pratt to support Lister. Fuchs and Lowe would then be dropped in the Theron Mountains with a dog team and 30 days' rations, there to conduct a detailed survey. Shortly afterwards, David Pratt, Blaiklock and Stephenson would be flown into the Shackleton Mountains to survey and geologise for up to three weeks. Finally, towards the end of September, the first four vehicles would begin their 270-mile journey to South Ice on the initial leg of the continental crossing. Having proved the route to South Ice, Fuchs and the two engineers would fly back to Shackleton in order to prepare the remaining vehicles prior to their departure, which would take place no later than 14 November. It was an ambitious programme and its success, as Fuchs well knew, would be entirely dependent upon the clemency of the weather at the beginning of the spring.

The weather, however, showed no signs of relenting. After a mild beginning to July, throughout the rest of the month the temperatures continued to plunge until, on the 29th, the thermometers registered -64°F, exceeding by one degree the lowest temperature recorded during the Advance Party's miserable year. More encouragingly, with every passing day, the ruddy glow on the horizon grew in intensity until, on 20 August, the sun finally nosed its way, albeit fleetingly, into the northern sky: its first appearance since May. 'Only a fraction of the top stood above the horizon,' wrote Lowe, 'looking at us quizzically like a Chad cartoon. But it was there – golden and blazing, the brightest sight we have seen for months.'[452] In a temperature of -35°F and with the 30-knot wind scouring their cheeks, the explorers stood close to the trapdoor of their entrance tunnel, basking in the feeble light. For much of the time, the flying spumes of snow obscured their view and, within an hour, the sun had disappeared – but their enthusiasm knew no bounds. From this point onwards, every day would add another 15 or 20 minutes to its stay and, to all intents and purposes, their winter was over.

Despite the cold and wind, preparations for the journeys continued whenever conditions allowed. Geoff Pratt, Lewis, Rogers and Lowe spent hours helping David Pratt to dig out vehicle spares, including tracks, fire extinguishers, bogey wheels, sprockets and tractor tyres – some 40 heavy crates in total, all covered in 3 feet of compacted snow. With this goldmine exhausted, the engineers then focused on bringing their vehicles to a state of readiness, checking wiring, greasing the Sno-cats' notoriously complicated tracks and welding on recovery equipment. Others concentrated on patching tents and clothing, refurbishing sledges and packing ration boxes, so that they would be ready to depart the moment Fuchs gave the signal. That signal would be a long time in coming.

The weather throughout August was appalling, with a temperature range of +8°F to -67°F. On five days the thermometer readings fell below -60°F and on 23 days to below -40°F. The average temperature for the entire month was -35°F with a mean wind speed of 20mph and gusts of over 60mph. Inevitably, such conditions made outdoor activity extremely punishing and it took the explorers fifteen hours of backbreaking work to dig out the Otter so that Weston could prepare it for the planned flight to South Ice. Inside the garage, meanwhile, Pratt and Homard turned their attention to overhauling the expedition's solitary Ferguson tractor and to fitting snow-proof brakes and wider tracks. It would then take a further week to permanently install Geoff Pratt's seismic apparatus in one of the Sno-cats prior to the initial journey. Given the circumstances, no one exhibited much surprise when Fuchs announced that he had decided to cancel the trial journey with the vehicles. 'This change of plan is a great disappointment to us,' he acknowledged, 'and is likely to put a slight strain on morale just when the winter should be over and we should all be getting the boost of field activity.'[453]

He was right to anticipate a dip in morale – but the delays caused by the weather were only indirectly responsible. Of far greater concern to the majority of the explorers during this tense period was Fuchs's style of leadership:

> We are not told anything except details and lack direction and decisions. We are enthusiastic to help but are not allowed to touch the all-important vehicles which are so behind in maintenance schedule ... Arrogance, the know-all attitude, the secrecy of decisions (or lack of them) is sapping efficiency more than the weather and all else.[454]

Even worse, when they approached Fuchs and Stratton with ideas of their own, they received very short shrift, Stratton telling one: 'You are not here to think, Bunny and I do that for you; you are here to do as you're told.'[455] Of course, such rebuffs were at least partly symptomatic of the anxiety felt by Fuchs and his lieutenant, but they were hardly calculated to inspire confidence.

'September has roared in like a lion', Lowe observed on the 4th. 'On 1st and 2nd days of the month the temperature stood at -60°F with clear skies and a light breeze from the south. Then on the night of the 2nd the south wind mounted and mounted to 20, 30 and then 40 knots and a gale has blown since with temp -40°F to -47°F and gusts to 54 knots.'[456] In these conditions, Weston found it impossible to complete work on the Otter though he made some progress on preparing the much smaller Auster after erecting a tent over its nose section. 'I am afraid that it may be October before the Otter flies,' wrote a depressed Fuchs on 11 September, 'in which case our plans will receive a serious setback.'[457] Even more worryingly, a few days later it became clear that the continuation of work on the aircraft might actually make all the difference between life and death.

On 17 September, Williams picked up an emergency call from the Royal Society's IGY base at Halley Bay requesting immediate assistance. While out skiing, the IGY base leader and doctor, Robin Smart, had fallen heavily and sustained internal injuries, including a suspected punctured liver. Initially Smart had attempted to treat himself, but his condition had rapidly deteriorated and he had lost consciousness. Help was urgently required. Weston immediately accelerated work on the Auster and on the first break in the weather, on the 20th, Haslop and Rogers flew off to render whatever assistance they could offer. But, as had so often been the case during the establishment of South Ice, as they approached their destination the weather once again closed in and Haslop overshot the Halley Bay base without seeing it through the dense banks of drift. With his fuel dwindling and the weather deteriorating, he decided that he must land and wait for conditions to improve. He put the Auster down within 50 yards of the ice edge and then radioed Shackleton to say that he and Rogers were safe but cold. 'Since then,' an anxious Lowe wrote on 23 September, 'cloud and wind have closed heavily about the sea and auroral interference has cut off radio links between here and Halley Bay.'[458]

Immediately upon receiving Haslop's transmission, Fuchs ordered that work should continue around the clock to prepare the Otter for a rescue flight, the main tasks being to de-ice the wings, fuselage and tail, which were packed with drift snow. Lewis, Geoff Pratt and Lowe began on the night shift (from 10.00pm until 8.30am) and Weston, Lenton, Fuchs and Stratton took over during the day. La Grange's meteorological observations continued uninterrupted and Williams stood by his radio, transmitting to Haslop and Rogers every fifteen minutes from

8.00am each morning. Those working throughout the night found the overthrow of their usual routine particularly disorientating but, as Lowe recognised, 'For Gordon and Allan sitting out their third night somewhere on the ice with no tent it must be very grim. The chances of their flying off when the weather improves are very slim indeed and I feel certain a relief flight in the Otter is the only way to help them out.'[459]

On 29 September the expedition breathed a collective sigh of relief when, after nine days of silence, the radio crackled into life and Haslop advised them that he and Rogers were fit – but hungry. Realising that they would probably freeze to death in the aeroplane's cockpit, they had spent their first night in what Haslop described as a 'two-man coffin' scraped in the ice and then covered with the Auster's engine cowling. Inside their thick down suits and sleeping bags they had spent a miserable night, lying head-to-toe and shivering and drowsing intermittently. They had with them a small primus, but with only 4 pints of kerosene they could only afford a 'brew up' first thing in the morning and last thing at night and, with no other means of melting the snow, thirst quickly developed into a major problem. For food, they relied upon RAF survival rations of which they had sufficient to last up to three weeks. Over the course of the following days, as they waited for a break in the weather, they had spent their time repeatedly turning the Auster into the wind and gouging out a larger hole, using their hands and a sheaf knife that Rogers had been carrying. By the end of the week, they had room enough to stand and niches for their sleeping bags. They had even fashioned shelves upon which they placed their belongings and another niche for the primus. As well as making them more comfortable, this work gave them an occupation and helped them to keep at least tolerably warm. But they could not survive indefinitely.

While the two downed aviators had been eking out their troglodyte existence, work at Shackleton had continued at a frenetic pace despite the fact that the blizzard and whiteout conditions showed no signs of relenting. By the time Williams picked up Haslop's second transmission the snow inside the Otter's wings had been melted, the rudder reattached and the engine started.

That same evening Lewis made a test flight but low cloud cover
limited the ceiling to 500 feet, forcing him to stay within three
miles of the base. On the 30th, weather reports from Halley Bay
indicated that a flight might be feasible and Lewis and Stratton
immediately took to the air, heading into an ominously dark and
murky sky to the north-east. Within minutes they were in serious trouble, as Fuchs recounted: 'Forced down by icing, unable
to see through the snow squalls, they were soon iceberg-hopping
at 50 feet, with a maximum speed of 75 knots on full throttle.'[460]
Realising not only that locating and rescuing the missing men
would prove impossible in such conditions but that a continuation of the flight might result in his also having to make an
emergency landing, Lewis had little option but to abort. Banking
to port, its engine racing, he turned the Otter westwards over
the Weddell Sea and headed for home. Rogers and Haslop must
spend yet another night in their ice cave.

The following day, having received another optimistic weather
report from Halley Bay, Lewis and Stratton made a second
attempt, determined to improve upon their frustrating experiences of the previous evening. Flying at 5000 feet, above the icing
zone but below the higher cloud, they reached Halley Bay in
two hours and twenty minutes and then commenced a search to
the south. After scanning a 70-mile stretch of coastline without
seeing any trace of the Auster or its occupants, they landed at the
IGY base, which was mercifully free of drift, refuelled and then
immediately commenced a search to the north. To their immense
relief, at a position some 50 miles beyond the IGY hut, they
began to pick up the signal transmitted by the Auster's 'Search
and Rescue and Homing' (or SARAH) beacon. A few moments
later, Lewis radioed the welcome news that he had spotted the
missing aeroplane and was preparing to land on a makeshift
runway marked out by Haslop and Rogers with fluorescent dye
and large chunks of ice.

As soon as the Auster had been fuelled and oiled, the two
machines again took to the air to make the short hop to Halley
Bay. By the time of their rescue, the two men had been on the ice
for eleven days and, even with careful husbanding, their remaining

fuel was down to a mere third of a pint. Even more worrying, the few good flying hours during 1 October turned out to be the last for some days and it was not until 4 October that the four men managed to make the return trip to Shackleton. The rescue could not have been timelier. Nor, as it turned out, had the long delay in reaching the Royal Society base produced any dire consequences for the injured Robin Smart. When Rogers stepped out of the cockpit at Halley Bay one of the first men to greet him was Smart himself who, without any medical attention, had made a miraculous recovery.

The Halley Bay emergency was not without its casualties however. Even before Haslop's forced landing Fuchs had admitted that his original timetable for the spring journeys was no longer viable. On 12 September he had cabled the expedition's headquarters in Victoria Street with a depressing analysis of the impacts of the appalling weather: 'Situation has now compelled me to telescope operations by cancelling first depot and seismic journey. Greatest loss will be development of vehicle safety crevasse technique before 300-mile journey to South Ice ... Everyone disappointed at delay of fieldwork.'[461] With the turn of the seasons providing such a tight window for the completion of the crossing, the expedition's timetable had always been ambitious – now it appeared that, unless conditions improved quickly, the TAE faced total disaster.

After Fuchs, the repeated postponement of the spring journeys probably affected no one more profoundly than the three men at South Ice. For Lister, Blaiklock and Stephenson every delay at Shackleton meant another day, week or month added to an isolation which, at times, seemed as though it might never end.

Within days of its completion in March, swirling drift had buried their tiny hut up to its chimneys, and when the men ventured outside, to take observations or to visit drift-recording or meteorological apparatus, they must first make their way down a 30-yard snow-tunnel and then climb a short ladder before exiting via a trapdoor to the surface. Off the tunnel, they had gouged various bays to provide storage, lavatory and rubbish pits, an

emergency refuge and another 50-foot-deep pit which became
the centre of Stephenson's ice crystal studies. At an altitude of
4430 feet above sea level and 270 miles inland from Shackleton,
South Ice generally experienced fewer blizzards than the expedition's main winter quarters but, with the temperature sometimes
dropping as low as -71°F, the hut's inhabitants quickly began to
refer to the Weddell Sea coastal area as 'the banana belt'. Less
amusingly, the punishing climate revealed an assortment of flaws
in the hut's design, as catalogued by Lister:

> The floor is usually at or very near freezing point while the
> ceiling temp is +80°F or nearly so if there isn't too much wind.
> The hut panels fit about flat onto each other instead of over-
> lapping to cheat drafts. The felt insulating strips are so hard in
> the cold that they don't make a seal between 2 flat surfaces
> … The aluminium framing conducts heat out of the hut and
> accumulates ice round the periphery of the inside walls at floor
> level … The indoor WC – chemical – was stupid … The Met
> bench is too big and the Glaciology bench too small.[462]

The list of defects grew to cover two closely-written pages
before, his spleen vented, Lister felt able to concede that, overall,
'It is a very fine base for 4 men and the furnishings by Morris
of Glasgow are a real pleasure and make much difference to our
comfort here.'[463]

Originally, the hut had been designed for four men and, as base
leader and chief scientist, Lister believed that he would need the
full complement in order to strike the right balance between the
day-to-day tasks essential to the efficient running of any polar
station and the onerous scientific programme he had planned. As
early as 24 February, he had employed this argument when urging
Fuchs to include a fourth man in the South Ice party. A month
later, while completing the hut's construction, he returned to the
subject: 'Certainly,' he wrote in a letter delivered by aeroplane,
'our programme requires 4 men working full time … Should you
think it impossible to send a 4th man, then I quite understand
and will cut our programme accordingly.'[464]

Despite Lister's less than subtle reference to a curtailed scientific programme – a barb surely designed to prick his leader's scientific conscience – Fuchs's response was a firm negative. 'The only possible men are George L and Gordon H,' he observed on 24 March. 'The former I consider should be at Shackleton to continue the pictorial record for the next seven months ... Then Gordon is the second pilot and if anything should happen to John L by mischance then we should not be able to relieve South Ice by air early next season. In any event it is late in the day suddenly to pitchfork another man into South Ice life without adequate preparation of mind and material.'[465] So far as Lister's companions were concerned, commenting on the breadth of the scientific programme designed for South Ice, Stephenson wrote of Lister that the 'scope of his interests and undertakings was limitless, and I understood why he asked for an extra man at the station.'[466] Blaiklock, on the other hand, later asserted that Fuchs's decision to limit numbers had been the right one all along: 'While we were kept busy enough,' he wrote, 'nothing was abandoned due to manpower shortage.'[467] In the event, Haslop's forced landing near Halley Bay in September would more than justify Fuchs's retention of both pilots at Shackleton. Besides, as Fuchs well knew, in the ice-bound isolation of the forward station, being kept busy would offer the best antidote of all to boredom and depression.

Throughout the long dark months, Blaiklock concentrated on meteorological observations, while also taking star sights to fix South Ice's precise location and plotting the results of the previous season's aerial surveys. Stephenson worked in the specially dug ice cave, focusing on petrology and on drawing and analysing ice core samples, which he studied microscopically to establish how snow gradually turns to ice without first melting. Finally, Lister prepared a detailed record of drift densities at various wind speeds – work that necessitated daily trips to an array of photocells and specially designed drift cylinders mounted on a dexion mast some distance from the trapdoor. By any standards, it was a complex and demanding programme and, when discussing Fuchs's decision to appoint Lister as base leader, Blaiklock noted that one of the primary benefits had been the expectation that since 'some of Hal's experiments were likely to fail ... with himself in charge he could choose what to abort.'[468] What Fuchs could not have foreseen, however, was the strength of Lister's reluctance to abandon any element of his programme and how successive failures to obtain high quality results would add to his spiralling frustrations. 'Time, time, time!' Lister exclaimed on 28 March, in the first of many such asides, 'How short we are of this. Yet we are progressing slowly – mustn't be impatient.'[469]

One of the first casualties in the battle between research and routine maintenance was hygiene. 'Some objection to Saturday clean and tidy up,' Lister complained on 30 March. 'The place isn't very dirty but it is untidy and would be more efficient and pleasant if a bit neater.'[470] A few days later, he recorded that 'Two of us suffering from "squitters". I'm sure this is due to the lack of cleanliness in the kitchen, especially washing dishes in a cupful of dirty water and drying them on filthy tea towels.'[471] Of much greater concern to Lister was his companions' apparent disregard for essential scientific equipment. The first major accident occurred when Stephenson smashed the party's only photoflash, rendering photography, particularly specialist drift photography, almost impossible. Even more troubling was the discovery that Blaiklock had mislaid a vital flux plate. 'This loss of an instrument of such importance to me is very annoying,' Lister wrote to his wife,

> ... especially when it is caused thro' slovenliness, arrogance – couldn't-care-less attitude. Ken may be a good traveller but on a scientific base of this size he is a menace ... I can't stand slovenliness, it is too expensive in time, temper and equanimity and isn't necessary.[472]

Fortunately, Blaiklock's cheerfulness and equable temper helped to make up for his carelessness, and Lister also grew to appreciate his conscientiousness in completing the regular meteorological observations and his willingness to undertake tedious chores like digging out the entrance and fetching fuel unasked. Over time, mutual respect and understanding served to cement a permanent friendship – in addition, as the winter stretched out and the pressures at South Ice escalated, Lister would come to rely upon Blaiklock as a valuable ally.

As the weeks passed and the darkness and cold intensified, it became increasingly difficult, and dangerous, to maintain the schedule of outdoor observations. By the end of May, with the temperature down to -60°F, the anemometers designed for measuring wind speeds began to freeze solid, so that after a day's work Lister found that he had too few readings to enable him to calculate an accurate wind speed profile. This in turn made it impossible to extrapolate the drag-factor generated by the drift, a key element of his pioneering work. 'Damn! Damn!' he scribbled on 30 May, 'What few results for the hours spent shivering and the fingers repeatedly whitened with frostbite. No wonder drift has never previously been studied in any detail.'[473]

On another occasion he came uncomfortably close to becoming a martyr to science when a blizzard descended and cut him off from the hut while he was out inspecting bamboo poles erected to assist in the measurement of drift accumulation. Just a few hundred yards from the trapdoor he found himself completely disorientated by a combination of thick, sizzling drift and a freakish change in wind direction. For two hours he stumbled among the sastrugi, blinded and directionless: 'I lay down for five minutes, walked ten yards and back and lay down again, sheltering behind a higher sastrugi, then repeated the process hoping someone would realise that I was outside longer than usual.'[474] Eventually, frostbitten and exhausted, he saw a light twinkling through the sheets of drift: a Tilley lamp suspended from the top of the dexion mast by an anxious Blaiklock. Wondering whether he was hallucinating, Lister staggered towards the beacon, his thick beard a mass of snow, ice and frozen mucus and his hands thrust into his armpits to protect them from severe frostbite. Eventually, the light led him to the mast and on to the trapdoor – Blaiklock and the Tilley lamp, he soon realised, had saved his life.

Despite the many obstacles, by mid-July Lister believed that Stephenson's glaciological work, at least, was beginning to show valuable results: 'The story of the progression from drift snow to near ice is unfolding very neatly and, with more analysis of the data, should make some first class papers.'[475] And yet Stephenson seemed very far from happy, becoming snappish and, at times, inclined to 'screaming defiance about results'.[476] Increasingly taciturn and moody, the young Australian spent long hours every day huddled in the eerie depths of his ice cave, deliberately cutting himself off from his companions, as an anxious Lister described:

> Jon terribly depressed, saying nothing unless asked a direct question and even then, only answering in a very quiet strained voice. Head in hands much of time and looking extremely miserable but says he is OK. Frequently much of day in bunk and nights spent working ... These periods of depression have become more frequent and this one is the most intense and alarming. Medical opinion at base could probably do little to help so best not asked for. Even Ken somewhat alarmed by Jon and asked me if I thought there was anything seriously wrong with Jon.[477]

The obvious explanation for this increasingly erratic behaviour was the psychological and physiological reaction to prolonged periods of darkness and isolation, known colloquially as 'cabin fever' – though Stephenson himself would later claim that 'at South Ice we experienced little of this.'[478] The condition, which is marked by restlessness, irritability, irrational frustration, disturbed sleep patterns and paranoia had been observed on previous polar expeditions – most notably on Adrien de Gerlache's *Belgica* expedition of 1897–99 – and is now known to result from a lack of sunlight, which in turn accelerates the pineal gland's secretion of melatonin. Unfortunately, as Lister recognised, the only effective antidotes would be the return of the sun and a change of scene – the first could be relied upon, but not for some weeks; the second seemed as far away as ever.

On 9 July, Fuchs radioed from Shackleton to provide a brief outline of his plans for the spring journeys – including, most importantly, the relief of South Ice by aeroplane at the beginning of September. 'This was very fine indeed since we have conjectured a little and now can be more certain,' noted Lister, 'tho' we would like more details.'[479] But detail remained scanty and the continuing uncertainty only served to add to the tension among the three men at the forward depot. On 2 September, sunlight finally returned to South Ice – three days later than expected because of the dense drift being hurled about by 30-knot winds but no less welcome for all that. Stephenson seemed to feel the benefit almost instantaneously: 'Jon much better now,' a relieved Lister recorded. 'Today he cracked first joke for many weeks. I hope the depressions never recur now the sun is back and we haven't long before leaving here.'[480] Two days later, however, the emotional pendulum swung back again when a bulletin from Shackleton revealed that appalling weather had put back the start of the initial journeys.

The three men continued with their observations and routine maintenance – but in a rather desultory and dispirited fashion and even the ultra-conscientious Lister admitted to feeling increasingly lethargic. Worse still, the bad news from Shackleton seriously undermined Stephenson's fragile recovery and, on the 12th, his moodiness erupted in an angry attack on Lister:

> In a burst of temper, Jon shouted orders at Hal. A brief tête-à-tête followed … Jon said he isn't depressed, just a bit taciturn and wishes to be left alone … Jon says he is sick of Hal and is to ask Bunny not to put the two together for the crossing. Ah! Well! There's little we can do about it save grin and hope the mood will pass.'[481]

Tension mounted still further the following day when Lister discovered that Stephenson had erased a cherished recording of his wife and baby son. 'Oh to get rid of the poisoned atmosphere,' he wrote that evening, 'and grow up and not be such children. Patience! Work!'[482]

The frenetic activity at Shackleton after Haslop's forced landing on 20 September served only to reinforce the South Ice trio's feelings of isolation and helplessness. Able to follow events by listening to Shackleton's transmissions, but unable to do anything or even to speak for fear of blocking the radio waves, the tension and feeling of utter impotence became almost intolerable. 'We don't contribute,' raged Lister, 'we just waste time and express ourselves. How puerile! ... we must take a back seat and only listen, and not talk, for Gordon and Allan are first on the priorities, poor devils.'[483] Unexpectedly, listening to the unfolding drama over the radio also left them feeling strangely listless. The Auster's first flight of the season may have ended in near disaster, but the very fact that the aeroplane had been able to fly at all clearly presaged the begin-ning of the spring journeys and made the continuation of the science programme seem somehow futile – even to Lister. Assuming that the Otter's preparation could be expedited and the rescue of Rogers and Haslop completed in the near future, the relief of South Ice must be imminent and Blaiklock and Lister could hardly disguise their excitement. They continued their observations and analysis but it became abundantly clear that their focus had switched to their planned survey journey to the Shackleton Mountains, which they would start after a brief visit to Shackleton.

After 196 days of complete mutual dependence, when the South Ice party eventually broke up, it did so with almost unseemly haste. On 7 October, the Otter arrived out of a clear blue sky carrying Haslop and Rogers – now both fully recov-ered from their eleven-day ordeal on the ice shelf. Blaiklock and Stephenson were caught almost by surprise and they dashed about like madmen, gathering their few possessions and fling-ing them into the aeroplane – then, with a brisk handshake, they were gone. The Otter had been on the ground for just 55 min-utes. Turning back to the hut with Rogers, Lister noted rather ruefully that 'Ken and Jon were delighted to leave.'[484] Now, prior to his own evacuation in a few days' time, his one remaining task was to tutor Rogers in the work of the base. In particular, the doctor would be expected to maintain the meteorological obser-vations and man the radio so that incoming pilots, flying in fuel and other supplies in readiness for the crossing, would be able to benefit from local weather reports. 'Turned in at 1 a.m. local,' recorded Lister that night, '… a natter with a new face takes a long time!!!'[485]

The following day Williams reported over the radio that, at last, four vehicles had started on the reconnaissance journey to South Ice: three Weasels, driven by Fuchs, David Pratt and Homard, and the Sno-cat equipped with the seismic apparatus, driven by Geoff Pratt. After months of delay and uncertainty it seemed that the Trans-Antarctic journey was finally underway. In the isolated privacy of South Ice, however, Rogers made no attempt to disguise either his relief at escaping from Shackleton or his opinion of the preparations for the journey. In recent weeks, he told Lister, life at Shackleton had been 'pandemonium'.[486]

9

Scott Base

Arriving back at Pram Point from the lower Skelton depot on 28 February, Bob Miller and his four companions found huge changes had occurred during the five weeks that some of them had been absent. Where, less than eight weeks earlier, there had been nothing but rock and virgin snow, there now stood a substantial polar station, complete in every respect. 'Just amazed with the comfort of this base,' Miller exclaimed the day after his return, 'every hour brings forth some new joy. It is amazing that such a base could have been built in six weeks yet that is virtually what happened.'[487]

The unloading of stores and equipment had been completed at the beginning of February and by the 5th, the last of the six main huts and three smaller scientific huts had been erected – a mere three weeks after the first foundations had been laid. In addition, a covered way allowed the men to move between the larger buildings without the need to don full protective clothing; three 6kw generators rattled and chugged around the clock, supplying electricity to the entire base; and nine radio masts enabled twice-daily radio schedules to be maintained with New Zealand. A radio telephone service had also been established, meaning that the explorers could speak regularly with their loved ones, and with the installation of a radio facsimile machine, a photograph could be transmitted straight from the Antarctic for the very first time. Captain Scott's hut might stand only a couple of miles distant at Hut Point but looking at the facilities of Scott Base, the Heroic Era seemed a world away.

There was, however, one astonishing oversight in the design of a base which, in all other respects, many considered to be the acme of its kind: the absence of a vehicle workshop. 'The Ross Sea Committee,' wrote a dumbstruck Gunn, 'abundant in absolute wisdom, had decided that we did not need a garage.'[488] The reason for this seemingly inexplicable decision was, perhaps, that the Committee, like many of the explorers themselves, believed that the tractors would be used only for the transportation of stores and hut materials from the ship to the base site, after which they would become largely redundant and would require only limited routine maintenance. 'I assumed that that was the purpose of the tractors,' remembered Richard Brooke, 'and I think most other people did as well.'[489] Given that Hillary had long since decided that the Fergusons would play a more substantial part in the expedition, it appears strange that he did not argue more strongly for the provision of a garage – but perhaps he wished to avoid too close an examination of his plans and felt confident that his mechanics would develop their own solution as, indeed, proved to be the case. On his own return from the Skelton Glacier on 20 February, Gunn discovered that Jim Bates had already started welding together steel fence standards to create the frame for a new hut. 'For the next six days,' he wrote, 'with Bates, Ellis and often Warren and Douglas, I cut, hammered and fitted until finally a large garage with double doors and a side door facing the door into the covered way, was completed … without it, life at base would have been largely without vehicles during the winter.'[490]

As the weather at Pram Point deteriorated, with night-time temperatures falling close to -20°F and frequent snow flurries reducing visibility to just a few yards, most of the explorers spent their time tidying up the base, burning refuse and chopping up seal carcasses for the dogs – a task which became increasingly difficult as the plunging temperatures made even the seals' blubber rock-hard. Hillary, meanwhile, turned his attention to one of the last major tasks to be completed before the end of the season: a comprehensive test of the tractors. Although the Fergusons had proved both rugged and dependable during the offloading of the stores and equipment for the base, it had yet to be established that they could complete a journey of significant length. 'The only way to prove this was to have a practical demonstration.'[491] For this purpose, he chose a 100-mile round trip to Cape Crozier, the easternmost tip of Ross Island and a spot made famous by one of the masterpieces of Antarctic literature, Apsley Cherry-Garrard's *The Worst Journey in the World*.

On 27 June 1911, during Scott's *Terra Nova* expedition, Edward Wilson, 'Birdie' Bowers and Cherry-Garrard had set out from their hut at Cape Evans to man-haul their way the 70 miles to Cape Crozier, where they intended to study the Emperor penguin rookery known to be located there. Their trek, in the dead of the Antarctic winter and with temperatures falling as low as -77°F, has long-since been acknowledged as one of the epics of polar endurance. In choosing Cape Crozier as the destination for his own expedition, Hillary realised that, as well as providing an excellent test for his tractors, a mechanised recreation of this historic journey across the Ross Ice Shelf would be sure to attract headlines and, in the public imagination, further strengthen the links between his expedition and earlier triumphs.

While they waited for conditions to improve sufficiently for the journey to commence, Bates and Murray Ellis concentrated on overhauling two of the tractors and on designing, building and fitting canvas canopies, which they hoped would shield the tractor drivers from the worst of the weather. With their modifications complete, when the skies cleared on 19 March, the expedition was ready to make a start. First to leave were Ellis and Mulgrew, whom Hillary sent ahead on skis to search for crevasses among the localised pressure ridges. Next, watched by the rest of the expedition, the heavily muffled Hillary and Bates clambered into their makeshift cabs and started the engines. Then, with a wave and a cheer, they were off: two bright red tractors, each pulling two sledges loaded with 3 tons of fuel, spares and camping equipment. The contrast with Wilson's expedition, which consisted of only three men and two man-hauled sledges each loaded with 757lb of supplies, could hardly have been more dramatic.

After its enthusiastic departure the tractor party quickly ran into trouble. The vehicles laboured in the soft snow between the pressure ridges while the skiers, despite their best efforts, found it practically impossible to identify the crevasses which the fresh snow rendered all but invisible. They had travelled barely half a mile when Hillary's tractor lurched sideways as the right-hand track broke through a snow bridge. 'For a moment,' he wrote, 'I thought the vehicle was tipping right over but it caught and balanced in a rather precarious position.'[492] Until the second Ferguson arrived to pull them to safety, Hillary and his machine hung suspended over the blue depths of the crevasse – and from that point onwards, he proceeded with greater caution. In worsening visibility the party paused to allow the engineers to repair a faulty track, but then they pushed on, driven as much by pride as by the need to cover more ground. 'We had no intention,' admitted Hillary, 'of camping here for the night as we could well imagine the laughs of the dog drivers back at base if they saw us in the morning camped a mere five and a half miles away.'[493]

Despite the poor visibility, the soft snow and the enforced halts, by the time they camped that evening, the party had covered a respectable 12.5 miles and Hillary felt very satisfied with progress. But the journey had only just begun. During the night the temperature dropped to -23°F and when the party tried to move off the next morning they discovered that the heavily laden sledges were frozen to the surface. When they tried to haul them free, the first tractor simply ploughed a furrow for itself without moving the sledges an inch and it took until 11.00am for the explorers to dig it out. Frustration continued to build throughout the day as the Fergusons struggled through snow which quickly became so deep that Hillary realised they must have entered a zone known as the 'windless bight', where the winds are deflected away from the surface of the ice, allowing the snow to lie completely undisturbed, sometimes for years. During their crossing of the bight, Wilson's party had encountered temperatures so low that the friction of their sledge runners had failed to melt the snow, generating such a drag on the sledges that the three men had been forced to resort to the depressing expedient of relaying their loads. On one agonising day they managed to cover only 1.5 miles after eight hours of backbreaking labour. Now, despite his initially high hopes and the tractors' 28 horsepower, Hillary, too, began to feel 'at times that it might prove too much for us.'[494]

After a long, cold and tiring day, they camped having covered another 12.5 miles – 'not much perhaps,' Hillary admitted, 'but we were pleasantly surprised that we'd been able to move at all in these conditions.'[495] The party spent an anxious night but the following day the soft snow quickly gave way to a much firmer surface, providing the tractors with such grip that they were soon tearing across the ice at a heady 6mph. 'We thundered on in great style for several hours,' enthused Hillary, 'until we came to where the barrier pressure ridges almost abutted on the slopes of Erebus … We climbed up and up along steep icy slopes and finally clawed our way onto an icy basin about a thousand feet above the barrier.'[496] Wilson's party had spent days wending its way through a complex field of crevasses in this area, but the tractor party encountered no real obstacles and closed upon Cape Crozier with surprising ease. By the time they pitched their tents at the foot of a prominent hill called the Knoll, Hillary and his companions had covered another 23 miles and were now 48 miles from Pram Point.

Close under the Knoll the cliffs of Cape Crozier fall precipitously 800 feet down to the Ross Sea below while, to the east, the 200-foot face of the Barrier comes into violent collision with the rocky coastline of Ross Island. The Barrier moves against the land at a rate of up to 1 mile per year, exerting colossal pressure on the compacted ice and forcing it up into huge contorted pressure ridges. The juxtaposition of mountains, sea and ice makes for spectacular scenery, as Cherry-Garrard described:

> The view from eight hundred feet up the mountain was magnificent … To the east a great field of pressure ridges below, looking in the moonlight as if giants had been ploughing with

ploughs which made furrows fifty or sixty feet deep: these ran right up to the Barrier edge, and beyond was the frozen Ross Sea, lying flat, white and peaceful as though things such as blizzards were unknown. To the north and north-east, the Knoll. Behind us Mount Terror on which we stood, and over all the grey limitless Barrier seemed to cast a spell of cold immensity, vague, ponderous, a breeding-place of wind and drift and darkness. God! What a place!'[497]

Somewhere in this tortured landscape, Hillary hoped to find the remains of the stone hut which Wilson, Bowers and Cherry-Garrard had built and where, 46 years earlier, they had deposited the various items of equipment they could dispense with on their return journey to Cape Evans.

After a blustery night, the four explorers emerged from their tents into a sunlit but cold morning to begin their search. With the mercury hovering around -20°F, they spent more than four hours searching an area of 2 square miles for any sign of Wilson's hut before Hillary almost literally stumbled upon it, a mere 500 yards south of their own campsite. 'I had reached the top of a little bump in the ridge when my eye caught sight of something unusual in the saddle beyond – it was a sledge, thrusting up above some low rock walls ... It was the hut all right – four rock walls half filled with snow and ice, and the sledge peeping over the top with its wood polished white by 45 years of this rigorous climate.'[498] No more than 2 feet high, the walls still held a ring of frayed, green canvas – all that remained of the sheet of Willesden tent material that had formed the roof of the hut while the 9-foot sledge, in a remarkable state of preservation and with its lashings still intact, had served as a ridge beam. Further excavations over the course of the next day brought to light nearly 100 separate artefacts, ranging from a tin of salt and a tea towel to three rolls of Kodak film – 'To be developed before May 1st, 1911' – and six thermometers, which had been faithfully recording the extreme temperatures of Cape Crozier for nearly half a century. All in all, as Helm and Miller later acknowledged, the finds constituted 'the most spectacular discovery of an historical nature to be made in the Antarctic for many years'[499] and practically guaranteed global press coverage for the expedition.

On 23 March Hillary decided to trace the route followed by Wilson and his companions down the precipitous slopes of Cape Crozier to examine the penguin rookery at its base. In July 1911, the climb had been arduous in the extreme, with the 'three crystallized ragamuffins'[500] alternately scrambling across moraine, floundering from one crevasse to the next and quite literally tunnelling through pressure ridges before they reached the colony. The prize for their courage and determination was, in Cherry-Garrard's words, to witness 'a marvel of the natural world ... the first and only men who had ever done so.'[501] For Hillary and his team, the reward must lie in the safe completion of the descent, as the colony would now be devoid of life. But they would be denied even that satisfaction. In the 46 years since it had first been visited, the Barrier edge and its associated pressure ridges had moved several miles further north, so their predecessors' route was impossible to follow. Hillary therefore decided to seek a path down the cliffs to the north of the Knoll – but without success: 'although I have no doubt that a route could be made down an ice rib close under the Knoll by using a few ice pitons, we had neither the time nor the inclination to attempt it.'[502]

Nothing now remained to keep the party at Cape Crozier and the next day they turned towards Pram Point, which they reached at 4.00am on 25 March, completing the entire return journey in an astonishing 15 hours. Despite the tractors' difficulty in negotiating areas of soft snow and the party's failure to reach the penguin rookery, the expedition could be counted a success. Most important of all, it had proved that the vehicles could haul heavily laden sledges over a range of surfaces in very low temperatures. 'We consumed 54 gallons for the 95 miles giving an average of 1¾ miles per gallon,' Hillary wrote on his return. '*Not good* but not too bad considering the frightfully soft going. We have a good team in Murray, Jim, Peter and myself.'[503] Buoyed up by this achievement, just a few days later he admitted to his diary that, with the vehicles' capabilities now effectively proved, he would 'if possible get two tractors to the Pole.'[504]

With their base built and fully operational and with all Hillary's objectives met so far as surveys and vehicle tests were concerned, the members of the Ross Sea Party could now begin to settle properly into their winter quarters. Douglas McKenzie, a Christchurch-based journalist, described the base as he saw it later in 1957; it possessed, he thought,

> ... something of the intimacy of a country general store. A kettle sang incessantly on an oil-burning stove; stamp sales were likely to be dealt with on one of the tables at any time; and the endless clicking of a Morse key from an adjoining room, and its answering chirps, were the vocal touches of the telegraph side of the business. Men off duty wandered in to saw a slice of bread from the loaf always sitting on the sideboard and to make toast to go with cocoa, instant coffee, or a pot of tea. Dressed in the usual fantastic range of polar clothing they sat at chairs to loll an elbow on a table and yarn, or they leafed through magazines, or put some discs on the record changer.[505]

In the opinion of Brooke, who could draw direct comparisons with his previous expedition, 'the facilities were fine, vastly better than what we had in Greenland.'[506] Perhaps the quality of the design was nowhere more apparent than in the degree of privacy it allowed the explorers. On all Heroic Era expeditions only the leader enjoyed the luxury of his own room; in contrast, every member of the Ross Sea Party benefited from a private, if tiny, cubicle, complete with bunk and desk – 'a fabulous bonus'[507] in Gerard's opinion. Excluding the bunk, each cubicle measured only 8 feet long by 33 inches wide but their existence meant that everyone could escape to his own sanctum in order to sleep, read or write in comparative peace. And, inevitably, even among the most gregarious, escape sometimes proved essential.

Although Brooke believed that the 'atmosphere was fine', he recognised that from the very beginning clear divisions existed within the Ross Sea Party. Employed as an expert dog-driver on an expedition which had begun to demonstrate a growing predilection for the use of mechanised transport, he was

particularly aware that the expeditionaries fell into two distinct camps: the dog-sledging champions and those in favour
of modern technology. 'I don't think it divided people in
their friendships,' he mused, 'but it certainly divided them,
I suppose, in their loyalties.'[508] For some, it also grated that
despite the long and honourable history of dog sledging at
the poles, they and their teams were looked upon increasingly
as 'back up' rather than as the preferred means by which to
explore. Marsh, in particular, already nettled by Hillary's clear
preference for the tractors, was horrified by the growing
rumours that they might even be driven as far as the Pole. 'Two
dog-teams and two men, that's all it would take, Bernie!' he
exclaimed to Gunn, 'What in God's name would be the point
of tractors?'[509]

Far more likely to generate discord, however, was the
potential for the explorers to split into camps for and against
Hillary himself. During the expedition's early days, Hillary's
preoccupation with the completion of the initial route surveys
and his resulting decision to spend much of his time either on
the *Endeavour* or at Hut Point, had made him a remote figure
to some of the explorers. Many, indeed, had come to accept
Miller as their leader in all but name. Now that they were all
gathered under one roof with Hillary once again at their head,
the differences between his old-school style of command and
Miller's more empathetic approach became apparent – and the
changes were not to everyone's liking.

The potential for conflict had first surfaced around the time
that the *Endeavour* prepared to sail for New Zealand in the last
week of February. In traditional fashion, Kirkwood had issued
invitations to a valedictory party on board but the captain had
made himself so unpopular that few among the expeditionaries
felt inclined to grace his wardroom with their presence – much
to Hillary's disgust. He wrote on the 21st:

At lunchtime I asked who was coming down to the ship to see
the chaps off. Only Wally Tarr put up his hand. I was *livid* and
therefore told them off a treat and advised them to all get ready

as they were all going down ... we had our niggles with the
Endeavour but we had a great deal of help.[510]

In the days preceding the altercation, Hillary had acknowledged
that the mad rush to complete the base had left everyone 'pretty
tired' and this may have made him unusually short-tempered and
his men unusually sensitive. Whatever the cause, however, while
Hillary believed that everyone 'had a thoroughly good time'[511] on
board the *Endeavour*, according to Gunn, the incident very nearly
resulted in open rebellion and only Marsh's diplomacy prevented
a damaging confrontation.

These differences were further reinforced by Hillary's decision
to impose what some perceived to be military-style discipline.
Vern Gerard asked rhetorically:

Was Scott Base a military establishment or a university field
station? It was BOTH, and there was some conflict because
different people saw it differently. The Hillary contingent ...
thought of Scott Base as a military outfit. The IGY people
thought of it mostly as a university field station.[512]

Although the scientists, in particular, were far from enthusiastic
about Hillary's penchant for military discipline, they accepted
some of its manifestations with a wry smile – such as his decision
to hold formal dinners once a week. 'Perhaps someone had been
reading *Voyage of the Discovery*,' wrote an amused Gunn, 'because
the same rules applied, one had to appeal to the President of
the Mess for permission to speak or tell a tale, no bets or use
of reference books allowed etc.'[513] But when the rules expanded
to include censorship of outgoing communications, amusement
very quickly gave way to anger – much of it being directed at
Gawn and Mulgrew, the wireless operators, 'who effectively
became the "boss pair" when Hillary or Miller were out exploring.'[514] Fortunately, the two men who might have served as a
focus for any anti-Hillary feeling would not allow such damaging
polarisation. Referring to the *Endeavour* argument, Gunn asserted
that Marsh

... was far too good and experienced an Expedition man to
cause an irrevocable rift, much as Sir E's manners or rather
lack of them, grated ... Good manners are the lubricant of
any society and it was not the last time Marsh employed his
native breeding, tact and wit to smooth over a rough spot in
the expedition.[515]

His comments could just as easily have been applied to Miller.

Whatever the atmosphere around the Ross Sea Party's mess
table, at least the expedition's food seldom gave cause for complaint. An employee of the Wildlife Division of New Zealand's
Internal Affairs Department and, until recently, a full-time
researcher into the life and habits of the opossum, Selwyn
Bucknell had taken the Army Cookery School's lessons very
much to heart. He excelled in the galley and the culinary gaffes
common to most expeditions were limited to Sundays, when
'Buck' took his rest and passed his ladle to one of the other
explorers. Brooke thought the food 'vastly better than we had
in Greenland ... We were supplied with lots of good meat and a
great big hole was dug in a snowdrift bank not far from the hut
which formed a natural refrigerator and so we kept all sorts of
things ... there was also quite a lot of booze if you wanted it.'[516]
The expedition could not boast a dedicated 'gashman', however,
and this role was undertaken in traditional fashion according to a
weekly rota.

Over the course of the previous weeks, the sun had been
sinking, inch by inch, behind the range of ancient volcanic
cones stretching from Mount Erebus to Cape Armitage and, on
14 April, it finally slid from view altogether. Now the explorers
must settle down to the long winter and to the sometimes mundane and largely static routine necessitated by the months of
darkness. Perhaps of all the members of the Ross Sea Party, the
scientists pursued the most carefully regimented programme.
As part of the International Geophysical Year, the team at Pram
Point would be focusing on investigations into meteorology
and related phenomena of the upper atmosphere including
aurorae, magnetic disturbances and ionospheric variations. In

addition, three seismometers recorded earthquake activity and a pulse transmitter registered radio propagation, while other equipment monitored solar radiation and tidal patterns beneath the sea ice. The International Geophysical Year would not start officially until 1 July but by 1 April a full series of observations was underway.

Although Gunn clearly exaggerated when he wrote of the winter that 'as far as science and exploring was concerned, our time was largely wasted,'[517] the scientists did encounter a number of obstacles which limited their effectiveness. As Gerard had anticipated, the proximity of Mount Erebus generated significant anomalies that interfered with magnetic observations and made the construction of a special hut from non-magnetic materials something of a joke. In addition, the all-sky camera froze solid, thereby curtailing the expedition's record of auroral displays. In Claydon's opinion, however, 'They never approached the spectacular beauty of the Auroras seen from New Zealand,'[518] so perhaps the loss was not very severe.

An additional problem for the scientists was the equal division of the duties of gashman and night watchman, with no allowance being made for the rigours of the scientific schedule. As a result, lack of sleep became a major problem for the scientists as they tried to meet the demands of both roles – but, as Gerard recognised, this 'just had to be endured'.[519] The scientists also had to deal with the journeys to and from their installations. 'For myself, I had to visit my magnetic (actually non-magnetic!) huts every 12 hours. This involved a trek by torchlight ... often on hands and knees if there was a bad blizzard, as was common.'[520]

Although both Gunn and Gerard would later claim that Hillary 'had little idea of what scientific work involved,'[521] Gerard acknowledged that their leader clearly appreciated the physical endurance and risks that completing observations in such a climate entailed. Recognising the danger inherent in a single individual working his way from the main hut to the scientific huts in continuous darkness, in a blizzard and with temperatures falling to -60°F, he personally erected a lifeline to minimise the risks of disorientation. Speaking of what he perceived to be Hillary's prioritisation of survey work over science, the usually acerbic Gunn also accepted that, in retrospect, 'what seemed like pure obstruction to me at the time was merely preoccupation with the crossing effort ... But I was not so patient in those days.'[522]

If, to some degree, the scientists had envied, or even resented, their companions who had undertaken exploratory work while they remained behind to build the base, some, at least, believed that the tables had now been turned. To Gerard it appeared that those not engaged in an all-consuming scientific programme such as his own must lack a meaningful purpose to their existence: 'I'm still not sure what Hillary and the other non-scientists like Ellis, Bates, Ayres, Brooke, Douglas were actually expected to do in winter.'[523] In reality, most of the non-scientists had ample work to occupy them and the engineers, in particular, would probably have scoffed at the suggestion that time hung heavy on their hands.

So far as Brooke and Marsh were concerned, their overriding priority was to complete the training of the dog teams. At its outset, the Ross Sea Party had been provided with a hotchpotch of animals, drawn from various sources. Of these, perhaps the least satisfactory were those obtained from Auckland Zoo. Despite their descent from dogs used by Admiral Byrd, Marsh considered them 'poor specimens, mentally as well as physically'.[524] At the other end of the spectrum were the animals donated by the Australian National Antarctic Research Expedition at Mawson Station. 'These dogs,' opined Marsh with perhaps just a hint of bias, 'were probably descended from FIDS stock ... They were large, powerful, and good workers, with an average weight of a little over 90 lbs.'[525] With the exception of any puppies born during the expedition, all the dogs would be left outside for the winter, as conditions in the Ross Sea area were known to be much more temperate than those at Vahsel Bay. 'The site was reasonably well sheltered and wind speeds were not generally high by Antarctic standards. The lowest temperature recorded at base was -68°F and the dogs did not appear to suffer any ill effects from this.'[526] Besides, in the doctor's expert opinion, except in the harshest conditions, 'It is preferable to keep dogs outside if possible; they become hardier and can better withstand the rigours of sledging.'[527]

The training of three teams had begun at Mount Cook and been perfected during the recent reconnaissance expeditions. The rest of the dogs, enough to make up a further three teams, were still completely raw and every opportunity had to be taken to teach them how to pull in a co-ordinated fashion – usually on runs of 10 or 12 miles during the winter. Following his own initiation during the traverse of the Ross Ice Shelf, Miller now championed dog sledging with the passion of a convert and even temperatures in the minus twenties and the ever-present danger of frostbite did nothing to dampen his enthusiasm. 'The joy of being a dog driver,' he wrote after one run, 'and of having a team of one's own is that of being able to show them the affection one might show one's children at home. This helps a lot to fill the void of home and family and loved ones.'[528]

While the great expanse of the Ross Ice Shelf echoed to the sound of the dogs and to the shouted commands of their drivers, back at base the RNZAF contingent also remained highly active. Throughout the autumn Claydon and Cranfield had continued to fly in both the Beaver and the Auster, the most significant flight being a reconnaissance of the newly discovered dry valleys between the Wright and Debenham glaciers on 21 March. It had always been assumed that with the arrival of winter both aircraft would be dismantled, with wings, propellers, undercarriage and tailplanes removed. Once in the field, however, it rapidly became clear that such extensive work would be impracticable. 'The extreme cold,' wrote Claydon, 'made working conditions almost impossible at times and it was quite obvious that if major dismantling work took place in the Autumn, it would be a very difficult task to re-assemble the aircraft in the colder temperatures of early Spring.'[529] As a result, only the wings of the Beaver were removed before the machine was towed into a shallow depression close to Scott Base, where it was tied down with a multitude of cables, before being left to be buried by the drift. The Auster was also bound down like Gulliver but then left completely intact and conditions proved so benign that it continued to be flown throughout the winter, albeit within a very limited compass.

The vehicle garage, too, had become, according to Hillary, 'a scene of extreme activity; of varying optimism and depression depending on our progress with preparations.'[530] As well as overhauling three Fergusons and a Weasel, Ellis and Bates constructed roll-bars to protect the tractor drivers in the event of their vehicles overturning; they sought to improve the draught-proofing of the homemade cabs; and spent long hours trying to improve the vehicle tracks and the tracking, to ensure maximum performance. In case these activities failed to keep them fully occupied, Hillary set them an additional task: the construction of a caravan. On the return journey from Cape Crozier, he had begun to appreciate just how uncomfortable tractor travel might become in the wilds of the Polar Plateau. For the drivers, partly protected from the wind by the canvas cabs and benefiting from at least some heat from the engines, the conditions were very uncomfortable but bearable. But as Hillary explained, 'If you weren't driving there was nothing to do except sit on a sledge. When you became too miserable you jumped off and ran alongside the tractors for a while in your cumbersome clothes until you either warmed up or your lungs gave out.'[531] It was during one such 'rest' that he had begun to consider how the lot of the passengers might be improved. His solution was the 'caboose': a 12-foot by 4-foot box, consisting of a framework of welded piping, covered in a sheath of plywood and an outer skin of thick canvas, the whole contraption being set on skis. Inside, he and the engineers squeezed bunks, cupboards, a cooking bench and the radio equipment. 'Despite its ludicrous resemblance to a horse-box,' wrote Hillary, 'we were very proud of it.'[532]

Inside the radio-room Gawn and Mulgrew were kept busy maintaining the planned radio schedules with New Zealand, with Shackleton Base and with the spontaneous effusions of enthusiastic radio hams across the globe. In addition, Gawn conducted regular classes in transmitting and receiving Morse, so that, by the end of the winter, all the members of the field teams became more or less adept. Miller, meanwhile, when not out with his dog team, drilled his companions in navigation and surveying and spent hours wrestling with the innumerable press releases and articles demanded by the world's media. Struggling to identify fresh subjects for so many articles, he sometimes found himself on very unfamiliar ground. 'I wrote a press article this morning on aurora and aurora-observing by Trevor Hatherton. This was worse than writing science fiction and read like it.'[533] He also found his companions' insistence on reading and criticising his work exasperating, especially since they showed so little inclination to shoulder any of the burden themselves. 'Damn them,' he exploded on one occasion, '– do they think it is easy to dish out stuff day after day. I can tell you it isn't.'[534]

Like most Heroic Era leaders, Fuchs believed that work and organised recreation were essential to the maintenance of harmony throughout the winter months. At Scott Base, a somewhat more relaxed philosophy prevailed, but some organisation of leisure still continued. In particular, Miller initiated a series of after-dinner lectures to be delivered by each of the explorers in turn. Ranging from his own 'Bull Fighting in Mexico' to Tarr's 'Development of Gas Turbine Engines', the talks were as diverse as the backgrounds and experience of the explorers themselves and the only rule of thumb 'was to avoid anything to do with the Antarctic and why we were there.'[535] Rather less demanding for those involved were the regular trips to the neighbouring American base, to visit the dentist, to watch films like *Captain's Paradise* and *The Man in the White Suit*, to play bridge and to socialise with a different crowd of men. But these gatherings did not appeal to everyone. 'I, personally, wasn't particularly interested in going there,' Brooke remembered, 'because I felt it was so out of keeping and most of the people there didn't want to be there.'[536] And even Hillary, who saw a great deal of the Americans and found them both hospitable and very likeable, thought that 'despite all this there is something about Hut Point that is distinctly depressing.'[537]

Another facility intended to reduce the feelings of isolation was the radio telephone. This meant that the explorers could regularly speak with friends and family, usually for only 4s 6d for a three-minute call. The pleasure was not unalloyed, however. Just like Goldsmith and Blaiklock in October 1956, some members of the expedition found that easy communications actually served to emphasise the gulf, both geographic and emotional, separating them from those at home. Brooke certainly felt uncomfortable with it: 'I know the others took a lot of advantage. I think I spoke, I don't know, once or twice at the most – I couldn't think what on earth I could say!'[538] Miller, meanwhile, found that the immediacy of the medium removed the ability to filter emotions: 'Fear I may have given a doleful account of life,' he wrote after one call to his wife and children, '– but that is how toll calls go.'[539] In contrast, Hillary entertained no such reservations and his calls to his wife, Louise, became so frequent that he began to fear 'wasting a packet of money on phone calls'.[540] Unfortunately, he would soon discover that, as well as providing a very welcome link with his loved ones, the radio telephone could also facilitate bureaucratic interference in the affairs of the expedition.

Since the completion of the autumn reconnaissance trips, Hillary's main preoccupation had been the planning of the spring and summer journeys – but in early April he received a telephone call that threw those plans into complete disarray. As early as July 1955, he had advised Helm that 'subject to the limitations of finance and shipping we should plan on the basis that … if organisation and time permits, or an emergency occurs, the Party could travel out as far as the South Pole.'[541] Thereafter, the Pole had continued to feature in his plans although, prior to the completion of the expedition to Cape Crozier, uncertainty regarding the Fergusons' capability meant that he considered any polar journey was more likely to be by dog sledge than by tractor.[542] Crucially, however, Hillary had never formally agreed the Pole as an objective with the Ross Sea Committee, which remained focused solely on the depot-laying intended to support Fuchs's crossing. While the Committee was not opposed to the completion of a limited additional programme of exploration and scientific investigation, any such activities must be compatible with, and subsidiary to, the depot-laying; in addition, they must not risk over-stretching the expedition's resources or generate conflict with the TAE's Management Committee in London or with Fuchs.

By the beginning of April – and perhaps providing evidence that the censorship of outgoing communications was not as effective as some assumed – rumours regarding Hillary's ambitions had begun to fly and, on the evening of the 8th, he found himself speaking, reluctantly, to the Honourable Charles Bowden, the Committee's chairman. 'He expressed the Ross Sea Committee's concern at the likelihood of my taking a party to the Pole,' Hillary wrote that evening, 'and spoiling Bunny's effort. Damned if I know!!!'[543] In a tense exchange, Bowden interrogated Hillary regarding his plans. In particular, he asked whether Hillary had consulted Fuchs and the TAE's Management Committee regarding his intention to push on to the Pole. Put on the spot, Hillary was forced to admit that he had not. According to the official account of the expedition, written by Helm and Miller, it was during this conversation that Hillary promised he would consult Fuchs at the earliest opportunity and report back. In his diary and in his published account, Hillary made no reference to any such commitment. Whatever promises may have been made during the conversation, Bowden clearly remained dissatisfied and perhaps even suspicious, while for his part Hillary wrote that this exchange 'was my first real indication that I might not see eye to eye with the Executive Committee as far as my field work was concerned.'[544] Worse was to come.

Fully recognising the danger of a rupture with the Committee, Hillary reluctantly recast his plans, admitting to his diary that 'The South Pole trip seems a bit of a dead loss.'[545] According to the revised programme the fieldwork would be prosecuted by three main parties. The northern party, consisting of four men and two dog teams, would travel over the sea ice along the Victoria Land coastline, exploring the dry valleys with their river and lake systems. The party would then ascend to the Polar Plateau via the Fry Glacier; cross to the Plateau Depot; and then complete the exploration and mapping of the Skelton-Ferrar area. The western party, consisting of four tractors and five men, would follow Miller and Carlyon's route across the Ross Ice Shelf to the Skelton Depot, where they would rendezvous with the southern party of four dog teams and four men, flown out in the Beaver. Together, the two parties would climb the Skelton Glacier, following the trail blazed by Brooke's team at the end of January. At the Plateau Depot, the parties would divide: the four dog teams of the southern party heading west and then south to establish Depot 480, before splitting into two teams, the first setting off to the east to map the mountains and valleys of the Mulock, Darwin and Barne glaciers while the second continued south to establish another depot (Depot 700) at 83°S, before undertaking survey work between the Beardmore and Shackleton glaciers. The western party, meanwhile, would head west from the Plateau Depot, taking as their objective the South Geomagnetic Pole.

In prefacing his proposals to the Committee, Hillary wrote that 'After discussion with Dr Fuchs and Mr Bowden I have decided to shelve any possible plans to get a New Zealand party to the South Pole.'[546] Having spoken with Fuchs on 15 April, he also wrote 'We'll go ahead with my latest plan and stay away from the South Pole. It's the South Geomagnetic Pole for us.'[547] Taken at face value, it was an important and no doubt galling concession – but Hillary appears to have been keeping his options open. Clearly, he chose his language carefully when communicating with the Committee – advising its members that he had 'shelved' rather than permanently abandoned his polar ambitions. In addition, while he had discussed the positioning and stocking of Depot 700 with Fuchs during their conversation of the 15th, he had studiously avoided any direct reference to an attempt on the Pole. Perhaps he considered that this omission would most effectively avoid an explicit and clearly articulated objection from that quarter: an objection that would serve only to bolster the Committee's position should the Pole again be discussed at some stage in the future.

Critically, when discussing the positioning of the depots, Fuchs had not revealed any nervousness or anxiety regarding the possibility of Hillary pushing farther south than originally planned. In outlining his decision to place Depot 700 at approximately 83°S, Hillary had acknowledged that the primary beneficiaries would be his own dog teams. But he had gone on to ask whether Fuchs would like any fuel stockpiling at this depot. 'Of course it would be useful,' Fuchs wrote in his diary that evening, 'but I doubt the effort being worthwhile.'[548] A few days later, when Hillary raised the subject again by telegram, Fuchs had given the matter further consideration and replied that he would 'like you to attempt placing six barrels petrol at D700 ... You ask how near Pole I want first depot; answer is D700 will do but Lat. 85 naturally an advantage.'[549] Quite unwittingly, by even suggesting that the depot might usefully be pushed farther south, Fuchs had provided Hillary with a perfect excuse – should one be required – for drawing ever closer to the Pole.

Despite the removal of the Pole as an avowed objective, Hillary's plans remained hugely ambitious – indeed, Bernie Gunn described them as 'perhaps the most comprehensive and daring plan of field activities ever proposed in the history of polar exploration.'[550] Confident that he had now appeased the Committee, Hillary concluded his proposal by claiming that 'Even modest success in all of these projects will provide a wealth of information about these comparatively unknown areas and provide the material for extensive maps.'[551] To his immense chagrin, the Committee agreed that the plans were ambitious – far too ambitious, in fact. In a long telegram of 9 May, Bowden wrote that, while it supported the completion of a reasonable programme of survey work which it believed would accord with the 'best Antarctic traditions', the Committee also felt

... that the programme was too ambitious and might stultify or prejudicially affect the primary and paramount objective of the New Zealand Party, namely the laying of depots and assisting the crossing party ... The main objection is to the

proposed northern and western parties, whose work, interesting or valuable as it might be, is nevertheless somewhat out of
our immediate territory and has nothing to do with the Trans-
Antarctic Expedition with which we are joined and our funds
are pooled.[552]

Having already compromised his plans, at least in his own eyes,
Hillary was furious – and he made no attempt to conceal his
frustration from his men. 'Sir E did not exactly roar with rage,'
observed Gunn, 'but with a face like thunder he stamped out and
pinned the offending document to the wall with a blow of the
fist!'[553] In his diary, Hillary recorded:

> Received a long cable from Bowden tonight squashing the
> northern and western parties in no uncertain terms. A most
> annoying and inaccurate document ... All I'm interested in
> doing is getting the fuel I want. I'll make my own plans for
> what we do with it.[554]

Fuming, he immediately drafted a tart reply, which he then asked
Miller to vet, prior to despatch. Although they did not always see
eye to eye, the freedom to conduct an extensive programme of
exploration and surveying lay close to both men's hearts and on
this occasion, instead of tempering his leader's wrath Miller actually 'suggested some pepping up in one or two places'.[555]

'I have never suffered direction easily,'[556] Hillary later admitted
and, from its outset, the final, uncompromising wording of his
reply to the Ross Sea Committee left its members in no doubt as
to his anger at their interference:

> Your cable was something of a surprise and a disappointment
> with its strong emphasis on safety which I would suggest has
> never been a part of 'best Antarctic traditions'... I would sug-
> gest that as long as the base is maintained as an effective going
> concern that decisions on the extent of the field operations we
> are capable of handling should be left by the Committee to the

expedition leader and his senior officers who have at least a first hand knowledge of the problems. Our party is particularly strong in capable and experienced field personnel and I do not intend to have them wasting their time sitting at depots or at base.[557]

He then went on to outline a number of minor changes he had decided to make to his plans. Specifically, the southern party would not divide until after Depot 700 had been established. In addition, in case the Beaver was rendered *hors de combat* before or during the stocking of depots 480 and 700, sufficient fuel would be flown to the Plateau Depot to enable the western tractor party to complete the aeroplane's work. Hillary was at pains to point out, however, that these alterations were the result of discussions with his officers and that they were not influenced by the Committee's remonstrance of 9 May. The implications were clear: while the Ross Sea Committee was at liberty to express its opinions – at a distance of 2000 miles from the scene of the action, unless it imposed the extreme sanction of removing Hillary from command it had little or no power to intervene. And, if matters did come to a head, for once Hillary could count on the full backing of the entire expedition – every one of whom resented the Committee's attempt to interfere in their affairs. Even Gunn afterwards wrote, 'We used to refer to him with a touch of sarcasm as "Our Leader", (considering, in our juvenile arrogance, that we needed little leading), but a real leader is there to make difficult decisions and stand by them, and by doing so he won our respect and support.'[558]

For nearly two weeks the Committee mulled over its reply. Hillary had conceded the polar journey; were the Committee to push for further concessions, it could face an extremely embarrassing and, thanks to the efficacy of modern communications, extremely public rift with the expedition's leader in the field. Clearly, the appointment of a world-famous figurehead capable of raising the expedition's profile brought disadvantages as well as benefits. Finally, on 22 May, Bowden articulated the Committee's decision to swallow its collective pride. The Committee, he wrote, 'has no wish to deny to you the functions of leadership and it should not be thought that our policy is merely safety first, but our views are based on recognition that as your main duty and purpose is first to establish Depots 480 and 700 and second to stand ready to make further advances south if request made by Fuchs it was deemed inadvisable to stretch out too far.'[559] He went on to remove the Committee's objections to the plans for the southern and western parties. So far as the northern party was concerned, Bowden agreed that Hillary might go ahead and plan the expedition along the lines indicated. His one caveat was that 'any decision or authorisation must be deferred until much more is known about the difficulties likely to be encountered and the prospect of success on the southern thrust.'[560] Both Hillary and Bowden knew that the Committee had been forced into an embarrassing climb down. Round one, in the form of a decision on the polar journey, had gone to the Committee, but Hillary had very definitely won round two. And there, for the time being, matters would have to rest: the deciding round would be fought amid the snow and ice of the Polar Plateau in the summer.

Throughout May, the squalls inside the Ross Sea Party's hut were matched by increasingly boisterous conditions outside. On 14 May, the first really severe blizzard struck the base: for several days the wind speed seldom fell below 40mph and sheets of drift snow reduced visibility to practically zero. 'Could not see more than two yards,' wrote Miller after venturing outside to feed the dogs, '– even light of a torch extinguished at 2 yards.'[561] Hillary, meanwhile, was becoming increasingly anxious about the stability of the buildings themselves. 'Very concerned about the roofs on the two New Zealand built generator huts. They are flapping about in a very alarming manner rising a good two inches in the middle. Let's hope they hold!'[562] Fearing that the roofs might be blown off altogether, he, Miller and others took turns to check and tighten the guy wires and, in the first decent lull, to fabricate reinforced trusses, to be held in place by wire cables. The arrival of the blizzard also brought a rise in the temperature to +11°F; the huts became increasingly muggy and uncomfortable and any man returning from outside covered in drift snow found that his clothes swiftly became sodden. Predictably, the billowing clouds of flying snow ferreted out every chink in the fabric of the walls and roofs and the covered way, in particular, began to fill with drift.

High winds and thick drift continued to dominate for the next few weeks until, on 15 June, another severe blizzard set in. Incarcerated, the men could only listen to the shaking and juddering of the huts as they took the full force of the gale, which occasionally gusted at over 90mph. Sometimes, the banshee-like wailing would be interrupted by a loud crash as a box or crate bounced from the hut's walls, causing the explorers to pause in their work to glance up at the wind speed indicator. When the blizzard finally began to die down, Brooke and Carlyon pushed their way outside, anxious to feed the dogs and check their condition. They found the landscape transformed. Huge drifts had formed in the lee of every hut and every loose item had either been blown away or become the nucleus of a secondary drift of its own. The dogs, however, though hungry, were still in good condition and would have leapt for joy at the sight of their masters, had the wire span to which their chains were attached not been buried beneath 2 feet of hard compacted snow.

In describing the blizzard, Claydon wrote that the 'worry of having a light aircraft exposed to the elements on occasions such as this made the days of waiting for a clearance an agony of suspense.'[563] When he, Cranfield and Tarr finally managed to make their way to the Auster they found it so deeply buried that only the tip of its propeller could be seen. Mercifully, though, it was still in position and still the right way up. Over the next week, the RNZAF contingent, ably supported by the rest of the expedition, spent long days at what Miller called 'the business end of a spade or shovel',[564] digging the machine free before dragging it out of its hole and onto the surface. 'Working conditions were wretched at this time,' reported Claydon, 'as a moderate blizzard was blowing and although the hole gave some shelter, drift was pouring like sand down the sides of the huge hole.'[565] By the time the aeroplane had been released it was a very sorry sight, with its fabric skin torn by the shovels of over-enthusiastic diggers. But, in spite of appearances, Tarr felt confident that he could soon return the battered Auster to flying trim. Looking back on a week of backbreaking and often excruciatingly uncomfortable labour, with tongue firmly in cheek, Claydon described it as 'an interesting exercise', which, in his opinion, 'helped to while away the long winter night, and at the same time gave plenty of exercise.'[566]

By the time Midwinter's Day arrived on 21 June, everyone felt that they had more than earned the superb meal prepared by Bucknell and served by the white-jacketed Hatherton and Marsh. It had been agreed that to mark the event the usual polar clothing should be eschewed and, instead, everyone should attempt an unaccustomed formality of dress. Over the previous days, and in the privacy of their cubicles, the explorers had rummaged through bags and trunks to drag out jackets, shirts and even ties that had not seen the light of day since the *Endeavour* sailed from New Zealand six months before. When these items were 'indignantly and protestingly stretched over waistlines and hips more demanding than of yore',[567] the explorers began to realise just how sedentary their lives had been during the winter months. Innumerable messages of congratulation flooded in from all quarters of the globe and greetings with Shackleton Base were exchanged by radio. With the bottles circulating freely, the Midwinter dinner became ever more boisterous and Miller admitted that, after the meal, 'the Highland dancing imported by Richard Brooke via Greenland was a little less orderly than usual.'[568] Finally, basing their actions upon the dubious assertion that Midwinter would fall at precisely 4.00am, in the early hours of the morning the entire party stumbled into the inky blackness to shout their encouragement to the sun as it began the long slow climb from its maximum declination. 'Next day,' wrote Miller, 'Scott was a much subdued place and the mess room was only by midday beginning to welcome signs of normal activity.'[569]

Despite the explorers' exhortations, the sun remained hidden beneath the horizon for another two months, adding insult to injury by finally appearing a full three days later than predicted by the almanac. Right up until 21 August the sky remained dark, with the thermometer indicating 65 degrees of frost and a 40mph wind hurling newly fallen snow into the eyes of anyone fool-hardy enough to venture outdoors. And then, as if by a miracle, the clouds began gradually to roll back and by the late morning of the 23rd the usually monochrome faces of the Western Mountains glowed a ruddy pink while the sea ice beyond Cape Armitage flickered as though it was alight.

'The simple joy of seeing the sun after an absence of five months is something that cannot easily be described,'[570] wrote Claydon with real feeling – and at 12,000 feet above Cape Royds it was the pilots who could best appreciate the transfiguration of the Antarctic landscape. The whole of Ross Island, McMurdo Sound and the coastline of Victoria Land, from Mt Discovery in the south to beyond Granite Harbour in the north, was transformed: details long concealed now being picked out in reds, amber and deep shadow. On the ground, the sledgers worked with renewed energy, dismantling and re-lashing sledges, reinforcing tents and packing rations – their eyes constantly, albeit often unconsciously, turning northwards to observe the gathering power of the sun as it climbed ever higher. As the light strengthened, the dog-teams rambled farther and farther across the sea ice towards a horizon which grew more distinct with every passing day. Writing of driving his team across the sea ice during the winter, Marsh had observed: 'When we travelled into the moonlight from shadow we always had a psychological feeling of warmth.'[571] For the time being, the sun's heat remained hardly less illusory than that of the moon, but its brightness and the realisation that the winter darkness had begun its slow retreat filled every member of the Ross Sea Party with optimism. 'The Antarctic orchestra is warming up after the long winter of apparent inactivity;' enthused Miller, 'each day with its increasing hours of sunlight brings a quickening of the tempo of outdoor activity.'[572]

As the Antarctic landscape revealed itself, the men's minds also began to expand beyond the limited compass of Scott Base and Hut Point. Now they could think of the spring and summer journeys not as distant prospects but as imminent realities. According to the programme agreed with the Ross Sea Committee, after a series of short trial expeditions, Hillary's main field teams would push out to explore the Victoria Land coastline, to force a route to the Magnetic Pole and, most importantly of all, to drive south-wards to establish depots as far as 85°S. Any decision to push farther south would be entirely dependent upon surface conditions and upon the performance of the Ross Sea Party's men, animals and vehicles. It would also hinge, of course, upon Hillary's appetite for direct and potentially damaging conflict: with the Ross Sea Committee, with the TAE Management Committee in London – and with Fuchs, 2000 miles away across the continent.

The latest in a long line of trans–Antarctic aspirants: Vivian Fuchs in the TAE offices in Victoria Street, London, 1955. The TAE's headquarters were just a stone's throw from Scott's *Terra Nova* Expedition's offices.

The overloaded m.v. *Theron* prepares to sail from Millwall Docks on 14 November 1955. The expedition's stores and equipment were stowed in the sealer's three insulated holds capable of storing 30,000 seal carcasses.

The explorers attempt to dig the *Theron* free of the pack ice of the Weddell Sea in January 1956. According to the BP photographer, Derek Williams, 'this was a time when the entire expedition looked as if it was going to founder.'

Unloading the *Theron* at Vahsel Bay, January 1956. To many of those involved the process seemed chaotic.

The Advance Party photographed from the deck of the retreating *Theron*, 7 February 1956. Fuchs wrote, 'I'm afraid they have an enormous task ahead of them.'

Shackleton Base under construction. Severe weather severely delayed progress and the Advance Party spent the entire winter living in tents and in the vehicle crate to the right of the picture. Theirs was the first expedition to over-winter under canvas at such high latitudes.

The Advance Party in their crate. From left to right: Homard, Goldsmith, Jeffries, Stewart, Williams, Blaiklock, Lenton and La Grange. All but Goldsmith, Stewart and Jeffries would eventually cross the continent.

Ken Blaiklock dog sledging near Vahsel Bay, November 1956. Blaiklock would become the last man to drive dogs to the South Pole – and the first since Amundsen.

Sir Edmund Hillary at Malte Brun Hut in 1956. He later admitted that his 'ideas of the Antarctic were hazy in the extreme'.

Crash landing on the Tasman Glacier. Fortunately, doubts about the untested combination of wheels and skis on the Auster had persuaded John Claydon to fly with the minimum of fuel.

Harry Ayres and George Marsh training dogs with a broken-down car chassis at Mount Cook in 1956. The effectiveness of the car's steering wheel was highly questionable.

HMNZS *Endeavour* prepares to sail for the Ross Sea, 21 December 1956. Hillary stands above the 'R' of Endeavour; to his right is Trevor Hatherton, leader of the IGY scientists.

Unloading dog teams and sledges from the *Endeavour*, January 1957. The wingless Auster stands on the ship's stern.

Fuchs in his office at Shackleton Base, perhaps consciously aping the famous photograph of Captain Scott taken during the *Terra Nova* Expedition of 1910–13.

Planning for the establishment of South Ice, January 1957. Foreground table, left to right: Fuchs, Lewis, Blaiklock, Stephenson (?) and Lister. Background table: Haslop, David Pratt and Stratton.

South Ice: Lister, Blaiklock and Stephenson spent over six lonely months, from 25 March to 7 October 1957, in this tiny buried hut.

Midwinter's Day celebrations at Shackleton Base, 21 June 1957. Left to right: Stratton, Homard, Weston, Lenton, La Grange, Lewis, Fuchs, Rogers (?), Geoff Pratt (?), David Pratt, Haslop, Williams, Lowe.

'Taffy' Williams wearing the Integrating Motor Pneumotachograph equipment devised by Dr Allan Rogers. The experiment proved so uncomfortable that Fuchs advised Rogers and his guinea pigs not to discuss it until they could do so without coming to blows.

An exterior view of Scott Base. The buildings' revolutionary method of construction proved highly effective – but at a huge cost.

The Ross Sea Party during one of the weekly group dinners instigated by Hillary. 'Perhaps someone had been reading *Voyage of the Discovery*,' wrote an amused Bernie Gunn.

Huskies on board the Ross Sea Party's Beaver aircraft, probably en route to the Skelton Depot, January 1957.

Cutting seal meat for the dogs at Scott Base during the winter of 1957. Even the blubber became rock-hard and sections of the sawn seals would be split with an axe, like logs.

Winter observations at Scott Base. The scientists considered themselves fortunate to have an all-consuming occupation during the long, dark winter months.

Hillary's converted Ferguson farm tractors, probably during their trial journey to Cape Crozier in March 1957.

The reconnaissance party led by Richard Brooke on the Skelton Glacier, February 1957. The Western Mountains are in the background; Mount Huggins is the tallest, cloud-capped peak on the right.

En route to South Ice, 8 October to 13 November 1957. Fuchs later wrote that 'the actual problems we had to overcome were far greater than we could possibly have envisaged'.

Ferguson tractor and Hillary's homemade caravan – 'the caboose' – at Hut Point.

The main journey: en route to South Ice, November–December 1957; Canadian-built Muskeg tractor in the foreground.

Crevasse trouble: a Tucker Sno-cat stranded after the collapse of a snow-bridge. Note the reinforced aluminium bridging spans inserted beneath the vehicle's pontoons.

Another dangerous vehicle recovery. The increased power of the sun rendered the crevasse fields doubly dangerous and left even the sure-footed Sno-cats vulnerable.

Fuchs and Hillary at the South Pole, 19/20 January 1958. In the face of growing criticism of his actions, Hillary had been reluctant to fly back for the meeting.

Blizzard during the descent of the Skelton Glacier, February 1958.

Bob Miller and George Marsh return to Scott Base, 23 February 1958. Both were highly critical of Hillary's 'polar dash', believing it to be a stunt that compromised the expedition's more valuable fieldwork.

Journey's end: the Crossing Party at Scott Base, 2 March 1958. It had taken 99 days to complete what Shackleton called 'the last great polar journey that can be made.'

10

Crevasse!

At Shackleton, the repeated delays caused by poor weather and the mercy flight to Halley Bay had lent a distinctly hectic air to the last days before the departure of the four vehicles for South Ice. In the garage, the two engineers had worked night and day, feverishly welding, tightening and lubricating – part of them dreading and part longing for the time when Fuchs would hold up his hand and say 'enough'.

That moment had finally arrived on 2 October, the day after the rescue of Haslop and Rogers. During an evening conference, Fuchs announced that further postponements could not be tolerated, not least because more delays would place even greater pressure on the engineers by reducing the time they would have for the preparation of the second group of six vehicles. 'I also stated,' he wrote, 'that our departure date of 14 November must be adhered to … If we did not succeed in keeping to the timetable it might mean that we should remain for another winter at Scott Base!'[573] Faced with such an unappetising prospect, the engineers had reluctantly agreed that they could be ready in three days – meaning that the route-finding party would leave on 6 October. The discussion had generated another mad offensive with spanners and grease guns, but despite the engineers' best efforts, it was not until the afternoon of the 8th that all was finally ready. At 1745 that evening, Fuchs, Homard, Geoff Pratt and David Pratt swung themselves into their cabs, started the engines and set a course for the Shackleton Mountains, 200 miles away across the Filchner Ice Shelf.

Anticipating a daily average of 20 miles, Fuchs had allowed 14 days for the 270-mile journey to South Ice but by the time the reconnaissance party camped that first evening they had made only 6 miles. Despite this hesitant start and temperatures that fell to -28°F during the night, morale within the group remained high with Fuchs acknowledging that 'At least we were away from base as an organised group and looking forward instead of thinking of last minute things to do.'[574] The next morning the vehicles took a lot of starting – but the engineers had expected this, knowing that, at low temperatures, the oil would be more viscous and the engines less inclined to fire, while battery performance would also deteriorate considerably. Once started, the engines needed to be revved hard in order to reach the optimum operating temperature – a process which, in sub-zero temperatures, could take up to 20 minutes. 'We used this time to search for anti-freeze leaks,' Homard recalled, 'and in digging out the vehicles and sledges. De-mister units were put to use to clear the windscreens of the frost and ice which formed rapidly when the cab was occupied. When the engines were thoroughly warmed up the radiator doors were adjusted and the vehicles used in low gear to break out the sledges.'[575] Rather more disappointingly after so many months of maintenance and modification, mechanical problems began to reveal themselves almost the moment they left their campsite, with Fuchs's Weasel refusing to haul its load in top gear. Eventually the entire party ground to a halt while Homard and Pratt struggled to tighten the fan belt and to reconnect a dislodged distributor lead. 'What incredibly bad design these Weasels have,' grumbled Fuchs in the first of many such asides.[576]

After three miserable hours during which Fuchs and Geoff Pratt could only sit in their frigid cabs or hover ineffectually at the engineers' elbows, the convoy at last moved on, with Fuchs leading in Weasel 'Able'. Now, more than ever, the ice shelf resembled a frozen sea, its wave-like undulations rising to crests spaced about a mile apart. For the present, though, this sea remained fairly benign, its gentle rises and falls presenting much less of an obstacle than the 'choppy', jagged, close-packed sastrugi which would be encountered later. With his Weasel's engine now running smoothly and with its fan belt no longer emitting an ear-piercing squeal, Fuchs made good progress, negotiating the wave-crests and the intervening troughs with so little difficulty that he soon found that he had left the rest of the party a mile or so behind. Growing increasingly impatient after so many delays, he waited for an hour for the rest to catch up before finally unhitching the sledge towed behind his vehicle and turning back. To his consternation, he found the three vehicles stationary and their drivers in the midst of a gloomy conference.

As it climbed the last gradient, Homard's Weasel had shed an upper-track bearing-roller; caught in the moving track, the roller had then travelled round until it fouled the drive sprocket, bending the axle in the process. Less than 8 miles from Shackleton and one of only four vehicles had already been disabled. The only possible plan was for Homard to limp the Weasel back to base and there carry out the necessary repairs. 'It is a great disappointment to Roy,' wrote Fuchs, 'and he talked of catching us up! I could not allow a single vehicle to move about on its own and it is not possible for us to delay for a moment.'[577] Pratt and a disconsolate Homard worked until 11 o'clock that night, stripping down the track and completing a temporary repair to enable Homard to return to the coast. To add to Fuchs's irritations, poor atmospheric conditions had so far prevented him from relaying the news to Shackleton by radio and that night he announced that if contact could not be established he would have to escort Homard for at least the first 4 miles to ensure that he was within easy striking distance of home. This would mean the loss of yet another valuable day.

Fortunately, the next morning, as the engineers completed their repairs, John Lewis flew overhead in the Otter, en route to the Shackleton Mountains with Lowe and Stratton. Good radio contact between the aeroplane and the ground party meant that when Homard finally departed he had a guardian angel to monitor his halting progress. A few hours later, a relieved Fuchs heard

that Weasel 'Charlie' had made it back without any further incident and that Homard was already hard at work on its repair.
In the meantime, Weasels 'Able' and 'Baker' and Sno-cat 'Charlie'
had made another 12 miles towards South Ice.

The following day, 11 October, the party continued across the
rises and falls of the ice shelf, occasionally picking out the flags
planted by Blaiklock and Goldsmith during their survey the previous year. Initially they made good progress but, after the first
few miles, Fuchs found his vehicle climbing a much rougher
slope than usual and he began to suspect the presence of crevasses. 'As I neared the crest, it became suddenly apparent that I
was passing over a succession of them and there was nothing to
do but continue steadily and hope to reach firm ground at the
top.'[578] As he would later admit, at this period, neither he nor
any member of his team had the slightest idea how thick a snow
bridge must be to sustain the weight of one of the vehicles and
how narrow the margin of error might be between making a safe
crossing and plunging into a concealed crevasse. He could only
hold his breath, cross his fingers and keep going. Although he
gauged that the crevasses were 8–12 feet wide, miraculously the
bridges held firm for both the Weasels with their 2.5-ton sledges
and for Geoff Pratt's Sno-cat, with its two sledges loaded with
4 tons of fuel, dynamite and rations.

The reconnaissance party's first experience of crevasses had
ended well but by the time they camped that evening Fuchs realised that they had entered a zone literally strewn with hundreds
of similar chasms – caused by the buckling of the ice shelf as it
collided with the nearby Shackleton Mountains. The following
morning near-whiteout conditions made it impossible to recognise the telltale rippling of the surface and the party had no
choice but to await better visibility. Conditions improved later
in the afternoon and anxious to make up for lost time they set
off at a breakneck pace of up to 8mph, little short of the Weasels'
optimum cruising speed. It wasn't long, however, before the vehicles began to buck and sway as the lids of the crevasses crumbled
beneath their weight. 'This was the country which I had observed
from the air last season,' Fuchs noted, 'and which I feared would

give us so much trouble for it is virtually a complex of crevasses and holes covered with a more or less continuous carpet of drift snow. I was therefore feeling particularly pleased that we were crossing it so well until at quarter to seven we hit real trouble!'[579]

Desperate to cover as much ground as possible, Fuchs had made the mistake of pushing too far and too fast, with potentially catastrophic results. 'The visibility had been going,' he wrote that night, 'and I was muttering to myself that I really ought to stop … when my Weasel began to sink.'[580] With the vehicle already in the mouth of an invisible crevasse, the only possible course of action was to keep going and hope that the caterpillar tracks would obtain some purchase on the far lip before the snow-bridge disintegrated. Fuchs's luck held and he felt the vehicle beneath him straighten up as it climbed back out and onto the level. The sledge behind fared less well: already weakened by the passage of the Weasel, the compacted snow fell away beneath its 2.5-ton weight, leaving the sledge steeply canted over and stuck as firmly as a cork in a bottle.

'Baker' and 'Charlie' were about a quarter of a mile to the rear and as he skied towards them to call for assistance, Fuchs could see that his Weasel and sledge had broken through a number of snow-bridges. Now, to help the other vehicles through this treacherous area, he skied in front of Weasel 'Baker', waving David Pratt forward when he believed he had identified a safe route. But within minutes of starting, Pratt's Weasel suddenly slewed sideways and heeled over, its right-hand track suspended over space, as incapable of movement as Fuchs's sledge. Except for the portion which had fallen beneath the Weasel's weight, the rest of the lid held firm, leaving the chasm itself invisible and making it look as though the vehicle had driven into sinking sand. Although, in his diary, Fuchs asserted that the party's predicament resulted from a recent snowfall blanketing the surface inequalities usually associated with a heavily crevassed area, he must also have known that his determination to keep moving in such terrain and in worsening visibility was little short of foolhardy. Luck not judgement had prevented the vehicles, their precious sledges and, indeed, the drivers from disappearing down a fathomless hole in the windcrust. As a result, in the gathering darkness, he and his team must retrieve a vehicle and a heavily laden sledge. Even more worryingly, because of the forced abandonment of the trial journey in the spring, the party possessed absolutely no experience in such complicated recovery procedures.

Pratt's Weasel had fallen sideways into the crevasse, so that one set of tracks was wedged against the nearest wall while the top of the cab rested against the far edge. Having studied the problem, Fuchs and Pratt decided to attach two steel hawsers to the stricken vehicle, one to the far side of the Weasel and one to its front. They fixed the opposite end of the first hawser to the Sno-cat, and that of the second to Fuchs's Weasel, with both recovery vehicles positioned on the near side of the crevasse. Having secured the cables, thereby, in theory at least, preventing Pratt's Weasel from rolling bodily into the hole, the unfortunate engineer then had the unenviable task of crawling back into his tilted cab. At a given signal, Geoff Pratt reversed his Sno-cat, using its considerable power to haul the Weasel into an upright position but leaving the right-hand set of tracks still hanging over the now visible abyss. Fuchs then pulled its front end round, so that the forward portion of both tracks could obtain some purchase on the lip of the crevasse and, with the aid of the second Weasel, draw away from the gaping hole. At last, settling into his sleeping bag at 1.00am, Fuchs acknowledged that 'Clearly with three near catastrophes in 300 yards we have reached an area from which it will be wise to remove ourselves as carefully and quickly as possible.'[581] To facilitate that process, he decided to take advantage of the improved atmospheric conditions to call for air support.

The next day, Lewis faced the challenge of landing the Auster on a 100-yard runway spanning no fewer than eight crevasses, any one of which might have swallowed the little aeroplane whole or, at the very least, caused it to flip over as its twin had done on the Tasman Glacier. But the luck that had brought Lewis safely through the Battle of Britain stayed with him and by lunchtime both he and Homard, who now rejoined the vehicle party, were safely on the ground. After a brief explanation of their difficulties, Fuchs took to the air, anxious to reconnoitre the surface of the ice shelf ahead and, if possible, trace a route out of the zone of half-concealed crevasses. To his immense disappointment, the flight quickly revealed that no such route existed; instead it became clear that by continuing in the same direction he and his companions would soon find themselves in terrain literally riddled with holes. The explorers' only option was to turn around and follow their own tracks northwards to the 50-mile depot laid by Blaiklock and Goldsmith towards the end of 1956. From there, instead of heading due south, they must attempt to strike west or southwest in an attempt to bypass the worst of the fissured surface. It was a depressing and a perilous prospect, as Fuchs acknowledged: 'The trouble is that by travelling in that direction we shall be running almost along the line of the crevasses, a dangerous manoeuvre but one which we will have to adopt in order to break through this 20–30 mile wide belt of broken ice.'[582] If more detailed reconnaissance flights had been possible before or during the winter, he might now have benefited from more knowledge of the ground conditions. Instead, the poor flying weather after the arrival of the *Magga Dan* and the delays encountered during the establishment of South Ice meant that he must thread his way almost blind through some of the worst vehicle country on the face of the planet.

Having salvaged Fuchs's sledge from its precarious lodging in the mouth of the crevasse, the party began to turn the vehicles and sledges around, ready for the retreat. 'Being encompassed on all sides by crevasses made the turning of the sledges a long and laborious task,' wrote Fuchs, 'involving the endless probing of the surface in order to determine the width of the crevasses over which we had to work the vehicles.'[583] As if to add to their discomfort, the ice beneath the explorers' feet had begun to boom and echo: the groans of the vast ice sheet as it ground its way inexorably to the Weddell Sea. 'One of the crevasses gave such constant sounds that we likened it to some men building a metal shed down below. Another just a few feet from our tents sounded as though boilermakers were at work!'[584]

At last, after hours of cautious manoeuvring, the vehicles all pointed in the same direction. Before starting, however, Fuchs

ordered that they should be roped together for the first time.
Anticipating this eventuality, one of the modifications made by
Homard and Pratt during the long months of preparation had
been the fitting of a double 1.5-inch wire cable around the entire
hull of each vehicle. As well as being fixed to the tow-bars, the
15-ton rope linking the three vehicles was now threaded through
these cables, creating an additional safety harness. 'This made
everyone feel safer,' observed Homard, 'and to feel safe is half the
battle.'[585] Hitched together like mountaineers, the party set off at
a sedate 3.5mph and, after a tortuous journey involving repeated
diversions around yet more crevasses, they finally reached
the 50-mile depot at 9.30 that evening. Only two days earlier,
the three vehicles had roared across this area at a heady 8mph,
scattering snow and ice in all directions and seemingly without a
care in the world – now the same party had been forced to retreat
with its tail firmly between its legs. The journeys into and out of
the crevasse field could hardly have been more different.

On 14 October, heavy drift reduced visibility to 100 yards, forcing the party to lie-up for another frustrating day. That evening
Fuchs wrote 'I cannot afford to take chances with the still heavily
crevassed area which we have to cross,'[586] but when he awoke on
the 15th to find that conditions remained unchanged, he felt that
he had no choice but to cast caution to the icy winds and push
on. For the next three days, and with the vehicles once again
roped together, they made steady progress, covering 25 miles on
the 15th, a total of 40 on the 16th, and 37 on the 17th. Initially,
Fuchs steered a course of 305°, hoping that this would send the
party across the crevasses at a reasonably safe angle. As he grew
more confident that the crevasses were well bridged, he ordered
the three machines onto a more southerly course of 275° and
then, ultimately, due south 'on a surface quite clear of hazards, as
far as we could tell.'[587] Although they caught fleeting glimpses of
the Shackleton Range on the southeastern horizon, for much of
the time they travelled in complete whiteout conditions, unable
to recognise any inequalities in the surface. It was, Fuchs admitted, 'a considerable strain to drive for hour after hour into a blank
white wall of falling snow.'[588]

Mechanical problems continued to dog the team, manifesting themselves firstly in a ruptured oil line on Weasel 'Baker' on the 15th and the next day, a 'run' big end on the number two piston on Fuchs's vehicle. 'This was really rather disastrous,' Fuchs acknowledged, 'for we cannot turn back now and even in a workshop the job is one of about 3 days as a Weasel is so constructed that the entire engine has to be removed to do even simple jobs, let alone this.'[589] On the ice shelf they had little option but to redistribute the sledge loads to reduce the burden on the failing Weasel and then push on in the hope that it would be able to crawl another 200 miles to South Ice. The story was not one of uniform disappointment, however. The Sno-cat covered the terrain with very little apparent effort, carrying 1 ton on board with another 4.5 tons towed behind. Amazingly, in spite of its great size, it also seemed to skate over crevasse bridges, causing far less disruption to the surface than the lighter Weasels. On the 17th an impressed Fuchs noted an increasingly rough surface made the Weasels 'pitch and toss exactly like small craft in a choppy sea. The Sno-cat sailed over the ridges and hummocks like a battleship in contrast.'[590]

Friday 18 October dawned fine and clear, with a temperature of -9°F – but, despite the ideal travelling conditions, the vehicle party remained stationary so that the two engineers could undertake repairs and routine maintenance. While David Pratt and Homard mended two broken 'U' bolts on one of 'Baker's' rear springs, replenished oil and did what they could to patch up the ailing 'Able', Geoff Pratt undertook his first seismic shots of the journey. Unfortunately, the completion of the four shots had unexpected consequences as the additional strain on the Sno-cat's batteries, when added to a night-time temperature of -30°F, meant that the next morning the vehicle could only be started with the aid of jump-leads. Eventually the convoy moved off, but not until the middle of the afternoon. Almost immediately they entered a zone of wind-sculpted sastrugi and soon the vehicles were bucking and rolling as they crashed through these natural tank-traps. 'The sastrugi running at right angles to our course continued to provide the most unpleasant conditions and for several hours I was constantly reduced to second gear to reduce the heavy plunging of the vehicle.'[591] Finally they broke free – but only when the sastrugi gave way to yet more crevasses. 'Unfortunately,' noted a despairing Fuchs, 'the change in terrain evidently marks the beginning of the bad area.'[592]

Snow bridges collapsed all around the vehicles as they drove forward but at first the crevasses were fairly narrow and progress, though painfully slow, remained constant. Then, just as they reached the day's 35-mile mark, a larger bridge disintegrated beneath Weasel 'Baker', leaving the vehicle on one side of a deep chasm and the sledge on the other. With night falling, Fuchs and his companions extracted the Weasel and sledge from their precarious position and then, tired and disheartened, erected their tent. Decisions regarding their next move would have to wait until the morning.

On 20 October, Fuchs requested another aerial reconnaissance but when Lewis told him that poor weather made flying impossible, he decided that he had no choice but to retreat – just as he had done on the 13th. In the hope of circumnavigating the crevasse belt, the three battered vehicles trundled back for 5 miles and then headed due west for another 5, before turning onto a course of 155°. With the vibration of the tracks, ice and snow tumbled away on all sides like sand slipping through an hourglass, revealing great, gaping fissures in the shelf. Turning onto the new course, Fuchs ordered that the machines and sledges should again be roped together and they continued in this fashion until 8.14pm. 'I had decided to stop at 8.15,' Fuchs recorded, 'and was looking for a nice solid bit of snow when "Able" gave a sickening backward lurch and stopped abruptly … Peering out of the side I found myself suspended over a 40-foot abyss which widened downwards in all directions.'[593] Closer examination revealed that the Weasel now rested against the back edge of the crevasse on its aft flotation tank, with only the front bogey clinging, as if by its finger tips, to the forward edge. Fortunately, the walls of the crevasse held firm, otherwise the vehicle would have plummeted into the blue depths dragging its sledge behind it. Watched by his companions, Fuchs climbed gingerly from the tilting cab, worked his way round to the front of the vehicle and then grasped their outstretched hands to be pulled to safety.

With their leader back on *terra firma*, the team probed the surrounding area, revealing in the process a web of small crevasses beneath the windcrust. They also discovered that some 15 yards to the left of Fuchs's lopsided Weasel, there was an apparently secure bridge wide enough and strong enough to take the rest of the vehicles. Geoff Pratt drove forward, his Sno-cat and two sledges weighing a total of 8 tons, and then, having passed over without incident, uncoupled the sledges and hauled out Fuchs's Weasel using a steel tow-cable. By the time the sledge had been pulled clear and the convoy had congregated on the south side of the crevasse everyone was exhausted and at 10pm they made camp.

The reconnaissance party had executed another entirely successful vehicle recovery and had further honed its skills – but this provided cold comfort to Fuchs. On top of all the delays before setting out, the party's progress had fallen far short of expectations and twice he had been forced to order a retreat, wasting yet more precious time and fuel. The following morning his calls for an aerial reconnaissance again went unanswered because of poor atmospheric conditions and, with his carefully laid plan unravelling before him, he could no longer disguise his growing anxiety. 'This is maddening, for we badly need air recce if we are to get out of this troublesome area in the dwindling days available. The only alternative is to take severe risks with the crevasses and in all probability lose one or more vehicles ... the days are passing – only 23 days to our departure date from Shackleton – and we are only halfway to South Ice and in real trouble with the route.'[594]

Another worry constantly nagging at his peace of mind was the uncertainty regarding his precise position in relation to the surrounding obstacles. In particular, he wanted to avoid running directly into a feature known as the 'Ice Wall': a 1,500-foot-high, near vertical barrier created by the Recovery Glacier as it descends from the mountains to meet the Filchner Ice Shelf. In planning his route, Fuchs hoped that by skirting around the foot of the Shackleton Mountains his vehicles would be able to scale the wall and reach the glacier by using a shallow slope which had been spied from the air during one of the early reconnaissance flights. Now, on the ground, he confided to his diary: 'Although I know from dead reckoning where we are I have little knowledge of the relation between that position and the physical features as we have as yet only a poor map of the area made from the air.'[595]

Having spent the whole of 21 October laboriously prodding the route ahead for 1.5 miles and listening for the telltale drum-like echo which indicated the presence of a crevasse, Fuchs decided to press on the next day despite the continuing absence of air support. The day dawned beautifully clear and bright, with visibility of 40 miles and a temperature of –26°F – but these wonderful travelling conditions did nothing to accelerate progress. As Fuchs glumly noted, 'Within twenty yards I broke through a fairly large crevasse but hauled across it. While David P. roped to me astern, was attempting to pull one side I went deep into another and as I write in the vehicle I am canted astern where the tracks once more hang in space. The Cat "Charlie" had only moved three or four feet before our journey came to an abrupt halt.'[596]

Matters improved somewhat when, at lunchtime, clear radio communications were at last established with Shackleton and by the early afternoon Lewis was airborne. While he waited for the Auster, Fuchs decided that the time had come to establish an air depot at a point about 40 miles to the east, where the dog teams were currently surveying. As well as facilitating improved radio communications and obviating the need for the aircraft to fly huge distances before they could do any meaningful work, such a plan would also facilitate local reconnaissance without the expedition being reliant upon good weather at Shackleton. The air depot would become a field base for the Auster and would be equipped with a 'chorehorse' generator and an engine heater. Haslop would be pilot, supported by George Lowe as ground crew.

When Lewis arrived, chilled to the bone in the Auster's unheated cockpit, Fuchs shared his new plans and then climbed aboard for a low-level reconnaissance of the terrain ahead. Circling over the campsite, he reported that 'it was immediately apparent that really bad country lay ahead'[597] and he therefore ordered Lewis to fly eastwards before diverting onto a course of 125°. Following this route they traced an area that seemed to promise relatively good going; but within a very few miles the Auster's shadow was once again being dismembered by a series of vicious-looking fissures covering an area at least 10 miles wide. 'If we can break through that belt we have a chance of decent going beyond,' Fuchs noted after landing. 'It is certainly going to be a tough job and a dangerous one but if we are to have a trans-Antarctic journey it has to be attempted and somehow we must be successful.'[598]

The following day the four men of the vehicle party began to retrace their steps in order to pick up the route identified from the air. Despite the immense anxiety of the last few days, his identification of a potentially viable new route filled Fuchs with renewed optimism, and he wrote of the day's trials and tribulations in an almost light-hearted fashion:

> I am not sure whether it is more pleasant to rumble over the gaping holes one has previously left behind or to break new ground wondering when the next sickening lurch tells you that your vehicle or sledge is about to descend into a chasm. There is no doubt that travelling over this sort of country with these heavy vehicles imposes a considerable nervous strain on the drivers. David Pratt, rather aptly, said that it reminds him of driving over a minefield in a tank – you never know when something is going to happen![599]

It took an hour and a half to retreat to the point at which Fuchs wanted to turn onto the new route. There, confident in the surface he had surveyed from the air, he ordered that the vehicles be unroped so that they could proceed independently. They drove in this manner for another 7 miles before Fuchs, still in the lead, noticed a grey shadow stretching across the snow in front of him: the bright sunshine had enabled him to observe a subtle variation in the surface which would have been invisible on an overcast day. Careful probing revealed a well-filled crevasse and, calculating that they had now reached the boundary of the broken terrain spotted the previous day, he ordered a halt. The perfect conditions encouraged a continuation of the journey but, having received confirmation from Shackleton that the air depot would be established that night, Fuchs decided to wait so that the best entry point could be identified from the air. A meal and a good sleep would also help to prepare the party for the ordeal before them. That night he wrote that 'the next ten miles are going to be, in my opinion, the make or break of the expedition, for we may well lose vehicles in the ground close ahead. With crash helmets, pilot's safety straps and vehicles roped together we have taken all the precautions we can for the safety of our own bodies.'[600]

Haslop and Lowe joined the party at midday on 24 October, having taken just 20 minutes to fly from their new depot, and in no time at all Fuchs was in the air. From above, the crevassed zone looked forbidding in the extreme and he observed that the 'level stretch through which we might hope to pass was clearly badly broken up with countless thousands of hidden crevasses of the peculiar basin-shape we have come to know on the Filchner Ice Shelf.'[601] With plenty of food for thought, he asked Haslop to fly up to the Ice Wall itself, so that he could better assess the ascent. As part of the planned geological expedition to the Shackleton Range, in the middle of October Stratton, Lowe, Blaiklock and Stephenson had flown to the mountains with two dog teams and supplies for 40 days. Between 14 and 17 October, while Lowe and Stephenson geologised, Stratton and Blaiklock had surveyed and flagged a route up the comparatively shallow incline to the top of the Ice Wall, marking particularly severe crevasses with red and white chequered flags. It was the feasibility of this suggested path that Fuchs now wanted to judge for himself. 'At first, I was appalled to see the route lead straight up over a complex of filled crevasses but after flying low over the route we had hoped to use from last year's recces, I saw that the way the dog party had found was probably infinitely preferable. I only hope that this early promise will be fulfilled for we badly need a bit of luck in our favour now.'[602]

Back on the ground, he decided that he had no option but to adopt the wearisome practice of probing every foot of the surface before the vehicles moved forward. As an accomplished mountaineer, well-accustomed to crossing crevasses, Lowe doubted the need for such a cautious approach, noting in his diary that 'The crevasse area ahead looked easy to me, a dead flat plane of unbroken snow with occasional hollows indicating covered crevasses from 9 inches to 4 ft wide.'[603] But Fuchs was in no mood to take unnecessary risks. 'Some of the monstrous caverns which we have discovered beneath the innocent surface have certainly justified the work,' he later asserted. 'Some of them would have accepted a double decker bus and there is no doubt that we should have lost at least one Weasel if we had not spent so much time on the ground.'[604]

With tedious regularity, each morning the team prodded and poked at the ice ahead using 6-foot aluminium poles. 'Just what that means in terms of monotonous labour is hard to describe,' wrote Homard with real feeling, 'quite apart from the never-ending risk of disaster.'[605] Once a crevasse had been identified, the explorers attempted to break a hole in the centre of the lid and, if they succeeded, they marked the area as being impassable and went on to test an alternative route to either side. 'Our practice', Fuchs recorded, 'has been to work at probing ahead all morning, go back to the vehicles and have lunch before the nerve racking drive over the "proved route" (usually ¾ mile), then more probing in the afternoon with a final run forward to camp at 8 p.m.'[606] The drivers' hearts continued to race as they rumbled across the booming caverns but, benefiting from the detailed survey work, mishaps to the vehicles became a rarity. Progress remained agonisingly slow nevertheless.

Between 25 and 28 October, the party made less than 2 miles per day, woefully short of Fuchs's planned daily average, and some members of the party began to wonder whether the dangers really justified the caution. 'Some largish crevasses were unearthed,' wrote a sceptical Lowe, 'but the work and time hardly repaid the 1.7 miles that was moved by the vehicles.'[607] Haslop, too, flying in the uninsulated Auster for up to 11 hours every day, began to question whether, instead of benefiting the drivers, his survey of the obstacles ahead simply made them more hesitant. Day by day the jovial New Zealander's disillusionment grew until he finally exclaimed: 'The biggest stumbling block to the vehicle advance is the air reconnaissance!'[608] Meanwhile, back at Shackleton, news of the constant delays and a dearth of real detail regarding the future strategy for the expedition – information that Fuchs seemed unwilling to share until he had consulted with Stratton – led to increasing unrest. 'Yet one must sympathise with them,' wrote Lister. 'They have a difficult job to do and should be able to call upon any aid they require.' However, he could not help adding the ironic remark, 'They don't use dogs as feelers ahead, perhaps too slow!'[609] Of course, in reality, no one felt more frustration than Fuchs. 'This was to have been our latest date for arriving at South Ice,' he observed dolefully on 28 October, 'but it must be now at least another week even with some luck with crevasses and weather.' He went on to assert that 'at least we shall have a known route for the next vehicles!'[610] But such claims had begun to sound very hollow indeed, even to his own ears.

News that Haslop had crash-landed the Auster in poor visibility, tearing off the tail-skid and leaving the aeroplane unusable until Peter Weston could be flown in to undertake the necessary repairs, threatened yet further delays. Fortunately, by the end of the 28th Fuchs felt confident that the party had at last drawn close to the far edge of the crevasse field, rendering aerial reconnaissance less vital. That evening he admitted: 'There is a great temptation to get into the vehicles and drive on but after all this careful and successful work in getting ourselves safely through an area such as I quite believe no vehicles have ever attempted before, it would be a great pity to make an error in the last stages.'[611] On the 29th, he skied ahead of the vehicles marking the last 2¾ miles before they finally debouched into an area mercifully free of crevasses. The next obstacle would be the towering Ice Wall and despite their relief at having got so far the explorers might be forgiven for thinking that they were about to step 'out of the frying pan and into the fire'.

After so many days of painstaking probing and crawling, the three vehicles travelled at what seemed like an amazing speed towards the wall, their tracks throwing up clouds of snow as they ground forward. At a point approximately 12 miles from the crevasses, a snow cairn came into view – built by Blaiklock and Stratton to mark the beginning of their recommended route up to the glacier. Before attempting the steep climb, Fuchs decided to ski forward for about 800 feet so that he could better assess a surface which, so far, he had seen only from the air. To his relief, it looked quite feasible, though not entirely devoid of crevasses. Once again the vehicles and sledges were roped together and the 1500-foot ascent began.

Almost immediately they ran into trouble: first, Fuchs's Weasel sank to its axles in soft snow and, with its tracks gaining no purchase, the Sno-cat had to be called forward to tow it clear. Hardly had 'Able' been dragged to safety when 'Baker' blundered into another soft patch and had to be similarly rescued. Even more troubling was the clanking and squealing coming from Fuchs's Weasel. Since 16 October, 'Able' had been running with a badly damaged big-end bearing; against all the odds, it had kept going, possibly aided by the limited demands placed upon it during the crossing of the crevasse zone. But now, after a much faster run of 12 miles and having been subjected to the additional strain resulting from Fuchs's attempts to drive it out of the most recent hole, the vehicle was clearly on its last legs. Despite its protests, Fuchs managed to nurse 'Able' across one last large crevasse marking the brow of the Ice Wall and then drew to a halt. The climb continued beyond this point but at a much shallower gradient and to his astonishment he found that even in a crippled Weasel he had surmounted with comparative ease what he had always believed would be one of the expedition's greatest challenges.

From this eminence, he wrote: 'We saw our tracks winding away into the distance across the ice shelf and also noticed a white track extending towards us from the east and could make out a dark spot at the head of it making it look like a 'plane and vapour trail far below us. This was, we realised, a dog team coming over to find us.'[612] It turned out to be Blaiklock and Stratton, who had travelled 19 miles in 9 hours to rendezvous with the vehicles. As Homard noted with evident glee, the dog team must now 'chase us up the "ice wall" whereupon, to the everlasting satisfaction of the mechanical snow vehicle fraternity, their sledge was towed by a Sno-cat.'[613] Shrugging off this ignominy as best he could, Stratton would now join the vehicles to gain some much needed experience, while Blaiklock and Homard sledged back to the survey party's camp before being air-lifted back to Shackleton. Once there, Homard would concentrate on the preparation of the remaining vehicles to be used on the crossing.

After the achievements of 29 October, the 30th proved extremely disappointing with the party covering a mere 3.5 miles. First, as Fuchs reported, 'poor old Weasel "Able" who has laboured on with a "run" big-end for 200 miles, finally gave up with a broken camshaft.'[614] This meant abandoning the vehicle and one sledge, loaded with a drum of fuel, 20 days' rations, half a gallon of paraffin plus other assorted spares and lubricants. The reconnaissance party had now lost 50 per cent of its original strength since leaving Shackleton three weeks earlier. Having cached the abandoned supplies to be picked up by the main Crossing Party, the two remaining vehicles moved off, heading eastwards along the line of some large but apparently well-bridged crevasses. Even before they crossed the first of these fissures, Weasel 'Baker' became bogged down in soft snow and had to be uncoupled from its sledge before being hauled free by the Sno-cat. 'As they moved across,' wrote Fuchs, who was standing to one side, 'I heard a tremendous rumble and the snow beneath me quaked, making me want to move rapidly to some other place, but as I had no idea where the noise originated, I stood where I was.'[615] As the vehicles crawled forward, a huge crater, 20 feet across and 40 feet deep, opened just 6 feet to the left of the Weasel, so suddenly that it almost seemed as if a bomb had fallen from the skies. The collapse sent a great cloud of ice particles high into the sky and a dumbstruck Fuchs noted that the 'hole was large enough to have swallowed Sno-cat, Weasel, sledge and all.'[616] It was only by the greatest good fortune that the chasm had not opened directly beneath the vehicles – had it done so they would have fallen together into the depths like a group of roped-up mountaineers peeling from a cliff face.

The next day the party finally cleared the heavily crevassed area at the top of the ice wall and reached, too, the end of the path marked by Stratton and Blaiklock. At its nearest point, the Shackleton Range was about 4 miles away, its thin rock ridges thrusting through the snow slopes like rusty knife blades pushed through a sheet, while, here and there, a rock face rose vertiginously, too sheer even for the snow to latch onto it. When they met with a handful of wide crevasses Fuchs ordered the drivers to move into the shadow of the mountains to their left, where the dangers would be less pronounced. The ground continued to rise sharply to the south as they motored on within half a mile of the rocky spurs and soon the vehicles had been reduced to 4mph in second gear. A little farther on and giant sastrugi, standing 4 or 5 feet high, gave the surface a ribbed appearance and the vehicles' route became ever more tortuous as they wound their way around the worst of them. That evening Fuchs wrote: 'We now believe we are 67 miles from South Ice in a direct line, but there are at least two crevasse zones and the Whichaway Nunatak climb to negotiate before we get there.'[617] Together, he knew, these obstacles would ensure that the line followed by the reconnaissance party would be anything but direct.

The first week of November proved to be one of the most difficult of the entire journey. Having spent much of 1 November on routine maintenance, in particular the greasing of 320 grease points on the Sno-cat tracks, the party moved off at 4.30 in the afternoon. Rising steeply before them, the Recovery Glacier created a disorienting false horizon, while the jagged sastrugi, running at right angles to their route, caused the vehicles to lurch sickeningly as they ploughed their way forwards at a maximum speed of 3mph. The next day, a few miles into the journey, the scenery began to change, with large hummocks and pinnacles of ice stabbing above the false horizon and giving early notice of even worse surface conditions to come. Reconnoitring ahead on skis, Fuchs found that the valleys between the high hummocks were interlaced with crevasses which gave the landscape, he thought, 'a queer lost world effect, as though, perhaps, we had suddenly begun to wander in some region of the moon.'[618]

Confident that the Otter would soon be making a flight to South Ice, Fuchs radioed Shackleton and asked that Blaiklock should travel on board so that he could undertake an aerial survey of the area ahead and identify a route through the crevasse zone. The aeroplane flew over at 6.25 that evening and, sure enough, Blaiklock reported that he had spotted what looked like a viable path to the east of the vehicles' current position. Grateful for the advice, Fuchs and his party moved 5 miles in the direction indicated but, to their frustration, they soon found their way barred by yet more crevasses. Rather than attempt to press on regardless, Fuchs asked Blaiklock to try again on the Otter's return flight from South Ice and just after 1.00am the aeroplane swooped overhead with Lewis, Blaiklock and Lowe on board. 'John and Ken talked on the radio,' noted Lowe, 'but Bunny and David S. could not get their suggestions on the route clearly. John landed and we bounced out while Ken gave a map with his observations sketched in place.'[619] Blaiklock had identified a more favourable route another 6 or 7 miles farther east. Despite this good news, Lowe could not help remarking that, after his four exhausting weeks on the trail, 'Bunny looked very worried and deflated.'[620]

Having waved off the Otter, the vehicle party headed east – but once again they found that the quality of the terrain only served to underline the inadequacy of aerial surveys, when even an experienced observer's impressions could be profoundly affected by tricks of the light. Initially the area pinpointed by Blaiklock looked significantly better: a great jumble of ice hummocks to the east and west gave the landscape the appearance of a harrowed field but in between stretched an area about 1.5 miles wide which appeared almost smooth. This was Blaiklock's suggested route. But when Fuchs skied forward to investigate further, he was dismayed to discover a mass of shallow depressions which indicated the presence of innumerable crevasses. 'This threatened much work in seeking a route, and so it has proved.'[621]

The party had no choice but to resort once again to the tedious and time-consuming expedient of prodding their way through the area using their 6-foot poles. 'This prodding is a deadly exercise,'[622] Fuchs complained, with very good reason. Day after day, the men crawled forward sounding the ice at intervals ranging from 6 inches to 3 feet depending on conditions, and never progressing more than half a mile after a whole day's excruciating labour. If anything, the work here was even more wearisome than when the party wended its way across the 11-mile wide crevasse zone on the Filchner Ice Shelf. 'This is because the snow surface is much harder with a number of ice layers. This makes it difficult to break through into the crevasses which are often only found because they are "boomers".'[623] Once they had identified a crevasse, the explorers chiselled away at the snow bridge until they had made a cavity wide enough for them to force through their head and shoulders in order to determine the width and orientation of the chasm below:

> Hanging head-down into a bottomless pit with sloping blue white sides that disappear into the depths gives the impression of gazing into deep water but it can also be somewhat alarming when you know that very soon you will have to drive a two- or three-ton vehicle with heavy sledges over the precarious snow bridge above the dark abyss![624]

The work was also acutely uncomfortable in temperatures which, now that the expedition had begun its long slow climb to the Polar Plateau, routinely fell well into the minus thirties. 'My stockings, leg duffel, three pairs of foot duffels, stocking and felt/plastic insole were all frozen together and to the inside of my moccasins,' Fuchs noted. 'Likewise gloves and inners were solid with rime and ice.'[625] Inevitably, despite all the probing, snow bridges routinely crumbled beneath the vehicles and on 4 November the Weasel broke through the windcrust twice in 100 yards. Two days later, in an area which had appeared relatively free of crevasses, a loud rumbling from beneath the surface presaged an imminent collapse. Seconds later two enormous holes, 40 feet long and 12 feet wide, appeared on either side of the vehicles. Incredibly, the

narrow bridge between the two chasms remained solid and the
vehicles passed over unscathed. Only 50 yards later, the Weasel
unexpectedly broke through again and remained precariously
suspended by the front bogey and a short length of track at the
rear. Had the crevasse been 6 inches wider, the vehicle would
have been left swinging like a pendulum, with only its safety rope
and the Sno-cat standing between it and a plunge into the depths.
The two vehicles finally broke free during the early evening of
7 November, though they continued roped up for another mile
in case they encountered any more isolated crevasses. It had taken
them four days to cover just 2.5 miles.

With the crevasse belt finally behind them, the following
morning the four men set off in high spirits, indifferent now to
the 25-knot wind and a temperature of -20°F. Although free of
crevasses, the route remained very demanding with the vehicles
crashing over 3-foot-high sastrugi and with high drift reducing visibility to a minimum. They pushed on all day, travelling at
between 2 and 3.5mph, until a gradual flattening of the surface
led Fuchs to suspect the presence of yet more crevasses. 'In half
a mile more, we passed over several large filled chasms almost
before becoming aware of them'[626] and, with the drift making it
increasingly difficult to distinguish the crevasses from the shining,
polished surface of the windcrust, he ordered a halt.

The high drift continued throughout the night and when the
explorers awoke the next day they discovered beautifully formed
snowdrifts had accumulated around their tents and behind the
vehicles and sledges. There was little enough time to appreciate
the scenery, however, and after breakfast the four men began the
tedious process of surveying the route ahead: Geoff and David
Pratt examining the cracks and crevasses in the immediate vicinity of the camp while Fuchs and Stratton skied forwards to map
a route through the fissures further afield. Beyond the last of
the sastrugi and just 3.5 miles from their camp they discovered
a series of great rifts, snow domes and ridges, the latter rising
to tower some 80 feet above the surface of the surrounding ice.
Clearly the gentler snow domes offered the best route for the
vehicles and Fuchs and Stratton soon discerned what appeared

to be a relatively easy course: 'one of our few bits of luck on this trip!' Fuchs enthused.[627]

Keen to take advantage of this piece of good fortune, the two men skied swiftly back to the tents, roped the vehicles together, and set off. After travelling just a quarter of a mile it seemed that they had escaped the local crevasses and the vehicles continued independently through the hillocks and rifts spotted during the early morning reconnaissance. Beyond this area a series of 50-feet chasms were clearly visible but, roped up again, they negotiated these hazards without the need for time-consuming and exhausting probing. They then enjoyed a clear run of exactly 4 miles before reaching the crevasse field lying below the Whichaway Nunataks. 'There we are now camped,' wrote Fuchs that night, 'with the rocks only two miles away but a fearsome looking mass of crevasses and hummocks lies between us and the steep glacier slopes up which we have now to find our way. This I hope is the last obstacle between us and South Ice which is 22 [nautical miles] from the Whichaways.'[628]

In the teeth of a bitter 20-knot wind, the next morning the explorers skied forward to investigate the route ahead. Soon they found themselves in the midst of a fantastic maze of hummocks of bare green-tinted ice, the intervals between scored by sinister looking crevasses and the whole sentinelled by the scarred heads of the nunataks. Time and again, a seemingly viable path petered away into a dead end, barred by some insurmountable incline or fissure. Foiled at every turn, Fuchs decided to climb the most easterly of the nunataks, hoping that, from an elevated position, he might be able to discern a feasible route through this obstacle course. For all their barrenness, the limestone of these buried mountains exercised an irresistible pull on men who had not placed their feet on anything but snow and ice for a nearly a year and Fuchs was soon fossicking about among the moraine in search of fossils. Stratton, meanwhile, scrambled to the top of the nunatak and soon reported that an area a mile or two to the west seemed to offer the least hummocked route for the vehicles. 'Passing westward over the blue ice of the glacier coming down between the nunataks,' wrote Fuchs, 'we headed for the "gap" and

found a difficult but we consider passable route. Then clambering
up and down the ice hill and dale country we returned to the
vehicles where we had our biscuits and cocoa.'[629]

By the time they camped that evening, the party had made
it to the mouth of the 'gap' after a run of 5 miles over a surface so smooth that the vehicles had accelerated to speeds of 8
to 10mph. Once inside the gap, however, crevasses slowed their
progress almost immediately and Fuchs decided to call a halt with
the intention of undertaking a further reconnaissance the next
morning. But, when the four men wriggled out of their tents
on 11 November, high drift and a 40-knot wind forced them to
abandon any hope of continuing the journey and instead David
Pratt took the opportunity to work on his Weasel, while his three
companions rested. Throughout the night the wind continued to
brush noisily against the sides of the tents and the next morning a low drift still swept off the surface – but it was no longer
thick enough to obscure the hummocks and crevasses and Fuchs
decided to prospect on skis a route to the glacier, which glides
between the two most easterly of the Whichaways.

Initially, he found the route fairly easy with the crevasses straight
and well bridged, if sometimes much wider than expected. But,
as so often on this journey, a region of comparatively easy going
soon gave way to a nightmare of intersecting and often fathomless
gashes in the surface. Every hummock seemed to be surrounded
by a field of cavernous holes. In this bewildering maze, the only
feature that seemed to offer any advantage to the traveller was
the quality of the ice. The walls of many of the crevasses over
which the vehicles had passed during the course of their journey
had been as unstable as ancient mortar, threatening to crumble at
every moment. Here, in contrast, the surface was as hard as iron
and probably far less prone to collapse. By 3.30pm, the route had
been surveyed and marked with flags and, after a scratch lunch,
the vehicles were brought forward.

Stratton and Fuchs led on foot, Stratton 50 yards ahead of the
vehicles, with Fuchs 30 yards behind him. While the former indicated the general course to be pursued, the latter ensured that
the vehicles lined up at right angles to cross the crevasses, thereby

exposing them to the least risk. Inching forwards at 2mph, the party headed for a particularly recognisable hummock which they had christened the 'obelisk' and upon which they had anchored their route up to the glacier. To everyone's relief the path prospected during the morning proved quite passable and when they reached the obelisk only a few hundred yards separated them from the upward slope of the glacier towards the nunataks. These last yards proved particularly hazardous with the crevasses often well bridged but so wide that when the explorers chiselled a hole to gauge their width, they couldn't see the walls on either side. For all their apparent stability, if such a long bridge collapsed, the crevasse below might swallow the leading vehicle, its sledge and its partner as well. As Fuchs had acknowledged so many times during the course of the journey, no matter how 'dicey' the route might appear, 'there was no alternative.'[630] Besides, standing at a vantage point three-quarters of a mile from the obelisk, he could see that all signs of crevasses disappeared another half a mile up the glacier slope. 'Much encouraged, and feeling that at last we were about to break through the last obstacles to South Ice, I returned to the vehicles which I could see below me edging their way through the last of the hummocks.'[631] But there was still one more challenge to overcome.

During the last few weeks the Sno-cat had more than proved its worth: time and time again, while the lighter Weasels floundered into crevasses and suffered from an array of mechanical problems, the Sno-cat had sailed on serenely through every type of terrain, so rugged and dependable that it had almost come to be taken for granted. Now, arriving back at the vehicles, Fuchs learned that, for the very first time, Sno-cat 'Charlie' had put one of its four tracked pontoons down a hole. 'The hole had been made by the Weasel on a bend,' he wrote, 'and this was what we all feared because it could be impossible to extract a sunken pontoon.'[632] Throughout the journey the concern had been that, if one of the cat's independent pontoons dropped into a crevasse so that its leading edge pointed downwards, when the vehicle moved forwards, the pontoon might become so firmly wedged against the front edge of the crevasse that it would become immovable. But

once again the Sno-cat – and David Pratt – proved their versatil-
ity. Pratt realised that driving forwards would result in the track of
the pontoon burying itself ever deeper in the crevasse wall, without any hope of its being freed. Instead, he and Stratton climbed
onto the dangling pontoon and, by bouncing on the rear end,
used their body weight to swing the front end upwards. At the
same time, Geoff Pratt drove the vehicle forward in its emergency
low gear so that, in a matter of minutes, it once again stood with
all four of its pontoons on firm ice. Another invaluable lesson had
been learned.

They completed the final leg of the journey to South Ice
the following day, 13 November. The party had camped the
previous night after an easy climb up the glacier slope, Fuchs's
assessment that the crevasses petered out a little over a mile
from the obelisk having proved accurate. 'What a sense of relief,'
he wrote that night, 'to be travelling over certain ground once
more and to know, almost for certain, that we had a clear route
to South Ice, 25 miles from the top of the ridge.'[633] Although the
last 25 miles were ribbed with rock-hard sastrugi, causing David
Pratt to remark that the surface was 'like running across a series
of railway lines',[634] the vehicles were able to by-pass the worst
and kept moving at between 2 and 6mph, their pace affected
more by the defective steering of the Weasel than by the natural
obstacles. As the distance diminished, Fuchs radioed ahead to
let Lister and La Grange, now manning South Ice, know that
the route-finding party was at last approaching. 'Presently, we
saw a black dot on the horizon which came and went with
the hollows into which we were running. Then suddenly there
he was quite close over the top of the ridge and at almost the
same moment David's Weasel ran out of petrol and Hal fell on
his knees over some sastrugi!'[635] Once the initial greetings were
over and the Weasel refuelled, the whole party continued the
last 3.5 miles to South Ice, the only visible parts of which were
the dexion meteorological mast, the wind generator tower and
two recently arrived dog teams spanned out as a series of black
dots against the snow. 'This evening,' wrote Fuchs, 'we had quite
a little party.'[636]

Looking back on the trials and tribulations of the journey to South Ice, in the official account of the expedition, Fuchs wrote: 'I had always expected to find difficulty in climbing from Shackleton to the inland ice sheet, but the actual problems we had to overcome were far greater than we could possibly have envisaged.'[637] Allowing for mishaps, he had estimated that the journey would take fourteen days; in fact it had taken 37 and had involved the loss of two out of four vehicles – though both had succumbed to mechanical failure rather than to crevasses. Of the two vehicles abandoned, one, Weasel 'Able', would be a permanent write-off. Even more disturbingly, Fuchs's carefully prepared schedule for the crossing now lay in tatters. To have any hope of completing the historic journey before the close of the season, everything would now have to go his way. Given his experiences to date, it seemed a wildly optimistic expectation.

11

Tractors to the Plateau

Unlike Fuchs, Hillary could be very satisfied with the events of recent months. In early September, a number of short expeditions had been launched from Scott Base, designed primarily to help the dogs to regain condition and to further test the tractors before the main summer journeys, but also to undertake some surveying and depot-laying. Using a rugged Greenland sledge, Brooke and Gunn had taken a dog team across McMurdo Sound and made the first traverse of the Blue Glacier. Miller and Carlyon accompanied them as far as the Stranded Moraines, but then diverted to the Ferrar Glacier where they were joined by Marsh and Guyon Warren who had crossed the Sound from Cape Royds. This party of four then made a second attempt to push up the Ferrar. They quickly found that the winter snows had done little to smooth the glacier's broken surface and, abandoning their attempt, they instead drove their dogs up the coast beyond Gneiss Point before returning to base. All the teams had pulled well and their performance seemed to bode very well for the main journeys. 'It's most encouraging,' enthused Hillary on their return, 'to find how well the dog teams and their drivers are going and if we can take most of their loads for them up the Skelton they should do very well on the Plateau.'[638]

While the huskies were taking their first real exercise of the season, Hillary, accompanied by Bates, Ellis, Mulgrew and Herb

Orr, one of the IGY technicians, had driven three tractors to Butter Point, where they replenished the depot laid there during the first days of the expedition. They too had made another abortive attempt on the Ferrar Glacier before heading north to Gneiss Point, where they established a depot for the use of the planned Northern Party. By the time it arrived back at base, the tractor party had covered 161 miles in eight days and, like the dogs, the vehicles had done extremely well.

The expedition had also provided the first opportunity to test Hillary's brainchild, the caboose. It had not lived up to expectations. On 10 September, he recorded that the homemade caravan had been 'magnificent all day and it kept pretty warm inside with the heater working on the tractor exhaust. However when it came to try to get ready for the night it was absolute bedlam and quite impossible. It is really much too small for five to sleep and change in.'[639] Worse still, when the convoy came to a halt and the caboose no longer benefited from the heat of the tractor's exhaust, the interior temperature plummeted. 'At 7 a.m. it was -33°F in the caboose,' Hillary noted a few days later, '– probably the same outside so our insulation is non-existent.'[640] Clearly, further modifications would be required before he subjected the caboose to the much harsher conditions of the Polar Plateau.

Although the spring expeditions had been wholly successful and enabled Hillary to look forward with confidence to the main journeys planned for the summer, their completion did surprisingly little to improve the mood at Scott Base. Indeed, if anything, differences of opinion and temperament among the explorers had become even more pronounced and a combination of homesickness and overwork left Hillary with little inclination either to engage with seemingly trivial personnel issues or to buoy up the flagging spirits of his companions. Observing that Claydon and Cranfield were 'feeling a little thwarted' at the increasingly large part that the tractors were playing in the plans for depot laying and that this disappointment was exhibiting itself in a prodigal use of aviation fuel on non-essential flights in the Auster, he simply wrote 'I've given up trying to restrict them – it's really quite hopeless … I periodically descend on them and clamp down a bit but now I don't care any more.'[641] Unfortunately, the advocates of tractor-travel felt no less jaded, despite their growing importance. 'Everyone is a bit scratchy and wishing they were home I think,' Hillary noted on 24 September. 'Jim is decidedly homesick and tired of working on tractors and the Antarctic in general, Murray is pretty similar.'[642] Miller, too, observed an increase in tension, remarking on the 29th that 'We had an attempt at a final Sunday dinner tonight but I consider it a flop because of one or two recent estrangements.'[643]

In this atmosphere, it came as something of a relief when the first of the main sledging parties, the Northern Party led by Brooke, left Scott Base on 4 October. In choosing his exact route, Hillary had given Brooke a remarkable degree of latitude: 'The only instruction that I got from him,' Brooke remembered gratefully, 'was simply to explore and geologise in the Western Mountains as far as we could but without leaving any major blanks, and how I did it was left to me and the others.'[644] To all intents and purposes, therefore, Brooke was now his own master. 'The initial plan,' he continued, 'was to go up to the Plateau Depot and then sledge north but I'm very glad to say that we got that changed because I was aware from Greenland that in the very early months of the year you get these terrible katabatic winds and it's very, very cold and the chances of doing any useful survey are slim – very slim.'[645] Instead, he decided that he, Warren, Gunn and Murray Douglas would undertake a circular journey, running along the northern coast of the mainland, before forcing their way up one of the many glaciers to the Polar Plateau. Having undertaken as much exploration and mountaineering as possible, the Northern Party would then cross to the Plateau Depot before heading back towards Scott Base via the Skelton Glacier. In executing this plan, their main problem would be deciding which glacier to use as their highway to the plateau. According to the programme that Hillary had presented to the Ross Sea Committee in May, the party would follow the Fry Glacier but, after a series of reconnaissance flights, Brooke decided to abandon the Fry in favour of the Mackay. Its ascent would undoubtedly be difficult but in comparison with the badly fractured surface of the other glaciers, it appeared to be just about passable.

'On the 4th,' wrote Gunn, 'we cleaned out our cubicles and stored our gear in the sledge room and at 11.00am went down to the dog lines bearing a tiny personal bag containing a book, a sewing kit, a diary, and a spare pair of gloves and socks. Other than that we had what we stood up in plus a spare anorak and jersey to be given to anyone of the party who lost one.'[646] And then, with the dogs howling as the whips cracked over their heads, they were off – heading across the sea ice under a leaden sky and with the thermometer registering in the minus thirties. It would be more than four months before any of them saw Scott Base again.

According to Hillary's plan the next to leave would be the tractor party, with an anticipated departure date of 9 October. While the tractors were still en route, Miller and Marsh would be flown to the Skelton Depot with their dog teams, where they would await the arrival of the vehicles. Once reunited, the entire party would scale the glacier to rendezvous with Ayres and Carlyon at the Plateau Depot. The dog teams would then head south, while the tractor party undertook routine maintenance and waited for the delivery of fourteen loads of fuel and other supplies by air before continuing their own journey. However the nature of that onward journey had changed radically.

As compensation for the shelving of his intended journey to the South Pole, in May Hillary had forced the Ross Sea Committee to agree to his pushing his tractors west from the Plateau Depot, taking the Magnetic Pole as their ultimate objective. Now he decided to relinquish the hard-won western journey altogether. Instead, once re-equipped and refurbished, the tractors would follow the dog teams to the newly established Depot 480. From there, the entire party would head south to establish Depot 700, where Miller and Marsh would separate from the tractors for the last time, diverging to the south-east to survey in the area of the Queen Alexandra Mountains. As for the tractors, whatever commitments he might have made to the Ross Sea Committee, Hillary's intentions were clear: once Depot 700 had been stocked, they would continue on towards the South Pole.

For the time being, Hillary shared the details of his ultimate objective with Mulgrew, Bates and Ellis – but with no one else. So far as Miller was concerned, given that Hillary had already accepted that the tractors might need to be used to stock depots 480 and 700 in the event of the aircraft being grounded, the decision to drive the tractors south instead of diverting them unnecessarily to the west probably seemed a sensible idea. Thrilled at the prospect of the journey ahead, instead of scrutinising Hillary's motives any further, he spent most of his time checking and reinforcing harnesses, gluing and stitching patches on to his tent, packing ration boxes and generally preparing for four months of sledging. But he and Marsh could not depart until the tractors were well on their way – and to Miller's impatient eye it seemed at times that the vehicles would never be ready. 'Geo and I are well prepared to leave next Monday,' he noted with increasing frustration on 7 October, 'but looks as if tractors will be late leaving so we may be held up ... We have planned to be as independent of tractors and aircraft as possible – in fact entirely after D480. This releases us from the worry of whether the tractors go or don't go.'[647]

In fact, the tractor party was suffering from far more than just the usual round of mechanical difficulties. Hillary believed that a team of five constituted 'the bare minimum for a tractor train of four vehicles'[648] and for three of his fellow drivers, he had selected the members of what he called the 'old firm': Jim Bates, Peter Mulgrew and Murray Ellis – all of whom had proved their mettle on the trial journey to Cape Crozier in March and on the more recent trip to Gneiss Point. As his fifth driver, he had chosen Trevor Hatherton, the IGY chief scientist, who had gained important experience in tractor driving during the Butter Point reconnaissance in January. In the months ahead these men would have to eat, sleep and work together as a closely-knit team – but the crowded conditions of the makeshift garage had only served to exacerbate inevitable and potentially destructive personality clashes. As early as 27 September, Hillary had admitted to being 'thoroughly sick and tired of the garage and Jim and Murray ... They are a couple of wet blankets and if I took any notice of

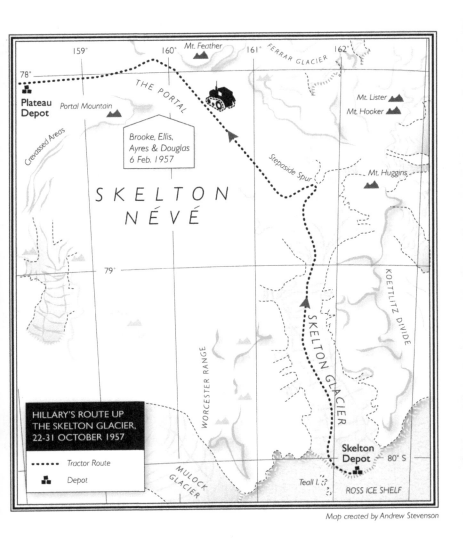

159° 160° Mt. Feather 161° FERRAR GLACIER 162°

78°

THE PORTAL

Plateau
Depot

Portal Mountain

Mt. Lister
Mt. Hooker

Crevassed Areas

Brooke, Ellis,
Ayres & Douglas
6 Feb. 1957

Stepaside Spur

Mt. Huggins

SKELTON
NÉVÉ

79°

KOETTLITZ DIVIDE

SKELTON GLACIER

WORCESTER RANGE

HILLARY'S ROUTE UP
THE SKELTON GLACIER,
22-31 OCTOBER 1957

•••••• Tractor Route

🏭 Depot

Skelton
Depot 80° S

MULOCK
GLACIER

Teall I.

ROSS ICE SHELF

Map created by Andrew Stevenson

them I'd never start any tractors at all.'[649] As if these tensions were
not bad enough, on the same day that Miller expressed his wish
to remain independent of the tractors, Hatherton announced that
his IGY responsibilities made it impossible for him to accompany
Hillary. When Hatherton's boss, Dr E.I. Robertson, Chairman of
the IGY Committee, sent a cable in support of Hatherton's decision, Hillary exploded. 'To hell with them all!' he raged, 'I'll get
this tractor trip going yet despite them all.'[650]

By 13 October a much-relieved Hillary had managed to
persuade Ron Balham, the expedition's meteorologist, to take
Hatherton's place – at least until the Plateau Depot – but it was
beginning to seem very unlikely that Bates would be able to
accompany the tractors. In order to release Bates for the journey,
Hillary considered it essential that a replacement engineer should
be despatched from New Zealand. In Bates's absence, this new
engineer would take on responsibility for the routine maintenance at Scott Base, particularly of the temperamental generators.
Hillary's request for an engineer had been approved and the ever-
obliging Admiral Dufek had agreed to transport the new recruit
in one of his Globemaster aircraft, which recommenced their
supply flights at the beginning of October. But with the planned
day of departure long-passed Bates's vital replacement was still
conspicuous by his absence. 'Blast the Yanks,' Hillary swore on
the 13th, momentarily forgetting the amount of US aid he had
already received, '– they transport down here urgently dozens of
useless loads such as reporters and cameramen – including three
New Zealanders – and leave behind essential men.'[651] The next
day he decided that he simply couldn't wait any longer – four
men, including just one engineer, would simply have to do. If and
when his replacement arrived, Bates would be flown out to join
the tractors by Claydon or Cranfield.

Of course, the journalists whose prioritisation over 'essential' men Hillary so deplored had all flown to McMurdo Sound
with the sole intention of reporting the departure of the Ross
Sea Party and when the tractors finally started up at 4.30pm on
14 October they did so, according to Miller, amid 'quite a hullabaloo of cameras and handshakes, admirals etc'.[652] When embarking

on his Cape Crozier trip in March, Hillary had been anxious to avoid any embarrassing mishaps in front of the dog-sledging aficionados. Now, with the world's press gathered to witness this much more momentous departure, it was almost inevitable that things would go awry. Instead of heroically surging forward to be swallowed up by the gathering snowstorm, the Heath Robinson convoy of three bright red tractors, a single drab Weasel, their Maudheim sledges and the caboose became bogged down almost immediately. And while Dufek and the other American officers waved and cheered encouragingly, the cameras clicked remorselessly. 'It was quite a sweat,' Hillary wrote that night,

> ... getting our loads around the pressure ridges ... It was reasonable going at first but after a couple of miles became rather softer. Then I was pulled up rather sharply and found that my Maudheim had broken through into a crevasse and was tilted well over with one runner right in.[653]

On closer inspection the crevasse turned out to be only 3 feet wide and 10 feet deep but even so it proved necessary to completely unload the twelve drums of fuel in order to extract the sledge. Hillary then ordered that the vehicles should be roped together before they continued over a sticky surface, which made for very slow going. After a day which he described as 'a rather tedious and infuriating one',[654] the party finally halted at 9.00pm having covered a meagre 7 miles. It had been an inauspicious start to the expedition but, as Hillary wrote that night, 'at least we've made the break and are on our way.'[655]

The following morning the tractors continued to flounder in soft snow. First one and then the next became so completely stuck that they had to be towed out and after several hours of hard labour they had covered barely a mile. 'Obviously we weren't going to get anywhere like that,'[656] Hillary observed, and realising that drastic action was required, he ordered that eight 350lb drums of fuel should be rolled off the sledges. After so much detailed work on fuel consumption and weight-to-power ratios, it was galling to abandon so much fuel within sight of base – but lightening the sledges at least meant that the tractors could make some headway. The alternative would be to relay the loads but that would be both exhausting and time-consuming and Hillary was anxious to cover as much ground as possible in the early days. 'We started on again and found that the lighter loads made all the difference and we could handle the snow satisfactorily. We slogged on for hour after hour only doing about 3mph and working very hard indeed and using masses of fuel.'[657] When the party made camp at 7.30pm, it had covered 23 miles, a reasonable total after such a hesitant start.

Hillary hoped to begin early on the 16th but even before they moved off from their campsite the Weasel overheated, forcing Ellis to spend the entire morning stripping down, cleaning and reassembling its cooling system. Since its departure from Scott Base, the tractor party had been moving against a stunning backdrop of mountain scenery, dominated by the smoking cone of Mount Erebus. Now they had reached a point nearly opposite White Island and could expect to enter the crevasse zone negotiated by the reconnaissance parties in January and February. The crevasses had presented a considerable obstacle to the dog teams and they would be even more dangerous for the much heavier motor vehicles. In an attempt to avoid the worst of the area, therefore, Hillary steered a course some 5 miles to the east of the known zone, straining his eyes all the while for telltale inequalities in the surface. Although he later acknowledged that 'this unknown factor brought a very real tension into my day,'[658] the strategy worked well. With no sign of crevasses, the drivers gradually grew in confidence, increasing their speed until the convoy was hurrying across the unexpectedly smooth surface in third gear. Seven miles into their journey, they paused to erect a snow cairn topped by a bright yellow 44-gallon fuel drum, and then turned due south. Although the weather rapidly deteriorated, with wind and drift increasing until Hillary could steer only by reference to the astro-compass mounted on top of his Ferguson's cab, they continued to make good progress and by the time they camped at 8.15pm they had covered another 30 miles, without encountering a single crevasse.

Despite a surface strewn with sastrugi, over the course of the next few days the convoy continued to cover the ground with surprising ease – in part aided by much improved weather. On 17 October, they made 32 miles and 38 on the 18th. That evening, the Beaver flew over their camp and Cranfield reported that he had just dropped Miller, Marsh and their dogs at the Skelton Depot, where they would await the arrival of the tractors. The replacement engineer had also shown up at last, meaning that Bates, too, could now be flown to the depot before the reinforced party proceeded up the glacier. 'It was with a feeling of some contentment that I crawled into my bag that night,' Hillary recorded. 'Everything was going very much according to plan – the vehicles were increasing their daily mileages; the dog teams were already waiting for us at the Skelton Depot; Jim Bates would soon be joining us to increase our engineering strength; and our success in dodging crevasses had been a great boost to our morale.'[659]

So far the vehicles had performed extremely well, with the only mechanical problems relating to the Weasel's cooling system. The Fergusons, in particular, seemed well able to cope with the rough surface, though the Weasel sometimes struggled amid the sudden rises and falls of the sastrugi. Then, on the morning of the 19th, disaster struck. The Weasel simply refused to start and it took Ellis some hours to identify a serious fault with the distributor drive. Had the snow surface been smoother, Bates might have been flown out from Scott Base to lend assistance – but Hillary and Claydon agreed that the sastrugi made this impracticable. Instead, while the rest of the party kept warm as best they could, Ellis struggled on alone to complete a temporary repair that he hoped would last until they reached the Skelton Depot, where he could undertake a more comprehensive overhaul. Unwilling to lose a whole day's travelling, when Ellis finally announced that he had completed the work at 5.00pm, Hillary decided that, despite the late hour, they should start and attempt to cover as much as possible of the last 50 miles to the depot. 'The going was good at first and we made excellent time but by midnight we were on some very rough, hard sastrugi which jolted us around.'[660]

The vehicles were now entering the tortuous area where the Skelton Glacier crashes into the Ross Ice Shelf, and as they lurched and plunged everyone expected Ellis's repairs to fail at any moment. To their surprise, the Weasel withstood the punishment and the team's confidence grew. But it was cold and uncomfortable work with the hunched drivers protected by nothing but the flimsy canvas sides of their makeshift cabs. Fortunately, the scenery offered some compensation for the trials of the journey. 'To the south of us,' observed Hillary, 'the sun was a molten ball of fire on the horizon and its low rays brought into sharp relief the jagged sastrugi and transformed their hills and hollows into a mottled patchwork of flame and shadow ... We were swimming along in a sea of glorious colour and for a while I forgot even the cold and the discomfort.'[661]

Just like Miller and Carlyon in mid-February, the drivers had to navigate very carefully among the pressure ridges and crevasses but by 6.00am they had picked their way through the worst of the area and found themselves under the great bluffs of Teall Island. Scanning the horizon, Hillary spotted a black dot to starboard that could only be the depot. They altered their course and soon the single dot separated into two and then three, the dots then gradually becoming distinguishable as tents, dog teams and fuel drums. 'It was good to see Jim, Bob and George again,' Hillary recorded shortly after their arrival at the depot, 'and to be greeted by the noise of the two dog teams. But we were mighty tired and fell into bed.'[662] It was 7 o'clock on the morning of 20 October and it had taken 13 exhausting hours to cover the 50 miles to the depot.

'Still at Skelton Depot,' Miller noted 24 hours later. 'Out early but no move. Tractors will be at least another day so no point in our going on too far ahead.'[663] In fact, it appeared that it would be little short of astonishing if the vehicles were able to move at any time in the immediate future. Even a fairly cursory inspection had revealed to Bates that the Weasel's distributor drive was badly broken and he told Hillary 'that it was a miracle that we had been able to keep going.'[664] It would now be necessary to remove the entire engine before comprehensive repairs could be completed.

In temperatures ranging from the minus twenties to the minus thirties and with a light wind blowing the loose surface snow around like confetti, Bates and Miller got to work while the others slept. First, Bates cut a large hole in the Weasel's roof; then he and Miller rigged a bipod from two large sections of bridging timber carried on one of the Maudheim sledges and used a block and tackle to pluck the engine from its housing. With the engine now fully accessible, Bates could begin. Fumbling with ice-cold metal tools and components with rapidly numbing fingers, it took nearly two days to complete the complex repair but, late on the afternoon of the 21st, the engine was bolted back onto its mounting and Bates declared the vehicle ready for test. Given that such an operation would have been considered demanding even in the garage at Scott Base, it was, as even the tractor-loathing Marsh acknowledged, 'a very fine effort'.[665]

The 'road test' proved the effectiveness of Bates's repair, but it also highlighted a weakness in one the Weasel's springs that necessitated further work and another frustrating delay. Nonetheless, at 9.30am on 22 October, Marsh and Miller set off to begin their ascent of the Skelton Glacier – the tractors would follow once the repairs to the Weasel had been completed. It proved to be a gruelling day for the dog teams and their drivers, with the rock-hard sastrugi causing a total of thirteen overturns and the polished surface making it incredibly difficult for men and dogs to keep their feet. 'Two chaps with a real heave can put a sledge on its runners again,' wrote a weary Miller that evening, 'but one must unload completely.'[666] And, of course, when both sledges capsized simultaneously, as often happened, the process took twice as long, with the two men struggling independently with their heavily laden sledges and tangled traces, often within sight of each other. 'The air was electric at my end,' Miller observed after one such incident, 'and Geo later said it was thunderous around him.'[667] Nonetheless, despite bruises and loss of temper, by the end of the day they had made an excellent 18 miles up the glacier. The tractors arrived at 2.00am. 'Did in just 4½ hours [the] distance for which we took 7 hours,' Miller noted. 'Pace about same but putting capsizes right cost us a lot of time.'[668]

Light snow and poor visibility forced the entire party to lie-up the next day but by the early afternoon of 24 October, conditions had improved sufficiently for Marsh and Miller to make a start. Appearances proved deceptive, however, and when dense drift reduced visibility to such a degree that the two men could no longer see each other let alone the landscape around them, Marsh decided that they must halt. 'We stopped and waited for the tractors so that we could shelter in the caboose until conditions improved. After about 15 minutes they passed us some 20 to 30 yards away. We only had a fleeting glimpse of them on account of the poor visibility and they showed no signs of having seen us.'[669] Unable to move forwards, after another 45 minutes of punishing exposure to the elements, they decided to camp:

> By this time it was blowing 50 knots down the glacier and it took the two of us over an hour to get the tent up ... We had four attempts before getting the two windward poles up and it must have been 1½ hours before the tent was entirely secured ... By 17.00 we were both inside and although there was not as much room as usual we were thankful.[670]

They had covered just 2.25 miles.

The tractor party fared rather better than the dog teams but even so they had what Hillary described as a 'torrid day'.[671] Thirty minutes after watching Marsh and Miller disappear into a cloud of drift, they too were lurching across sastrugi that ran lengthways down the glacier. In the swirling drift none of the drivers saw the dog-teams when they passed them and by 2.30pm Hillary admitted to feeling 'rather worried about Bob and George and knew they must have had a helluva time with their dogs.'[672] They paused for 90 minutes in the hope that the dogs would catch up and then, with still no sign of them, Hillary trundled back down the trail for a mile or so, but with no success. The weather showed no signs of relenting but as the tractors seemed well able to battle against the strong wind and their tracks obtained plenty of grip on the hard surface, he decided to push on as far as possible.

For another two hours they ground their way slowly forwards, steering into the wind and navigating by reference to the mountain peaks jutting through the haze of drift. Eventually the tractors began to break through into a series of crevasses bridged over with a thin layer of ice, but still they kept moving. 'The bridges now were giving way with almost unfailing regularity,' Hillary remembered, 'and each time we crossed a crevasse our vehicles would lurch violently and then carry on. It was no place for too much caution or crossing the area would have taken us days.'[673] For the last hour the party climbed steadily up among magnificent peaks, the wind easing and the ice gradually giving way to firm, wind-packed snow. By the time they camped at 8.00pm they had covered more than 19 miles despite appalling surface conditions and immediately ahead lay the slopes of the Lower Staircase.

Describing this feature, Hillary subsequently wrote that 'Here we could expect our greatest difficulties – particularly in getting our heavy loads up steep slopes of soft snow.'[674] But when his party halted the following evening, he admitted to being 'very pleased indeed with our progress'.[675] Poor weather had prevented an early start, but the wind dropped around midday and by 1.30pm the conditions had improved enormously. The first of the snow slopes proved surprisingly easy to climb but as the gradient gradually increased, the tractors began to lose traction and then to dig themselves into the much softer snow surface. Relaying became necessary. With lighter loads, the Weasel and the Fergusons continued to claw their way uphill in low gear. At each terrace, the sledges were unhitched and the tractors then roared back downhill to collect their next load. The relaying was time-consuming but the party's progress over what Hillary had always believed would be one of the expedition's greatest obstacles exceeded even his most sanguine expectations. 'By 4 p.m. the wind had dropped and the weather was superb with glorious views of Mt Huggins and the surrounding peaks. We reached the Twin Rocks satisfactorily and then started climbing up the great snow gully that led between areas of crevassing finally up onto the Landing at 3,500 feet.'[676] Here, having covered a very steep

12 miles, they decided to camp and await the arrival of Marsh and Miller.

The dog teams eventually caught up late the following afternoon having managed to maintain 3.5mph since their enforced halt on the 24th, despite the steep slopes and their 650lb loads. Very satisfied with the dogs' performance, at camp Miller observed a marked difference of opinion among the tractor drivers regarding their own progress of the previous day: 'Tractors just moving according to Jim B,' he recorded. 'Easy going according to Ed. All in point of view. The fact remains that this is where Ed expected trouble and they have made the first Staircase successfully.'[677] Complete whiteout prevented any further travelling on 27 October but, despite only a marginal improvement in conditions on the 28th, Hillary decided to push on regardless of the fact that he knew the party had camped amongst crevasses, which the flat lighting would render nearly invisible. His one concession to safety was to send the dog teams ahead of the heavier tractors. Miller:

> Off to smooth start at 8.10 to and around Stepaside Spur and on to Upper Staircase. Dogs of both teams going well – long pulls up hill ... Increasingly bad light as we worked on up Staircase – could only see dim outline of horizon ahead and frequently nothing at all.[678]

Aerial reconnaissance and Brooke's survey of the previous February had revealed that a wide belt of crevasses ran out from the rocky outcrop of Stepaside Spur but by diverting well to the right before turning in under the Spur, the dog teams managed to avoid the worst of the fissures. 'After running to just short of the highest point on the Spur,' wrote Marsh, 'we swung out on to the glacier and steered on the magnetic compass ... From here we began putting out trail flags at varying intervals to help the tractors to follow us.'[679]

Some distance behind, Hillary noted that the 'whiteout today has been as bad as you get'[680] and, to make matters worse, at times the tractor party found the gradients so severe that they were forced to relay their loads as they climbed over a series of parallel folds in the glacier's surface. Sometimes it proved impossible to pick out the paw prints and sledge tracks of the dog teams and eventually Hillary dismounted and walked ahead of the vehicles in an attempt to maintain progress. 'Even so,' he wrote with surprising sang-froid, 'I had to bend down practically to the snow to identify the tracks and my course was a shambling weave as I stumbled over unseen roughnesses in the surface. I could have walked on to a crevasse and not seen a thing!'[681] As the party gained more height and the rocky buttresses of Stepaside Spur fell away to be enveloped in the blanket of drift, he began to consider halting because of the appalling visibility. Then, just as he was abandoning hope, he caught sight of the first of the dog party's route flags and these enabled the tractors to continue their climb towards the nevé above.

Eventually, after 7½ hours of driving in near-zero visibility, the tractors reached the dog party's camp. 'We are now on edge of the nevé proper', wrote a delighted Miller, 'and beyond that the Plateau – the boundless Plateau. Tractors in between 4.30 and 5.30 p.m. having done much better than I would have ever expected of them because much of the going was incredibly soft. A freshening wind arising tonight and dogs quiet after their splendid day's work.'[682]

All told, the party had climbed another 2400 feet and could rest satisfied in the knowledge that, very soon, they would leave the glacier behind them and enter the plateau itself. The day had ended well – but Hillary could not deny that he had taken a severe risk in travelling among crevasses in such poor visibility and that it was only by great good fortune that they had suffered no casualties. 'Think we should probably not have travelled today, but feel some satisfaction in having got up the Upper Staircase and into the crevasse free nevé.'[683] A dangerous precedent had been set.

Despite his acknowledgement of the risks he had taken, over the course of the next few days Hillary showed no inclination to adopt more caution – much to the annoyance of some members of his team. When strong winds and severe drift prevented the

dog teams from moving on the 29th, the tractors set off without them, with Hillary and Miller agreeing that the whole party
would rendezvous at a point no more than 20 miles from the nevé
camp. A lull in the weather eventually allowed the dogs to move
forward on 31 October but visibility remained extremely poor,
with landmarks such as the Portal and the Lashley Mountains
appearing only fleetingly. The uphill going was extremely tough
for dogs and men and Miller and Marsh both looked forward
to making camp at the 20-mile point agreed with Hillary – but
when they reached that spot, there was no sign of the vehicles. By
the time they camped, having covered nearly 22 miles and at a
point approximately 24 miles from the Plateau Depot, both men
were infuriated by Hillary's apparently cavalier disregard for the
agreed plan and, ultimately, for their safety. Miller fumed:

> Tractors were to have stopped after 20 miles from last camp …
> They certainly have not camped so far and we are puzzled as
> they contracted to go no further until they know that aircraft
> could safely land on surface at depot. Puzzled? But it's the same
> old please self story. One day these changed plans are going to
> kill someone and it is not going to be me.[684]

The tractor party had reached the Plateau Depot on the afternoon of the 31st after two days of cold, uncomfortable travelling
in poor visibility and over a surface which varied from rough sastrugi to deep soft snow. On the 29th, John Claydon had reported
by radio that deterioration in surface conditions had forced him
to land Harry Ayres, Roy Carlyon and their dog teams approximately 3 miles from the original Plateau Depot and he had
provided Hillary with the exact co-ordinates of the new depot's
location. This re-location of the depot would involve the tractor
drivers in a tedious transfer of the supplies cached the previous
season – but there was no choice in the matter. On reaching
the new depot, where he and his companions received a warm
welcome from Ayres and Carlyon, Hillary admitted that his first
feeling was one of enormous relief, not least because his navigation had proved so accurate. 'To see our four battered vehicles

and the laden sledges at the Plateau Depot,' he later remarked, 'seemed to be the fulfilment of an impossible dream. I don't think that ever before, even on the summit of Everest, had I felt a greater sense of achievement.'[685]

Despite their success, the tractor party continued to be dogged by the tensions that Hillary had first commented on in September and which he had hoped would dissipate once they were in the field. 'The tractor party is a pretty capable little bunch,' he observed on the 31st, 'but I wouldn't say that they are easy to deal with. Murray is a professional pessimist; Peter usually optimistic; Jim goes from the heights of one to the depths of the other. But I'm afraid that irrespective of their feelings I know what I want and I'm going ahead with it.'[686] Of the 'old firm', he admitted to liking Bates the best, not least because of the veteran engineer's enthusiasm and resourcefulness. Mulgrew, too, he thought both loyal and 'a pleasant companion most of the time'. But Ellis he found extremely difficult. 'Murray is a very capable and useful chap in many ways,' he admitted, 'but I never feel his heart and soul [are] in the venture and he's so damn pessimistic and depressing about everything. I may be wrong but I sometimes feel he hates my guts.'[687] This jarring of personalities also left Hillary feeling introspective and self-doubting. 'I suppose I'm pretty impossible at times. Once I decided to use tractors I subjugated everything else to it and I suppose this rather got on people's nerves … I know I get rather irascible at times but I'll just have to try and calm down and keep things rolling along. I know what I want and I'm determined to see it carried through if I possibly can – but heaven forbid that I should ever lead an expedition again.'[688]

After two days of hard travelling in poor weather Marsh and Miller eventually reached the Plateau Depot on 2 November – but the pleasure of reuniting the party was short-lived. Immediately after their arrival, Hillary announced that, for what a disgruntled Marsh described as 'some reason best known to themselves',[689] he and Mulgrew would fly back to Scott Base with Ron Balham. According to the original plan, the four dog teams were to depart for Depot 480 as soon as the dogs in Miller's and Marsh's teams had recovered their strength. Now, instead, Miller, Marsh, Ayres and Carlyon would be obliged to linger at the Plateau Depot to help Ellis and Bates to transfer all the cached supplies from the old depot and to assist them with the maintenance of the tractors. Even worse, Hillary refused to alter his plans when, on the morning of the 3rd, Ellis strained his back so severely that he became temporarily paralysed. Although Ellis swore that the injury was an old one and he would recovery quickly, Marsh was altogether less confident. Unless the engineer's condition improved rapidly, then he too would have to be evacuated and the dog sledgers would simply have to wait at the Plateau Depot until a replacement could be flown in to keep Bates company. They found it a very bitter pill to swallow.

Mulgrew had flown to Scott early that morning and, by lunchtime, Hillary and Balham were also winging their way back to Pram Point on board the Beaver. 'We had a superb flight over the Skelton area and down the south branch of the Ferrar,' Hillary enthused, apparently oblivious to the anger of the men left behind on the windswept plateau. 'It really is a most beautiful area.'[690] The magnificence of the craggy mountains, slashed with their deep gorges and shimmering glaciers and, finally, the dramatic hump of Erebus with its twisting ribbon of smoke, made Scott Base seem small and dreary in comparison. 'Found base very tidy but slightly depressing,' Hillary noted after his brief tour of inspection. 'I will be glad to get back on the plateau again and on with the job.'[691]

The magnitude of the difficulties associated with that job was once more pressed home when, two days later, Ellis also arrived at Scott Base – persuaded by Marsh to retreat when his condition showed no signs of improving amid the Spartan comforts of the Plateau Depot. As soon as the crippled engineer reached the base on 5 November, Hillary drove him over to Hut Point where the two American doctors diagnosed a severe sprain and prescribed a couple of weeks' rest. 'Murray is adamant he'll be OK in a few days but I doubt it,' observed an anxious Hillary. 'That reduces my party to 3. I'll have to get some more men somewhere.'[692] The need for further recruits became even more acute when, the next day, Ellis revealed that even if he did make a miraculous recovery, he had no wish to accompany the tractors beyond Depot 700, preferring instead to join one of the dog teams. 'I've been expecting this,' Hillary wrote angrily, 'so it was no surprise but seems a pretty weak and wishy-washy attitude all the same. Well I'll just have to try and get someone else.'[693]

As well as presenting Hillary with yet another unwelcome obstacle to the fulfilment of his polar ambitions, Ellis's words provoked a further bout of pained self-analysis:

> I'm learning a lot about human character – especially not to try and judge it. It's a reflection on my ability to judge character that of the five chaps that I personally knew and chose for the party (Ayres, Bates, Douglas, Ellis, Gunn) to my mind only Bates and Gunn have lived up to my mental pictures of them. Ayres, Douglas and Ellis have all done a pretty good job I guess but they have individually lacked that spirit of enthusiasm and loyalty I expected.[694]

Hillary had considered that five men constituted the bare minimum for a convoy of four vehicles. Hatherton's withdrawal and Balham's decision to accompany the tractor party only as far as the Plateau Depot had forced him to consider making the onward journey with only four men. Now he was faced with the prospect of travelling beyond Depot 700 with only three tractors and three men. While he had shown himself willing to take a number of risks during the ascent of the Skelton Glacier – risks which Fuchs would never have countenanced – he believed that embarking on such a journey with so few men was simply too dangerous. He must, therefore, find another driver. 'My only hope now,' he wrote on 6 November, 'is Derek Wright.'[695]

An employee of the New Zealand National Film Unit, the 28-year-old Derek Wright had accompanied the Ross Sea Party as official cinematographer when it first sailed for McMurdo Sound and he had tried his hand at driving a Ferguson during the unloading of stores from the *Endeavour*. He had sailed back to New Zealand in February but had always intended to return to the Antarctic to continue filming during the expedition's second

summer. Now Hillary hoped that the moviemaker might be persuaded to take an altogether more active part in the expedition. 'I
sent off a telegram to Admiral Dufek', he wrote, 'explaining the
position and asking if it would be possible to expedite his passage.
The reaction from Admiral Dufek was generous and immediate,
and to my delight I was advised that Derek would be arriving by
Globemaster early on the morning of November 7th.'[696] As so
often before, the Americans had come to the rescue.

Since Ellis's evacuation from the Plateau Depot on the 5th,
poor weather had made it impossible to fly in a replacement to
keep Bates company and Hillary was under no illusions regarding
the feelings of Marsh and Miller, who had now been stationary
since 2 November. They would, he wrote, 'be furious, I guess, at
being held up.'[697] Moreover, as the days passed, his own uneasi-
ness began to grow, and he could no longer ignore the fact that
his decision to return to Scott Base, Ellis's injury and the poor
weather were all conspiring to compromise the expedition's
fragile timetable. 'I started haunting the windows,' he remembered, '– keeping an eye on the clouds and waiting impatiently
for a break – but heavy clouds and mild temperatures persisted
all through November 6th.'[698] By the 7th there were indications
that restlessness was giving way to recklessness and after a radio
schedule with Scott, Miller recorded that he had 'had to knock
Ed back on a suggestion that we leave Jim Bates on his own.'[699]
Fortunately for Bates, Miller rejected the proposal absolutely, telling Hillary that 'on no account' would he agree to it and later
that same day the visibility improved sufficiently for Cranfield to
fly Mulgrew back to the depot. At last the dog teams could prepare to start out towards the proposed site for Depot 480.

The prospect of an imminent departure did little to curb the
irritation of the dog sledgers. Reading a press release brought in
by Cranfield, an irate Miller noted that 'Ed has told the country that those at the depot stayed from choice – like hell. If he
could have heard the comments over mucking us up for at least
two days by not sending back a replacement for Murray while
the holidays go on he would not have said "They stayed from
choice". I know what he did mean – but a bloody silly way to say

it.'[700] Inevitably, during their long wait for the end of what Miller derisively called 'the holidays', the members of the plateau party had also discussed Hillary's plans for the tractors – and Miller, at least, was appalled at what he heard. 'I cannot get Jim's comments on objects of tractor effort out of my mind,' he wrote on the evening before he and Marsh set out for Depot 480, '– such selfishness and personal ambition.'[701] Given this strength of feeling it was perhaps as well that Hillary was unable to fly back to the Plateau Depot until after Miller's departure.

'November 9th,' Hillary remembered, 'was possibly the most depressing day I experienced throughout the whole expedition.'[702] Not only had the weather closed in immediately after Mulgrew reached the depot, preventing further supply flights and the return of the drivers, but that morning Mulgrew reported over the radio that he had fallen from the roof of the caboose while fixing an aerial, breaking a number of ribs. Just two days after his return to the depot he would again need to be evacuated and the tractor party's numbers were once more depleted. Finally, a radio schedule with the dog sledgers brought the news that they had made incredibly slow progress since starting for the planned location of Depot 480 on the 8th. 'The surface,' Marsh observed, 'although it looks alright, is appalling.'[703] Eventually they had found it necessary to unload twelve cases of dog pemmican, two boxes of man rations, four gallons of paraffin and a complete set of survey equipment – all of which would have to be picked up by the tractors. 'Even after this, progress was interminably slow, with the dogs stopping at every patch of new snow and these are becoming more frequent.' For Hillary, after so many days of waiting, the news could hardly have been worse, as a surface which the dogs found so difficult might well prove impassable for the Fergusons. 'Looks like trouble ahead: a lot of relaying,' he noted despondently. 'Probably puts the pot on our Pole dash.'[704]

At last, on the evening of the 10th, the clouds rolled back from across Ross Island and a favourable weather report from Mulgrew and Bates 290 miles away persuaded Claydon that it was worth making an attempt to reach the depot. 'We were off the airstrip by 9.45 p.m.,' noted Hillary, 'and flew across the Sound under a heavy overcast. However the head of the Blue Glacier was clear and we flew up into the sun and then in excellent weather crossed the névé.'[705] By the time they reached the Ferrar Glacier, the cloud lay far behind and brilliant sunshine glinted from its uncrossable surface, giving it a star-spangled beauty. As they approached the plateau, Claydon began to pick up the depot's radio beacon and he began his descent. After so many delays because of poor weather, the flight had been remarkably easy.

With the Beaver's engine still running to reduce the combined effects of cold and altitude, Hillary and Bates quickly unloaded and then helped Mulgrew to climb painfully into the cockpit for his return flight. Although his injuries clearly made it impossible for him to drive one of the tractors, his condition did not appear so serious that it would prevent him from operating the radio at base; this being the case, Hillary had decided to ask Ted Gawn, the senior radio operator, to replace Mulgrew as a driver, at least until his ribs healed sufficiently for him to rejoin the tractor party. Gawn had willingly stepped into the breach, but the prospect of his driving a tractor across the plateau filled Hillary with something akin to dread: 'Ted was our most expert radio operator and would be fully at home as far as field radio communications were concerned,' he later wrote, 'but he would be the first to admit his weaknesses as a tractor driver. His flair for breaking tracks and generally getting into vehicle trouble had become a byword at Scott Base.'[706] However, as Hillary would have been the first to acknowledge, circumstances no longer allowed him the luxury of being fastidious in his choice of companions.

The Beaver made two more flights that evening, bringing in the remaining supplies and the two new volunteer drivers in conditions so perfect that, according to Claydon, 'one of the passengers made history, being the first Antarctic explorer to arrive on the Polar Plateau – asleep!'[707] Despite having managed to recruit enough drivers to continue with four vehicles, Hillary's relief at being back 'on the job' was short-lived. Although Bates had worked conscientiously during his ten days at the Plateau Depot, soon after Hillary's arrival he revealed that he shared Ellis's strong reservations regarding the planned expedition to the Pole. 'Soon after I arrived back,' Hillary wrote that night, 'Jim said he and Murray had had a talk and neither were keen on going past D700 as they thought the vehicles would be shot by then and anyway they'd be beyond the range of the Beaver. Told Jim we had to *get* to D700 first before we could worry about not going beyond it.'[708] Although Hillary later asserted that his confidence in his engineers' abilities far exceeded their own and that he 'decided not to be too much influenced by their misgivings,'[709] Bates's words were an unwelcome blow – and they hinted at another battle to come.

The tractors finally got underway at 6.30pm on 12 November and almost immediately they began to struggle with the soft snow encountered by the dog teams a few days earlier. Each vehicle in turn ploughed its way into the surface and had to be towed free and Hillary admitted to being 'aghast to find how easy it was for the Fergusons to bog into the soft surface.'[710] With a gross load on the sledges of 11 tons, after many hours of hard labour the party had covered less than 7 miles. That evening Miller sent an encouraging report to the effect that the surface improved significantly about 25 miles from the Plateau Depot but, despite this good news, the day had been, as Hillary later acknowledged, 'a discouraging beginning when I thought of the 900-odd miles that separated us from the South Pole.'[711]

In three days the party managed to cover just 35 miles, the soft snow and increasing gradient making it necessary to resort to relaying loads. The increasing altitude also severely reduced the Fergusons' performance and fuel consumption soared. Moreover, these appalling conditions constituted an enormous challenge for the inexperienced members of Hillary's party. 'The more we struggled the more we became bogged and I bitterly regretted the loss of Murray and Peter. My new team could hardly hope to have the skill and timing of the old one and we churned in again and again.'[712] Now, for the first time in the whole expedition, the Weasel, which had generally been considered the sick man of the party, came into its own. With the Fergusons floundering, Hillary unhitched a 2-ton sledge from the tractor-train and fastened it behind the Weasel which, despite a colossal load of 5 tons, continued to make good headway.

On the 15th, they at last reached the 25-mile point and, as predicted by Miller, the surface improved so markedly that the loads could be rearranged more evenly. The day was not without its problems however. Since the arrival of the first US planes of the season, influenza had been spreading like wildfire through the Ross Sea Party and Hillary had been sickening even before he rejoined the tractors. Since the 14th he had felt too ill to drive the lead tractor and had instead retreated to the rather more luxurious and better-heated cab of the Weasel, while Bates took point. On the 15th, the party's main objective was to reach a snow cairn built by Miller's team 35 miles from the Plateau Depot to mark the spot at which they had changed course from due west to 215°. By Hillary's reckoning the tractors should have reached the cairn by 8.30pm but there was still no sign of it. Puzzled, he scanned the horizon with his binoculars and eventually picked it up in a position a long way to the east. It seemed that the astro-compass, Bates's steering or his own calculations must be seriously at fault – an error of 6 miles in 35 came as quite a shock with the best part of 1000 miles still to travel. 'And then to cap it all,' groaned Hillary, 'we struck soft snow climbing up to the cairn and the tractors bogged down ... Poor old Jim was thoroughly cheesed off. I hope I feel well enough to take over the widetrack again tomorrow.'[713]

At the cairn Hillary and Bates took the time to examine the astro-compass attached to the cab of the wide-tracked Ferguson that Hillary usually drove and they discovered that the baseplate had worked loose, so that the tractor's vibration caused the instrument gradually to pivot to the right and thus throw the party off-course to the left. But the discovery gave Hillary scant satisfaction. 'Whatever the reasons, and excuses,' he later admitted, 'the fact remained that the navigation was my particular responsibility and I crawled into my sleeping-bag with the rather lugubrious thought that I'd made a proper hash of it.'[714]

Despite much stronger winds and drift, progress improved significantly over the course of the next few days with the tractors moving much more easily over a hard surface. Hillary also chose to switch to night driving, as the sun compass would be easier to operate with the sun in front of the vehicles as they pursued a south-westerly or southerly heading. On the 16th, with Hillary once again in the lead, they made 18 miles and their campsite that night gave them splendid views of Mount Feather and Mount Harmsworth to the east and the jagged ridges of the Western Mountains on the horizon. The radio schedules that evening also brought the welcome news that Fuchs's reconnaissance party had reached South Ice three days earlier and that Brooke's Northern Party was making excellent progress and had begun its climb up to the Polar Plateau. Less reassuringly, Miller reported that his party had not only been delayed by poor weather and was still only 85 miles from the Plateau Depot but that it had also encountered crevasses some 72 miles from the depot.

Miller's warning persuaded Hillary to steer a course slightly to the west of that followed by the dog teams, and on the 17th the tractor party managed to skirt round the crevasse zone, covering an impressive 30 miles. It was by far the best day's total since they had left the depot. Despite a much more compact snow surface, which favoured the Fergusons, strong drift-laden winds slowed progress the following day and by the time they camped on 18 November the tractor drivers were chilled to the bone. 'We did 21.6 miles today,' Hillary scrawled in his diary, 'but I'm blowed if I know if it was worth it as we had a thoroughly miserable time ... It's a serious weakness not having an extra driver as it makes things so much easier on personnel. I'll have to see what I can do for the D480/D700 trip.'[715] The one consolation was that the party had covered 105 miles in the last six days and was now more than half way to the planned location of Depot 480.

Improved visibility and a firm surface enabled the tractor party to make excellent headway on the 19th, with the vehicles sometimes travelling at an unheard of 5mph. The surface, however, also proved extremely rough in places and the constant jarring took its toll on both the sledges and the lashings that kept their cargoes in place. At one point a 44-gallon drum of fuel broke loose, halting the convoy while Gawn and Hillary trundled back for a mile to retrieve it. Despite this accident, the party chalked up a total of 34 miles and Hillary thought this 'was the best surface we

had struck on the southern journey and we revelled in it.'[716] The
party also enjoyed the unspoken satisfaction of at last overtaking
the dog teams, whose progress had been seriously hampered by
the weather, though the vehicles' slightly different heading meant
that the two parties were separated by some 7 miles and saw
nothing of each other as they passed.

The following day, high winds and dense drift made another
day of high speeds and significant distances seem unlikely, but
the sun's glow was still sufficiently discernible for the use of the
astro-compass and Hillary decided to press on. Driving in a temperature of -30°F and in strong winds was a miserable business
and soon the drivers' extremities were bitterly cold and their
clothes coated in ice, but the good surface and their ability to
maintain reasonable speeds persuaded them to keep going despite
their discomfort. 'We plugged on for hour after hour, stopping
only when we had to for a quick warm up or a hot drink, and
after ten hours going we were absolutely worn out so we stopped
and camped. We'd done thirty point three miles and it had been a
struggle every inch of the way.'[717]

After their exhausting ten-hour drive, the drivers slept until
8.30pm on 21 November – but two messages received during
the routine radio schedule that evening startled Hillary back into
full wakefulness. The first telegram, dated 19 November, was from
Fuchs, 'giving all the gory details of their trip to South Ice'[718] and
sharing with Hillary the revised departure date of the Crossing
Party from Shackleton:

> Owing to thirty-nine days spent forcing route to South Ice
> our start delayed ten days giving 200 miles to catch up to
> maintain twenty miles per day. This will be attempted ... Air
> reconnaissance to 85°S indicates Shackleton to South Ice most
> difficult section to Pole. Not certain twenty miles per day can
> be maintained to South Ice but expect over 20 miles per day
> thereafter. Could be up to fortnight late arriving Scott Base but
> will endeavour [to] reduce this though possibility remains we
> do not arrive till 9th March. Hope [to] improve this pessimis-
> tic statement on passage. If conditions difficult we can accept
> intended D700 at 600 miles ... Time so gained may be useful

to you for your works on mountains. As it seems unlikely we can meet at D700 would appreciate guide from Plateau Depot if possible. Delighted you have vehicles on plateau and going so well. Congratulations from all.'[719]

Though not greatly surprised by the contents of the telegram, Hillary felt far from satisfied. 'They are certainly having a packet of trouble and I'm not at all happy about the very late dates … He talks of March 9th at Scott Base – which probably means later still.'[720] For the Ross Sea Party the most significant impact of any further delays would be the potential need for some at least to remain in the Antarctic for another winter. It was a prospect that few among the New Zealanders – including the homesick Hillary himself – would relish.

According to Hillary's later account of the expedition, the second most troubling – and the most surprising – element of Fuchs's telegram was 'Bunny's lack of appreciation of the weight of momentum we were getting behind our southern tractor journey, as was indicated by his suggestion that we might prefer to put the final depot at 600 miles instead of 700 miles.'[721] In Hillary's view, with the tractors now only 250 miles from the 700-mile point, their arrival there was almost a certainty: 'It was what would happen beyond D700 that occupied my thoughts and plans.'[722]

The second telegram – from John Claydon, paraphrasing a telephone call from the Ross Sea Committee – crystallised those thoughts. 'Committee interested in your prospects reaching Pole,' wrote Claydon, 'and whether you have considered this. If you are prepared to go for Pole committee will give you every encouragement and full support following formal approval from London. If you intend to proceed Helm requests you seek committee approval for the venture following which they will get OK from London.'[723] Reading Claydon's telegram immediately after that from Fuchs, Hillary could only assume that both the Ross Sea Committee and its counterpart in London had become extremely anxious about the Crossing Party's chances of traversing the continent before the close of the season. Fuchs's journey time might be reduced if Hillary provided him with a

fully surveyed route and a guide who could lead him from the
South Pole to Scott Base. That Hillary's polar aspirations had
already been deliberately quashed by the Ross Sea Committee
some six months earlier seemed to have been conveniently
forgotten. 'They (and London),' exclaimed Hillary, 'are now
anxious that we go on to the Pole presumably so that the route
can be proved and so make it easier for Bunny (what a change
of mind!!)'[724] Nor, apparently, had it crossed anyone's mind that
whatever the committees might think, Fuchs had certainly not
requested any such help — his stated requirements extending no
further than the provision of a guide from the Plateau Depot
onwards. If nothing else, his telegram made it absolutely clear that
the idea of Hillary progressing to the Pole, with or without the
committees' approval, had never even occurred to him.

Hillary later wrote of the Ross Sea Committee's message that
he found it 'most encouraging, largely because of an error in my
interpretation of it. It was handed to me scribbled out on a rough
piece of paper, and in reading it through I gathered from the terms
"following formal approval from London" that this approval had
already been obtained ... As I discovered later, London had never
been approached on this matter and I had in fact misinterpreted
the meaning of the message.'[725] Considering the full text of the
message — particularly the entirely unambiguous statement that
'If you intend to proceed Helm requests you seek committee
approval for the venture following which they will get OK from
London' — many, particularly among the British, found it difficult
to understand how it could have been misunderstood. Certainly
Claydon was under no illusions: 'The arrangement,' he wrote
in his official report, 'was that following a request by Hillary to
the Ross Sea Committee for permission, the formal approval of
the London Executive of the TAE would be sought.'[726] In reality,
however, such debates were irrelevant. While Hillary might derive
some satisfaction from being able to write 'I now have official
sanction for my Pole dash,'[727] he would probably have been the
first to admit that the denial of such sanction would have made
absolutely no difference to his plans. His 'Pole dash' was already a
foregone conclusion — no matter what the consequences.

12

The Starting Line

With the clock ticking and still no certainty as to when the route finding party might reach South Ice, by early November the atmosphere at Shackleton was little short of frantic. Communications between the field party and base had become ever more sporadic and most of the explorers felt that they had been left completely in the dark regarding Fuchs's plans to make up for lost time. 'Conjecture on the future moves of the expedition are everywhere,' George Lowe noted on 5 November, after another prolonged radio silence. Two days later, he observed: 'Some say we cannot possibly leave by 14th November ... Whatever the future events the days are dribbling out and the vehicles have not managed to average 10 miles per day in the run to South Ice ... I feel some drastic recasting of the plans or approach to progress must be made immediately.'[728]

For his part, Fuchs acknowledged that the demands of the journey had forced him to push communications to the very bottom of his list of priorities and he understood that this would lead to apprehension among his men – and to some irritation when, from a position of almost total ignorance, they were left to field questions from outside agencies. 'Rather naturally,' he wrote on 12 November, 'they have been getting anxious about the passing of time, the preparations they have to make and the pressure for information from home, particularly from the BBC.'[729] Like

so many others before and since, the members of the TAE were
discovering that courting publicity (and the funding it attracted)
brought disadvantages as well as benefits; in particular, improvements in technology meant that fêted explorers could no longer
out-distance pursuing journalists and committees. Inevitably,
demands for information became ever more strident when things
appeared to be going wrong. 'Even while travelling,' Fuchs continued, 'I receive the repercussions of the numerous requests for
newspaper articles, broadcasts and such information. I have been
compelled to keep rather clear of this manoeuvre as our days
have been far too long as it is and there is certainly no time for
writing articles, awaiting radio schedules etc.'[730]

Despite his growing understanding of the pressures his deliberate radio silence was generating – an understanding that was
reinforced when he learned that his men had conceived the
'extraordinary idea of flying in to collect us wherever we were!'[731]
– Fuchs did little or nothing to improve communications, even
after his arrival at the forward base. Watching proceedings at South
Ice, Lister remarked that 'little was said to base over the radio,
which was a pity since I knew they felt very sore at base, with
some justification.'[732] At Shackleton, meanwhile, Lowe could no
longer contain his anger: 'We had had no effective contact with
them for several days,' he scribbled irritably. 'Messages arrived
from Scott Base – from Ed who was in the field at "Plateau
Camp" – and from the office in London. All wanted answers to
pertinent questions. No answers were received.'[733] Once again,
Fuchs had failed to appreciate to what extent his own actions,
no matter how well intentioned or justified, could sap the confidence and morale of the TAE on both sides of the continent.

Poor visibility prevented Lewis from collecting the drivers until the afternoon of 15 November and by the time they
reached Shackleton that evening, they had been absent for
39 days. Although Fuchs was not always the shrewdest observer
of his men's state of mind, even he could not fail to recognise
the air of disquiet and depression. 'It was very noticeable that the
general and individual morale of the base had sunk to a low ebb!'
he wrote a few days later. 'Largely this was due to their inability

to understand the problems, and therefore the delay, which faced our field party. Second they did not have anyone to tell them not to fuss about a bit of wasted time.'[734] A remarkable comment from one who had frequently plumbed the depths of despair during the course of the previous month. However, having taken the time to interrogate his team regarding their anxieties and to describe in detail the trials and tribulations encountered en route to South Ice, he felt confident that during the course of the following days 'the troubles in the minds of many gradually disappeared and the unit morale went up 100%.'[735] But not everyone was satisfied by his pep talk. Lowe, in particular, felt far from convinced by what he heard: 'A new date is given of 24th November,' he wrote immediately after the discussion. 'This is very late and we can never make up the lost mileage or days. Ed, I feel, has every reason to feel disappointed with the lack of contact and our lack of progress.'[736]

Since flying back to Shackleton at the end of October, Homard had been working hard on the preparation of the six vehicles – three Sno-cats, two Weasels and one Muskeg – which would now make the journey to South Ice. With David Pratt's arrival on the 15th, this work accelerated. The other explorers, meanwhile, concentrated on packing and dividing their equipment and chattels into four categories: those items which were to be carried in the vehicles; those which would be flown to the American base at Ellsworth for onward transmission to the Royal Society base at Halley Bay; those to be flown direct to Halley Bay in the Otter; and, finally, those non-essentials which would be abandoned at Shackleton. As this work continued, it became increasingly apparent that despite all the months of preparation, some aspects of Fuchs's plan were still evolving, with such obvious decisions as the selection of the men for each element of the journey still not made. Lister had expected to join the vehicle party at South Ice but on the 19th, and with no explanation, he was told that he would accompany them from Shackleton. 'Suddenly Bunny told me on the radio that I was to return to base immediately an aircraft could reach us (planned for next day) and then I would travel with the vehicle team. Ah well! How plans do change.'[737]

Despite such last-minute alterations, by the 22nd the explorers had begun to load the sledges with the 20 tons of food, fuel and material that would be needed on the main journey and, with the work progressing well, that evening Fuchs felt confident enough to hold a party to mark the expedition's imminent departure.

Two days later they were at last prepared to start. Loading and lashing had continued until the early hours of the morning and the men's tiredness delayed the departure by a few hours; but everything was now ready – or ready enough. According to Homard, at the moment of departure he and Pratt 'were still holding hacksaws and spanners and wishing we could have "just one more day".' But with the expedition already a fortnight behind schedule, even the engineers accepted that 'there could be no further delay so long as each vehicle was a "runner".'[738] Fuchs had expected Finn Ronne to fly into Shackleton in order to see off the expedition but bad weather prevented flying. Instead, during the afternoon, a small party of Argentinians turned up unannounced, having travelled the 20 miles from their station in a Weasel. Diplomatic relations between Britain and Argentina remained extremely tense as a result of conflicting claims in the region, but at a local level, feelings were much more cordial and at 6.30pm the Argentinians enthusiastically joined the RAF contingent in waving and shouting encouragement as the vehicles pulled away, heading south. The crossing of Antarctica had begun.

'Six vehicles thundered and clanked away on a grey evening to run 17 miles before we camped,' Lowe recorded. 'We were pulling some twenty odd tons of fuel and food and bowled along at about 7 miles per hour.'[739] The running order consisted of a Sno-cat now named 'Rock 'n' Roll', driven by Fuchs and Stratton; Sno-cat 'County of Kent', driven by Homard and Lenton; Sno-cat 'Able' driven by David Pratt and Blaiklock; and the Muskeg 'Hopalong', driven by Jon Stephenson. The two Weasels brought up the rear: 'Rumble', driven by Rogers, and 'Wrack and Ruin', driven by Lowe. The bad weather that had prevented Ronne from reaching Shackleton had also delayed Lister, who would now be dropped in by aeroplane as soon as conditions allowed. Geoff Pratt would replace Lister at South Ice, where he and La

Grange would continue the scientific observations and wait to be picked up by the vehicles before the united party of twelve men made for the Pole.

The soft snow surface allowed the vehicles to move at speed despite the fact that the sledges ploughed furrows 6 to 9 inches deep as they moved, and when they reached the filled chasms a few miles from Shackleton they crossed with ease before camping. They had made good time but already Fuchs was worried. In particular, it was obvious that the crevasse bridges had begun to soften and sag with the increasing power of the sun : 'This looks ill for the rest of the journey to South Ice.'[740] The next day grey skies stripped the landscape of all contrast and intensified the danger posed by crevasses – but all agreed that they must press on regardless. Lowe wrote that 'the party set off in line like ships at sea tossing and rolling and throwing a spray of snow away from the tracks like a bow wave.'[741] They bowled along, occasionally pausing for a crevasse, but making good headway until at around midday they reached a point some 14 miles from their last campsite. There disaster struck. Moving at speed, the leading cat, 'Rock 'n' Roll', suddenly burst through the lid of a crevasse 15 feet wide. The vehicle's nose plunged down but just as it seemed that it would topple in altogether, the front pontoons buried themselves in the far wall and the drag of the sledges behind prevented a headlong fall into the chasm. Beneath the cat gaped a black, hungry-looking fissure some 60 feet deep and Fuchs and Stratton had what Lowe called 'a tricky two minutes'[742] clambering to safety. Both were visibly shaken.

The recovery took five exhausting hours and Fuchs admitted that, when he first looked at the position of the Sno-cat, he thought 'it seemed almost an impossibility'.[743] Realising that the vehicle might be irretrievable, they cautiously removed everything of value and then used a steel-wire hawser to hitch the stricken vehicle's rear end to the two remaining cats. The two Weasels were then driven over a rather insecure-looking snow bridge and attached to the front, to prevent it dropping when the cats began to pull from behind. 'All was set', recorded Lowe, 'and the two thundering powerhouses, the cats side by side, churned the snow and roared.' [744] 'Rock 'n' Roll' lurched and her nose dipped visibly, but the Weasels held her and she came free, miraculously undamaged. 'These excitements,' continued Lowe, 'and the sharp reminder that the vehicles were very easily lost – even when the journey had hardly begun – became a lesson taken to heart by all.'

That night improved visibility enabled Haslop to drop Geoff Pratt at South Ice and to collect Lister and by 11.30pm the vehicle party was at last up to its planned strength for this stage of the journey. The following day it quickly became apparent that the vehicles had entered a belt of crevasses which the warm summer temperatures had rendered far more dangerous than had been the case in mid-October. The Crossing Party had covered just 40 miles since leaving Shackleton and already it was obliged to start the tedious process of prodding the surface to identify crevasse lids. 'These lids cannot be seen from the surface contour,' wrote Lowe, 'and will easily allow to pass a man or dog team and sledge and never be noticed; but they cannot and do not take six vehicles pounding over them with 35 tons in all. They break.'[745]

Inching forwards, often in near whiteout conditions, it took them until 30 November to force their way through the crevasses, moving no more than 2–3 miles a day and with the more expendable Weasels always in the vanguard. 'The party is feeling very depressed by our slow progress as indeed I am myself,' Fuchs admitted on the evening of the 29th, 'but I am resisting all suggestions of moving rapidly over this now dangerous territory as I have no intention of losing men or vehicles by carelessness. This is only the sixth day of the journey and it is no time to panic about slow progress and perhaps prejudice the success of the whole venture by pressing on regardless!'[746] The party's mood darkened further when Homard and Pratt identified serious wear in the inboard rollers and running rail of one of 'Rock 'n' Roll's' pontoons. The engineers couldn't be sure how long the vehicle might last but they dismally assured Fuchs that a failure would necessitate an entirely new pontoon being flown out from Shackleton. This news was particularly depressing because, up to now, the Sno-cats had been by far the strongest of the vehicles. If they began to fail so early in the crossing, what hope could the party have of completing the journey?

They finally broke free of the crevasses the following day and plunged forward to cover a total of 27 miles. 'It was remarkable,' wrote Fuchs, 'to see the more gloomy and somewhat grumbling members of the party change their whole outlook to one of cheerfulness! A pity that an early setback, or is it the laborious prodding, so reduced their morale.'747 On 1 December they made 41 miles, travelling in beautiful weather over perfectly smooth but soft surfaces. The landscape, the convoy's constant rolling motion and the unvarying quality of the light, gave the experience an almost dreamlike quality on days like this:

> The land itself, the colour, the changelessness is like porridge without salt. It never rains, there is no thunder, no lightning, no crisp clouds in the sky; now, the sun never sets and beats down always from the same height going round and round and round. A strange emasculated place that goes on and on – there is nothing to become very attached to and we are trying to drive across it.748

This dreamlike continuity was interrupted that evening when they discovered that 'Rock 'n' Roll's' damaged pontoon was beginning to disintegrate, while Homard's Sno-cat, 'County of Kent', arrived at the campsite firing on only five of its eight cylinders. A day of emergency repairs enabled them to continue on the 3rd and, much to everyone's relief, none of the vehicles broke down despite covering 65 miles in 13 hours. 'The weather was clear and warm,' enthused Lowe, 'the surface superb. The cats in front ploughed forward in line like cruisers going into battle with flags and pennants flying and puffs of snow spray flying. I never cease to be impressed by the sight.'749

The vehicles were now approaching the 11-mile wide crevasse belt at the foot of the ice wall and on the 4th Stratton and Fuchs had just spotted the chequered flag marking the beginning of the crevasses when 'Rock 'n' Roll' broke through. 'The first we knew was a horrible sinking sensation,' Fuchs recorded, 'with the bonnet seeming to rise in front of us, a pause and then a further lurch as the back went further down.'[750] Closer inspection revealed that the second drop had occurred when the four heavy-duty bolts holding the tow bar had sheered off completely; even worse, the steering rockers under the chassis had snapped in two and the pontoon bars were seriously distorted. Fortunately, Homard and Pratt had brought sufficient spares to effect a repair but it would take two days to complete once 'Rock 'n' Roll' had been hauled out of its hole by Sno-cats 'Able' and 'County of Kent.' 'Meanwhile,' groaned Lowe, 'the big prod started in earnest.'[751]

It took the party seven days to work their way through the crevasse belt – as long as it had taken the reconnaissance party in late October. The days were unusually hot and windless and the men began to sweat and strip amid the snow and ice. Lowe described the scene:

> Looking along the line of prodders was like looking along the pilgrim track to Badrinath where devout Hindus crawl or measure their length and do all manner of uncomfortable antics to acquire merit as they go to Holy Vishnu's shrine. Here most were stripped to the waist in the world of snow, each with a stick and a glazed devout look to all the sky, moving a step then thrusting into the snow and forcing it down to the hilt until he was bent double with his ear and muscles tensed to listen and feel – then up with a jerk and another glazed step forward ... Every twenty yards or so the pole would push through to nothingness underneath and here the devout pilgrim changed his religion – from Hindu to Moslem. The inspection hole was made and looking along the line could be seen Moslems with their bottoms in the air and their heads on the ground praying to Mecca![752]

Progress was agonisingly slow but the need for caution was again brought home to everyone on the 8th when Sno-cat 'Able' dropped through a snow bridge already weakened by the passage of the other vehicles.

The recovery proved to be the most difficult to date. Only the leading tips of 'Able's' front pontoons rested on the lip of the crevasse while the rear pontoons hung in space. Ken Blaiklock thought the recovery looked quite impossible: 'It was so precariously pitched,' he remembered, 'there was one pontoon out there and one pontoon out here, and everything dangling. Whichever way you pulled it you'd have got it on a bit of wire hanging down a crevasse.'[753] Clearly the cat could not be hauled backwards and it was equally obvious that the rear pontoons would have to be supported when it moved forwards – but how could they be supported given that they were now hanging completely free? Looking into the crevasse's blue depths, the explorers noticed that it narrowed at a point some 25 feet below the surface – by shovelling snow into the crevasse they might be able to block it at this point and create a foundation from which to build a temporary bridge. Such a recovery had never been attempted before – but it appeared to be the only option. Having secured 'Able' by steel hawsers, to the other cats at the front and to the Weasels at the back, everyone set to with shovels, gradually plugging the crevasse with tons of snow. Then, roped to the vehicles for safety, some of the men lowered themselves into the crevasse where they began to cut ledges in the walls; these ledges then served as corbels supporting sections of reinforced aluminium bridging spans, set at precarious angles across the width of the fissure. The greatest risk was that, once the cat moved forwards, its rear would drop heavily onto the bridges and, to prevent them collapsing under the shock, steel rope slings were looped about their ends and then secured by dead-men driven into the snow surface above.

Finally, after some five hours of intense labour, the moment of truth arrived. David Pratt climbed nervously back into his cab and with a hoarse roar the two Sno-cats began to draw the stricken vehicle forwards, while the two Weasels, acting as anchors, gradually gave way behind.

As 'Able' started to move we held our breath; there was a loud crunch as the ledges under the bridging gave way and the vehicle lurched sideways to sink momentarily deeper, but the 'dead-men' held; then, like some monster rising from the deep, it appeared to heave and wallow its way to the surface, finally to come safely clear.[754]

The recovery had been brilliantly and flawlessly executed.

Without experiencing any more near misses, the convoy finally broke free of the crevasses on 10 December and by 1.15am the following morning the entire party was camped at the foot of the ice wall. 'Tonight', wrote Fuchs, 'we change to Greenwich Mean Time which advances our clocks three hours and at the same time change to night travel in order to have crisper snow surface and perhaps some increased strength in the snow bridges upon the "ice wall" and the Recovery Glacier.'[755] The move would also synchronise the travelling times of Hillary's and Fuchs's parties and, in theory at least, make radio communications easier. After a day's rest, work began again at 2100 GMT on the 11th.

As expected, the hot sun of recent weeks had seriously weakened a number of the snow bridges and crevasse lids on the route over the ice wall: some sagged visibly while others had collapsed altogether, leaving jagged holes in the windcrust. Nonetheless, having reconnoitred on skis, Fuchs felt confident that they could force a passage and, in the event, only one of the Weasels came to grief on the ascent. Driven by Allan Rogers and with Lister perched rather unwisely on top of the cab in order to spot crevasses, 'Rumble' had just reached the brow when it fell sideways into an invisible chasm. 'My trousers were ripped to ribbons as I dropped past the open door of the Weasel which has a sharp corner,' noted the unfortunate Lister – but he was lucky to have escaped so lightly, being thrown onto soft snow instead of into the bowels of the crevasse itself. 'The recovery procedure,' he continued, 'was just as in Greenland – haul horizontal and then motor out ... Of course our experts considered the matter for an hour while a few of us sounded around to permit other vehicles to manoeuvre.'[756]

Lister's sideways swipe at 'our experts' was just the latest expression of a complaint that had first been made by Goldsmith during the unloading of the *Theron* nearly two years before, and which Lister himself had angrily articulated three weeks earlier while waiting to be airlifted from South Ice. 'Our leadership,' he wrote then, 'has more dogged enthusiasm than experience and hence we waste time relearning things which many know already but we are not allowed to demonstrate ... We are dogged by FIDS tactics. Nothing else is accepted, indeed nothing else is worth thinking of!'[757] Fuchs was far from unusual in his resistance to what he perceived to be new ideas. Other highly experienced FIDS veterans, like the Albert medallist Kevin Walton, fully shared his view that the Antarctic was the last place in which to trial new methods and equipment. Defending such conservatism, Walton wrote that 'to the polar traveller who intends to explore and to return with his results, it is sound common sense.'[758] What Fuchs failed to recognise, however, was that in refusing to capitalise on the experience of Arctic veterans like Lister, he was nullifying the logic that had led him to recruit those men in the first place – particularly when their experience related to vehicles, of which most FIDS veterans were almost entirely ignorant. It was also highly unfortunate that his conservatism sometimes found expression in terms that the non-FIDS participants in the expedition found objectionable, thereby undermining the singleness of purpose so essential to polar travel.

'Rumble's' mishap proved to be the last on the road to South Ice. Having safely crossed the belt of crevasses at the top of the ice wall, at 9.00am on 13 December, the ten explorers were camped opposite the western edge of the Shackleton Mountains. That night they travelled another 31 miles over sastrugi so severe that La Grange compared it to 'driving over a vastly magnified sheet of corrugated iron'[759] but by the end of the day they had reached the first zone of crevassing in the centre of the Recovery Glacier. They began probing during the evening of the 14th and, aided by the markers laid down a month earlier, they crossed the belt with astonishing ease. 'We are now camped on the south side of this very bad area,' Fuchs wrote delightedly, 'after one long day's work (14 hrs) instead of the 4 days it took us last trip. As a result we are now 9 days ahead of the pioneer trip in October and November.

If our luck holds we can reach South Ice in another three to four days.'[760]

Their luck did not hold. The following day, after five hours of routine maintenance, the convoy set off into worsening weather. As the vehicles crunched their way across a field of sastrugi, thick clouds rolled across the sky from the west and soon there was almost complete whiteout. 'Being in the lead in Rock & Roll', wrote Fuchs, 'I drove by feel alone, accelerating up the hummocks and easing down the far side. Maintaining course was also difficult as the two sledges, each laden with two tons, tended to swing the cat's tail on the uneven ridges.'[761]

Conditions worsened and on the 16th they managed to cover only 5 miles before the presence of crevasses made it impossible to continue in such appalling visibility. They remained stationary the following day but on the evening of the 18th blue sky could be seen to the east and with the surface whiteout significantly reduced, Fuchs, Stratton, Blaiklock and Lister undertook a survey on skis before the vehicles were brought forward to the edge of the crevasse zone at the foot of the Whichaway Nunataks. The delays caused by the whiteout had been immensely frustrating, but with conditions apparently improving it seemed probable that the Crossing Party would be able to reach South Ice within the next two days. When Lenton tuned into the BBC that evening, however, any satisfaction Fuchs may have felt at this prospect rapidly dissolved at the startling news that Hillary, apparently with the Ross Sea Committee's approval, had announced his intention of attempting the South Pole. 'Bunny,' observed Lister, with masterly understatement, 'is naturally a bit fed up.'[762]

Perhaps inevitably, the news bulletin heard by the Crossing Party painted a very incomplete picture of recent events on the far side of the continent. Hillary's party had reached the site of Depot 480 on 25 November, after a difficult journey across hummocks, sastrugi and crevasses, sometimes travelling in near whiteout conditions. The last 18 miles to the depot site had proved particularly hazardous and on the 24th a Ferguson had become trapped in a crevasse for the first time. It had been extracted by the very simple, if somewhat brutal, method of tying its front to the rear of the three remaining vehicles, which then accelerated hard and in unison. 'The strain came on with a jerk,' remembered Hillary, 'and for a moment the tracks skidded in the snow and I thought, "We're not going to do it!" Then we shot forward again like a cork out of a bottle and I knew the tractor was out or the rope had broken.'[763] Fortunately the Terylene rope had held.

Hillary had hoped that the stocking of Depot 480 would begin immediately after their arrival but once again poor weather made flying impossible and the members of the tractor party had no choice but to wait for conditions to improve, occupying their time with routine repairs and maintenance and readjusting the sledge loads for the onward journey. At 4 o'clock on the afternoon of 28 November, Marsh, Miller, Ayres and Carlyon reached the depot, their scabbed faces and bleeding lips showing that they had had a tough trip from the Plateau Depot. Dogs and men were all tired and Miller and Marsh were disgruntled, pointing out that the depot was a good 8 miles from the position previously agreed. 'We all thought that this was a little too inaccurate,'[764] Marsh noted tersely, and it was only by the merest chance that they had found the depot at all.

Hillary's seeming indifference to accurate plotting and the trouble it could cause for the other teams attracted further comment on the 29th, when Claydon at last set out in the Beaver, carrying supplies of pemmican and fresh seal meat for the dogs as well as rations and fuel for the men. Flying over unknown terrain and already struggling with wildly inaccurate maps, Claydon was furious to be told only at the last minute that the location of the depot had changed. 'During the later stages of the first flight into the Depot,' he recorded, 'the trail party nonchalantly mentioned over the radio that they had fixed their position more accurately – 8 miles away from the previous point. In striking contrast to the white desert below, the air was blue for miles!'[765]

Hillary's flawed navigation and his nonchalance regarding its inherent dangers were not the only causes for dissension at the depot. On the morning of 30 November, he joined Marsh and Miller in their pyramid tent to outline his plans for the expedition after Depot 480 had been fully established. After some discussion, he agreed that the tractor party would stock a new depot, 'Midway', at a position to be chosen by Marsh and Miller but to be located approximately 130 miles out from Depot 480. He also agreed that Ayres and Carlyon – the weaker of the two dog parties – would no longer need to proceed all the way to Depot 700. Instead, they would strike east from Midway Depot to survey around Mount Albert Markham, before restocking at Midway and then returning to Depot 480. The supplies at Midway Depot would also provide extra security for Marsh and Miller on their return from establishing Depot 700. Finally, by using the tractors to cache a supply of petrol at Midway, Hillary would reduce the amount of fuel that would have to be flown to Depot 700, thereby limiting the number of long-range supply flights that would have to be made by Claydon and Cranfield.

All three agreed that this revision to the original plan made good sense. There was altogether less enthusiasm, however, when Hillary at last shared his plans for a tractor journey to the Pole, citing Claydon's telegram of 21 November as his official sanction. 'It appears,' observed Marsh, 'that he has every intention of going on to the Pole. Regarding this he said the Ross Sea [Committee] had agreed to this plan following approval from London. I think he has read the message as meaning that approval had already been obtained but follows this up by saying that in any case this makes no difference. Bob immediately expressed his disapproval of "stunts" and this was not well received.'[766] 'I can't see any justifiable point in it,'[767] Miller scribbled irritably, but, fully realising that nothing he could say or do would dissuade Hillary, he instead sat down to write letters on the subject – to his mother, to his wife, to Arthur Helm and to the Ross Sea Committee. The following day, 1 December, Miller and Marsh were glad to get away from the depot, leaving Carlyon and Ayres with the tractors, and by the time they camped they had covered 16 miles in 6 hours, travelling over an undulating surface marked by large sastrugi. 'After our high living at the Depot,' noted Marsh that evening, 'we are back on sledging rations once again, but it is good to be on the way once more.'[768]

While the dog sledgers hacked their way across country towards the planned location of Depot 700, Hillary and the tractor party remained at Depot 480, completing their repairs and waiting for the pilots to make the last of their supply flights. Confident of its approval, on 5 December Hillary also took the opportunity to send a telegram to the Ross Sea Committee, summarising his plans. 'On establishment of D700 the tractors carrying sufficient fuel to reach Pole will continue south to meet Fuchs. Unless Fuchs requires the assistance of the vehicles, which is unlikely, we will continue on after meeting him and leave our vehicles at the Pole station ... I will join Fuchs at the Plateau Depot and guide him down the Skelton and across the Ross Ice Shelf.'[769] Of course, this plan once again hinged upon American support – specifically on the Americans agreeing to fly the New Zealanders from the Pole to Scott Base so that Hillary could then fly back out to the Plateau Depot to meet Fuchs. To remove any doubts on this subject, immediately after receiving what he had interpreted as the Committee's sanction on 21 November, Hillary had contacted Admiral Dufek and obtained his agreement. With the ever-obliging Dufek falling in with his plans, there now appeared to be nothing in his way.

Hillary's last major concern, the recruitment of a suitable number of drivers for the onward journey, was also resolved during the enforced halt at Depot 480. Having waved off Ted Gawn, who gratefully retreated to Scott, the tractor party welcomed back Ellis and Mulgrew, now both recovered from their injuries sustained at the Plateau Depot. In addition, on 6 December, they greeted Douglas McKenzie, a Christchurch-based journalist and one-time RAF bomber pilot, who had met most of the explorers during their training on the Tasman Glacier some sixteen months earlier. In order to report on the expedition's progress, McKenzie had sailed to the Antarctic on board the *Glacier* and had now asked if he might travel with the tractors for a short period. 'On the face of it,' he later wrote, 'this was to be only a return journey to allow an hour with the tractor party for the story, but I was cunningly laying the ground to join the party for at least the next leg of their travels.'[770] What McKenzie did not realise was that Hillary was as anxious to recruit an additional driver as he was to volunteer. 'There was room in a tent for another man,' Hillary recalled, 'and all the necessary equipment. On the spur of the moment I made the decision and, somewhat to his surprise, Doug Mackenzie found himself a full fledged member of the tractor party bound for D700.'[771] With this addition, Hillary's tractor party now numbered six: Hillary himself, Bates, Mulgrew, Ellis, McKenzie and Wright.

On the same day, Claydon delivered the last load of supplies to Depot 480 and at 6 o'clock that evening the tractor party set off in pursuit of Miller and Marsh, leaving Carlyon and Ayres to start their own journey the following day. 'In perfect weather we rattled along over an easy surface, crossing fold after great fold and rarely dropping below four miles per hour.'[772] Bates's work on the tractors, including a retune, had clearly paid dividends and by midnight the party had covered 25 miles. Sitting down to a 'midday' meal of bacon and mashed potatoes in the cramped confines of the caboose, Hillary admitting to feeling highly pleased: if they could maintain this rate of progress they would reach the site of Depot 700 in just five days – 'and then,' he enthused, 'wasn't it only another 500 miles to the Pole?'[773] His jubilation received a sudden check, however, when Mulgrew, who had been manning the radio, handed him a message from the chairman of the Ross Sea Committee.

Hillary had long since learned to dread any telegram from Bowden, and with good reason. After the conventional congratulations on the expedition's progress, the telegram read:

> Overriding consideration is that nothing should be done that involves any risk whatever of endangering primary objective of this whole great Commonwealth project, namely, successful crossing of Antarctic Continent … From this it follows that Depot 700 must not be left unmanned since experience proves that this may make it impossible to find under certain climatic conditions …
>
> In view of many uncertainties which cannot be resolved yet the Ross Sea Committee cannot at present agree with your proposals. We feel for instance we must await the actual

establishment of D700 and Fuchs's arrival at South Ice after which his future movements might be more clearly indicated.[774]

Hillary's reaction to the cable followed the pattern established over many wearisome months of fencing with the Committee: 'I'll treat it in the same manner I do most of their instructions – ignore them. They really are a bunch of clots and seem to change their minds with the weather.'[775]

Worse still, he now found himself fighting a battle on two fronts: with the, in his view, overly cautious but honourably intentioned bureaucrats of the Ross Sea Committee in New Zealand, and closer to home with Miller and Marsh, who had now reached the position selected for the Midway Depot. Following receipt of Bowden's message, Hillary kept a radio schedule with the two dog-sledgers who were far from pleased with what he told them. According to Marsh, Hillary advised them that he wanted to 'put Midway Depot in a position chosen and fixed by himself. Neither of us are very happy with this arrangement … it would be better if the Depot was placed where we had originally decided.'[776] As usual, Marsh's reaction to this news was measured; Miller, on the other hand, was furious, believing that Hillary's navigation was slapdash and his approach to safety, and anything other than maintaining progress, cavalier at best. 'We have established this Halfway Depot and they now say (they is Ed) they may not bother to look for it if they are too far forward,' he stormed. 'What a nerve. Catch us up at all costs – that's all he has in mind. We take time and care over Nav [navigation] – why can't he? It would hold him back that's why. I have told him to come in here as there are no difficulties and tomorrow will sched [schedule] him again insisting as our safety depends on this on our return.[777]

McKenzie, too, believed that Hillary's primary concern at this point was to beat Miller and Marsh to Depot 700. If he succeeded, he would prove that tractors were superior to dogs not only in the weight they could carry but also in speed:

This is what Hillary seemed determined to prove; and it was perhaps important for him to do so to justify not only the work and time which had gone into modifying the vehicles during the winter, but also his presence on the plateau gambolling about in farm tractors at all.[778]

Rubbing salt into Miller's wounds, Hillary also announced that, prior to leaving Depot 480, he had agreed a significant change in the plans for Ayres and Carlyon. Even more galling, the changes had been made without consulting Miller, the expedition's senior surveyor. Instead of travelling east to explore the area around Mount Albert Markham as had been previously agreed, Hillary now told Miller that Ayres and Carlyon would examine the head of the Darwin Glacier, before descending the glacier to then be flown out from a newly established Darwin Depot. '[They] will be languishing back in Base before end January,' fumed Miller. 'A perfect disgrace that anyone should be back in Base before end of February. And the waste of the best dog team (Harry's) in not undertaking a full season's work ... I am afraid Ed is more and more showing his lack of appreciation of what really matters in Antarctica.'[779] The following day Miller sent off another cable, telling Hillary that he considered it 'essential you lay Midway Depot [at] our marked site as previously planned and agreed. Site carefully fixed with regard our safety [on] return journey and TAE.'[780] Whether as a result of poor atmospheric conditions or Hillary's unwillingness to debate the issue, Miller received no reply and he could only hope that the message had been received and understood – and that it would be complied with. In the meantime, he and Marsh continued their drive south – their ambition pricked by the news that the men at Scott had begun to bet on which party would arrive first at the spot selected for Depot 700.

According to Bernie Gunn, beneath George Marsh's 'polished and urbane exterior ... lurked an unsuspected ambition,'[781] that ambition being to beat Roald Amundsen's daily average of 20.8 miles during his famous journey from the Bay of Whales to the Pole and back. Given this personal 'grail-quest', the very suggestion of a tie between dogs and tractors simply acted as an extra spur to one whose loathing of mechanised transport and

determination to push himself and his dogs as hard as possible
had already been marked by less ambitious sledgers like Ayres and
Carlyon. Miller, despite being a comparative novice, proved an
ideal sledging partner for Marsh and admitted to 'shouting and
pleading, raving and yes, cursing'[782] to drive his own team forward as fast as possible. 'I was thrashing poor old Andy with a ski
stick today,' he admitted rather shamefacedly on 10 December,
'and he took a blow on the head by ducking – knocked him out
for a minute or two but he was soon pulling again. Had me worried for a moment or two as I can ill afford to lose a dog.'[783] Cruel
though these methods might seem – particularly when adopted
by a man whose affection for his dogs was beyond doubt – in
terms of the distances travelled, they paid off. The two dog teams
had covered nearly 180 miles in the ten days since they had left
Depot 480.

In comparison with the helter-skelter rush of the dogs, to a
casual observer the motion of the motor vehicles might have
seemed distinctly unhurried. Looking at the tractor train with
fresh eyes, McKenzie thought it powerfully reminiscent of a
rather down-at-heel camel caravan labouring across the deserts
of North Africa. 'It had the same agglomeration of lumpy bun-
dles and incongruous, homemade equipment;' he wrote, 'it had
garish colour, and a roped continuity. Its locomotion – certainly
no faster than the plodding of camels – swaying and joggling,
conveyed through the length of the train, like a wriggle down a
worm, each hillock surmounted by the leader.'[784] But appearances
could be deceptive. For all their apparent clumsiness, the tractors
covered over 52 miles on 7 December and 41 the following day,
despite the presence of numerous crevasses, which Hillary continued to charge with all the abandon of a steeplechase jockey.
This rapid progress only slowed on the 9th when the Weasel's
clutch disintegrated. Despite time-consuming repairs, the need to
redistribute loads to relieve the burden on the failing vehicle and
a large area of soft snow which plucked at the Fergusons' tracks,
they still managed to cover a respectable 27 miles.

With the low sun glittering on the ice ahead, the tractor party
picked up the tracks of the dog sledges late in the evening of the

9th. Now, just as a lost airman might follow railway lines to reach his destination, the tractors latched onto the dog-sledge tracks and stayed glued to them until they reached the 10-foot-high snow cairn Marsh and Miller had built to mark their favoured position for the Midway Depot. Having found the cairn Hillary no longer had any reason to consider locating the depot elsewhere and he and the other drivers unloaded six drums of fuel for the Crossing Party plus eight tins of pemmican, two ration boxes and a jerrycan of kerosene. They rested for the remainder of the day and then set out for Depot 700 at 8.00pm on the 10th. Hearing the news the same day via Scott Base, Miller commented that 'they are just leaving the depot Halfway. We gave our ETA Depot 700 as Friday and apparently tractors have done the same. Will be a dead heat – suspect interest at Base is high as to our relative progress.'[785]

Hillary had hoped to cover the remaining 100 miles to Depot 700 in the next two days but, as he wrote in his diary, 'It's amazing how plans go awry. We started off from Midway Depot at 8 p.m. all set for a good run. But after a couple of hundred yards we stopped as the Weasel was making disturbing noises.'[786] The convoy immediately halted and the two engineers began to delve into the Weasel's innards. It didn't take them long to diagnose a failed bearing in the differential but with no suitable spares there could be no question of a proper repair. Instead, they had no option but to drive on, turning a deaf ear to the bearing's squeals, and waiting for the differential to seize completely at any moment. When it did, they would simply have to abandon the vehicle.

Although Miller and Marsh had encountered a belt of crevasses about 10 miles south of Midway Depot they had radioed Hillary to tell him that the crevasses appeared 'harmless'. But, as a disgruntled Hillary wrote later on the 10th, 'this was far from the case. They really were extremely unpleasant. Nothing more than four feet wide but bottomless. No danger to life I suppose but rather frightening.'[787] Cutting across the crevasses at right angles, the tractors broke through bridges repeatedly, leaving holes that appeared to grow in width with every yard travelled. Just a few feet away the drivers could see the tracks of the dog teams that had skimmed across the area effortlessly, and Hillary admitted that 'This sharp experience confirmed our growing conviction that it was unwise to take too much notice of the opinions of the dog drivers on the crevasse-free nature of any route.'[788] Finally, at 1.00am, he decided that they must halt so that he, Ellis and Mulgrew could rope-up and survey a route on foot.

They flagged a zigzag course for about a mile and then returned to the vehicles for a meal and a hot drink before bringing the tractors forward. The route through the crevasses required a number of very sharp changes of direction – always difficult for the heavily laden Fergusons – and soon 'there was much sweating and swearing as a consequence.'[789] During one of these manoeuvres, the rubber track belonging to one of the vehicles caught in the drawbar of its sledge and snapped. With the tractor perched on the lip of a crevasse, the repair would be complex and dangerous – but there was no choice and, as Hillary acknowledged, 'Murray and Jim attacked the problem with courage and determination.'[790] Working with bare hands in temperatures in the minus twenties it took the engineers some hours to complete the job but eventually the convoy got underway again and by 6.30am on 11 December they had at last cleared the zone. It had taken a gruelling and nerve-racking eight and a half hours.

After another 90 minutes of relatively easy going, Hillary ordered a halt at 8.00am, on the edge of another belt of crevasses. While the others surveyed the route ahead, Ellis and Bates stayed with the vehicles and attempted a temporary repair of the Weasel's differential, which was clearly reaching the end of its tether. They spent more than five hours fabricating a bronze bush to replace the shattered bearing but despite their efforts Bates considered the chances of the repair lasting were very slim. The party moved on again at 3.00am on the 12th and almost immediately Bates's fears were realised. Within half a mile, the bearing had become red hot and smoke was pouring from the differential into the Weasel's cab. With an imminent risk of the Weasel bursting into flames, Hillary realised that the time had come to abandon it. They stripped it of everything useful; pumped its remaining fuel into the tanks of the Fergusons; and redistributed the sledge loads again. Then, at 5.00am, they moved off. 'As we left the Weasel behind it looked mighty lonely perched by itself amongst the sastrugi and I felt quite a sense of loss,' Hillary noted at the end of the day. Like all the TAE's Weasels, it had given good service but it had also given the engineers an enormous amount of trouble.

Despite its ominous appearance, the surface ahead proved remarkably good. It was littered with crevasses as much as 70 feet wide but all of them appeared well plugged with only their narrow outer edges posing any obvious risk. Of course, an entire plug might collapse under the combined weight of the tractors and their sledges but, with his usual insouciance, Hillary wrote, 'We didn't regard this with any great seriousness.'⁷⁹¹ On this occasion, his optimism proved well founded and the tractors crossed the fissures without incident and soon they began to peter out, giving way to a firm but rough area of sastrugi. According to McKenzie, who was seeing this type of scenery for the first time, 'The face of the plateau where the snow had become crusty was infinitely marked with designs of incredible delicacy and beauty – flutings and ripples joined into grander devices resembling anything from toy staircases to a carving by Epstein.'⁷⁹² But, while he looked upon these 'figures of perfection' with amazement and delight, he also recognised that, for the other drivers, familiarity had bred contempt, or at least indifference, and now they viewed the delicately sculpted sastrugi merely as obstacles to be dodged or overcome. Above all else – and certainly above the beauty of his surroundings – speed remained Hillary's key concern and by the end of the day his party had covered another 26 miles. 'We are now 58 miles from D700,' he enthused, 'and if all goes well might make a big push tomorrow.'⁷⁹³

All did not go well. On 13 December a complete whiteout prevented the convoy from moving off until 2.00am, some five hours later than planned. Then, as the tractors descended into a wide basin stretching for miles in all directions, they hit deep snow. 'The very soft snow of several hollows will probably slow [the tractors] somewhat,'⁷⁹⁴ Miller had predicted on the 11th, and he was right. Progress was reduced to a crawl and when the vehicles began to bog down completely there was no option but to start relaying the sledges across the depression. It took hours to complete the crossing, with the sun beating down so strongly into the sheltered hollow that the drivers could feel their skin tightening and cracking under its glare. At last the party reassembled on the far side and they began to climb back out. Gradually the soft snow gave way to a firmer surface and the tractors climbed more swiftly towards the crest of the slope. 'I had just started to relax,' Hillary recalled, 'and was ruminating on the fact that I was feeling a bit chilly when I saw the lead tractor give a terrific lurch, its nose poked in the air for a moment, and then it shot forward on to a level keel again and stopped.'[795] The party had struck yet more crevasses and the yawning hole behind Ellis's tractor showed that he had had a lucky escape.

It took until 11.00am on 14 December to cross the crevasse belt and when he picked up his diary before retiring to his sleeping bag Hillary admitted that 'I really find all this a bit of a strain and think I've really lost my dash for crevasse country.'[796] Thirteen hours later they were underway once more and very soon they might have been forgiven for thinking that they had been caught in a time warp. Within only a short time of setting off, they once again found themselves on top of a ridge looking down onto another vast depression, an exact replica of the one that had cost them so much time, energy and fuel the previous day. This time, by careful driving, they managed to traverse a quarter of the basin before one of the Fergusons became completely stuck, with the deep snow nearly level with the top of its tracks. They dug it free and began to relay and eventually climbed their way back out and onto the plateau – but the effort had been wearying and vexing in equal measure. By 1.00pm only 10 miles separated the tractors from Depot 700 – but the surface ahead was slashed with yet another network of crevasses.

Hillary drove forward in the lead tractor and almost immediately found his Ferguson falling beneath him as a wide bridge gave way: 'suddenly there was a thud beneath me,' he later wrote, 'and my tractor tipped steeply backwards. I almost fell out of my seat but had sufficient presence of mind to lean forward and flick the throttle full on. The bridge had gone and I was going with it!'[797] With its nose pointing skywards and its tracks scrabbling at the lip of the crevasse, it looked as though the tractor and its driver were about to topple backwards but then, miraculously, the tracks obtained just enough purchase to pull the vehicle the vital few inches forward so that it fell heavily onto the far side of the chasm.

It had been a very close shave and with everyone 'a bit shaken up'[798] Hillary decided to camp for the night and continue refreshed the next day. On 15 December a brief survey showed the crevasse belt to be extensive and very dangerous. When prodded with an ice axe, bridges tumbled away to reveal enormous rifts which might easily swallow a tractor. Perhaps the worst of all was the last, some 3.5 miles from where the convoy was parked: this was large and easily recognisable but the bridge appeared to be very insecure and Hillary thought he could detect signs of recent movement. Despite testing a stretch some 800 yards long neither he nor Mulgrew could identify a genuinely safe bridging point and at last they decided that they must depend upon a section which, though still flimsy, seemed as though it might be marginally more stable; they were wrong. When Bates, in the lead tractor, reached the central portion of the bridge 'there was a tearing sound, the bottom dropped out of the lid, and in almost slow motion the tractor sank back into the crevasse.'[799] To everyone's relief Bates proved to be as lucky as Hillary and just when it seemed that the Ferguson must roll backwards into the chasm, the rear section of its cab caught on the lip of the crevasse and the slide came to a halt, leaving the vehicle rearing upwards.

Once a scared looking Bates had climbed to safety the rest of the party gathered around the hole to plan the retrieval. The first requirement was to bring the other tractors forward so that they could pull the trapped vehicle out of its hole; this meant finding an alternative crossing point. The search for a safe route soon made it clear that Hillary's own impatience was at least partly the cause of the accident as a few hundred yards further to the east than he had previously prodded, the large crevasse petered out altogether to be replaced by a tracery of much smaller ones.

Having brought the two remaining Fergusons to the south side of the crevasse, they were then roped in tandem to the front of Bates's vehicle before Mulgrew volunteered to clamber into its cab to put it into neutral. At a given signal, Hillary and Ellis then accelerated hard and fast to jerk the tilting vehicle from its precarious lodging. The plan worked perfectly and with one tremendous heave the Ferguson was pulled out onto the level. 'Despite the fearful jar there must have been on the rear tractor,' wrote a relieved Hillary, 'it seemed to have come to no harm whatsoever – a distinct compliment to its rugged construction.'[800]

They finally reached Depot 700 at 1.00pm on 15 December, having covered the 230 miles from Depot 480 in nine days. They found that Miller and Marsh had been waiting for them since the 13th, having maintained their daily average of 18 miles. The first of the tractor party to arrive was Derek Wright, who walked ahead of the vehicles in order to film Hillary's approach. 'There was also Doug McKenzie, Press Correspondent,' wrote a disapproving Miller. 'Ed certainly is watching his publicity with both the correspondent and cameraman in his party. With six men to drive the vehicles now I consider this a distinct overloading on publicity to the detriment of the other parties such as the northern group which is doing such excellent work.'[801] He would soon have even greater cause for irritation.

On the 16th, while they awaited the first of the supply flights, Hillary joined the two dog-sledgers in their tent to discuss their next move. Having completed everything that had been expected of them with regard to the laying of depots for the Crossing Party, Miller and Marsh were keen to begin what they considered to be the most interesting and important work of the expedition: the survey and exploration of the Queen Alexandra Mountains to the south-east of Depot 700. To enable the dogs to push as far as possible, they asked that the tractors should lay a small depot between Depot 700 and the mountains. Hillary refused. With his attention fixed exclusively on his planned polar journey, he told them that he could spare only one drum of fuel for such purposes. One drum would carry the three tractors only 12 to 15 miles from Depot 700, rendering the effort essentially futile.

His one concession was that the Beaver could be used to drop a small depot at whatever point the dog teams had been able to reach two days after leaving Depot 700. The Beaver would not be able to lay a depot beyond the point attained by the dogs without being forced to land on a completely unknown surface – and this was a risk that Hillary was not prepared to take. Inevitably this decision would limit the distance that could be safely travelled by the survey team and Miller was livid, calling Hillary's decision to concentrate on his own objectives at the expense of all else 'despicable'.[802] Three days later, when en route for the mountains, he returned to the subject: 'Ed should be ashamed. To be there in a position to help us and all he can think of is his own damned southern circus which has not a skerrick of justification.'[803]

So far as Hillary's next move was concerned, there could be very little doubt about it: he would push on to the Pole, as he had always intended. His one frustration was that poor weather at Scott prevented Claydon from flying in the necessary fuel and supplies, without which his tractors could not move. He could only wait and occupy himself with sifting the sledge loads to minimise the weight to be towed to the Amundsen-Scott South Pole Station, another 500 miles due south.

On 17 December he received two telegrams. The first was an extraordinarily optimistic message from Fuchs advising him that the Crossing Party expected to reach the Pole between Christmas and the New Year. In his published account of the expedition, Hillary wrote that 'This was a much more promising report, although I couldn't quite see how he was going to do it without a marked increase in his rate of progress.'[804] So far as the impact on his own polar ambitions was concerned, he went on to state that 'As long as we were within a couple of days march of the Pole when Bunny arrived there I thought he would be agreeable to us carrying on and finishing the journey with the Fergusons.'[805] But that was definitely not the way he saw it at the time. On the 17th, he wrote in his diary that Fuchs's forecast 'if true will put the pot on us getting to Pole I suppose. Well at least we can prove the route out a few hundred more miles which will be a worthwhile job though I'd have liked to reach the Pole. I'll keep trying anyway.'[806] In his reply to Fuchs, he simply confirmed that 'On completion of D700 intend heading south-west with three Fergusons to try and clear crevasse areas and get clear running towards Pole. I don't know how far we will get but will keep you advised of progress.'[807] Once again, he had dropped hints but stopped short of an unambiguous statement of his intent.

The second telegram was from Bowden. 'In considering your future programme, you should know that the Committee recently agreed that if Fuchs or London Committee requested you should carry on toward Pole the Committee would raise no objection provided this could be done within existing resources … you should now make every endeavour to discuss your next steps as fully as you can with Dr Fuchs personally.'[808] Hillary's response to this typically cautious recommendation was unusually tame. 'I think he's afraid we may offend TAE if we head for the Pole,' he observed simply. 'Perhaps he's right.'[809]

The following day improved weather at Scott enabled Claydon to complete the first of four supply flights into Depot 700. On the third flight, completed on the 19th, he brought surprising news of the Crossing Party's progress: 'He says that Bunny won't be leaving South Ice until about December 25th,' exclaimed an exasperated Hillary. 'Ye Gods who is one to believe!! Well we'll just plug on [with] our original plan and try to get to the Pole as soon as we can. I think we can do it!'[810] More formally, he wrote to the Ross Sea Committee, completely ignoring their instructions of 17 December, and telling them that he would continue to push southwards.

What Hillary admitted neither in his diary nor in his later published account – but what he must have appreciated nonetheless – was that the collision of Fuchs's retarded progress and his own unyielding ambition would have potentially devastating consequences for the unity of the TAE. Having reached 80°30'S, Fuchs was still short of South Ice – but he was almost exactly 500 miles from the Pole. This meant that, with 1000 miles separating them, the Crossing Party and Hillary's tractor party were almost exactly equidistant from the bottom of the world. With the world's press watching the expedition's every move, Hillary was canny enough to realise that the respective positions of the Crossing Party and his own meant that any further move south must inevitably be viewed as a competition, no matter how unintentional. Only by delaying his journey – potentially by weeks – or by aborting it altogether would he be able to defuse the situation. But, as Hillary had repeatedly asserted in his diary, there could be no question of his relinquishing his long held polar ambitions. The race was on.

13

The Race to the Pole

Fuchs's reaction to the news of Hillary's 'Pole dash' was one of stunned disbelief. 'I cannot imagine,' he wrote incredulously, 'that Ed would have set this ball rolling without letting me know what he wanted to do ... While there is no objection to his going on to the Pole, there is also no value for he can do no work on the way.'[811] Clearly, the idea of Hillary pushing on to the Pole had never so much as occurred to him and his astonishment reveals just how little conception he had either of the New Zealander's ambition or of how, over the course of the expedition, Hillary's confidence in and regard for him had diminished – a process which had begun even before the *Theron* reached Vahsel Bay in January 1956.

At a more practical level, there was the realisation that Hillary's party possessed a strength which, instead of being used to alleviate the problems of the Crossing Party, would now be wasted on what Fuchs considered a completely pointless journey: 'Had we known that he could carry sufficient fuel for another 480 miles, it would have made our task easier and safer to have had the use of it. After all, the New Zealand part of the Expedition was mounted entirely for this purpose and not for local jaunting.'[812] In his frustration, he appears to have forgotten that, as early as April, when asking how much fuel the Crossing Party required at Depot 700, Hillary had offered to depot more petrol closer to the Pole, if required – a suggestion which Fuchs had not taken up, perhaps believing that Hillary was over-stretching himself. 'No doubt when I get news from London,' he concluded uncertainly, 'we shall find that Ed has in fact had nothing to do with this proposed arrangement. If he has, I cannot say that any of us will feel that the party on the far side have kept faith with us.'[813] In the meantime, rather than obtaining clarification direct from Hillary, Fuchs satisfied himself with 'seeking correct information, in rather acid comment, from London'.[814]

On 20 December route prodding continued through what Fuchs described as 'a far worse crevassed area than we realised in November.'[815] Weeks of 24-hour sunshine had significantly weakened the crevasse bridges and, while the innumerable punctures in the windcrust could be avoided easily enough, no one could predict when the ground might drop from under his feet. Twice on the 20th, they nearly lost Blaiklock when, without warning, bridges collapsed beneath him. On the first occasion, he was left resting on his elbows while his skis dropped irretrievably into the bowels of an 80 foot-deep crevasse; on the second, the sudden appearance of a 4 foot-wide hole left him standing suspended over nothingness, with only the tips of his skis preventing him from plummeting to an icy grave.

'As a result of prodding today,' Fuchs recorded on the 21st, '98 flags were put in to mark the tortuous and extremely difficult route through the most incredible maze of dark caverns and crevasses which we crossed so blithely after a morning's prod by three people in November.'[816] But the hard work paid off and by the close of the day, all of the vehicles and personnel had zigzagged their way to safety and they could confidently look forward to reaching South Ice the next day. 'Phew!' exclaimed Lister, 'It was a great relief for it was a horrible area and probably would have been almost impossible to recover any vehicle which plunged into the maze of underground caverns.'[817] In the minds of most of the explorers, the safe traverse of the Recovery Glacier represented a hugely important step towards the crossing of the continent and, as Blaiklock enthused, 'we knew whatever lay ahead couldn't be any worse.'[818]

They eventually arrived at the forward base that night, having taken 8 hours to hack their way across the remaining 31 miles of sastrugi in brilliant sunshine. 'We drove at our ease at last,' remembered Homard, 'free from a knotted stomach, enjoying the undulating country and the coming and going from view of many nunataks. The course was steered by vehicle compass ... and quite suddenly, it brought us over a hill to South Ice.'[819] They were met by La Grange and Geoffrey Pratt and very soon all twelve men were squeezed into the tiny hut, celebrating their arrival with tea and rum – 'I had too much on an empty stomach,' Lister confessed, 'and was soon high, then sick – disgusting!'[820]

While Lister retched, Fuchs sent a message to Hillary, outlining the Crossing Party's progress and confirming that he intended to depart from South Ice on Christmas Day. 'Distance travelled in 29 days 349 miles, but expect rapid travel from here on. Thanks for your information and proposed crevasse recce. Hope you will be able to mark route through or limit of area with snow cairns or stakes ... Happy Christmas to you all.'[821] Extraordinarily in the circumstances, while he acknowledged Hillary's offer to survey the crevasses south of Depot 700, he made no reference to the BBC's report of a polar dash, and chose not to elicit a more precise explanation of Hillary's plan to 'get clear running towards Pole'.[822]

On the 24th, while the Crossing Party continued the process of sorting and re-lashing loads for the onward journey, Fuchs received a telegram from Hillary. It confirmed that the stocking of Depot 700 had been completed and that the New Zealanders had vacated the depot the previous day with 3 Fergusons, 20 drums of fuel and 5 men – McKenzie having flown back to Scott in order to report on other aspects of the Ross Sea Party's work. The tractors' onward journey, Hillary continued, was to be made 'with the intention of proving the route out another 200 miles and then, if the going proves easy, doing a trip to the Pole.'[823] For the first time, Hillary had given Fuchs explicit notice of his intentions. Even more surprisingly, he went on to state that he would 'scrub southward jaunt if vehicles and fuel can be used in any way to expedite your safe crossing either by a further depot or anything else you suggest.' Until he heard from Fuchs, he would continue south for 100 miles or so, building cairns to mark the crevassed areas. The obliging tone of this message made Fuchs 'wonder if there was a radio intercept of my message to London? Anyway today I have accepted Ed's offer, explaining why I consider it necessary and have also told London no further action is necessary.'[824] So far as Fuchs was concerned, a potentially unpleasant rift had been satisfactorily bridged – assuming, that is, that Hillary received his message and acted upon its contents.

A thousand miles away across the continent nothing seemed less likely. On the same day that the Crossing Party reached South Ice, Hillary had noted in his diary that he was 'aghast' at their delay. However, in an unusually pliant frame of mind, he also admitted that 'any mad dash for the Pole at the moment would be a bit premature so I'll have to quell my ambitions and do the best I can for Bunny. Oh well we've had a good run so we can't complain I suppose.'[825] As was so often the case, confirmation of Fuchs's progress coincided with a missive from Bowden – and this time the chairman of the Ross Sea Committee was uncharacteristically brusque. 'Before commenting on your telegram of 19th, we require to know if you have received my telegrams of 5th and 17th and whether your projected movements fit in with the requirements outlined therein, meanwhile you should not proceed beyond depot 700.'[826] 'He certainly is playing tough!' Hillary observed sarcastically. '... I've sent a pretty insubordinate note to the Ross Sea Committee but they can fire me if they like.'[827] Crucially, however, despite its mutinous tone, Hillary's message also contained the commitment not to proceed more than 100 miles beyond Depot 700 without having first obtained a clear statement of intent from Fuchs.

Three days later, with Depot 700 now 117 miles to the rear, Hillary was once again feeling bullish. Firstly, he had received another telegram from Bowden 'in much more subdued vein'.[828] Bowden again stated his view that Hillary 'should not have proceeded beyond 700 without explicit approval from Dr Fuchs' and that his projected trip to the Pole 'should not be attempted without the full willing consent of the commander in the field'[829]

– but he and the Committee had accepted Hillary's assurances regarding the limit of his advance. Secondly, Hillary had received Fuchs's telegram of 22 December, in which he was asked to build snow cairns – but received no veto of his planned polar journey. Hillary later wrote that he was 'very pleased to get this message for, apart from its being our first real confirmation for some time of his position and plans, he had asked for no further assistance and had raised no objections to our move south.'[830] Nonetheless, he decided to send one last message to Fuchs: 'We are 390 miles from Pole,' he advised. 'Have cairned two areas of crevasses since D700 but last fifty miles has been clear going. Waiting one day here then will push on ... Best of luck, happy Christmas and an early New Year at the Pole.' Having sent this message, he turned to his diary in jubilant mood: 'Well I'm going to push for the Pole and have announced the fact,' he enthused. 'Doug McKenzie reckons there is enormous [?] interest in New Zealand and I don't think we'll disappoint them ... We'll depart at 7 p.m. tomorrow and really push it hard.'[831]

He was not the only one now intending to 'push it hard'. On 23 December Blaiklock and Stephenson had left South Ice with the two dog teams which had been picketed at the forward base since November, their mission to reconnoitre the completely unknown route towards the Pole ahead of the vehicle party. After what Homard described as 'as good a Christmas dinner as was possible under the circumstances ... a glass of port wine and ... the Queen's speech,'[832] the complete party of eight vehicles – four Sno-cats, three Weasels and one Muskeg – followed in their tracks on the 25th. 'It was a gay sight,' observed Fuchs as the convoy motored away from the now abandoned South Ice hut,

> ... for being Christmas Day everyone seemed in a decorative mood ... the whole column sprouted with chequered red and white crevasse flags, black and white trail flags, a white ensign, an RAF flag and various coloured banners. Ralph even sported coloured paper streamers and two small Chinese lanterns, till the Muskeg, which he is now driving, looked almost like a carnival float.[833]

Despite its exuberant departure, the party made only poor progress as it battled with a combination of iron-hard sastrugi and
deep, soft snow in the intervals between. The sledges in particular
suffered from the violent crashing across the ridges and 2 tons
of barrels and jerrycans had to be re-lashed almost immediately.
The next morning whiteout conditions persuaded Fuchs to stop
but at least the unscheduled halt enabled Geoff Pratt and Lister
to undertake seismic shots and the glaciology that Lister believed
had been much neglected of late. By 3.45pm the skies had cleared
and once again they moved off over the corrugations, following
a course marked every 5 miles by 6-foot snow cairns built by
Blaiklock and Stephenson. They covered just 25 miles in all and
camped next to the dog team's 35-mile marker.

The poor surface was not the only problem encountered that
day. During the late afternoon, Lister's Weasel developed a series
of leaks in its cooling system and by the time the rest of the party
camped, Lister and David Pratt, who had been chaperoning the
ailing Weasel in his Sno-cat, were nowhere to be seen. With
no radio link between the vehicles, their condition remained a
cause for some anxiety. Radio communications generally were
proving extremely disappointing, with no contact made with
Shackleton, Halley Bay or the American polar station. 'This is
particularly unfortunate today,' noted Fuchs, 'as it was our first
attempt this morning to contact Ed Hillary and Depot 480 direct.
Nothing heard.'[834]

No matter how unfortunate the poor radio communications
might appear to Fuchs, to Hillary they soon proved to be little
short of a godsend – at least when judged by their impact upon
his polar quest. As planned, his tractor party had moved off at
7.00pm on Christmas Day. The surface was excellent and with
their lighter loads the Fergusons bowled along almost effortlessly. Narrow crevasses and areas of soft snow slowed them in
places but by the time they camped at 7.30am on 26 December,
they had covered a very satisfactory 56.7 miles and were now
only 335 miles from the Pole. A little over twelve hours later they
moved on again and, despite difficult surface conditions and a
steady rise to more than 9000 feet, they still managed to cover

44.5 miles. Complete whiteout prevented their starting again until 8.30pm on the 27th and the first 2 miles proved to be very hard going indeed, with the Fergusons labouring through deep, soft snow. Conditions improved during the early morning of the 28th and when they drew to a halt at 8.00am, they had added another 41 miles to their total. At 86°24'S, the tractors were now almost exactly half way between Depot 700 and the Pole. And here, at last, Hillary received Fuchs's message of 24 December accepting his offer of an additional depot at the expense of Hillary's dearly held polar ambitions.

In his lengthy telegram, Fuchs confirmed his plan to abandon three of his eight vehicles 'at optimum distances' and then went on to outline his proposals for reducing the risks still facing the expedition:

> If our planned abandonment of three vehicles is followed by any breakdown among remaining five, our only means of augmenting fuel would be by further reduction of numbers at [a] time when mechanical condition and weather are deteriorating … This risk was accepted when we thought you would have difficulty stocking D700. In interests of whole expedition I do not feel we should continue to accept this risk, and am in difficult position of feeling I must accept your offer to clear present crevasse area then establish additional fuel depot at appropriate position from D700 thus abandoning your idea of reaching Pole. Know this will be great disappointment to you and your companions, but the additional depot will enormously strengthen the position of the crossing party which cannot afford at present to deviate from the direct route.[835]

Had he received this message a few days earlier, Hillary would have been outraged. Fuchs's belated request for an additional, unplanned, depot would have forced him either to abandon his polar journey or to appear both insubordinate to the overall commander in the field and callous about the safety of his fellow expeditionaries. In the event, Hillary claimed, the delays in relaying the messages from one party to the other meant that by the

time he received Fuchs's request he was no longer in a position
to comply without compromising the safety of his own team.
'He now wants a depot establishing but I'm afraid he's too late,'
Hillary scrawled in his diary that night.

> We've come too far now – our only safe place is the Pole.
> Fuchs is 32 miles south of South Ice and doing 25 to 30 miles a
> day. What on earth is wrong with him – doesn't he realise that
> he has only covered 300/400 miles and that he still has 1,700
> to go – what a mess up they're making of it.[836]

His reply to Fuchs was rather more diplomatic but equally
uncompromising.

> Your message has arrived too late, as we are now 240 miles from
> the Pole with only ten drums left. Have neither the food nor
> fuel to sit here and await your arrival … Your previous messages
> gave no indication of your concern about your fuel so I pre-
> sumed you were satisfied with the depot stocking as arranged.[837]

More fuel could be flown into Depot 700, he told Fuchs, and if
there was any doubt about the Crossing Party's being able to reach
Depot 700, the Americans at the Pole station would no doubt
be able to supply them with as many barrels as they required to
get them there. In the meantime, he expected to reach the Pole
within six days and, once there, he would instruct Claydon to fly
more fuel to Depot 700.

Overall, there can be very little doubt that both Fuchs and
Hillary were attempting to manipulate the situation for their own
ends. Though he never acknowledged it, Fuchs knew that there
would be added cachet in being the first motor vehicle party ever
to reach the South Pole and the first expedition to reach the Pole
overland since Amundsen and Scott more than four decades earlier. The prospect of being beaten by his own lieutenant – a man
whose presence in the Antarctic was originally intended solely
to support Fuchs's own effort – must have been galling in the
extreme. An extra cache of fuel would have provided additional

security – but it had never previously been considered essential. Fuchs's request for a depot south of Depot 700 must be seen, in part at least, as a ploy to scotch Hillary's polar ambitions.

As for Hillary, by making his dash for the Pole, he was defying the oft-repeated instructions of the Ross Sea Committee and operating entirely independently of Fuchs. No one knew better than he the vagaries of long-distance radio communications in the Antarctic and he allowed only the bare minimum of time for a message from Fuchs to reach him before he pushed south. Indeed, Peter Mulgrew, who was responsible for the tractor party's radio communications, went much further. In his opinion Hillary 'carefully planned the radio messages that I sent in such a way that should we receive an instruction either from Fuchs or the Ross Sea Committee not to proceed, it would be too late as we would have passed the point of no return.'[838] Certainly Hillary later claimed that, by the time he received Fuchs's message 'We had enough fuel to go either to the Pole or back to D700. The only place we could establish a depot was where we were, and we didn't have the food to sit around for a month or more until the crossing party reached us – and there was always the chance they wouldn't reach us.'[839] In fact, he could have returned to Depot 700, asked Claydon to fly in more fuel, and then laid a depot at any point between Depot 700 and the halfway mark between Depot 700 and the Pole. Laying an additional depot would almost certainly have required more than one trip and would have placed additional strain on the tractors and on the pilots, who would have been required to make additional flights at the outer limit of their aircraft's range – but these were not considerations that had ever stopped Hillary before. There would also have been no need for the drivers to wait at the new depot – having laid it, they could have returned to Depot 700 and been evacuated by air.

Of course, in order to fulfil his offer to stock Depot 700 with more fuel, a party on the ground would be needed to assist with unloading the aeroplane. A few days later Miller and Marsh, now well on their way to the Queen Alexandra Mountains, heard that this task would fall to them, necessitating their immediate return to the depot. Given that this would mean abandoning their own survey work, Miller's reaction was a combination of anger and suspicion. 'It would appear,' he fulminated, 'that Ed had received [a] request from Bunny for more fuel in a depot between 700 and Pole which John [Claydon] says he was unable to meet – WHY? Now he is only 120 miles from Pole. WHY? All sounds rummy to me … why should I curtail the programme I have set my heart on just to do something he had the chance to do to help the general purpose of TAE but would not because of selfish glory.'[840] The answer, of course, was that Hillary recognised that the establishment of a new depot or a return to Depot 700 would have put an end to his dream of reaching the Pole – and that was not a price he was willing to pay, particularly when he knew that the new depot would be of only secondary value. He was, however, willing to dispense with survey work which, in the eyes of many, had a far greater value than his own polar journey. Unfortunately, he didn't stop there.

News of Hillary's decision finally reached Fuchs on the morning of 28 December after two trying days during which his party had become strung out over more than 30 miles, with Lister and David Pratt trailing to the rear and, in the vanguard, Geoff Pratt and La Grange undertaking seismic shots well in advance of the main party. 'News of Ed Hillary going to Pole … displeased Bunny very much,' noted Lister, 'but really Ed cannot be blamed!'[841] In his own diary, perhaps bowing to the inevitable, Fuchs merely recorded that 'It now looks as though we should have more fuel flown to D700 and if we are short of vehicles, use one or more of Ed's tractors on from the Pole. He will wait there for us and I hope that he and his mechanic Bates will continue back with us to Scott.'[842] Following the tracks of the lead vehicles, which were in turn following the tracks and snow cairns of the dog teams, the dawdlers finally caught up with the main body of the convoy at 2.00am on 29 December. Later that day they moved on again, lurching across the undulating surface, which threatened yet more damage to vehicles and sledges with every rise and fall. And then, after some 25 miles of grinding and crashing, the surface improved: 'suddenly the scene changed', wrote a relieved Fuchs, 'and for the next 9 miles there was a shining, smooth, even surface over which we trundled at 9–10mph. What a relief! ... When I arrived the camp had been set up and once more we are all together.'[843]

After five weeks on the trail, camp life had settled into a fixed pattern which, in its details, hardly varied from the routine first established by Scott, Shackleton and Mawson half a century earlier. Having chosen the site for each two-man tent, its occupants began by stamping the snow flat. Next, they pulled their tent from its canvas bag, opened it and drove the projecting ends of the four corner canes a foot into the snow. The skirt at the base of the tent walls was then spread out horizontally and loaded with freshly cut snow blocks, providing the structure with some protection from the violent winds scouring the plateau. Once he had assured himself of his temporary home's stability, the 'inside man' crawled through the entrance funnel to receive the ground sheet, two blankets, two sheepskins, two double-layer sleeping bags and the cooking and ration boxes from the 'outside man'. Having tended to dogs or vehicles, or assisted with the scientific work, the latter also climbed inside, carefully brushing the snow from his clothes and boots in the space between the inner and outer walls of the tent. When fully inside, both men removed their outer garments and hung them up to dry. 'A plume of steam could often then be seen issuing from the ventilator,' wrote Allan Rogers. 'Most people then sat in their double layer sleeping bag to cook, or eat or write, still wearing underwear, shirt, pullover, socks and trousers. This was partly for warmth and partly because the only other working position was kneeling which became quite painful after a time.'[844]

The evening meal usually consisted of pemmican mixed with potato powder, pea flour or some dried onion, sultanas, raisins, cheese or curry powder in what all too often proved a vain attempt to vary the flavour. A standard primus stove served for cooking, for heating and for drying clothes and once it was lit the temperature at the apex of the pyramid tent would rise to about 100°F within a matter of minutes. In order to keep down the loads to be man hauled, the sledgers of the Heroic Era had been compelled to make do with an inadequate fuel ration with the result that their clothing was very seldom fully dry. This meant that when they dressed in the mornings they were faced with the prospect of trying to squeeze into clothes that had set like steel and, once thawed, their dampness caused painful rawness and boils, which made the backbreaking work of manhauling ever more debilitating. In contrast, in what Rogers described as 'one of the most important changes in sledging routine in the last fifty years',[845] on the TAE each tent was allowed 2 gallons of paraffin for fifteen days – enough to permit the deliberate drying of clothes every night. Even so, the need to conserve fuel and to prevent fire meant that primuses could not be left lit all night, and in the mornings the men usually woke to temperatures 20 degrees or more below freezing.

The explorers tried to time their bodily functions to coincide with the routine stops during the day. In reasonably clement weather, the shelter provided by a sledge or vehicle gave adequate protection from frostbite, while their sledging diet tended to generate large, soft and easily passed stools, limiting the time that the men were exposed to the elements. Always alert to the physiological quirks of the environment, Rogers observed what he termed an 'amusing phenomenon' when the men urinated into recent snow: 'The wind soon cut away the adjacent softer snow (as in the wind carving of sastrugi) leaving the hard ice behind like an upside down yellow fir tree. These were christened "Uromites".'[846] During blizzard conditions, however, the need to prevent open garments filling with drift snow made it impossible to leave the tent. In these situations, the explorers used empty food tins for urination, always taking the greatest care not to spill the contents onto their sleeping bags, and, so far as possible, they tried to defecate immediately before striking camp.

With a working day that often stretched to sixteen hours or more and with sleep restricted to six hours a day, some of the expeditionaries found that the demands of the journey were having a strange, dislocating effect on their relations with their fellow travellers. Each man would, perforce, spend hours with his tent and driving companion, but he might hardly meet the others for days on end: 'you meet at the stops maybe,' observed Blaiklock,

> ... but it's too cold to do much chatting ... and you just get some choccy out or get a cocoa or pat a dog or check something and off you go again. And when you're coming up to night time you've all got your separate jobs ... So you meet one or two people, but you don't meet many for very long – even on the journey. It's surprising how isolated it is.[847]

Adding to this feeling of dislocation was the sheer monotony of the scenery on the Polar Plateau, which hardly varied for mile after mile, day after day. And when whiteout descended, the effects became even more extreme, with low cloud blotting out the sun and erasing any contrast in the landscape. Gusts of wind whipped across the polished surface of the plateau, snow fell and the visible world contracted to a whirling vortex of whiteness in which only the lumbering orange hulks of the nearest vehicles could be discerned.

The last few days of 1957 proved particularly frustrating for the Crossing Party. Maintenance and repairs took far longer than expected and when they did manage to move off at 8.30pm on the 31st Lowe almost immediately snapped a heavy Maudheim sledge runner in two when he collided with a particularly vicious sastrugi. 'He must have hit a hard mass at far too great a speed,' grumbled Fuchs, 'lessons of this kind seem always to be learned too late!'[848] In the first of their planned vehicle drops, the party had abandoned the Muskeg, 'Hopalong', at their last camp, having first stripped it of all useful equipment. But then, only 7 miles into the journey, Rogers's Weasel broke a track and could not be repaired because of a lack of spare parts. Inevitably, this meant returning to the campsite and bringing the Muskeg back into commission so that it could tow the abandoned Weasel's loads. They were fortunate that the Muskeg was still so near at hand, but the swap inevitably wasted yet more valuable time and fuel. Lister wrote that night: 'We feel a little sad about our ill luck but now we have less sastrugi and hope for better distances since we are rapidly getting into a serious position. BBC news told of Ed Hillary and 4 companions being 90 miles from the Pole.'[849]

Despite their best efforts Fuchs and his team were consistently failing to meet their planned daily mileage and with every passing day they slipped farther and farther behind schedule. 'Today we have covered 39 miles,' he recorded dolefully on 1 January 1958, 'but even this is a disappointment as we had hoped to do 50.'[850] With the convoy entering another vast belt of sastrugi and the vehicles struggling in first or second gear all the way, the next day he could only report: 'Another 30 miles today, but what a labour ... The strain on vehicles and sledges is prodigious, particularly I worry about the gear boxes, for these constant hours of heavy work in low gear is bound to tell on them.[851]

He was right to be worried. The Sno-cat 'Rock 'n' Roll' was beginning to emit ominous noises and during the day's run two sledges, one towed by the Muskeg and one by a Weasel, suffered broken hairpin tow-bars, which took yet more precious time to replace. The party finally fell into their sleeping bags at 4.30am on the morning of 3 January after another exhausting and discouraging day.

'Progress is dogged,' wrote George Lowe, summing up his experiences of Antarctic travel for a friend,

> ... even my companions, especially the leader is dogged ... This mechanical form of travel is so very different from Scott man-hauling his sledges or from Amundsen swishing quietly along with dogs. Our method is warmer – with long boring periods of just sitting while the motors roar – dirtier with grease and petrol fumes, faster when the going is easy and maddeningly slow when the way is difficult.[852]

Throughout the 3rd the vehicles continued to plough their way across the field of sastrugi, sometimes smashing their way through the ridges and at others clawing their way upwards to then crash down into the soft snow trapped in the interstices. Tow bars and hairpin connections broke with infuriating regularity and soon most of the vehicles were linked to their sledges by steel hawsers, which placed even greater strain on the gear boxes, as the sledges were constantly being jerked violently into motion. 'We have now driven for 57 miles constantly in 1st or 2nd gear,' wrote a desperately worried Fuchs, '– how long will the gear boxes last?'[853]

That evening as Fuchs mulled over the expedition's predicament, Lenton handed him a message just received from Hillary. It proved to be another bombshell. With the distance between the two parties now substantially reduced, direct contact was at last possible and Hillary had composed the message that very evening, at a position just a few miles from the Pole:

> I am very concerned about the serious delay in your plans. It is about 1,250 miles from the Pole to Scott Base, much of the travelling from D700 north being somewhat slow and laborious with rough, hard sastrugi. Leaving the Pole late in January you will head into increasing bad weather and winter temperatures, plus vehicles that are showing signs of strain. Both of my mechanics regard such a late journey as an unjustifiable risk and are not prepared to wait and travel with your party. I agree with this view and think you should seriously consider splitting your journey over two years. You still probably have a major journey in front of you to reach the Pole. Why not winter your vehicles at the Pole, fly out to Scott Base with American aircraft, return to civilisation for the winter and then fly back in to the Pole Station next November and complete your journey.[854]

For the second time in just over a fortnight, Fuchs found himself reeling at a bulletin from the far side of the Pole. On 18 December he had been caught completely by surprise by the news that Hillary had stolen a march on him and expected to reach the symbolic milestone of the Pole before him, effectively stealing his thunder and inviting unwelcome accusations of a rift in the TAE's command. Now, Hillary had added insult to injury by suggesting – just as he himself was about to reach the Pole – that Fuchs should drastically alter his plans at the last minute and abandon his attempt to cross the continent in a single, continuous journey. With the expedition's objectives publicised across the globe, such a decision would certainly open the TAE and its leader to accusations of, at best, a Shackleton-like heroic failure in the face of overwhelming odds; at worst, there might well be suggestions of incompetence, the crowing of vindicated nay-sayers and even accusations of cowardice and abject failure. No wonder that, when he climbed into his sleeping bag that night, Fuchs had little prospect of any sleep.

After sending his message telling Fuchs that he had gone too far towards the Pole to turn back safely, Hillary and his com-panions had continued their journey on the evening of 28 December. Despite a combination of soft snow and an alti-tude of over 10,000 feet, which seriously inhibited the Fergusons' performance, by 8am the following morning they had covered 44.2 miles and had reached latitude 87°02'S. By contrast, in the radio schedule that evening they heard that the Crossing Party had made just 15 miles the previous day, reaffirming Hillary's confidence in his decision not to wait for Fuchs. 'Take them a long time at that rate!' he noted caustically.[855]

Despite their much faster progress, there was little enthusi-asm among Hillary's party for the task in hand. 'Driving along for hour after hour with nothing to see but miles of snow in every direction and absolutely no relief for the eye became inexpressibly tedious,'[856] he later wrote, and the combination of the never-changing landscape and the hours of gruelling labour for no obvious gain left the men testy and discontented. 'Everyone damn tired and sick of this slow going,' he observed on 31 December. 'We were away at 7 p.m. and immediately struck deep soft snow. During the next 6 hours we covered 6 miles. It was heartbreaking. Bottomless stuff in which the Fergies were helpless and we were chewing up the petrol at a great rate.'[857]

With the tractor engines now misfiring and prone to stall, fuel consumption had become Hillary's most serious concern and he knew only too well that he had very little margin for error – a realisation that was made all the more uncomfortable by the fact that the bubble sextant, upon which he relied for navigation, had developed a serious flaw and could not be relied upon with any confidence.

'Still 104 miles from the Pole and fuel is worrying me a good deal,' Hillary wrote on New Year's Day 1958. 'Nothing but deep soft snow and more soft snow. Terribly worried about petrol consumption as we are very low.'[858] A day later, he recorded that the party had struggled on for another 27.7 miles over a glue-like surface that caused fuel consumption to soar. 'The mileage is OK,' he noted lugubriously, 'it's the petrol that's worrying me. We have 4 drums left and 70 odd miles to do. If I can bring us bang on to the Pole we'll probably make it with a gallon or two in the tank.'[859] Equally worrying was the undeniable fact that the tractors were now struggling to such a degree that it would take very little to immobilise them altogether. If the worst happened, Hillary would either have to call upon American aid or his reluctant team would be forced to man-haul the remaining miles to the Pole. Either scenario would be an ignominious anticlimax to his much vaunted and long planned 'polar dash'. In addition, and as he no doubt fully appreciated, while his insubordination to the Ross Sea Committee and to Fuchs would probably be forgiven if he arrived at the Pole triumphant, he could expect little sympathy from his critics if he limped into the Pole Station having left his tractors mouldering on the plateau miles from anywhere – a permanent monument to his own hubris.

News of the Crossing Party's progress was no more reassuring, with its position being reported as 380 miles from the Pole on 3 January. In his diary entry for 28 December, Hillary had written that 'If Bunny is as late as I think he'll be I'll try and persuade him to abandon his effort for this year and fly out with the Yanks, then fly back in next year and complete the run.'[860] Now he returned to the subject:

Bunny hopes to arrive at the Pole in 14 to 16 days – 'If he gets reasonable luck.' He wants me and one of our engineers to meet him at the Pole and to travel through to Scott Base with him. Neither Jim or Murray will have it on. They reckon it's

suicide at such a late time in the year. I feel the same and will
have to do a campaign on Bunny to try and persuade him to
stop at the Pole and then complete the job next summer.[861]

While Hillary considered how this suggestion might be expressed
most persuasively, the tractor party continued to trundle onwards
until, at 8.00pm on the 3rd, Hillary, in the lead tractor, spotted
something black in the distance. To his immense relief he quickly
realised that it was a marker flag designating the boundary of the
Amundsen-Scott South Pole Station. 'We'd done 60 miles in the
day, and had come directly in onto the base which pleased me
a good deal ... We're all very tired. I feel decidedly seedy and
ragged these days. I think I've just about had enough but it's good
to have succeeded in our effort with the old Fergies.'[862]

Instead of pressing on to the station itself, which was still some
20 miles distant, the party camped next to the marker flag and
Mulgrew called up Scott Base to transmit the single word 'rhubarb'
– the agreed code to notify safe arrival at the Pole. This message
would then be forwarded to *The Times* and to the BBC, who
shared the rights to the expedition's story. Next, Mulgrew began
to transmit to Fuchs, following the text just drafted by Hillary.

At 9.30am the following morning the tractor party set off to
cover the last few miles to the American base and, with the sun
shining brilliantly and the mist of the previous day dispersed by
its rays, visibility was excellent. An hour into the journey they
climbed the latest in a series of great folds in the plateau and, at
last, the huts and aerials of the base came into view. 'And now our
leisurely progress seemed more annoying than it had ever before
... our minds were winging freely towards our objective but our
tractors chugged on at the same old pace.'[863]

At 12.30pm, still 11 miles from the station, they were welcomed by Dr Vernon Houk, the base commander, and by Major
'Mogy' Mogesson, the chief scientist, who had travelled out to
greet them in a bright red Weasel sporting the Stars and Stripes.
After much shaking of hands and slapping of backs, Hillary's team
remounted their Fergusons for the last time and headed for the
circle of drums and flagpoles marking the geographic South Pole.

Reporting for the *Daily Mail* Noel Barber, who gloried in being the first Briton to reach the Pole since Scott, noted that the two Americans 'sheered off at right angles from Hillary's machines, and came back by a circuitous route, so that nobody could ever say that Hillary had not come in on his own.'[864] It was, as Barber observed, a 'very pleasing gesture' and typical of the generosity that the Americans had shown to the expedition.

In addition to Barber, three American journalists had been flown to the Pole to witness the climax of Hillary's journey and as he and his drivers climbed stiffly from their cabs, bearded, bedraggled and with their clothing torn and dirty, they were surrounded by clicking cameras and subjected to a barrage of questions and congratulations, one mingling with the other. 'In the manner of modern life,' wrote Barber,

> ... the historic moment had to be relived several times for the photographers. The 'original' handshake had to be performed over and over again, and then the grimy but grinning team assembled, and moved into closer formation so that all could perpetuate the moment.[865]

It was, Hillary noted in his diary, 'The usual hullabaloo but a very pleasant reception.'[866] Before being led inside for a celebratory lunch of sausages and beans, he paused to look at the three battered farm tractors with their sledges and the ungainly caboose.

> There was no doubt about it, our tractor train was a bit of a laugh! But despite appearances, our Fergusons had brought us over twelve hundred and fifty miles of snow and ice, crevasse and sastrugi, soft snow and blizzard to be the first vehicles to drive to the South Pole.[867]

They had completed their epic trek with just enough fuel left to drive 15 miles more.

While Hillary had been preparing for the last leg of his journey, Fuchs had been mulling over the suggestion that he abort the crossing. 'This evening,' he wrote after reading the telegram for the umpteenth time, 'I received what I can only regard as a panic message – Ed saying that he thought we ought to abandon the expedition at the Pole owing to the delay in our progress. He has also decided he does not want to wait at the Pole to go back to Scott with us!'[868]

That night, as he lay in his bag, he began to compose his reply. In his view, any decision to break the journey at the Pole would jeopardise his mission altogether and there could be no question of abandonment – temporary or otherwise. Seeking to dismiss the suggestion comprehensively, his final wording was blunt:

> Appreciate your concern but there can be no question of abandoning journey at this stage. Innumerable reasons make it impracticable to remount the expedition after wintering outside Antarctica. Our vehicles can be and have been operated at minus 60 but I do not expect such temperatures by March. Whiteout and drift will be our chief concern. I understand your mechanics' reluctance to undertake further travel and in view of your opinion that late season travel is an unjustifiable risk I do not feel able to ask you to join us at D700 in spite of your valuable local knowledge. We will therefore have to wend our own way using the traverse you leave at the Pole.[869]

He also took the opportunity to report the development to the Management Committee in London. 'Have received message from Hillary,' he told them, 'urging me to abandon journey at Pole … He states his agreement with his mechanics' views that continuation of journey late in season is unjustifiable risk. I do not agree.'[870]

The following morning, before moving off again after yet another day of whiteout and essential repairs, Fuchs called his team together to tell them of Hillary's recommendation and of his own reply. He had not sought his men's opinions before rejecting the suggestion but after discussing it with them he was able to write with obvious satisfaction that 'There certainly seems to be no sympathy with the idea among us here.'[871] Plain-spoken as ever,

Homard called Hillary's recommendation 'a bloody cheek'.[872] Blaiklock, meanwhile, considered it completely impractical:

> I think there would have been no possibility of returning the following year, for a number of reasons. Not only finance, but also the possibility of a number of the party being unavailable because of other commitments, as well as the inability or avail-ability of the US to transport us back to the Pole, and lack of support from the UK … I was also dismayed at his lack of loy-alty and personal support for Bunny, and his own self-interest in his plans.[873]

Lister, as always, was more willing to look at the matter from both sides. 'I sympathise with Bunny feeling sad at our lateness,' he confided to his diary, 'and angry at Ed's stealing the thunder at reaching the Pole so early. I also sympathise with Ed wanting to get to the Pole when he was doing so well. A pity we contribute yet another soiled page to the already extensive book of polar intrigue.'[874] And soon, to Fuchs's dismay, a much wider audience would be turning those soiled pages.

Hillary read Fuchs's telegram while sitting in the unaccus-tomed comfort of the South Pole Station, waiting for a US plane to transport him back to Scott. Of course, the subtext would have been obvious to him – and to anyone else reading the mes-sage. If Fuchs and his fellow travellers considered the risks of the onward journey to be acceptable, in claiming that they were 'unjustifiable', Hillary was being, at best, excessively cautious. To the conqueror of Everest – and to a man whose attitude towards crevasses and other obstacles had sometimes bordered on reck-lessness in the previous months – such a suggestion would have been a very bitter pill to swallow. But, surprisingly in the cir-cumstances, he kept his temper. 'Thanks for message', he replied. 'Suggest we wait and see at what time and in what conditions you arrive at Pole. Am returning to Scott Base today with party except Peter Mulgrew who will maintain radio network from caboose. Expect transport to be available to return to Pole on your arrival and discuss matters with you then.'[875]

Crucially, however, rather than let the matter rest there, he decided to repeat his suggestion regarding a break in the journey to the Management Committee in London, copying the message to the Ross Sea Committee, as a 'formality':

> Have expressed my view to Fuchs that with extreme delay in his programme and the punishment his vehicles are sustaining that he would be most unwise to attempt to continue on over the 1,250 miles to Scott Base this season. This journey could only be done at considerable risk to men and at the sacrifice of any effective seismic programme ... When I advised Fuchs of my views, he replied more in sorrow than in anger, and expressed himself determined to go on despite all ... To my mind enough prestige will have been gained by the arrival of Fuchs and ourselves to enable of modification of the plan to allow the task to be carried out in a reasonable and safe manner over a two-year period whereas a forced march late in the season could well cause most unfavourable publicity. Your instructions are the only thing that can enable Fuchs to save face and adopt a modified plan so I would earnestly request that the Management Committee should give this matter its earliest consideration.[876]

This message and Fuchs's of 4 January were read to the Management Committee in London on the 6th. Eleanor Honnywill, who took the minutes of the meeting, later told Fuchs that, after a few moments of 'absolute stunned silence', the Committee members rose one by one to give Fuchs their ringing endorsement while Frank Corner, the New Zealand High Commission's representative on the Committee, 'looked acutely miserable and stared into his lap.'[877]

The Committee's Chairman, Sir John Slessor, expressed the Committee's joint opinion more forcibly than most: 'What the hell has prestige got to do with anything,' he roared after reading Hillary's telegram, 'and what is all this nonsense about face-saving?'[878] Having agreed to endorse Fuchs's decisions and to dismiss the opinions 'of a young man who has just done one Polar journey with a couple of farm tractors'[879] the Committee sat down to consider more calmly the tenor of its replies. To Fuchs, they wrote that they had 'considered your telegram and Hillary's … We have full confidence in you and your judgement as leader of the expedition. We support your decision and any other you may make.'[880] This message was then copied to Hillary and to Bowden, with the added assurance that Hillary's recommendation had been given all due consideration – prior to its being rejected unanimously. 'Whatever we may have thought of the Committee, God bless them, sometimes in the past,' enthused Honnywill, 'when they thought it had come to "backs to the wall" there wasn't one single hesitation – there wasn't even a discussion!'

Its business completed, the Committee broke up for the day, everyone agreeing that the telegrams and the discussion they had engendered were 'dynamite and must be kept absolutely secret'. Nothing, the members agreed, must be discussed outside the committee room: the girls in the office were to be kept in ignorance and the telegrams themselves must be kept locked in the office safe, away from prying eyes. And then, according to Honnywill, the Committee members donned their bowlers and took each other off to lunch – to be met outside the door of 64 Victoria Street by banner headlines in all the lunchtime editions and the newsboys crying out 'Big Row in the Antarctic'. 'If it hadn't been so tragic,' she wrote, 'it would have been very funny. To say we were flabbergasted is putting it mildly. We were stunned and speechless, and then absolute pandemonium broke loose. Within minutes the telephone lines were red hot and without time to think out the Party line we were being battered from all sides to make official comments, and foolish admissions carefully designed to fan the flames.'

How, everyone wondered, had the press learned of the fracas, when the Committee itself had only just become aware of it? The answer lay in what Hillary described as 'a mix-up at the Ross Sea Office in Wellington'.[881] Whether by accident or design, his message had been released to the newspapers and in a matter of hours the story was making headlines across the globe. 'Dr Fuchs Rejects Advice to Halt at the Pole',[882] reported *The*

Times in measured tones, while the Christchurch *Evening Post* proclaimed a 'Deep Split Between Fuchs and Hillary'. As well as dismissing Hillary's dash to the Pole as a piece of 'melodramatic opportunism', *The Economist*, meanwhile, chastised Hillary for his 'attempt to force his views on Dr Fuchs' and for 'invoking the "concern" of the American expedition at the pole, which it is up to the Americans, if they feel it, to express for themselves.'[883] With reporters camped on its doorstep clamouring for details and with the papers filled with speculation in the absence of hard facts, the Committee quickly decided that its only course of action was to release the text of all the telegrams. 'The Party line was obvious,' continued Honnywill, 'even if we didn't exactly convince ourselves':

> 'No – there is no quarrel – there is no rift and no sort of dis-
> sension – there is simply a difference of opinion. Of course
> Sir Edmund is entitled to make suggestions if he wishes – the
> Committee have not accepted it and the matter is therefore
> closed. Of course Sir Edmund is now helping Dr Fuchs – of
> course they are not on bad terms – of course we love him – of
> course we don't think he stinks – much!'[884]

Although some papers, like the *Illustrated London News*, accepted the official line and seemed content to report that the telegrams represented a 'disagreement on policy not a quarrel',[885] many others were far more interested in the more sensational aspects of the story and coverage would continue long after all parties had left the Antarctic far behind them.

In Britain and in New Zealand the commentary rolled on and on and, over time, much of the coverage became increasingly partisan in tone. 'Of course the more it went on the more Ed's reputation suffered and the better you came out of it,' gushed Honnywill, '– which was our only ray of comfort. The man in the street, the grocer's assistant, our hairdressers – everyone we met was terribly disappointed when we maintained solidly that we were one big happy family and all buddies together, and of course Ed hadn't done any damage at all.'[886] The mask occasionally slipped, however. When asked by the BBC whether he thought Hillary had sent his cable direct to London in an underhand attempt to bring extra pressure to bear on Fuchs to abandon the crossing, Slessor's reply, for all its terseness, carried a wealth of meaning: 'it might so appear', he told his interviewer.[887]

Antarctic worthies from the Heroic Era were also drawn into the debate. Sir Douglas Mawson, the only surviving expedition leader of the period, told *The Times* that he thought Fuchs had 'done a magnificent job' and that he would like to see the Crossing Party continue its journey after reaching the Pole. But, Mawson continued, 'he must weigh the chances himself. If he decides to go on I hope he does his damnedest.'[888] Tryggve Gran, the Norwegian ski expert on the *Terra Nova* Expedition, also asserted that 'The Scott tragedy must not discourage him!'[889] Rather less encouragingly, Sir Philip Brocklehurst, a veteran of Shackleton's *Nimrod* Expedition, wrote to the *Daily Telegraph* to express his view that the whole enterprise was 'rather a mediocre affair' in comparison with the achievements of the Heroic Era and that the risk of the entire crossing was 'considerably less than that incurred in crossing a Yorkshire grouse moor on a stormy winter night.'[890]

Still over 200 miles from the Pole, Fuchs was horrified by news of the growing press frenzy, which constituted a deeply unwelcome distraction from far more pressing matters. 'Ed Hillary has apparently released his suggestion and my reply to the Press for we are hearing about it on the BBC news,' he wrote at latitude 86°09'S on 7 January. 'This seems to have been particularly impolitic as the Press are building it up into a dispute between Ed and I. There is no dispute as all that has happened is that he made a proposal which I could not accept and said so.'[891] Lister, too, thought it 'a very unsavoury business'[892] and rather naively expressed his disappointment at the BBC agreeing to cover the story.

The degree to which these events preoccupied Fuchs is perhaps best reflected in the fact that, on the 7th, he completely failed to mention in his diary that John Lewis, Gordon Haslop, Taffy Williams and Peter Weston had safely completed their transcontinental flight in the Otter. After securing Shackleton Base on

27 December, the four airmen had flown to South Ice to refuel
and to await suitable weather for the longest leg of their journey.
After an abortive attempt on 29 December, they had eventually
taken off at 11.48pm on 6 January and, in a remarkably trouble-
free flight, had covered the 1430 statute miles to Scott Base in
exactly eleven hours. 'We had a wonderful run across the Ross Ice
Shelf,' reported a jubilant Lewis. 'Gordon Haslop was flying and
as we came in to Scott Base, Taffy Williams called them up on the
radio and we ordered our beer. Two Americans flew out to escort
us in, and as you can imagine we were jolly pleased to get here.'[893]

Despite these distractions, throughout the first week of January
the Crossing Party had maintained its slow but steady progress
southwards, travelling over a continuous field of low, hard sastrugi which continued to punish vehicles and sledges alike. On
the 6th, they had finally dispensed with the Muskeg and the
Maudheim sledge that Lowe had damaged so severely a week
earlier. 'Together with fourteen empty fuel drums,' remembered
Fuchs, 'this formed a memorial pile to "Hopalong", a hard working and still active friend, whose life ended in latitude 85°15'S.'[894]
Despite Fuchs's moment of nostalgia, in reality few of the men
had developed any real affection for their vehicles – at least in
the opinion of Blaiklock. 'I'm talking as a dog man, of course,' he
recalled, 'but I suspect most people just regarded them as a lump
of metal to get from A to B. Certainly the Weasels I don't think
had any [admirers] … They were damn awkward things to drive;
they were cold because you had to have the window open. No, I
don't think there was any attachment in that way.'[895]

Even as 'Hopalong' was lost to view, Fuchs was already considering which vehicle to abandon next. As he wrote on 8 January:
'The problem is which Weasel to drop for Hal's has good tracks,
engine cab and equipment but bad suspension system, while
George's has given no trouble so far (except carburettor and
thermostat and exhaust leak) but has an engine using 1 pint of
oil every 5 miles.'[896] Eventually, the decision was taken out of
his hands when, on the 14th, an irreparable oil leak resulted in
Lister's Weasel seizing completely – a development which disappointed no one more than Lowe, who had been praying that his

own vehicle, 'Wrack and Ruin', would fail first and allow him to transfer to a Sno-cat. 'We have left a trail of £1,000s of equipment from Shackleton right to here,' noted Lister as his Weasel disappeared into the distance. 'What next will we be leaving?'[897]

During the first week of January the party's rate of progress had gradually increased, despite sastrugi and routine maintenance, so that by the 10th Fuchs could note with satisfaction that they had managed to maintain a daily average in excess of 20 miles since leaving South Ice and were now 192 miles from the Pole. Based upon the aerial reconnaissance of the previous season, he anticipated that surface conditions would gradually improve from this point onwards – but it proved a vain hope. A combination of whiteout and continuous sastrugi dragged their daily average back down to less than 16 miles over the course of the next four days and, as Lister remarked, the delays 'made us reflect on winter and our late position.' But, as he went on to state in the same diary entry, 'Conjecture is entertaining too and we laugh and pull each other's legs about next winter, a bitter March, etc. Yet we all hope to get out before it becomes too late.'[898]

By 17 January, they had reached 88°45'S – approximately 85 miles from the South Pole. After covering 30 miles on the 17th and another 29 on the 18th, the Crossing Party began its final approach on the morning of the 19th over a surface free at last of sastrugi. As Fuchs observed, the day was a brilliant one, without a cloud in the sky, with only a light breeze and with the sun glinting from the smooth, undisturbed surface of the snow:

> As the party moved towards the Pole, I looked back and thought it looked a brave sight. The orange Cats and Weasel together with the loaded sledges bearing many fluttering flags of different colours. Besides the national Commonwealth flags, there was that of the city of Bristol, a TAE flag embroidered by Ralph, chequered crevasse flags, trail pennants, and a green one embroidered by Hannes with a brown antelope of South Africa.[899]

Above the convoy, streaming from the high, open exhausts of the Sno-cats, a great plume of condensation billowed and the 'curious damp, cold' air remarked upon by Scott was filled with the screeching and grinding of the vehicle tracks and the hoarse roar of their engines.

The surface began to undulate gently and as the convoy climbed a ridge from which the plateau fell away in one long continuous sweep, the Pole Station came into view at last, its huts and masts and the tracery of guy ropes standing out darkly against the otherwise uniform whiteness. 'Although it could only just be discerned with the naked eye,' Fuchs later wrote, 'it seemed so short a distance from us that our first instinct was to drive straight to the beckoning black spot in the white expanse.'[900] Unfortunately, a direct approach was impossible as Major Mogesson had radioed Fuchs to ask that the convoy avoid the snowfield which his scientists were busy studying and that they instead travel along the 24° meridian. The drivers therefore turned south-east along the crest of the ridge and drove on until they discovered a line of flags marking the route they were expected to take.

As they entered the final approach, two Weasels drove out from the base towards them but then stopped 2 miles short of the convoy. Initially puzzled, Fuchs quickly realised that the Weasels were towing two sledges crowded with upwards of 30 people, all armed with cameras which they kept inside their jackets until the last moment to prevent the shutters from freezing solid. Followed by the now exhausted dog teams, the Sno-cats and the solitary Weasel rumbled forward, their tracks throwing up showers of loose snow which sparkled in the sun, and finally drew up in the centre of the reception committee. This included, as well as correspondents and the base personnel, Admiral Dufek and Hillary, who had flown back to the Pole in a Neptune the previous day. 'On jumping out of the Cat,' recorded Fuchs, 'I first shook hands with Ed, then George Dufek and the base leaders. There was such a press of photographers and recorders that it was quite difficult to move about.'[901] The greeting between the two explorers was simple and undemonstrative: 'Hullo, Bunny,' said Hillary. 'Damn glad to see you, Ed,' replied Fuchs.

For the next ten minutes around 40 men in a wide variety of clothing milled, chatted and moved from one group to another as the cameramen recorded the scene for posterity – and for immediate despatch, by radio facsimile, to the outside world. Doug McKenzie, another of the recent arrivals, observed that 'The gaiety and animation and *bonhomie* of this moment seemed to have more in common with a ski-jumping prize-giving in the French Alps than with the sinister business of polar travel.'[902] Noel Barber, meanwhile, noted that 'Everything had to be done several times "for the record". Shaking hands, close-ups of Hillary and Fuchs, of the two explorers with the Admiral, even the poor dogs had to be put into action again for the cameras.'[903] When the first excitement of the meeting had subsided, Dr Houk and Admiral Dufek climbed into Fuchs's Sno-cat so that he could drive them to the base. Hillary, however, chose to follow with George Lowe, causing McKenzie to make the wry remark that 'more than three in a Sno-cat's cabin is a crowd.'[904] And then, 56 days after leaving Shackleton Base, the five surviving vehicles of the Trans-Antarctic Expedition drove the last 2 miles to the Geographic South Pole and there turned off their ignitions. 'At last,' Hannes La Grange enthused, 'we had reached it, with its ring of empty oil drums encircling the flags of the United Nations and United States, and the cluster of huts and radio masts used by the Americans ... It was a great day.'[905]

Despite the excitement of the throng, McKenzie later wrote that he thought the meeting of Hillary and Fuchs at the Pole 'a pitiful flop as an expedition highlight'.[906] With America rapidly becoming the dominant presence in the Antarctic, from its very inception Fuchs had wanted to emphasise his expedition's Commonwealth origins and to avoid American influence and aid so far as possible. That being the case, ideally the meeting between the two arms of the expedition would have been an exclusively Commonwealth affair. Instead, their presence at the Pole gave the Americans proprietorial rights and they became the TAE's *de facto* hosts. As a result, in McKenzie's opinion the meeting became an American event – 'or so much American that the rest did not greatly matter ... The meeting was taken out of its context as a major event in the crossing of Antarctica and shown to be a meeting between three people rather than two – the three who had arrived on the Pole ice by mechanical means: Dufek by aircraft, Hillary by tractor, and Fuchs by sno-cat.'[907]

Among the Crossing Party, too, not everyone shared La Grange's enthusiasm. Indeed, for many the overwhelming feeling was one of anticlimax. Over the course of the previous days the expeditionaries' thoughts had turned increasingly to the events of 46 years earlier and to the horror of Captain Scott's party when, on 16 January 1912, they had discovered a Norwegian camp at latitude 89°42'S, just a few miles short of the Pole. 'This told us the whole story,' a despondent Scott had written in his diary. 'The Norwegians have forestalled us and are first at the Pole.'[908] In very different circumstances, the TAE too had been forestalled – not by the Norwegians, but by the Americans. And just as many of the Ross Sea Party had looked upon the straggling US base at Hut Point with something akin to dismay, Fuchs's men found that the drab appearance of the South Pole Station, with its ring of rusty drums and tawdry internationalism, stripped the moment and the place of its romantic associations. Jon Stephenson, the youngest in the party, summed up the thoughts of many when he wrote that 'in looking around the Pole and its surroundings, I felt no deep sense of place or history, apart from a realisation that the historic South Pole is nothing more than the ultimate point in south latitude. I felt swamped by all the strangers and by the large, busy station with a different style and culture from those to which I was accustomed.'[909]

Perhaps sensing this disappointment, before they entered the base proper, Fuchs took the opportunity to address his men and to articulate, in the words of Homard, 'something that we were all feeling.'[910] After so many trials and tribulations, he told them, the expedition had reached the South Pole, a key milestone in their epic journey. 'It was a pity,' he acknowledged, 'we could not have arrived at a "great white desolation" and decided for ourselves that here was the South Pole. However, the US Station was already set up and we must accept the fact.'[911] The incident passed quickly, but it marked an important moment of solidarity within the expedition that might otherwise have been lost amid the clicking cameras and mutual backslapping. It marked,

too, a degree of empathy with his men that many had thought
Fuchs incapable of feeling. But now, as they descended the snow
slope into the American base, Fuchs must turn his attention away
from the concerns of his own small party and instead focus upon
the perceptions and expectations of the wider world. As he prepared for the inevitable press conference, he knew that for all
their cordiality and enthusiasm, the waiting reporters would be
scrutinising his every word and gesture for signs of division and
antagonism in the aftermath of the 'race to the Pole'.

14

The Hundred Days

Fuchs gave his press conference in the Pole base's refectory, its walls covered with statistical charts and dog-eared notices and the air filled with the fug of tobacco smoke and the odour of the reporters, base personnel and explorers pressed onto its long benches. Wearing a white roll-neck sweater and with his jaw adorned with a thick beard, Fuchs looked, McKenzie thought, 'every centimetre an explorer in the old tradition'.[912] Seemingly unperturbed by the phalanx of arc lights, cameras and tape recorders, he rested his elbows on the table, lit his pipe, and calmly prepared to field the journalists' questions. As expected, they focused on three main topics: the dangers of the onward journey and the wisdom of proceeding so late in the season; the race to the Pole; and the rift, real or imagined, caused by Hillary's attempts to persuade him to split his journey over two years. If they had hoped for angry recriminations or signs of a bitter feud, the journalists did not know their man.

According to McKenzie, Fuchs swept through the conference 'with the brisk efficiency of a scoutmaster who is not going to let strangers see that his troop-leader has been difficult.'[913] Even Noel Barber, who had infuriated the TAE's Management Committee with his vocal support for Hillary, admitted to being immensely impressed 'with the quiet efficiency of this man with pale blue eyes, ruddy complexion and reddish blonde beard, who behaved like the complete master of the expedition, not aggressive in any way, but quite definitely the boss.'[914] Fuchs exuded confidence. 'We see no reason why we shouldn't make it,' he told the reporters. 'If we do not and winter overtakes us, it is just hard luck.'[915] Of course the Crossing Party had made slower progress than he had hoped and the Pole was far short of the halfway mark, being only 900 miles from Shackleton and 1250 miles from Scott. But the worst part of the journey lay behind them and, by abandoning the dog teams at the Pole, from where the Americans would fly them to Scott Base, and by spacing the seismic shots more widely, the convoy should be able to increase its daily mileage significantly. The route ahead had also been surveyed and crevasses marked and, once beyond Depot 700, the convoy would be within the range of the Otter and Beaver aircraft, which could drop supplies if required. Taken together, these factors should alleviate many of the difficulties encountered so far. 'And about that controversial Hillary suggestion that Fuchs should break off the expedition at the Pole,' wrote Bertram Jones of the *Daily Express*, 'and continue later in the year, Dr Fuchs said: "He made a suggestion. I could not accept it. There was no argument." He smiled as he said it.'[916] Finally, when asked for his reaction to Hillary's dash to the Pole, Fuchs drew quietly at his pipe before answering with the same sphinx-like inscrutability. 'I have nothing against it,' he said. 'He was in a position to do it. So jolly good show.'[917] As a consummate, if entirely false, expression of unity of purpose and mutual regard, the performance could hardly have been bettered. One key member of the expedition, however, was conspicuous by his absence.

Hillary's attempt to exert pressure on Fuchs by appealing to the Management Committee in London had backfired seriously, with much of the resulting pressure being imposed not on Fuchs, but on Hillary himself. Writing to Charles Bowden on 6 January, Sir John Slessor expressed his committee's opinion that, in the event of the Crossing Party being delayed any further, 'the duties of the supporting parties under Hillary become correspondingly greater. We consider these duties should include the laying of additional depots, including 800, should Fuchs so require … Emphasise, as previously, that Hillary's primary job is to make as

certain as humanly possible that Fuchs reaches Scott Base this
season.'[918] Although the Ross Sea Committee had always held
the same view, and had only endorsed Hillary's actions when to
do otherwise would have been to openly acknowledge its own
powerlessness to control him, Slessor's telegram – which the
London Committee also released to the newspapers – must have
rankled. In the face of the growing furore – and the widening
gulf between the British and New Zealand elements of the expedition – the next day, the Prime Minister of New Zealand, Walter
Nash, felt compelled to back his nation's favourite son, publicly
affirming his confidence in Hillary, who, he said, 'would do the
best thing for all the parties concerned.'[919]

'I seem to have turned into the big bad wolf,' Hillary noted
after hearing of Nash's intervention, '– well to hell with them!
I'll go on as before as I know the majority of this emotion is
sparked off by the fact that we reached the Pole first – due solely
to Bunny's bungling efforts.'[920] Despite his characteristic bull-
ishness, however, Hillary knew that the eyes of the world were
now turned fully upon him. He knew, too, that to most observers, what Walter Nash called 'the best thing' could have only one
meaning: the stocking of an additional depot in line with Fuchs's
request of 24 December. But with Depot 700 positioned at the
outer limit of the Beaver's range and with no tractors in position to transfer the fuel further south, the laying of an additional
depot had become a practical impossibility. The best he could
hope to do, as he had told Fuchs on 28 December, would be to
fly in more fuel to Depot 700. Unfortunately for Hillary, flying
in more fuel required the active and immediate participation of
the survey party in the field – and Miller and Marsh were in no
mood to comply with his requests. In the routine radio schedule
of 7 January, he again asked them to bring forward their return
to Depot 700 in order to operate the radar beacon and to meet
and unload the Beaver, but Miller's response was uncompromising. 'Ed spoke wanting us to bring in aircraft to D700 – have said
will not be there until Jan 16th which is two days earlier than
we stated a week ago. He seems very anxious to get this in for
Bunny – I wonder why? ... He can wait. He had his chance to

comply with Bunny's wishes earlier so now he can sweat ... How transparent he is.'[921]

Miller and Marsh finally reached Depot 700 on 15 January after a highly productive month, during which they had covered more than 400 miles on sledge and foot, collecting some 40lb of geological specimens in the process. Most important of all, they had completed a thorough exploration of the Queen Alexandra mountain range to the west of the Beardmore Glacier, and had been able to establish that the range actually consisted of five distinct mountain chains. The day after their return to Depot 700, seven additional drums of petrol were flown in from Scott Base and with Fuchs still 100 miles from the Pole, Hillary had successfully avoided any embarrassing failure to fulfil his pledge to the Crossing Party. Nonetheless, it had been an uncomfortable couple of weeks and he felt very little inclination to return to the Pole for a public meeting with Fuchs – a meeting which, so far as both men were concerned, could serve very little practical purpose since Hillary would not join the Crossing Party until it reached Depot 700. But, as Admiral Dufek appreciated, while the meeting might be purely symbolic, to avoid it altogether would be to court speculation on the part of the press. On the 17th, Dufek hosted a cocktail party at Hut Point and announced that he intended to fly the assembled reporters to the Pole the following day. He also took the opportunity to have a quiet word with Hillary who confided to his diary that the Admiral 'gave me some fatherly advice and persuaded me to go too. What a nuisance!'[922]

Having followed Dufek's well-meant advice and dutifully given the journalists their photo-opportunity at the bottom of the world, Hillary felt no urgent need to attend the press conference, deciding instead to 'give Bunny a free lash to say what he liked.'[923] Afterwards, the two men spent a few hours together discussing logistics and the onward journey to Depot 700. Although he later wrote of Fuchs that 'I was more than a little impressed by his unswerving spirit,'[924] in his diary, Hillary was rather less complimentary. 'We cleared things up quite satisfactorily,' he wrote immediately after the interview, 'but I'm afraid Bunny depresses me. He's so dogged and stubborn and secretive and lacks the confidence of most of his party. He confidently speaks of March 1st at Scott Base but all the others are hoping for March 15th ... What a mess up it all is!'⁹²⁵

During the previous months, Hillary had exhibited a considerable degree of self awareness, acknowledging, at least to himself, the potential destructiveness of his single-minded determination to pursue his own goals no matter what the consequences – and recognising that his obstinacy had a tendency to alienate some members of his team. In close proximity to Fuchs, however, he appears to have been shorn of his ability to self-analyse and he concluded his diary entry with the comment 'Bunny's party are obviously a far from happy group and as George [Lowe] says "It's a one man show". Apparently no one knows what is happening at any time except Bunny and David [Stratton].'⁹²⁶ In repeating Lowe's description of Fuchs's faults as a leader, Hillary might just as easily have been quoting Miller's analysis of his own shortcomings – but the irony seems to have been lost on him entirely.

Having provided Fuchs with the details of the route to Depot 700, there was nothing to keep Hillary at the Pole and later on the 20th he and Dufek flew back to Scott, leaving the Crossing Party to prepare for the next stage of their journey. It was a decision which came as a relief to both men, as the ever-observant McKenzie remarked:

> Apart from their official meetings neither had any obvious interest in the other's company; they did not seek out each other. They were two men who had been thrown together by force of circumstances and they were apparently without common ground for social intercourse. Their politeness towards each other was unfailing, as between strangers.⁹²⁷

The Crossing Party's stay at the Pole saw very little reduction in its activity – and Fuchs's decision to switch from Greenwich Mean Time to New Zealand Time did nothing to alleviate his team's tiredness, the net result being that they worked around the clock. 'I decided we should change over to their time at once by treating

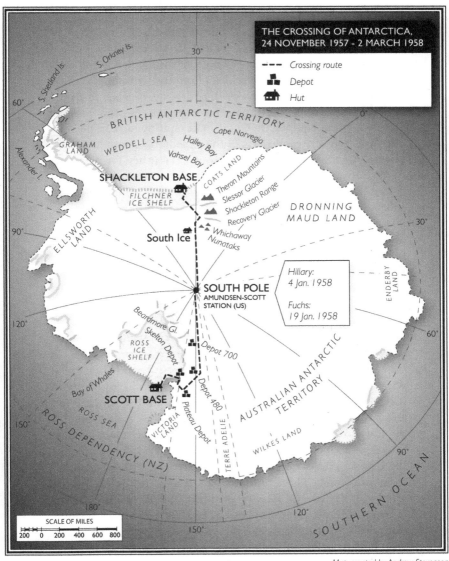

THE CROSSING OF ANTARCTICA,
24 NOVEMBER 1957 - 2 MARCH 1958

- - - Crossing route
Depot
Hut

S. Shetland Is.
S. Orkney Is.
30°
60°
S. Shetland Is.
0°
BRITISH ANTARCTIC TERRITORY
GRAHAM LAND
WEDDELL SEA
Cape Norvegia
Alexander I.
Halley Bay
Vahsel Bay
SHACKLETON BASE
FILCHNER ICE SHELF
COATS LAND
Theron Mountains
Slessor Glacier
Shackleton Range
Recovery Glacier
DRONNING MAUD LAND
ELLSWORTH LAND
South Ice
Whichaway Nunataks
90°
30°
ENDERBY LAND
SOUTH POLE
AMUNDSEN-SCOTT STATION (US)
Hillary:
4 Jan. 1958
Fuchs:
19 Jan. 1958
120°
Beardmore Gl.
Skelton Depot
ROSS ICE SHELF
Depot 700
60°
AUSTRALIAN ANTARCTIC TERRITORY
Bay of Whales
Depot 480
SCOTT BASE
VICTORIA LAND
Plateau Depot
ROSS SEA
WILKES LAND
90°
150°
ROSS DEPENDENCY (NZ)
TERRE ADÉLIE
120°
180°
150°
SOUTHERN OCEAN
SCALE OF MILES
200 0 200 400 600 800

Map created by Andrew Stevenson

our night as day,' he wrote, 'and going to bed early if individuals wished. In fact I think most of us have missed a complete night's sleep.'[928] But at least the base's facilities meant a huge improvement in their working conditions. In particular, the Americans insisted that they abandon their tents in favour of the base's accommodation and removed their own vehicles from the workshop in order to allow Homard and Pratt to work under cover for the first time in many weeks. While the engineers repaired broken tow bars and battery heating equipment, Geoff Pratt continued with his seismic shots and other members of the expedition concentrated on rearranging the sledge loads for the onward journey. Fuchs, meanwhile, answered correspondence and radio messages – including congratulations from the Queen, from Prime Minister Harold Macmillan, from Walter Nash the New Zealand Prime Minister and from a host of other dignitaries from around the world. Not all the official correspondence was quite so welcome, however. George Lowe opened one envelope to discover a final demand from the Inland Revenue, which had been conscientiously pursuing him from continent to continent for months.

In January 1957, American visitors to the recently completed hut at Shackleton had described it as 'quaint'. Now, looking at the facilities at the Amundsen–Scott Base, the Crossing Party could understand why. In addition to its well equipped workshop and a state-of-the-art laboratory that left the long-suffering Lister green with envy, the base boasted some facilities which, to men who had spent so long among the Spartan surrounds of Shackleton and South Ice, must have seemed almost other-worldly, including hot showers and a 24-hour cinema. But these unaccustomed luxuries and the generosity of their hosts did nothing to reduce the Crossing Party's desire to push on to Scott Base as hard and as fast as possible. Their attitude puzzled some of the Americans, who shared Hillary's views regarding the risks of the onward journey so late in the season, but, as Hal Lister observed, in addition to their natural desire to complete their journey, the fracas with Hillary acted as a further spur to keep moving:

> Many are surprised at our continuing the journey when we are so late, but really we must. I hope, we all sincerely hope, to

get out this summer-autumn … Certainly we must see the job thro' especially after the Hillary-Fuchs controversy, which we hope is over now and will be forgotten.[929]

Fuchs had planned to leave the Pole no later than 23 January, but high winds and thick drift slowed the completion of Pratt's seismic work and the departure was eventually delayed until the 24th. Before beginning their long journey north, all the members of the expedition were encouraged to 'run round the world' by making a circuit of the ring of fuel drums marking the Pole. 'I ran around the world in less than three minutes;' noted La Grange with satisfaction, 'a South African record!'[930] Having completed their circuit, each man received a coloured testimonial in the style of a 'Crossing the Line' certificate and, in return, and as a token of thanks for the kindness they had been shown, Fuchs presented the base with the TAE's pennant. There was no doubting the genuineness of the Americans' hospitality but, in Stephenson's opinion, the hosts were perhaps no less pleased to see their guests depart than the guests were to leave. 'The goodwill, generosity and patience of our friendly American hosts at the Pole were impressive. But towards the end of our time there, I sensed we had outstayed our welcome; the station men had busy routines, scientific and otherwise.'[931] It was time for the Crossing Party to move on.

After the inevitable last-minute vehicle repairs, the convoy finally set off at 4.55pm on the 24th, first driving around the Pole itself and then thrusting out along the 156th East meridian, like a satellite using a planet's gravitational pull to slingshot it into outer space. The Americans had marked the route with flags for 18 miles, terminating with a snow cairn where they had deposited additional fuel and food. 'This we had been pressed to take with us,' Fuchs noted, 'but in keeping with my policy that this shall be an unaided Commonwealth expedition we did not touch any of it.'[932] Apparently, at least to Fuchs, the facilities provided over the course of the previous days and the Americans' willingness to fly the TAE's exhausted dogs to Scott Base did not count as aid.

A combination of a 20-knot wind, poor visibility, a soft snow surface and a temperature of -14°F made driving distinctly unpleasant but by midnight the party had covered 25 miles.

Owing to the surface conditions and the high altitude of the Polar Plateau, which here reached approximately 10,000 feet above sea level, fuel consumption soared, with Fuchs's Sno-cat using nearly a gallon every mile. Despite near-constant whiteout and a soft surface, over the course of the next two days the vehicle train continued to make slow but steady progress, covering 35 miles on the 25th and 40 miles on the 26th. They made another 40 miles on the 27th and during the course of the day the surface gradually improved until the cats were making 8mph. Much to Fuchs's satisfaction, even the last of the Weasels, which had been suffering from continual vapour locking because of the altitude, had been able to make between 6 and 7mph for the last 5 miles and when he climbed into his sleeping bag at 4.00am on the 28th, he felt quietly confident.

Work began again a few short hours later with a routine seismic shot. The charge failed to detonate, however, and when David Stratton walked over to Sno-cat 'Haywire' to consult with Geoff Pratt, to his horror, he found the geophysicist in a heap on the floor, struggling for breath, his face an unhealthy pink, his pupils dilated and his limbs twitching. Stratton called for Allan Rogers who quickly diagnosed severe cumulative carbon monoxide poisoning. During the Heroic Era, a number of explorers had come close to being asphyxiated, usually when their hut chimneys became blocked by drift snow, allowing toxic fumes to accumulate. Pratt's poisoning was simply a modern twist on this old problem, his vehicle's heater having pumped carbon monoxide into the enclosed cab. But the danger was no less significant in 1958 than it had been in 1908. In particular, the rarefied atmosphere at high altitude increased the risk of heart failure and brain damage. Rogers administered oxygen from the cylinders used for welding, but this supply would not last for more than five hours and, on the doctor's advice, Fuchs felt compelled to ask Admiral Dufek if he would fly Pratt to Scott Base, where the higher oxygen content of the air at sea-level would aid his recovery.

As usual, the Admiral responded immediately to this call for help and a little after midnight, two Neptune aircraft could be heard circling high above the British camp, having taken off from

McMurdo Sound four hours earlier. On board one was Griff Pugh, a physician with the British Medical Council and a specialist in carbon monoxide poisoning who, by a happy coincidence, happened to be undertaking a physiological programme at the US base during the summer season. Over the radio, Pugh discussed Pratt's condition with Rogers and advised him that the combination of poor visibility and the high altitude of the plateau made the American pilots reluctant to attempt a landing except in a dire emergency. Given that Pratt's condition had stabilised, the two doctors agreed that the best course of action would be to drop two large oxygen cylinders and breathing apparatus by parachute and a few minutes later Fuchs's men were carrying the heavy metal tubes to Pratt's tent while the Neptunes began their 800-mile flight back to the coast.

The Crossing Party had covered a mere 10 miles on the 28th, but with Pratt's condition rapidly improving, the following day they managed to travel another 60 miles through a severe whiteout. The area was covered with sastrugi but now the vehicles were running parallel with the ridges instead of driving across them, making the journey less gruelling. Despite these improved surface conditions, it had become clear that the last Weasel was reaching the end of its useful life and it had been towed the last 5 miles into camp. The altitude had inhibited its performance to such a degree that Fuchs had been forced to reduce its load to a mere three-quarters of a ton and its fuel consumption now equalled that of the much larger and more powerful Sno-cats. Rather more positively, that evening Fuchs could report that as a result of the continuing oxygen treatment, Pratt had made a complete recovery 'and really appears to be his normal self again'.[933]

After a day of maintenance, the expedition moved off again at 10.15 on the morning of 31 January and, to Lowe's delight, they abandoned Weasel 'Wrack and Ruin' at their camp. All twelve explorers were now travelling in the roomier and more comfortable Sno-Cats – though only a man who had spent the last two months in the confines of a Weasel's cabin could ever describe a Sno-cat as comfortable. The temperature in their cabs usually hovered between -15°F and -20°F when the men first climbed into them, and even after the heaters had been pumping hot air (and carbon monoxide) for an hour, it seldom rose above 40°F, while, at floor level, it remained well below freezing. Being the furthest from the heater vents, the back seats, in particular, became extremely uncomfortable for their occupants after hours of inactivity. 'To sit out of the sun in an aluminium box at -10°F with frost and ice accretion on the roof and engine fumes coming in really makes each day rather trying and exhausting to no purpose,' grumbled Lister.[934]

Although a temperature of -26°F and a soft surface made the early stages of the journey difficult, the expedition made excellent progress on the 31st, covering 70 miles in eleven hours. 'For the first time since long before the Pole I have been able to drive in top gear!' Fuchs enthused. 'This is the greatest distance we have accomplished at any time in one day. Certainly the surfaces this side of the Pole are a great improvement.'[935] The following day, they made another 45 miles, continuing on a course which ran parallel with the welt-like sastrugi and gently descended from the Pole across a series of long shallow steps. 'This, at any rate,' wrote Homard, 'was a little more satisfying than a dead flat ice sheet.'[936]

Rather less satisfying were the telltale signs of imminent failure among the Sno-cats. On the 31st, Homard had discovered that the outer main bearing of a pontoon on 'County of Kent' had disintegrated and required replacement, constituting what Fuchs later described as 'the first of the series of different Sno-cat troubles that now began to haunt us.'[937] In particular, over the course of the next few days, all of the vehicles in turn suffered problems with their complicated caterpillar tracks. Each track possessed 148 steel links, every one of which must be tightened at 100-mile intervals with a special spanner, an individual track taking around an hour to complete. Even more frustrating, the design meant that the links could only be tightened and not slackened by hand, so that the explorers constantly fretted about the risk of placing too much strain on the tracks. This, Fuchs recalled, 'tended to make the operator over careful, and he would end his task only to find that the track was still too loose. Then the operation would have to be begun all over again.'[938] None of the tracks had been tightened since the departure from the Pole and by the 2nd, their slackness was causing them to jump regularly from their guide rails, then jam solid with a violent wrench.

In order to address this problem, the 4th was designated a maintenance day and, as well as tightening the tracks, the expeditionaries took the opportunity to top up each of the cats' two differentials and two gearboxes. In addition, each vehicle's 320 grease nipples were lubricated – a tedious job even in a heated garage and triply so on the Polar Plateau, with a temperature of -20°F and a wind blowing at 25mph. 'And imagine what a grease gun does in a stiff breeze,' groaned Blaiklock, 'you get oil everywhere, all over your anoraks – filthy!'[939] As well as being very unpleasant, allowing one's clothing to become impregnated with grease is also extremely dangerous in a polar environment. The grease prevents the fabric from breathing and body moisture becomes trapped. As a result, the clothes lose their insulation and the wearer becomes more prone to frostbite, despite having taken all the usual precautions.

Hitherto, a maintenance day had usually meant no travel, but Fuchs was now determined to press on to Depot 700, 'and not put it off till tomorrow as most people hoped, I fancy.'[940] Despite a late start, they made 33 miles – although Geoff Pratt's Sno-cat did not crawl into camp until 2.30 on the morning of 5 February, after yet more trouble with its tracks. 'It is good to press on now,' wrote Lister, voicing the views of many, 'but oh, we are rather tired, sleeping little.'[941] Fuchs believed that the convoy had already passed the first belt of crevasses reported by Hillary but at 8.30pm on the 5th Stratton halted with the front pontoons of his vehicle resting on the lip of a fissure about 12 feet wide. 'Skiing on a quarter of a mile to climb a high hummock for a view,' Fuchs wrote, 'I crossed 9 more large parallel crevasses which boded ill for our progress. From the relatively high point I could see at least two more miles of these great cracks directly ahead while to the right and left they could be seen to extend into the indefinite distance.'[942]

The belt proved to be 3.5 miles across and consisted of some 50 crevasses varying in width from 12 feet to 75 feet and the following morning a party of four began the tedious process of

prodding a route ahead on foot. At the same time, Fuchs and
Homard brought two of the cats as far forward as possible and
the rest of the team assisted Geoff Pratt with the firing of the
morning's seismic shot. Three shots totalling 10lb of explosives
were fired, hurling snow and ice particles hundreds of feet into
the air, and to his horror Fuchs observed that, for the first time,
the resulting vibrations caused the crevasse lids to crack and
sag visibly. This, he acknowledged, 'was scarcely encouraging to
one who was about to pioneer a route across a whole series of
unpleasant looking chasms.'[943] Despite the ominous appearance
of the crevasse belt, all the vehicles passed over it without accident
and perhaps their good fortune made Fuchs a trifle complacent
when, around 25 miles farther on, he recognised another crevasse,
apparently no more than 3 feet wide. Having already crossed
much wider chasms, he ploughed on confidently, only to feel
his rear pontoons dropping beneath him, indicating that the crevasse was much wider than it had at first appeared. The Sno-cat's
momentum carried it and its sledges across without damage but
following behind in 'County of Kent' Homard was less fortunate.

Crossing the crevasse at a point to one side of the gaping hole
left by Fuchs's vehicle, 'County of Kent' also broke through the
crevasse lid and only just managed to claw its way to safety, cracking its large, cast-aluminium rear steering platform in the process.
Since the expedition carried no spare, once again Homard's inge-
nuity came to the fore and over the course of the next few hours
he succeeded in patching the broken element using nothing
more sophisticated than a block of timber and a rope. Not long
afterwards, David Pratt also ran into trouble, shearing the pin
which linked the forward steering arm of Sno-cat 'Able' with the
steering platform, necessitating another time-consuming repair.
While the engineers laboured on, Fuchs, Stratton and Lister surveyed the area ahead and discovered that the convoy was now
confronted by a series of parallel crevasses running at right angles
to its course. None of the fissures was more than 15 feet wide, but
the wind crust appeared thin and brittle and certainly incapable of supporting the vehicles' weight. The crevasses petered out
about 2 miles from their current position but only to be replaced
by an equally dangerous area of hummocks and punctures. As

so often before, just when it appeared that the expedition was within striking distance of a key objective, in this case Depot 700, from where Hillary would be able to guide the Crossing Party to Scott Base, new obstacles rose in its path.

Fuchs scoured the area in the hope of finding Hillary's crossing point marked by the tracks of the Fergusons and by the snow cairns built by the New Zealanders – but found no sign of either. Disappointed, on the morning of 7 February, he decided that he had no option but to push across the crevasses at a point about 6 miles southeast of where the leading Sno-cats had first run into trouble. Here the prevailing winds had caused thick drifts to form across the crevasse bridges, giving them, in theory at least, extra strength and stability. With the repairs to David Pratt's cat still incomplete, rather than delay the whole party, Fuchs now split it into two: 'County of Kent' and 'Rock 'n' Roll' forming the vanguard while 'Haywire' and its crew kept company with 'Able'. In the tried and tested manner, four men on skis painstakingly zigzagged their way through the area, crossing nineteen crevasses in the process and planting chequered warning flags, before waving the Sno-cats forward. The second half of the Crossing Party should be able to follow the safe route using the crevasse flags and the vehicle tracks left by the pioneers. Given that experience had proved the near impossibility of a single Sno-cat being able to extract another that had become trapped, it was a dangerous strategy – but, for all his confidence before the reporters, Fuchs was now as anxious as the rest of his party to maintain momentum.

As the two leading cats drove on, the landscape gradually became more and more undulating until the vehicles were rising and falling over a series of ridges that surrounded shallow basins a few miles wide. The north facing slopes were hard and rough and bore large sastrugi, while the southern slopes were relatively soft and smooth. It seemed to Fuchs that the ridges probably indicated that the ice sheet here was already being distorted by its collision with the mountains to the east. The mountains themselves were not yet visible – but these telltale signs, like ripples from the fall of an unseen stone, were very welcome indeed to men who had seen not seen rock since the Whichaway Nunataks.

At last, at 8.40 on the evening of 7 February, Fuchs detected a
dark speck about 3 miles ahead and a few degrees to starboard.
It could only be Depot 700. Thirty-five minutes later, the two
cats came to a halt beside the pile of fuel drums and ration boxes,
all surmounted by a fluttering marker flag. The depot stood at
82°58'S, 146°02'E and at an altitude of 8370 feet above sea level.
Averaging 34.5 miles a day, it had taken the expedition 15 days
to travel the 521 miles from the South Pole. In addition, over
the 1427 miles from Shackleton, the convoy had now brought
its daily average up to 19 miles. This was still 1 mile per day short
of the minimum that Fuchs had predicted for the journey after
South Ice, but now the party would be travelling over a known
route and, with Hillary to guide them, they should be able to
increase their pace still further. After setting up camp, Fuchs
climbed into his sleeping bag and, with obvious relief, confided
to his diary that he 'felt a real sense of accomplishment in at last
joining up with depots laid from the far side of the continent –
the first time this has been done.'[944] Now he must wait for Hillary.

Over the course of the previous few days, news of the Crossing
Party's rapid progress had wrought an astonishing change in
Hillary's outlook. After so many months of scepticism, at last he
began to believe that Fuchs might actually live up to his confident predictions. 'Bunny making excellent progress and now
250 miles from Pole,' he noted cautiously on 31 January. 'Looks
like my gloomy forecast could be wrong as Bunny has pulled
his finger out and is hurrying along. Well, this is one occasion I'd
be delighted to be proved wrong.'[945] Two days later, he recorded
that the Crossing Party had covered 340 miles since leaving the
Pole and hoped to reach Depot 700 by 6 February. 'This puts a
completely new complexion on things,' he enthused, 'and maybe
we'll reach Scott Base by the end of Feb. I'll certainly try to hurry
things along. If we make good time this could be quite a pleasant
trip down the Skelton.'[946]

As well as finding that his pessimism regarding Fuchs's chances
now seemed unjustified, Hillary was also buoyed up by recent
discussions with Dufek. Over the past weeks, he had regularly

quizzed the Admiral regarding the planned departure dates for the American ships and aircraft, his persistence reflecting his own urgent desire to return to his wife and children and finally to turn his back on the Antarctic – something which, for all his independence, he knew he could not do until Fuchs had completed his journey safely. On 25 January, he learned at last that Dufek planned to retain two Neptunes and two Globemasters on standby at Christchurch from where they could fly back to McMurdo Sound when Fuchs arrived at Scott. The Admiral also confirmed that he intended to keep back the icebreaker, *Glacier*, until 10 March in order to evacuate the swarms of reporters who had descended on Hut Point to witness the closing stages of the trans-continental journey. So long as the powerful *Glacier* remained in the Sound, the *Endeavour*, which had arrived on 30 December, could also stay – Kirkwood being guaranteed a navigable route through the pack ice. 'This is excellent news,' wrote a relieved Hillary, 'as it means we are assured of evacuation.'[947] But not everyone would wait for Fuchs. Since many of the New Zealanders had completed their work, there was no longer any pressing reason for them to remain. In addition, the Crossing Party might still be delayed seriously and forced to over-winter at Scott, in which case the base would become seriously over-crowded. The only way to ensure that an over-wintering party remained tolerably comfortable was to commence the evacuation of all non-essential personnel.

Some members of the Ross Sea Party viewed the prospect of the homeward voyage with mixed emotions. Commenting from his position close to Depot 700, Bob Miller had noted after a routine radio schedule that there had been an 'Absolute collapse of morale at Base; it appears everyone going home in all directions – deplorable.'[948] Miller ascribed this collapse to 'the ballyhoo of the NZ Pole journey' and, in large part, he was right. In particular, Jim Bates and Murray Ellis had become the focus of much negative press attention when they announced their unwillingness to assist Fuchs's engineers on the last leg of the crossing. 'I flatly refused to stay at the Pole,' Bates had told one journalist. 'I felt I had done my job and that was that. I did not interest myself in

Fuchs's plans.'[949] Naturally, given Bates's position as a key member
of a party whose primary function was to support the crossing,
such a statement could only inflame speculation and a number
of newspapers even began to ask whether the engineers should
be disciplined for insubordination. 'This nastiness has removed
any pleasure I might have had left in the expedition,'[950] Hillary
complained, though without acknowledging that the attacks on
the engineers were a direct result of his own decisions on the
plateau and of the pressure that he had applied to them. For Bates,
this personal criticism was the last straw. Weary and disillusioned,
he was delighted to become the first member of the Ross Sea
Party to retreat north – travelling on board the *Private John R.
Towle* in company with three members of the IGY party, Trevor
Hatherton, Herb Orr and Peter Macdonald.

Whatever tensions they might have experienced during
their year in the Antarctic, the members of Hillary's team had
grown accustomed to one another and the sudden break up of
their company, with the expedition returning to New Zealand
piecemeal instead of as a unified and victorious whole, inevitably
affected morale. When Richard Brooke and Bernie Gunn flew in
from the Skelton Depot on 7 February after four months in the
field, they found that fourteen of their friends and colleagues had
already left, the USS *Greenville Victory* having followed the *Towle*
on the 4th, with Ellis, Mulgrew, Douglas, Warren, Gawn, Balham,
Ayres, Carlyon, Bucknell and Sandford on board. Describing
their arrival back at Scott, a disappointed Gunn wrote: 'We set
out full of hope and excitement, I had thought often of returning
the same way, dashing up with light sleds, dogs yelping, waving to
the men, pats for the dogs, handshakes and congratulations but
instead, we had, exactly nothing ... I don't believe that ever again
have I felt so totally depressed.'[951]

Anticlimactic though its return might be, the Northern Party
had been spectacularly successful. In the 127 days since 4 October,
its four members had sledged well over 1000 miles, collecting sufficient data in the process to complete, for the first time, a detailed
topographic and geological survey of the 20,000 square miles
of the mountain country between the Mulock and Mawson

Glaciers. As well as filling a huge blank in the map of the continent, they had climbed an astonishing 31 mountains. Most of these – including the 12,247 foot cone of Mount Huggins – had never previously been scaled, though Brooke modestly asserted that 'not much mountaineering technique was required to get up that,' and 'for virtually every other mountain we climbed … it's simply a question of just walking up.'[952]

Warren and Douglas had been flown out of the Plateau Depot on 15 January in order to catch the *Greenville Victory*, but Brooke and Gunn had stayed on for another three weeks to complete their work. In fact, according to Brooke, one of the party's greatest problems lay in choosing the exact limits of their programme – the freedom that Hillary had allowed him when defining his objectives meaning, in practice, that there was always one last ridge to climb. 'That was the difference between our trip and probably most polar journeys. It was difficult to apply a specific aim that was our goal … there was always, basically, a bit more you could do.'[953] In summing up the Northern Party's achievements half a century later, Gunn wrote of Brooke that he 'was prepared to travel hard, perhaps harder than any polar explorer before or since'[954] and there can be little doubt that aeroplane-supported dog-sledging exploration, which lasted from 1920 to the advent of the skidoo in the early 1960s, can have had few more outstanding exponents.

With all the members of the Ross Sea Party, except Miller and Marsh, now either back at base or en route for New Zealand and with the Crossing Party waiting at Depot 700, Hillary focused his attention on reaching Fuchs. But just as poor weather had hindered his plans to rejoin the tractor party at the Plateau Depot during the early days of his own polar journey, the weather now closed in at Scott and kept him pinned down. Watching the snow falling and the thick clouds rolling sluggishly across the sky, for once he felt almost pleased to hear that further mechanical troubles had delayed the progress of the two rearmost Sno-cats and that Fuchs's convoy had not yet reformed at Depot 700. At least this meant that his own absence was not contributing to the Crossing Party's enforced halt.

On 9 February, the sky over McMurdo Sound cleared but poor conditions on the plateau delayed the outbound flight until 4.00pm, when a brief window of opportunity opened at last. With the weather so unpredictable, the long-range flight would be risky but, as John Claydon reported, 'As it was important not to hold Fuchs up at D700 it was decided to proceed with the flight on a "hit or miss" basis.'⁹⁵⁵ Since the Beaver's tanks could carry only sufficient fuel for a one-way journey, if Claydon missed the depot because of poor visibility he would have no option but to try landing on an unknown surface to await rescue. Given the experiences of Haslop and Rogers in September, the prospect seemed very unappealing. Nonetheless, heavily overloaded with fuel and supplies and carrying Hillary and Derek Wright, who wanted to complete his movie sequence with the Crossing Party, the Beaver staggered into the air that evening, leaving deep ruts in the fresh snow covering the airstrip.

Low cloud and snow flurries over the ice shelf forced Claydon to pioneer a new route up the Barne Glacier and for five hours he struggled against a 20-knot headwind, sometimes flying between cloud layers and relying solely upon his instruments for navigation. The air temperature dropped so low that the Beaver's vapour trail turned to ice crystals and hung motionless in the sky, while the surface below, when it appeared fleetingly through the clouds, looked so fractured that an emergency landing would have been quite impossible. In such conditions, it came as a great relief when Claydon at last picked up the radar beacon at Depot 700 and soon afterwards he completed a faultless landing next to the four Sno-cats, 'Haywire' and 'Able' having drawn into camp just an hour earlier.

The new arrivals were given an enthusiastic welcome by the vehicle party, the warmth of the reception increasing still further when the New Zealanders handed out sacks of mail and luxuries in the form of eggs and fresh fruit – though Fuchs, who had been suffering from acute toothache, noted rather warily that 'The apples and oranges are … hard as rocks and it will be quite a problem to thaw them sufficiently to eat them.'⁹⁵⁶ Such reservations aside, he greeted Hillary cordially and soon the two leaders were discussing the next stage of the journey. Though the prospect probably possessed very little appeal for either man, they also agreed that from this point onwards they would share both a tent and a Sno-cat – perhaps hoping that this would serve to further suppress speculation regarding their differences.

Hillary certainly felt far from comfortable at the idea of working so closely with Fuchs. 'I viewed the onwards journey from D700 with very mixed feelings,' he later admitted, 'and I knew I would need to make a major change in my approach to the venture.'[957] In particular, up to this point he had been very largely a free agent – far too free, indeed, so far as Fuchs and the two management committees were concerned. At Scott Base and during his polar journey he had been undisputed leader; now he was reduced to the rank of guide and advisor, with all decisions resting ultimately with Fuchs. Moreover, in the unlikely event of an open quarrel, his own deeply unpopular suggestion regarding a break at the Pole rendered it highly improbable that he would win any meaningful support from Fuchs's followers.

After retiring to their sleeping bags at 3.00am on 10 February, by 8.00am the party was up and about again and a little over 90 minutes later the Beaver was hurtling across the snowfield with Claydon and Wright on board at the beginning of their long flight back to Scott. For his part, Claydon had thought it 'grand to see the boys of the *Theron* days again',[958] though what he described as 'a dreadful meal of pemmican "hoosh"' – the sledgers' traditional soup of melted pemmican, water and hard biscuits – no doubt made him glad to return to the comforts of the base. On the ground, the vehicle fuel tanks and the empty drums on the sledges had already been replenished from the supplies at the depot and at 10.00am the convoy moved off. For 10 miles the cats ploughed on relentlessly and a hugely impressed Hillary noted that they 'ran magnificently over the firm roughish surface and really are an enormous change from the poor old Fergie.'[959] Their pace slowed considerably, however, when 'Rock 'n' Roll' broke through the lid of a crevasse. Fuchs, Hillary and Lister took to their skis in order to probe the route ahead, but fortunately the belt proved to be only 2.5 miles wide and they cleared it without suffering any serious mishaps. Shortly afterwards, they picked up Hillary's two-month-old tractor tracks and again they increased their speed, covering a very satisfactory 52 miles by the close of the day.

Given this rate of advance, Fuchs would no doubt have been highly nettled by Hillary's later assertion that, in joining the convoy, 'the speeding up of progress was to be my main aim'[960] – the implication being that he would achieve as much by chivvying as by path finding. He went on to state that he 'also had some interest in observing the crossing party in action, in taking note of their various techniques, and in making the inevitable comparisons.'[961] Of course, these comparisons were highly unlikely to favour Fuchs. The following morning, after watching the preparations for departure, Hillary observed: 'I'm afraid that this party is very inefficient at getting away and much time is wasted.'[962] Despite this supposed inefficiency and a series of obstacles including a rough surface, huge filled chasms, and a 3-mile-wide belt of crevasses, the party made another 53 miles during the course of the day, reaching Midway Depot at 4.20am on 12 February. After the trials and tribulations of the journey to the Pole, such distances seemed almost incredible and a delighted Lister confided to his diary that 'For the first time I have some confidence that we will be off the plateau in time to get the ship.'[963] For the glaciologist it was a watershed moment as he admitted in the same entry that, up to this point, he had known 'in my heart that we would be too late for the ship.'

This sudden surge of optimism made the events of the next five days seem particularly cruel, with a combination of mechanical problems, whiteout and routine maintenance reducing the convoy's daily mileage over the period to a pitiful 13.5 miles. The 12th had been scheduled as a maintenance day, but the party had again become separated when David Pratt's Sno-cat, 'Able', had first of all fractured a weld on its main steering cross bar and then suffered failure in its transmission box. Homard had driven back in 'County of Kent' to assist him and as the two missing vehicles carried much of the essential equipment, the rest of the expeditionaries could only sit and await their return. Pratt,

Homard and the tools turned up at 2.30 the following afternoon but by the time the maintenance was completed whiteout made it impossible to continue. 'We must travel tomorrow,'[964] Lister noted dolefully that evening and, as if in answer to his prayers, the next day they made 50 miles despite the unbroken whiteout. But it proved to be a false dawn: on the 15th the convoy was again struck by mechanical troubles and ground to a halt.

Rather optimistically, Fuchs had hoped to cover the remaining 80 miles to Depot 480 during the day, but shortly after starting he found that the steering of 'Rock 'n' Roll' was behaving erratically. At first he put it down to the drag of the sledges as they slid sideways off the hummocks but then, 18 miles into the journey, the steering failed to answer altogether and after describing a lazy 'S' bend 'Rock 'n' Roll' came to an abrupt halt. Climbing down from their cab, Fuchs and Hillary found the vehicle's front and rear pontoons pointing in different directions and Fuchs immediately realised that the steering cross bar system had failed, just as it had on 'Able' a few days earlier. 'Looking underneath, I could see the welds had torn apart in several places and very, very bad welds they had been. What a pity Tucker spoils a good idea with such appalling workmanship!'[965]

On inspecting the other cats, they discovered that exactly the same problem had begun to develop on 'Haywire' and 'County of Kent'. As the only spare had already been used on 'Able', the engineers now had no choice but to begin the arduous process of re-welding the failing joints in temperatures below -35°F. 'For the main part,' Homard noted stoically, 'outside repairs are uncomfortable, to say the least, and take very much longer than they do under cover.'[966] The welding job proved no exception and the following day Fuchs learned that the two engineers had worked continuously until 5.30 that morning, coaxing the welder into life and attempting to complete their work so that the convoy could move on. Despite their best efforts they had failed and the vehicles remained stationary until 10.30am on 17 February. The only person who seemed blissfully unfazed by the delay was Geoff Pratt, who spent the entire period fast asleep. 'The probability is that he needs it,' Fuchs commented, 'but it would irk the others more if they had not observed his astonishingly deep and long sleeping at Shackleton.'[967]

It took a little over 12 hours to reach Depot 480 on the 17th, with the tracks of Hillary's Fergusons showing up clearly in the bright sunshine and making route finding easy. The following day, however, a combination of flat lighting and the accumulated ice on the double-glazed windscreens often made it quite impossible to see the tracks and sometimes they remained invisible even when Hillary and others searched for them on foot. In these conditions, the sun compass also became totally redundant and the drivers were forced to rely on the magnetic compass – but so close to the South Magnetic Pole this, too, behaved erratically, with the magnetic pull drawing the needle downwards. The effects were dramatic, as Fuchs described: 'I was driving with eyes firmly fixed on the compass, when David Stratton drew my attention ahead. There I saw three Sno-cats coming towards me!'[968] Intent on his twitching compass needle, Fuchs had described a circle and was driving back along his own path. Clearly a new approach was needed if the Crossing Party were to have any hope of making any meaningful progress in the whiteout.

A few days earlier, Hillary had commented in his diary that 'There is certainly an urge to get out as quickly as possible ... and I'm carefully fostering it.'[969] Now, in order to maintain momentum, he proposed a new method to ease the problems of navigation. Although Fuchs favoured waiting for the sun to reappear, after some debate Hillary persuaded him to mark a course using bamboo poles and flags. Keeping the magnetic compass still, in order to allow the needle to settle, the navigators set up two poles on a compass bearing, one a few yards from the other; next, two men skied as far forward as they could without losing sight of the poles; making sure that the poles were still in line, one behind the other, they then planted a flag as a marker for the drivers to steer towards. The skiers then moved forward and repeated the process, establishing a series of 'stepping stones' that enabled the drivers to remain on course. 'We did this for several hours and made about 5 miles,' Hillary noted. 'Then realised what clots we were and persuaded Bunny to try using vehicles for it. I poked my head out of trapdoor in cab of cat and shouted directions to Bunny at the wheel as I sighted on flags behind. Ken and Jon on sledge behind leapt off every 100 yds and put in another flag.'[970] The strategy of steering by flags and poles was not new, having been used by the British in Greenland and by the Americans, but using vehicles to speed up the process was novel and Hillary could be justifiably pleased that he had significantly increased the party's rate of travel.

Route flagging continued on the 19th, but the team further refined their approach by having the driver lean out of the door of his cat and look backwards so that he could steer without being dependent upon shouted instructions. Forward vision and accelerator control were provided by the passenger. 'This certainly speeded things up,' Fuchs recorded that night, 'but the strain on the driver's arm and neck is considerable, especially as his left hand must be constantly through the door window to ensure that the lurching does not pitch him out under the 'Cat rear tracks.'[971] Leaving the doors open also meant that the cabs became bitterly cold and frequently filled with flying drift snow, but the discomfort was a price worth paying. Using this method, they trundled forward at between 6 and 8mph and by the end of the day they had nearly tripled their mileage of the previous day, covering a total of 42 miles.

'So it went on,' remembered Fuchs, 'maintenance on the 20th followed by 25 miles of route flagging, another 39 miles flagged on the 21st; then relief the next day when slight visibility made it possible to see surface irregularities, and for 15 miles we went "sastrugi hopping" – that is, driving from one selected ridge to the next, thereby maintaining a reasonable course.'[972] After so much anxiety, and in spite of their tiredness, the men's spirits soared as the risk of being marooned for another year retreated and their minds were filled less with the question of whether they would get out and more with the uncertainty over whether their evacuation would be by sea or air. 'Really, I prefer to fly,' Lister noted, 'since the ship will be so crowded and rolling.'[973] Not so very long ago the idea of being choosy about his means of escape would have seemed ridiculous.

The 21st, in particular, was a red-letter day because, after so many weeks of monotonous whiteness, the explorers saw ahead of them the mountains marking the rim of the Polar Plateau. The last rock they had seen was that of the Whichaway Nunataks, now some 1500 miles to their rear. In improving visibility, the convoy covered a total of 52 miles on the 22nd with more and more mountain peaks rearing up over the horizon. 'This was the most enjoyable part of the journey', wrote Homard. '... The whole scene became more and more beautiful as we entered a huge ring of mountains while travelling uphill and down all the way.'[974] By the time they camped, Mount Feather was clear against the blue sky, forming an excellent marker for the Plateau Depot some 36 miles distant.

The following morning the four cats climbed to about 8275 feet over a series of crevasse-free undulations, reaching the lip of the plateau and then beginning their long descent towards the Ross Ice Shelf. 'Everyone very cheerful and really feel we are getting near home,'[975] Hillary had written the night before and soon it seemed that this excitement had been transferred to the sledges themselves, as they surged forward under the force of gravity and for the first time threatened to overtake the Sno-cats as they headed downhill. Marker cairns erected by Hillary's tractor party soon came into view followed almost immediately by the fuel drums and flags of the Plateau Depot itself, just 1.5 miles to the north. 'Rock 'n' Roll' drew into the depot at 8.30pm but the other vehicles had been delayed when the forward steering arm of 'Haywire' had dropped and been twisted below the still-moving Sno-cat. A repair would take some hours, so while they waited, Fuchs, Hillary and Stratton began to dig out the fuel and ration boxes from the drifts.

Just as they completed the excavation, there was a roar as the Otter and the Beaver flew low overhead, piloted by Claydon and Lewis who had been told of the party's imminent arrival over the radio by Ralph Lenton. The planes circled and then landed a few yards away and soon the pilots were tossing out boxes of luxury items and, even more welcome, bags stuffed with mail. As the unloading continued, the remaining Sno-cats rolled into camp and soon the entire party was enjoying an impromptu party, squeezed into the Otter's narrow fuselage, swilling down the bottles of beer brought by Lewis and yelling at each other over the noise of the aeroplane's engine, kept running to prevent freezing. Then they began to stow surplus material from the depot along with a Nansen dog sledge. Finally, Blaiklock and Stephenson clambered aboard. The two dog-sledgers hoped to undertake their own expedition to the Horlick Mountains the following spring and were keen to slaughter seals for dog meat and to check on the condition of the teams that had been flown out from the Pole station. Of course, this decision meant deserting the convoy in the very last stages of the crossing – but in Stephenson's opinion the sacrifice was not so very great. 'Without our dogs,' he later wrote, 'Ken Blaiklock and I felt demoted and dislocated … The prospect of our own, small-scale expedition excited my imagination, as I'm sure it did with Ken.'[976]

Once the two aeroplanes had departed, the rest of the party finished pitching camp and laying out the seismic gear for the last shot of the expedition the next morning. As they completed their task, they paused to watch the sun sinking below the southern horizon – a stark reminder, were any needed, that the sledging season was rapidly drawing to a close. 'With the clouds lit red by the hidden sun,' Fuchs recalled, 'and the snow mauve in semi-shadow, yet flecked by darker colours in every hollow, we walked to our tents, knowing that the next day we should plunge over the edge and wind our way down through the unfamiliar scene of rocky mountains and towering cliffs.'[977]

They began the long descent of the Skelton Glacier on 24 February – but a combination of poor visibility and mechanical trouble dashed the party's expectations of a quick run. Clouds rolled in from the south, obscuring the sun and forcing them to proceed by poling and flagging their route. A temperature of -38°F, combined with a katabatic wind of 35mph made the process of hanging out of the cab door to watch the retreating poles more than usually uncomfortable, as the drivers found themselves facing directly into the onrush of bitterly cold air. Then 'Haywire' developed further faults, delaying the entire party. Disappointment and extreme discomfort left the explorers exasperated, with their circumstances and with each other. 'Time lost in waiting and wondering probably equals all other time lost on the whole trip,'[978] grumbled Lister as he waited for La Grange and Pratt to show up. Finally, at 8.45pm the whole party halted in the centre of the Portal, having covered 20 difficult miles and dropped by 1000 feet.

On the morning of the 25th, the tents were still being lashed by the blizzard but confident that the further they pushed down the glacier the better conditions would become, Hillary urged Fuchs to continue. For some hours it seemed that his prediction had been far too sanguine. Although there was sufficient sun to permit the use of the sun compass for navigation, high drift continued to billow around the vehicles and rasp noisily down their high sides. Then, one after the other, the Sno-cats' engines began to splutter as the fine drift found its way into the engine compartments to be sucked into the carburettors. They cleared the carburettors and carried on, but the process had to be repeated again and again. 'In this fashion and with frequent halts we fumbled our way down through the Portal,' Hillary remembered,

> ... and then, with a suddenness that was quite spectacular, the
> level of the high drift around us dropped to a few feet above
> the surface and we looked out on to the stupendous sweep of
> the Western Mountain, bathed in cold sunshine and thrusting
> up clear and sharp into the blue sky.[979]

The glimpse was a brief one and by the time the party camped under a huge bluff the wind had picked up again and was pouring down the glacier with tent-splitting violence – but they had still covered 52 miles. Not everyone was satisfied, however. In particular, Hillary admitted to being somewhat resentful at what he saw as the lack of appreciation of his efforts in preparing the route. He observed:

> I'm sure all the chaps will regard this as a memorable day, but I
> can't help feeling that they don't realise the work that has gone
> into the route and how close we came to unpleasant crevasse

areas at times. Anyway it was a day of some strain for me and I was glad to get them down.[980]

He was right to suspect that not everyone was as appreciative as he might wish. Like his fellow surveyor, Bob Miller, Blaiklock was distinctly unimpressed by what he saw as Hillary's haphazard efforts at route mapping. 'Ed could claim that he had proved that the route was passable,' he recalled, 'but against that he took no trouble, took no survey detail whatsoever; did nothing ... So we didn't actually find his route all the time ... there was quite a significant amount where we couldn't find his tracks because they'd faded away and he had no traverse you see.'[981] Perhaps to Hillary's surprise, Fuchs was much more generous, noting in the official account that 'all the way down the glacier Ed's first-hand knowledge saved us many hours of route finding and possible difficulty.'[982]

They positioned the Sno-cats to act as a windbreak but all night the explorers' tents twisted before the continued buffeting of the gale-force winds, their tent poles bending and the canvas flapping and snapping ominously. When they awoke, the wind was still tearing down the glacier at 40mph, but as soon as the drift eased sufficiently for Hillary to gain his bearings, they set off downhill. At first, great swirling curtains of drift obscured nearly everything but within a mile the weather changed completely: the wind dropped miraculously and the sun burst through the clouds, bathing the mountainsides and the slopes ahead in a glorious light. The drift diminished too, though it continued to scud across the surface of the glacier, collecting in hollows and every now and then shooting up in spirals. No one could look upon this vista without being moved and for the members of the Crossing Party, now nearing their journey's end, the effect was profound. The sun, wrote an astounded Lister, 'tinged the beautiful sculpted mountains; the highlights, and deep shadows etching the gaunt white walls into ridges, corries, basins, cliffs, peaks and domes; all combined to make a really breathtaking panorama of some of the finest scenic beauty I have ever seen.'[983] Homard, too, was thrilled by the mountains and hanging glaciers, calling the descent of the Skelton 'one of the finest experiences I have had.'[984]

As the convoy continued down the steep inclines of the Skelton Glacier, the drivers found that the smooth, wind polished blue ice caused the sledges to slide uncontrollably from side to side. This didn't present any real danger where the sledges were connected to the cats by rigid tow bars – but the sledges drawn by 'County of Kent' were linked by flexible steel rope hawsers, which came close to causing disaster.

They had travelled only a few miles when a terrific crash caused Homard to brake sharply. The sledge towed behind had caught up with the cat on the slippery surface, smashing into the vehicle's rear and forcing an overhanging balk of 4-inch by 2-inch timber straight through the steel back door, missing Lister's head by just a few inches. During the course of the journey, in many ways Lister's admiration for his leader had grown. In particular, he was impressed by Fuchs's stoicism and, having travelled in the same vehicle for much of the time since the abandonment of his own Weasel, he found both Fuchs and Stratton very good company. But this near-miss made him furious and brought to the surface all the old complaints, most notably Fuchs's conservatism and obstinate refusal to take advice:

> Bunny refused to accept that wire tows were dangerous, but that was 18 months ago … Now he has learned a great deal and tho' still unwilling to accept anyone else's idea or experience, he has now enough experience to be nearer the expert that all the papers embarrassingly claim.[985]

As well as nearly impaling the hapless Lister, the collision broke the cat's rear steering platform and for a time it seemed that the vehicle might have to be abandoned, until the ingenious Homard managed to rig up a temporary repair using a crowbar and a length of rope. Whether this botch would last until the convoy reached Scott, only time would tell.

All day the vehicles wound their way round and down over innumerable crevasses, the blue ice continuing for about 15 miles before it gave way to a much softer snow surface, which gradually became more and more ridged as the vehicles approached Teall Island. Fuchs compared the ridges to small sand dunes, two to three feet high, and for mile after mile the Sno-cats pounded on, sometimes rising with the ridges, sometimes simply squashing them flat. And then, to everyone's relief, a collection of black dots became visible: the Skelton Depot, at the very edge of the Ross Ice Shelf and just 180 miles from Scott Base. 'The last and easiest stage was now ahead of us,' wrote a relieved Hillary, 'and I felt my work was almost done.'[986]

The following day, 27 February, the Crossing Party dug out the supplies which they needed, or which Fuchs was reluctant to leave in the field, and worked on the vehicles. This would be their last day of maintenance and, as Fuchs admitted, 'We were happy to think that it would be some time before we would have to fill a grease gun again, or become covered in a mixture of oil and drift.'[987] The convoy was about to leave the Skelton Glacier and enter the Ross Ice Shelf, meaning that it would have to work its way through the belt of pressure ridges and crevasses crossed by Miller and Carlyon during their reconnaissance of February 1957. Fortunately, Hillary's tractor party had already proved that vehicles could negotiate the area without undue difficulty and that evening the Crossing Party covered 20 miles without mishap and camped on the smooth surface of the ice shelf itself.

They started late the next day, but still managed to make another 64 miles and camped a little way to the east of the low rocky tongue of Minna Bluff. Before setting off at noon, the party had been visited by the TAE's two aircraft, bringing Stuart Heydinger, a photographer from *The Times*, and Dr Pugh, who wanted to join the Crossing Party for the last few miles to Scott. The aeroplanes also brought in a crowd from Scott Base, keen to congratulate the Crossing Party and to cheer them on as they embarked on the last few miles of their epic journey.

Although the arrival of the two aeroplanes on 28 February had been expected, it had prevented the party from moving on until much later than planned. Fuchs was therefore in a much less welcoming frame of mind when, the following day, a US Navy Otter arrived unexpectedly, threatening yet another delay. According to Fuchs, on sighting the Otter, he fired a two-star-red flare 'as a gesture of *joie de vivre* before starting'.[988] Lister told a different story. According to his account, on seeing the aeroplane 'Bunny said, "Hurry inside and start moving; I don't want to meet American Press men now or we'll never get away".'[989] The result was an accident that might have proved catastrophic. Either confused by the flare or distracted by the aeroplane as it came into land, David Pratt in Sno-cat 'Able' didn't see that 'Rock 'n' Roll' had slowed down and he careered into Fuchs's sledge. 'Able' reared up over the static sledge and in the process crushed a wooden box containing hundreds of detonators used in the seismic shots. Had the detonators exploded, they would almost certainly have destroyed the sledge and the cat and either seriously injured or killed the crew of 'Able'. It had been a lucky escape. Even so, the incident was not without its casualties, as Lister explained. 'Later we heard that the pilot was the one who risked his neck to fly out our dogs,' he wrote angrily,

> He was one of the pilots who dropped in the oxygen when we desperately needed it. Naturally, these people were upset. They had come to say Hello, welcome, well done, etc and to bring a bottle of whisky. A refused welcome turns sour very quickly. We were boorish and ill mannered and ungrateful for open handed aid and offers of aid.[990]

Despite this embarrassing and potentially damaging incident, the party made excellent headway over the smooth surface of the ice shelf, travelling 74 miles in the course of the day – the greatest distance covered in a single day during the entire traverse – and leaving just 30 miles before they reached Pram Point. By the time the vehicles came to rest, Ross Island was in clear view and Hillary noted: 'It was with some emotion that I made out the familiar shapes of Castle Rock and Observation Hill on the horizon.'[991] Erebus and Terror were also clearly visible, the former tinged pink by the rays of the setting sun.

After more than 2,000 miles of arduous travelling, it was perhaps as well that the members of the Crossing Party were granted this moment for reflection before they reached their journey's end and the inevitable fanfare and barrage of questions and photography. Fully aware of the significance of the moment, but also typically self-effacing, in his last diary entry of the expedition, an awed Lister chose to dwell not on the trials, tribulations and hugely impressive achievements of the TAE, but on the extraordinary record of those who had gone before. 'The names of all these places strike notes of recognition,' he wrote, captivated by the panorama before him,

> ... and I wonder just who and what happened in and about this region since 1902 when Scott first got in here. It is remarkable what those early explorers achieved under the conditions they accepted. That is the outstanding thought here, seeing the terrain and remembering the early equipment. Just how did the human being survive – and come back for more?! Stupendous![992]

Before starting the next morning to cover the last few miles to Scott, the expedition members took a few minutes, not to conduct a seismic shot, but to deck their battered vehicles with flags and bunting. Once they were satisfied with the effect, they climbed into the Sno-cats for the last time and began heading for the blunt pinnacle of Castle Rock. As the black shadows and gleaming white faces of an icefall on the Scott Base side of the rock came into view, they adjusted their steering and very soon they saw an empty petrol drum supporting a windsock on a 10-foot pole. This marked the beginning of a line of flags that would lead them down a path bulldozed across the pressure ridges by the Americans. As they ran in towards the island, the citrus yellow buildings of Scott Base came into view, starkly visible against the dark rock of Pram Point. Then a motley collection of Weasels, tractors and even Bren Gun Carriers began to stream towards them, carrying American personnel from the Hut Point base, sailors from the *Endeavour*, the few remaining members of the Ross Sea Party, the TAE members who had flown on ahead – and, of course, innumerable reporters and photographers.

'Soon we joined up,' Fuchs recalled, 'and, as the Sno-cats thundered and weaved between the ridges, escorted in front and behind by a variety of vehicles, scores of figures stood, camera in hand, at every vantage point.'[993] One of the escorting Weasels flew a flag emblazoned with the words 'The World Press Salutes the TAE' and, as the convoy drew up in front of Scott Base, the party's ears were assailed by the efforts of an impromptu brass band, the lack of expertise among the players being more than made up for by their enthusiasm. Never before had an Antarctic expedition, whether of the Heroic or Modern eras, received such a welcome.

With multicoloured Very lights arcing overhead and the band trumpeting and crashing in the background, at 1.47pm Fuchs and Hillary climbed down from the cab of 'Rock 'n' Roll' for the last time. According to one observer, Fuchs looked 'almost dazed in the face of the excitement around him'.[994] He was not too overwhelmed, however, to quip to the incredulous reporters that the crossing of Antarctica, 5 years in the planning and over 2 years in the execution, had been 'a piece of cake'.[995] Then, in a final ostentatious display of unity, he linked arms with Hillary and rather self-consciously the two men made their way through the crowd of applauding spectators to the mess room, where 'a vast and disjointed party at once began'.[996] Within a few moments Fuchs was handed the first sheaf of the congratulatory telegrams that had already begun to pour in from all corners of the globe and soon he slipped quietly away to read them, leaving his men, still dressed in the tatty stained clothes that they had not removed since leaving the Pole and each with the first of many drinks in his hand, to respond to the questions being fired at them from all sides.

Shortly afterwards, La Grange summed up their feelings:

Looking back now, after 99 days and more than 2000 miles of trek, the arrival ... for a few seconds seemed unreal. I could not realise that it was all over. The terrific welcome, the massed brass band, a hot meal, drinks, haircut, bath, cables pouring in – yes we had succeeded in completing what Shackleton had called the last great journey on earth left to man.[997]

Epilogue

On 5 March 1958, Fuchs, Hillary and their teams sailed from McMurdo Sound and into a furore of press attention and public adulation not experienced by a returning Antarctic expedition since Shackleton's arrival in New Zealand at the end of his *Nimrod* Expedition 49 years earlier. Unlike Shackleton, however, who took great pains to safeguard the news of his epic polar trek until he could wire the story to the *Daily Mail*, Fuchs had completed his journey in the full glare of publicity. Indeed, the news of the TAE's triumph had circled the world even before he climbed down from the cab of his Sno-cat. Wireless, radio telephones and an effective air link with New Zealand had ensured not only that reports on the expedition's progress had been swiftly conveyed to a waiting world, but also that journalists were present at key moments in the expedition's life, such as the relief of the Advance Party in January 1957 and the arrival of Hillary and Fuchs at the South Pole a year later. In the case of Douglas McKenzie, a reporter had even taken part in the expedition itself, exchanging the role of observer for that of tractor driver.

As she sailed into Wellington harbour after a stormy twelve-day passage across the Southern Ocean, a flotilla of small boats crowded with well-wishers mobbed the *Endeavour*, an excited hooting rose from the sirens of the larger ships lying at anchor and a flight of RNZAF Vampires swept low overhead, adding

their deep roar to the cacophony of welcome. Most satisfying
of all to the returning explorers was the sight of the red-hulled
Magga Dan, which steamed out to meet the *Endeavour* and then
shepherded her towards her berth. On her deck, almost within
arm's reach, stood the wives and families of the explorers, shouting, waving, blowing kisses and, in the case of Dr Anne Lister,
holding up the one-year-old son who had been born after Hal's
departure for the Antarctic.

The New Zealand welcome was on a lavish scale, with thousands of spectators crowding the bunting-strewn wharves to
greet Fuchs and Hillary, 'the two knights of the Antarctic',[998]
who stood together, bareheaded and smiling on the *Endeavour's*
bridge. At the foot of the gangway they were greeted by Clarence
Skinner, the Acting Prime Minister, but the exchange of official
compliments was kept mercifully brief and in no time at all the
explorers were embracing their families – much to the frustration
of the waiting pressmen who tried desperately to herd them back
together for the obligatory group photographs.

Morning tea on the wharf was followed by a more formal Civic
Welcome at the Town Hall and then a drive to the Parliament
Buildings for a state luncheon and lengthy and rather tedious
official eulogies from Skinner and the Leader of the Opposition.
Given that some of the men had spent more than two years in the
Antarctic they were allowed very little time to acclimatise, being
hustled from place to place, feeling shell-shocked and looking
like scarecrows in suits that now hung baggily on their thinner,
tauter bodies. 'We had five different places to visit in one day with
welcoming Cocktail Parties at each,'[999] complained Lister, who
would much rather have spent the time with his wife and baby
son. As for Fuchs, he later admitted that the most disconcerting
element of the whole reception had been the sudden switch
from the lumbering Sno-cats, which had seldom achieved 10mph
during the 2000 traverse, to an open-top limousine travelling at a
full 30mph through the cheering crowds of Wellington. It was, he
claimed, 'one of the most frightening experiences of my life!'[1000]

Driving at speed was not the only novelty to which Fuchs
had to become accustomed over the coming days. While sitting

freshly shorn and soapy in a bath at Scott Base he had received a cable from 10 Downing Street advising him that, like Shackleton and Mawson, but ironically, unlike Scott himself, he was to receive a knighthood in recognition of his achievements. Now, he must become used to being addressed not as 'Bunny' but as 'Sir Vivian'. The knighthood proved to be just the first in a series of honours showered upon him by British, Commonwealth and foreign institutions over the coming days and weeks, including the Special Gold Medal struck in his honour by the RGS – only the fourth such medal to be issued in 128 years and the first since Robert E. Peary's conquest of the geographic North Pole in 1910; a further clasp to his Polar Medal; honorary degrees; and medals from geographical and other societies at home and abroad.

The ecstatic hubbub continued uninterrupted on the expedition's arrival in Southampton on board the MV *Rangitoto* on 12 May. 'The red carpet was rolled out in style for us,'[1001] wrote Jon Stephenson and, after a civic reception hosted by the Mayor, the explorers were whisked to London on a special train, where they were greeted at Waterloo Station by Alec Douglas Home, Secretary of State for Commonwealth Relations. A cavalcade of open-topped cars drove them through cheering crowds lining the damp streets of London and on to a press conference and reception at the RGS in Kensington Gore. Here, among others, they met veterans of Watkins's and Rymill's expeditions, themselves one-time trans-Antarctic aspirants. Two days later Fuchs received his knighthood from the Queen, and the rest of the expedition members their Polar Medals or clasps to their existing medals. Lunches, dinners and parties followed in quick succession, with speeches made and numerous toasts drunk at each. 'Oh, we had a marvellous time!' Blaiklock enthused. 'In the first month it was just party after party.'[1002] Perhaps the most memorable of all was a government reception at Lancaster House, at the end of which Harold Macmillan, the Prime Minister, helped to roll back the carpets and ordered the Guards orchestra to put away their sheet music and strike up popular dance tunes instead.

Fuchs and Stratton delivered the first lectures, to the fellows of the RGS and then to the general public at the Royal Festival Hall, with the Queen, the Duke of Edinburgh and Princess Margaret in attendance. These were followed by a tour of the country by one of the Sno-cats, beginning in Trafalgar Square, and by a nationwide series of lectures delivered by various members of the expedition, though the itinerary proved that the expedition staff had a far better grasp of Antarctic geography than that of the United Kingdom. 'My home was in the north of England,' Lister observed wryly, 'so I was asked to do the requested public lectures in the north. Very soon I was given all the lectures north of Potters Bar. It is remarkable how near the wild country begins!'[1003]

For Fuchs, the greatest remaining challenge was to write the official account of the expedition, which his publishers were anxious to have ready in time for the Australasian Christmas market. So anxious, indeed, that they had even suggested flying him home from New Zealand so that he could concentrate on writing. Under intense pressure to meet the deadline, Fuchs recalled that as he completed each chapter 'it was rushed to the station literally hot from the typewriter, where it was handed to the guard of the London train to be met by a representative from Cassells at Waterloo. Soon the galley proofs were arriving back to us, and as we got to the later chapters we received the earliest ones in page proof, the more recent ones in galleys all at the same time. No time for second thoughts or revision, it was confusing to say the least.'[1004] Although Jon Stephenson thought the finished book, *The Crossing of Antarctica*, only 'a modestly gripping account',[1005] it quickly became a best seller and was translated into no fewer than fourteen languages, including Hebrew and Japanese.

With the book finished, Fuchs could at last take up the post of Director of FIDS, which he had been offered on his return. Fortunately, however, the Colonial Office was happy to support the ongoing publicity and over the coming months he continued to lecture, touring Europe and North America, where the applause for the expedition was just as vociferous as it had been in England. Fêted by heads of state, including General de Gaulle and President Eisenhower, who presented him with the National Geographic Society's Hubbard Medal, Fuchs continued to give television and radio interviews and to lecture continuously until May 1959.

Meanwhile, the other members of the expedition were picking up the threads of their own lives. For many, this meant returning to a rather more prosaic existence. Lewis, Haslop, Taffy Williams and Peter Weston resumed their duties with the RAF and Homard returned to the Army. Geoffrey Pratt continued his geophysical work with British Petroleum and David Pratt joined the Commonwealth Development Corporation. Others, like Richard Brooke, already had further adventures lined up. Disappointed by the piecemeal return of the Ross Sea Party, immediately on his own return to civilisation Brooke accepted a role in the British Services Expedition to the Himalayas and took part in the first ascent of the 25,550-foot Mount Rakaposhi in the Karakoram Range. Unfortunately, the timing of the expedition meant that he had to abandon the development of his Antarctic survey results, but as he later admitted, the temptation was simply too great: 'I shouldn't really have accepted but I did … I'm afraid the opportunity was something I couldn't resist.'[1006] After travelling 2000 miles, either driving a broken-down Weasel or freezing in the back of a Sno-cat, George Lowe, too, was happy to turn away from the Antarctic and resume mountaineering, taking part in expeditions to Nepal, the Russian Pamirs, Ethiopia and Greenland.

Four men – Ken Blaiklock, Hannes La Grange, Bob Miller and Rainer Goldsmith – would soon return to the Antarctic. Indeed, Blaiklock and La Grange had hardly returned from the TAE before they volunteered for their next expeditions. Blaiklock joined the Belgian Antarctic Expedition of 1959–61, for which he was awarded the Belgian Order of the Crown to add to his Polar Medal (with three bars) and his OBE, while La Grange led the first South African National Antarctic Expedition of 1959 and in the process became the 'father' of South African Antarctic exploration. Bob Miller, too, took command of his own expedition, leading a team to map and study the geology of Oates Land and Victoria Land in 1963. He remained active in Antarctic affairs throughout his career, advising the New Zealand government on

Antarctic matters and becoming President of the New Zealand
Antarctic Society as well as chairman of the Royal Society of
New Zealand's National Committee for Antarctic Research. In
1979, he was knighted for his services to the Ross Dependency,
conservation and surveying. Viewed with suspicion by Fuchs for
his refusal simply to accept the established way of doing things,
Goldsmith continued to challenge received wisdom, returning to
the Antarctic with Operation Deepfreeze V in 1960 in an attempt
to isolate the virus causing the common cold, and in 1980 with
the International Biomedical Expedition to study the effects of
cold on the human body and mind.

Hillary also hoped to continue his association with the
Antarctic and, in particular, with the Ross Dependency. From the
earliest days, both he and the New Zealand Antarctic Society had
seen his involvement in the TAE as a means by which to encourage their nation to become an active participant in Antarctic
exploration. In the many interviews he gave at the end of the
expedition, he continued to advocate a continued New Zealand
presence, pointing out that Scott Base would provide an excellent
long-term centre for such activities. His arguments prevailed and
in the immediate aftermath of the TAE, the New Zealand government established the Ross Dependency Research Committee
to plan, co-ordinate and supervise a scientific programme for
the 1958–59 summer season and for the further development
of investigative work after the conclusion of the International
Geophysical Year on 31 December 1958. It also acknowledged
that 'the excellent equipment at [Scott] base, enables work to be
done of considerable significance to world scientific problems,
particularly in upper atmosphere, physics and seismology.'[1007]

Hillary, however, would play no part in this work. According
to Douglas McKenzie, who published his account of the TAE
in 1963, 'Edmund Percival Hillary had been a bad boy; and in
New Zealand the business of quietly dropping him was pressed
forward with a sufficient delicacy that perhaps it might not be
unduly noticed.'[1008] Hillary's single-minded determination, his
impatience of authority and his willingness to allow substantial
autonomy to ambitious sledgers like Brooke and Miller had all

contributed to the expansion of the Ross Sea Party's objectives to include a remarkable series of long-distance surveys. After leaving Depot 700 in December 1957, Miller and George Marsh had discovered two new mountain ranges; they had proved that the Queen Alexandra Range was made up of five distinct chains; they had discovered four new glacier systems; and they had confirmed the height of Mount Albert Markham. Meanwhile, Brooke and his team had explored and surveyed 15,000 square miles of new territory. But the single-mindedness and independent spirit that had helped to produce these journeys had also led Hillary to compromise the exploratory journey into the Queen Alexandra Mountains; had risked endangering the completion of the crossing; had led to a very public rift in the leadership of the expedition; and had rendered the Ross Sea Committee impotent. Within the Ross Sea Party, opinions of his leadership and decisions would remain divided: Brooke, for instance, remained forever grateful to Hillary for the latitude that he had been given when planning the northern journey; Miller and Marsh, on the other hand, would never forgive him for prioritising his illicit and essentially valueless dash for the Pole over their own far more valuable work. So far as the Ross Sea Committee and its successors were concerned, Hillary was simply too independent and unreliable to be counted on and, much to his chagrin, he would never again be offered any official role in New Zealand's Antarctic programme.

While the New Zealand authorities considered the nature of their ongoing commitments in the Antarctic and Blaiklock, La Grange and Goldsmith planned their future expeditions and packed their gear, the scientists of the TAE began to work up their results in readiness for publication. These results were mixed. Most important of all, Geoffrey Pratt's seismic and gravimetric investigations proved conclusively that the Antarctic continent was a single landmass rather than a series of islands bound together by ice. Indeed, the 34 seismic stations completed between South Ice and McMurdo Sound revealed that the ground beneath the ice cap dipped below sea level in only two places in the entire course of the traverse. However, as Fuchs acknowledged in his introduction to the scientific reports, 'considerable errors may exist because of the limited depth (10m) at which it was possible to fire the shots.'[1009] The gravity observations, too, he continued, 'suffer from lack of heighting and are given as raw gravity.'[1010]

So far as geology was concerned, Stephenson's work confirmed the nature of the rock formations of the mountain ranges discovered during the expedition, with the plant fossils recovered from the Theron Mountains and the Whichaway Nunataks proving to be Permean and therefore over 250 million years old. Examination of the striations also indicated that at one time the mountains, and therefore the whole of the continent, had been submerged beneath a much thicker ice sheet. Finally, when asked by the Labour politician, Clement Atlee, whether the expedition had located any valuable mineral deposits, Stephenson was able to assure him that none had been discovered. 'Thank goodness,'[1011] had been Atlee's response, the spectre of an international scramble for the riches of Antarctica well and truly exorcised.

Less satisfying were the results of Lister's glaciological studies, which had been severely hampered by the breakage or loss of vital equipment at South Ice, which in turn led to unavoidable errors in the interpretation of snow accumulation and ice flow. Despite, or perhaps because of these frustrations, in presenting his findings to the RGS, Lister made the rather optimistic assertion that 'another expedition is surely warranted,'[1012] but he never returned to the Antarctic and throughout his life he would continue to bemoan the fact that he 'never did justice'[1013] to his studies at South Ice. Perhaps the most frustrated of all the scientists, however, was Allan Rogers. On his return to the University of Bristol, he discovered that the breath samples collected during his laborious and physically uncomfortable work with the Integrating Motor Pneumotachographs had been contaminated and rendered useless as a result of defective ampoules. He also found his other physiological data to be so voluminous and its interpretation so complex and time-consuming that it discouraged any assistant sufficiently qualified to help him. In the event, as he dryly acknowledged in the report which he finally published in 1971, the 'delay in starting the analysis was a blessing in

disguise since until comparatively recently there was no com-
puter available in the region that was large enough to handle the
mass of data which amounted to approximately a million bits.'[1014]

The paucity of these results when compared with the
multi-volume scientific reports of the Australasian Antarctic
Expedition (AAE) of 1911–14 or the *Discovery* investigations of
the 1920s and 1930s might have been expected to cause grave
disappointment among the TAE's sponsors. In fact, the bestowal
of so many awards within days of the expedition's return, and
long before the publication of any scientific papers, proved that
in the eyes of most observers the great appeal of the TAE lay not
in its scientific programme but in the idea of the crossing as a
magnificent adventure. On greeting the expedition at Waterloo
Station, Alec Douglas Home had told Fuchs that 'To all of us you
have done something much greater than your scientific achievements. You have provided [*sic*] that in this twentieth century the
spirit of adventure is still alive.'[1015] An article in *The Times* the
same day made the inevitable link with seafarers like Drake and
Raleigh, calling Fuchs 'a man worthy to be named with the first
Elizabethan explorers', and going on to assert that 'adventure
beckoned him as she did them and he set about wooing her
in the same courageous, businesslike spirit.'[1016] Even the Prime
Minister picked up the theme, arguing that the TAE proved that
the Elizabethans' 'courage and spirit of endeavour and adventure
is as alive in this country today as it ever was.'[1017] As for Fuchs,
while he continued to assert his conviction that the scientific
results would 'justify the early faith and vision of all those who
supported us in the beginning, and sustained us to the end,'[1018] in
the immediate aftermath of the expedition, he seemed content
to let the newspapers concentrate on the adventure and to let
the science slip quietly into the background.

In fact, though no one could seriously doubt Fuchs's conviction that the TAE would serve the cause of science, the spirit of
adventure that appealed most to the public imagination probably
also played a much greater part in his motivation than he would
have cared to admit. According to Blaiklock, from the very outset
Fuchs had 'realised that the crossing had to take precedence'[1019]

and once the expedition was in the field, science became so secondary that Lister, in particular, complained bitterly that his experiments were either rushed or abandoned to the cause of increased daily mileages. Derek Williams, too, to whom perhaps Fuchs spoke more openly than to any permanent member of the expedition, confirmed the primary motivation:

> The exploration side, the emotional side, is the dominant factor and the scientific dimension is the secondary factor. The expedition leaders who said otherwise ... were to some extent either deluding themselves or hypocritical on this matter ... I believe that this expedition, like the other preceding expeditions in the great outburst near the time of the First World War, were all based on the quest for fame and fortune.[1020]

In this context, it could be argued that Duncan Carse, whose plans for an Antarctic crossing had been rejected in part because of his decision to downplay the importance of science, had been more honest, if rather less shrewd, than Fuchs.

One man intimately familiar with the spirit of adventure was Hillary and in writing of his first meeting with Fuchs on 18 November 1953, he stated that, in his view, the primary motivation for the expedition 'whether Fuchs would admit it or not, came more from an honest love of adventure and the pride and prestige that he felt would accrue to his country and himself if he were first to succeed in such a long and hazardous undertaking.'[1021] Perhaps, had Fuchs been more willing to acknowledge his adventurous streak, he and Hillary might have found that they had much more in common than either of them believed. However, he was very little inclined to discuss his internal springs of action with anyone, least of all Hillary, and as late as 1991 La Grange wrote of Fuchs's autobiography, *A Time to Speak*, 'It is a great pity that he did not write it before the TAE! – we would have known him so much better.'[1022]

Of course, science and adventure had not been the only imperatives behind the expedition. In seeking the government's financial and moral support, Fuchs had also been at pains to emphasise the importance of the prestige to be garnered by the Commonwealth nations that took part. Scientific discoveries would constitute but a small part of that prestige, and he knew it. Far more significant was the message that Britain's willingness to undertake such a costly endeavour would convey to the countries of South America and, in particular, to Argentina, which had repeatedly challenged Britain's hegemony in the region. At the same time, if successful, the expedition would serve to bolster national pride in a period when the British people veered between the confidence resulting from victory over Germany and Japan and the crumbling self belief engendered by near bankruptcy, the loss of empire and, during the course of the expedition, the very public humiliation of the 1956 Suez Crisis. Any undertaking which helped to achieve these objectives must be appealing to the government – and when the cost of the undertaking was to be borne, in part at least, by private sponsors, the appeal was even greater.

In terms of international prestige, the success of the expedition – and the ministerial posturing that it generated – certainly served to underpin Britain's commitment to the region in the eyes of the world. More importantly, it demonstrated to Argentina and others that Britain had both the ability and the willingness to undertake an expensive and logistically challenging exercise on the far side of the world. Although it is difficult to determine if, and to what degree, the TAE influenced Argentinian policy, it is true that Argentinian aggression was effectively held in check for nearly a quarter of a century. Only in April 1982, when cuts in government funding seemed to indicate both a waning interest in the region and a reduction of military capability, did General Galtieri, acting president of Argentina's ruling military junta, choose to launch his ill-fated invasion of the Falkland Islands. However, the potential for militarisation of the region and the risks of an escalation of the kind of confrontation that had taken place at Hope Bay in February 1952 were far more effectively curbed by Article 1 of the 1959 International Antarctic Treaty, which forbade military activity south of latitude 60°S. So far as influence on the wider world stage was concerned, Britain's possession of a nuclear arsenal and its position as a permanent member of the United Nations Security Council held far more sway than an increasingly shaky and under-funded presence in the Falkland Islands Dependencies.

The TAE also did absolutely nothing to slow down the juggernaut expansion of the United States' influence in the Antarctic. Although the Americans made no territorial claims in the region, during the course of the expedition they adopted an attitude not very far removed from the amused patronage that an adult might give to a precocious and wilful child – an attitude certainly not undermined by Hillary's willingness to call repeatedly upon American logistical aid. With the establishment of their air base at Hut Point and of the Amundsen–Scott South Pole station, the US firmly established itself as the most dominant power on the continent, a position it retains to this day.

So far as personal prestige was concerned, with the completion of the crossing Fuchs became the most celebrated explorer of his day, fêted by governments, geographic and scientific institutions and by the general public. Among polar aficionados, his reputation remains high and as recently as 2000, Phillip Law, leader of the Australian National Antarctic Research Expeditions from 1947 to 1966, opined that the record of his achievements 'surpasses the accomplishments of any of the Antarctic leaders of the Heroic Era'.[1023] But for all the claims made at the time of the TAE that 'the name of Fuchs will go down to history among those of other famous explorers like Scott and Shackleton,'[1024] in reality Fuchs's name no longer has any hold on the popular imagination. By the time he died aged 91 on 11 November 1999, he had outlived his celebrity and his epic journey had been all but forgotten. Given his achievements, it is ironic that the name of Shackleton, whose plans for a continental crossing ended in shipwreck, both real and metaphorical, should have become a household word while that of Fuchs, no less determined and, ultimately, much more successful, should have sunk almost without a trace. Indeed, the TAE as a whole might be described as the greatest polar expedition ever forgotten. A number of factors have contributed to this undeserved obscurity. Not least among these is the current obsession with the Heroic Era of polar exploration. In recent decades this fascination has generated a mass of biographies and studies of the expeditions launched in the first two decades of the twentieth century. In contrast, there has been no major study of either the hugely successful BGLE (British Graham Land Expedition, 1934–37) or its successors.

In fact, although it was launched more than three decades after the death of Shackleton – the event which most historians agree marks the end of the Heroic Era – the TAE was, in many ways, a product of the tradition that included the far more celebrated expeditions of Scott, Shackleton and Amundsen. Certainly the men who took part believed themselves to be the inheritors of the heroic tradition. Two years after the TAE returned to civilisation, George Lowe linked the expedition to those of Scott and Amundsen:

> Although we used vehicles we still clung to camping and eating rules of the past ... Then, Amundsen with his dogs or Scott on foot walked the 1800 desperate miles. Amundsen averaged 17 miles a day with his dog teams and returned according to plan; Scott averaged a dozen miles a day and died tragically within a hundred miles of his base ... in the future there will be no place for the lightly equipped hardy dash which was the spirit in which our expedition was conceived.[1025]

More recently, and rather more succinctly, Rainer Goldsmith called the TAE 'the last of the heroic expeditions – full stop!'[1026]

In some people's minds, the TAE's energetic pursuit of a detailed scientific programme and its use of state-of-the-art technology, including radio, aeroplanes and caterpillar tractors, might serve to divorce it from the more muscular form of heroic exploration championed by Shackleton and to diminish its appeal to the imagination. But every Heroic Era expedition included scientists – or at least variously gifted amateurs charged with the completion of observations in fields such as geology, meteorology, magnetism, biology and bacteriology. Admittedly, Shackleton viewed science as yet another means by which to attract funding but others, like Douglas Mawson, placed it at the very heart of their plans. Scott, indeed, took his scientific responsibilities so seriously that he even chose to burden his exhausted sledge team with geological specimens collected during his trek to the Pole – a decision which some believe contributed to the death of his entire party. Fuchs, like Mawson, was a professional scientist – but he, too, used science as much as a means to an adventurous end as an end in itself.

As for equipment, innovative technology formed a part of almost every early foray into Antarctica: Scott used a hot-air balloon on his *Discovery* Expedition and tractors on his *Terra Nova* Expedition; Shackleton trialled a motorcar on the *Nimrod* Expedition and various types of motorised sledges on the *Endurance* Expedition; and Mawson's Australasian Antarctic Expedition took wireless and a converted aeroplane. Shackleton and Mawson, in particular, also used advanced vehicle technology as a hook upon which to snag public interest; Shackleton admitted to the mandarins of the RGS that his motorised tractors would be as useful for raising the profile of the expedition as for hauling sledges, while Mawson even went so far as to charge for joyrides in his expedition's Vickers REP monoplane (although the machine's plunge to earth on 5 October 1911 quickly cut off that particular source of income). Not surprisingly, most of the technological innovations adopted by the explorers of the Heroic Era failed; but technology and heroism have never been considered mutually exclusive.

However, if the TAE exhibited many of the Heroic Era's attributes of courage, stoicism and innovation, it also suffered from many of the earlier period's negative characteristics, most notably a reliance upon obsolete and inadequate equipment (including some of the field radio transmitters and the Weasels) and a failure to benefit from the ideas and inventiveness of other nations – particularly the United States. Certainly as far as the Weddell Sea Party was concerned, the recent developments in such areas as prefabrication and the use of lightweight materials might never have occurred, while the problems resulting from the logistical support of the Crown Agents would not have been alien to Sir James Ross – or even to Nelson. This failure to keep up with the times was perhaps best captured by US Navy captain, Edwin A. McDonald, when, as mentioned earlier, he described the Shackleton Base hut as 'quaint.'

Despite these shortfalls in attitudes and equipment, however, the fact remains that the TAE was astonishingly successful, achieving many of its scientific and all of its geographical goals – and doing so without the loss of a single man. Nor was this in a period when the Antarctic environment had been rendered in any way 'safe'. At the time of the TAE, the establishment of the IGY bases across the continent resulted in a grim catalogue of accidents and fatalities. In October 1956, one of the first US P2V Neptunes to land at McMurdo Sound crashed on the ice, killing three men outright and mortally injuring a fourth. Two years later a Globemaster crash at Cape Hallett killed another six. Three tractor drivers died as a result of plunging through the sea ice or into crevasses at McMurdo Sound, Little America and Mirny, the Soviet base. Worst of all, in October 1958, an Argentinian supply vessel, the *Guarain*, foundered in the Weddell Sea with the loss of 36 hands. Despite the development of better vehicles, aircraft, radio beacons and other safety equipment, travel in the Antarctic, even in the immediate vicinity of well established bases, remained an extremely perilous undertaking.

Taking all of these factors into consideration, why has the TAE been forgotten? To understand this anomaly properly, the expedition must be considered within the context of its times. Comparison might be drawn with Mawson's AAE which also delivered huge achievements, sledging across 2600 miles of previously unexplored territory and completing a scientific programme of unparalleled complexity in some of the harshest conditions encountered during any Heroic Era expedition. Nor was the AAE devoid of the dramatic and tragic incidents which appeal to historians and the general public alike: one man fell to his death down a bottomless crevasse; another died of malnutrition during a 300-mile trek back to the expedition's winter quarters; and a third went insane. And yet Mawson's expedition is largely forgotten, mainly because the AAE returned to civilisation just as that civilisation was about to launch into four years of unparalleled horror and bloodshed on the Western Front. By the summer of 1914, Antarctic exploration, successful or otherwise, had become an irrelevance.

Like Mawson, Fuchs had the great misfortune to return from his epic adventure at an historical watershed – albeit a significantly less tragic one. On 12 April 1961, 3 years after the return of the TAE, Yuri Gagarin was propelled into orbit of the earth; six weeks later, on 25 May, President John F. Kennedy announced to a joint session of Congress his decision to commit the United States to a manned lunar landing by the end of the decade. Taken together, these events effectively switched the world's attention from terrestrial to space exploration. The resulting impact on Fuchs's reputation and on that of the TAE as a whole is perhaps best captured in a cartoon of 3 March 1958 by Leslie Illingworth of the *Daily Mail*. In that cartoon, Fuchs, looking the very epitome of heroic endeavour in fur-lined anorak and with ice-encrusted beard, flings open a door into a hut populated by

The TAE cavalcade en route to the Royal Geographical Society, 12 May 1958. Fuchs's reception rivalled those given to Scott and Shackleton half a century earlier.

Fleet Street journalists. 'Nonsense, gentlemen,' he cries, 'it CAN be done!' But the journalists can hardly spare him a glance, so preoccupied are they with the latest headlines of a space race and inter-continental ballistic missile threats. Heroic or otherwise, the TAE was the last hurrah of a bygone age.

It is now well over half a century since the British Commonwealth Trans-Antarctic Expedition completed its remarkable journey. Sir Vivian Fuchs died in 1999 and Sir Edmund Hillary in 2008. Most of the other expeditionaries have also passed away – but a few remain: veterans of one of the most extraordinary and most successful exploratory enterprises of the twentieth century. This book is intended as a tribute to all the men of the TAE – to their courage and their endurance in the face of Nature at its most hostile and unforgiving.

Notes

Abbreviations

BAS   British Antarctic Survey
SPRI   Scott Polar Research Institute
TNA   The National Archives

1   See Margery & James Fisher, *Shackleton*, p.297
2   Scott, *Gino Watkins*, p.306
3   'Project of a British Antarctic Expedition, 7 January 1932', quoted in Scott, *Gino Watkins*, p.310
4   Spencer Chapman, *Watkins' Last Expedition*, p.4
5   *The Times*, 16 May 1932
6   Ibid, 20 June 1932
7   Quoted in Scott, *Gino Watkins*, p.329
8   Fuchs, *A Time to Speak*, p.44
9   Fuchs, diary, 12 July 1929. Quoted in Fuchs, *A Time to Speak*, p.53
10   Fuchs, *A Time to Speak*, p.60

11   Ibid, p.62
12   Ibid, p.64
13   Ibid, p.64
14   Shackleton, *South*, dedication
15   Fuchs, *A Time to Speak*, p.173
16   Ibid, p.175
17   Ibid, p.196
18   Ibid, p.217
19   Fuchs, diary, 16 August 1948
20   Fuchs, *A Time to Speak*, p.206
21   BAS, AD1/D1/5.18, Fuchs, 'Trans Polar', 16 August 1948
22   Fuchs, *A Time to Speak*, p.218
23   Ibid, p.218

24 BAS, AD8/1/64,
Pierce-Butler to Robin,
3 September 1948
25 Fuchs, *A Time to Speak*, p.44
26 Clifford to James Griffiths,
Secretary of State for the
Colonies, 24 March 1950.
Quoted in Fuchs, *A Time to
Speak*, p.218
27 Ibid, p.219
28 TNA, CO78/253/1-3,
Clifford to Peter A. Carter,
23 May 1950
29 Colonial Office to Clifford,
12 December 1950. Quoted
in Fuchs, *A Time to Speak*,
p.219
30 Quoted in Fuchs, *A Time to
Speak*, p.220
31 BAS, 2005/3/B/I/a/1,
Fleming to Duncan Carse,
20 April 1953
32 Clifford to Fuchs,
28 March 1953. Courtesy of
Peter Fuchs
33 Ibid
34 Trendall, *Putting South
Georgia on the Map*, p.16
35 BAS, DC64, Carse to
Roberts, July [?] 1945.
Quoted in Trendall, *Putting
South Georgia on the Map*,
p.22
36 BAS, DC64, A/11/b/14,
Carse to Fleming, 6 January
1950. Quoted in Trendall,
*Putting South Georgia on the
Map*, p.25
37 BAS, 2005/3/B/I/a/2,
Carse, 'Proposal for a
Trans-Antarctic Crossing',
23 March 1953

38 Ibid
39 BAS, DC64, Carse to
various recipients,
3 April 1953. Quoted in
Trendall, *Putting South
Georgia on the Map*, p.68
40 Ibid
41 BAS, 2005/3/B/I/a/1,
Fleming to Carse,
20 April 1953
42 Ibid, 8 April 1953
43 Fuchs to Clifford,
7 July 1953. Courtesy of
Peter Fuchs
44 BAS, 2005/3/B/I/a/1,
Bertram to Carse,
14 April 1953
45 Ibid, Carse to Robin,
17 April 1953
46 BAS, 2005/3/B/I/a/2,
Carse, 'Proposal for a
Trans-Antarctic Crossing',
23 March 1953
47 Fuchs to Clifford,
7 July 1953
48 Fuchs, 'Trans Antarctic
Journey', July 1953. Courtesy
of Peter Fuchs
49 Ibid
50 BAS, 2006-72-6, Fuchs, 'A
Consideration of Political
Factors Affecting the
Proposed Trans-Antarctic
Expedition', 1955–57
51 Ibid
52 Ibid
53 Robin, 'Trans-Antarctic
Journey', 12 March 1950.
Courtesy of Peter Fuchs
54 Fuchs to Robin,
19 February 1953. Courtesy
of Peter Fuchs

55 Fuchs, 'Trans Antarctic Journey', July 1953. Courtesy of Peter Fuchs

56 Ibid

57 Ibid

58 Ibid

59 Ibid

60 TAE, Minutes of the Inaugural meeting of the General Committee, 24 June 1954. Courtesy of Peter Fuchs

61 SPRI MS1507/2/1, Clifford to Wordie, 14 June 1953. Quoted in Trendall, *Putting South Georgia on the Map*, p.69

62 SPRI MS1507/2/7, Clifford, 'Analysis of the relative merits of the Carse and Fuchs TAE plans', 26 November 1953. Quoted in Trendall, *Putting South Georgia on the Map*, p.69

63 Clifford to Fuchs, 22 September 1953. Courtesy of Peter Fuchs

64 Ibid

65 Fuchs to Clifford, 7 July 1953. Courtesy of Peter Fuchs

66 Ibid, 30 October 1953. Courtesy of Peter Fuchs

67 Ken Blaiklock to Jon Stephenson, 16 August 2006. Courtesy of Ken Blaiklock

68 Colin Bertram to Fuchs, 30 March 1954. Courtesy of Peter Fuchs

69 Quoted in a letter from an unnamed RGS official to N. Pritchard of the Commonwealth Relations Office, 2 February 1954. Courtesy of Peter Fuchs

70 Ibid

71 C.R.L. Parry, '64 Victoria Street', *Geographical Magazine*, 1961, vol. 34, No. 4, p.235

72 Minutes of the Inaugural meeting of the General Committee, 24 June 1954. Courtesy of Peter Fuchs

73 Minutes of a Meeting of the Trans-Antarctic Executive Committee, 30 November 1954. Courtesy of Peter Fuchs

74 Reprint of a speech by Sir Anthony Eden, 4 November 1955. Courtesy of Mary Lowe

75 Fuchs to C.R. Coote of the *Daily Telegraph*, 12 May 1954. Courtesy of Peter Fuchs

76 The expedition would eventually cost around £750,000

77 Fuchs, lecture at the National Education Conference, Durban, c.1958

78 Author's interview with Rainer Goldsmith, 3 May 2009

79 See Margery & James Fisher, *Shackleton*, p.308

80 Fuchs, lecture at the National Education Conference, Durban, c.1958

81 Author's interview with Ken Blaiklock, 1 June 2009

82 Author's interview with Roy & Enid Homard, 3 July 2009

83 Fuchs, *The Crossing of Antarctica*, p.6

84 Pratt, 'Performance of Vehicles Under Trans-Antarctic Conditions', Institution of Mechanical Engineers, 'Proceedings of the Automobile Division', 1958–59, No.6, p.196

85 John Giaever, *The White Desert*, p.158

86 D.E.L. Homard, 'The REME Contribution to Polar Exploration', *Journal of the Royal Electrical & Mechanical Engineers*, 5, No.1 (1959), p.6

87 Ibid

88 Homard, 'The British Trans-Antarctic Expedition, 1956–58', *British Army Review*, No.7 (1958), p.34

89 C.R.L. Parry, '64 Victoria Street', *Geographical Magazine*, 1961, vol. 34, No. 4, p.235

90 Fuchs to Professor N.E. Odell, 19 October 1954. Courtesy of Peter Fuchs

91 *Morning Advertiser*, 20 January 1954

92 Notes of a Meeting on Antarctic Policy and Proposal for a Commonwealth Trans-Antarctic Expedition, 21 September 1954

93 Fuchs, *A Time to Speak*, p.224

94 Hillary, *No Latitude for Error*, p.13

95 Ibid

96 Fuchs to Professor N. E. Odell, 19 October 1954. Courtesy of Peter Fuchs

97 Fuchs to L.B. Quartermain, 24 November 1954. Courtesy of Peter Fuchs

98 C.R.L. Parry, '64 Victoria Street', *Geographical Magazine*, 1961, vol. 34, No. 4, p.236

99 Ibid, p.235

100 *The Times*, 4 November 1955

101 Rainer Goldsmith, diary, 14 November 1955

102 Fuchs, *The Crossing of Antarctica*, p.10

103 Goldsmith, diary, 14 November 1955

104 *The Times*, 15 November 1955

105 George Lowe, diary, 17–22 November 1955

106 John Claydon, Report by Officer Commanding RNZAF Antarctic Flight 1955–58, p.5

107 Quoted in Hillary, *No Latitude for Error*, p.21

108 Author's interview with Derek Williams, 5 July 2009

109 Ibid

110 Ibid

111 La Grange, 'Across Antarctica – A South African at the South Pole', *Journal of the Mountain Club of South Africa*, No.61, April 1959, p.2

112 Goldsmith, diary, 19 November 1955

113 Ibid, 8 December 1955

114 Author's interview with
Derek Williams, 5 July 2009

115 Author's interview with
Rainer Goldsmith,
3 May 2009

116 Author's interview with
Derek Williams, 5 July 2009

117 Goldsmith, diary,
16 December 1955

118 Alister Hardy, *Great Waters*,
p.161

119 Goldsmith, diary,
20 December 1955

120 John Claydon, Report
by Officer Commanding
RNZAF Antarctic Flight
1955–58, p.7

121 Fuchs, *The Crossing of
Antarctica*, p.14

122 Author's interview with
Derek Williams, 5 July 2009

123 La Grange, 'Across Antarctica
– A South African at the
South Pole', *Journal of the
Mountain Club of South
Africa*, No.61, April 1959, p.1

124 Author's interview with
Derek Williams, 5 July 2009

125 Goldsmith, diary,
24 December 1955

126 George Lowe, diary,
25 December 1955

127 Fuchs, *The Crossing of
Antarctica*, pp.15–16

128 Fuchs, diary,
5 December 1955

129 Ibid, 23 December 1955

130 Author's interview with
Derek Williams, 5 July 2009

131 Goldsmith, diary,
26 December 1955

132 A.S. Helm & J.H. Miller,
Antarctica, p.112

133 Author's interview with
Derek Williams, 5 July 2009

134 George Lowe, diary,
31 December 1955

135 Auckland Museum, MS
2010-1, Hillary, diary,
31 December 1955

136 A.S. Helm & J.H. Miller,
Antarctica, p.111

137 Fuchs, diary, 2 January 1956

138 George Lowe, diary, 4–5
January 1956

139 Fuchs, diary, 8 January 1956

140 Goldsmith, diary,
2 January 1956

141 Ibid, 18 January 1956

142 Quoted in Hillary, *No
Latitude for Error*, p.33

143 George Lowe, diary,
20 January 1956

144 Fuchs, *The Crossing of
Antarctica*, p.20

145 John Claydon, Report
by Officer Commanding
RNZAF Antarctic Flight
1955–58, p.12

146 Goldsmith, diary,
20 January 1956

147 George Lowe, diary,
22 January 1956

148 Goldsmith, diary,
23 January 1956

149 Auckland Museum, MS
2010-1, Hillary, diary,
25 January 1956

150 Goldsmith, diary,
26 January 1956

151 Author's interview with
Derek Williams,
5 July 2009

152 Fuchs, *The Crossing of Antarctica*, p.26

153 Ibid, p.28

154 Goldsmith, diary, 28–29 January 1956

155 Auckland Museum, MS 2010-1, Hillary, diary, 29 January 1956

156 John Claydon, Report by Officer Commanding RNZAF Antarctic Flight 1955–58, p.15

157 Goldsmith, diary, 28–29 January 1956

158 Fuchs, *The Crossing of Antarctica*, p.32

159 Fuchs, diary, 30 January 1956

160 Goldsmith, diary, 31 January 1956

161 Auckland Museum, MS 2010-1, Hillary, diary, 30 January 1956

162 Helm & Miller, *Antarctica*, p.115

163 John Claydon, Report by Officer Commanding RNZAF Antarctic Flight 1955–58, p.18

164 Hillary, *No Latitude for Error*, p.40

165 Author's interview with Derek Williams, 5 July 2009

166 Lowe, diary, 30 January 1956

167 Goldsmith, diary, 31 January 1956

168 Ibid

169 Fuchs, diary, 31 January 1956

170 Lowe, diary, 1 February 1956

171 Goldsmith, diary, 1 February 1956

172 Ibid

173 Ibid

174 Fuchs, diary, 1 February 1956

175 Ibid

176 Helm & Miller, *Antarctica*, p.116

177 John Claydon, Report by Officer Commanding RNZAF Antarctic Flight 1955–58, p.18

178 Fuchs, diary, 1 February 1956

179 Ibid

180 Ibid

181 Hillary, *No Latitude for Error*, p.44

182 Goldsmith, diary, 4 February 1956

183 Lowe, diary, 5 February 1956

184 Goldsmith, diary, 9 February 1956

185 Ibid, 6 February 1956

186 Fuchs, diary, 6 February 1956

187 Ibid

188 Fuchs, diary, 6 February 1956

189 Author's interview with Derek Williams, 5 July 2009

190 Ibid

191 Fuchs, diary, 7 February 1956

192 Author's interview with Derek Williams, 5 July 2009

193 Fuchs, diary, 7 February 1956

194 Author's interview with Derek Williams, 5 July 2009

195 Lister, *Ice – High and Low*, 2005, p.89

196 Goldsmith, diary, 7 February 1956

197 Blaiklock, draft chapter for *The Crossing of Antarctica*, 1958, p.1

198 Goldsmith, diary, 7 February 1956

199 Homard, 'The REME Contribution to Polar Exploration', *Journal of the Royal Electrical & Mechanical Engineers*, 5, No.1 (1959), p.5

200 Blaiklock, draft chapter for *The Crossing of Antarctica*, 1958, p.1

201 Goldsmith, diary, 14 March 1956

202 Blaiklock, draft chapter for *The Crossing of Antarctica*, 1958, p.3

203 Author's interview with Ken Blaiklock, 1 June 2009

204 Goldsmith, diary, 17 March 1956

205 Blaiklock, draft chapter for *The Crossing of Antarctica*, 1958, pp.3–4

206 Goldsmith, diary, 24 March 1956

207 Homard, 'The British Trans-Antarctic Expedition, 1956–58', *British Army Review*, No.7 (1958), p.38

208 Goldsmith, diary, 22 March 1956

209 Ibid, 27 March 1956

210 La Grange, 'The Beginning: 1 Taking part in the Trans-Antarctic Expedition', *South African Journal of Antarctic Research*, vol. 21 No. 2 (1991), p.93

211 Blaiklock, draft chapter for *The Crossing of Antarctica*, 1958, p.4

212 Ibid

213 Author's interview with Ken Blaiklock, 1 June 2009

214 Goldsmith, diary, 28 March 1956

215 Quoted in *Berkshire Chronicle*, 7 June 1957, p.9

216 Blaiklock, draft chapter for *The Crossing of Antarctica*, 1958, p.6

217 Goldsmith, diary, 7 May 1956

218 Goldsmith, diary, 7 May 1956

219 Author's interview with Ken Blaiklock, 1 June 2009

220 Quoted in Goldsmith, diary, 16 May 1956

221 Goldsmith, diary, 15 May 1956

222 Blaiklock, draft chapter for *The Crossing of Antarctica*, 1958, p.7

223 Goldsmith, diary, 16 May 1956

224 Homard, 'The REME Contribution to Polar Exploration', *Journal of the Royal Electrical & Mechanical Engineers*, 5, No.1 (1959), p.9

225 La Grange, 'The Beginning: 1 Taking part in the Trans-Antarctic Expedition', in *South African Journal of Antarctic Research*, vol. 21 No. 2 (1991), p.93

226 Quoted by George Lowe, diary, 13 January 1957

227 Quoted in *Berkshire Chronicle*, 7 June 1957, p.9

228 Goldsmith, diary, 21 June 1956

229 Blaiklock, draft chapter for *The Crossing of Antarctica*, 1958, p.8

230 Ibid, p.9

231 Goldsmith, diary, 7 August 1956

232 Blaiklock, draft chapter for *The Crossing of Antarctica*, 1958, p.10

233 Goldsmith, diary, 20 September 1956

234 Goldsmith, diary, 25 September 1956

235 Blaiklock, draft chapter for *The Crossing of Antarctica*, 1958, p.10

236 Goldsmith, diary, 30 October 1956

237 Ibid, 1 November 1956

238 Author's interview with Ken Blaiklock, 1 June 2009

239 Ibid

240 Blaiklock, draft chapter for *The Crossing of Antarctica*, 1958, p.12

241 Ibid

242 Ibid

243 Goldsmith, diary, 30 December 1956

244 Blaiklock, draft chapter for *The Crossing of Antarctica*, 1958, pp.13–14

245 Gunn, *Land of the Long Day*, Chapter 5 (unpaginated)

246 Ibid

247 Goldsmith, diary, 31 January 1956

248 Auckland Museum, MS 2010-1, Hillary, diary, 5–7 June 1956 [sic]

249 Fuchs to A.S. Helm, 29 March 1955; quoted in Helm & Miller, *Antarctica*, p.48

250 Helm & Miller, *Antarctica*, p.120

251 Hillary, *No Latitude for Error*, pp.49–50

252 *The Times*, 29 December 1913

253 *The Trans-Antarctic Expedition & The International Geophysical Year*, pamphlet issued by the Ross Sea Committee, 1955

254 Gunn, *Land of the Long Day*, Chapter 5 (unpaginated)

255 Marsh, *Report on Dog Sledging of the New Zealand Party of the TAE*, p.5

256 Gunn, *Land of the Long Day*, Chapter 5 (unpaginated)

257 Quoted by Gunn, *Land of the Long Day*, Chapter 5 (unpaginated)

258 John Claydon, Report by Officer Commanding RNZAF Antarctic Flight 1955–58, p.27

259 Helm & Miller, *Antarctica*, p.125

260 Gunn, *Land of the Long Day*, Chapter 6 (unpaginated)

261 Helm & Miller, *Antarctica*, p.132

262 John Claydon, Report by Officer Commanding RNZAF Antarctic Flight 1955–58, p.37

263 Alexander Turnbull Library, MS90-304-2, J.H. Miller, diary, 22 December 1956

264 Author's interview with Richard Brooke, 8 August 2009

265 Alexander Turnbull Library, MS90-304-2, J.H. Miller, diary, 24 December 1956

266 Ibid, 29 December 1956

267 Ibid, 30 December 1956

268 Author's interview with Richard Brooke, 8 August 2009

269 Auckland Museum, MS 2010-1, Hillary, diary, 30 December 1956

270 Author's interview with Richard Brooke, 8 August 2009

271 Auckland Museum, MS 2010-1, Hillary, diary, 30 December 1956

272 Ibid

273 Gunn, *Land of the Long Day*, Chapter 7 (unpaginated)

274 Author's interview with Richard Brooke, 8 August 2009

275 Gunn, *Land of the Long Day*, Chapter 7 (unpaginated)

276 Author's interview with Richard Brooke, 8 August 20

277 Alexander Turnbull Library, MS90-304-2, J.H. Miller, diary, 4 January 1957

278 Helm & Miller, *Antarctica*, p.144

279 Hillary, *No Latitude for Error*, p.72

280 Ibid

281 Auckland Museum, MS 2010-1, Hillary, diary, 4 January 1957

282 Alexander Turnbull Library, MS90-304-2, J.H. Miller, diary, 6 January 1957

283 Auckland Museum, MS 2010-1, Hillary, diary, 5 January 1957

284 Gunn, *Land of the Long Day*, Chapter 8 (unpaginated)

285 Ibid

286 Ibid

287 Hillary, *No Latitude for Error*, p.75

288 Auckland Museum, MS 2010-1, Hillary, diary, 8 January 1957

289 Fuchs, *The Crossing of Antarctica*, p.59

290 Fuchs, diary, 12 January 1957

291 Lowe, diary, 13 January 1957

292 Lister, *Ice: High and Low*, p.89

293 Stephenson, *Crevasse Roulette*, p.40

294 Fuchs, diary, 14 January 1957

295 Lowe, diary, 15 January 1957

296 Goldsmith, diary, 29 January 1957

297 Lister, personal diary, 13 January 1957

298 Goldsmith, diary, 29 January 1957

299 Ibid

300 Fuchs, diary, 19 January 1957

301 Quoted in Stephenson, *Crevasse Roulette*, p.28

302 Fuchs, diary, 1 February 1957

303 Lowe, diary, 21 January 1957

304 Fuchs, diary, 1 February 1957

305 Lowe, diary, 21 January 1957

306 Fuchs, diary, 1 February 1957
307 Lister, personal diary, 25 January 1957
308 Fuchs, *The Crossing of Antarctica*, p.107
309 Stephenson, *Crevasse Roulette*, p.41
310 Fuchs, diary, 1 February 1957
311 Ibid
312 Lister, personal diary, 1 May 1957
313 Ken Blaiklock to the author, 27 May 2010
314 Lowe, diary, 4 February 1957
315 Stephenson to Fuchs, 9 February 1957. Courtesy of Peter Fuchs
316 Lowe, diary, 9 February 1957
317 Lister, personal diary, 1 May 1957
318 Lister, *Ice: High and Low*, p.95
319 Lowe, diary, 11 February 1957
320 Lister, personal diary, 1 May 1957
321 Lowe, diary, 11 February 1957
322 Ibid, 18 February 1957
323 Fuchs, diary, 22 February 1957
324 Lister to Fuchs, 24 February 1957. Courtesy of Peter Fuchs
325 Stephenson to Fuchs, no date. Courtesy of Peter Fuchs
326 Ken Blaiklock to the author, 14 June 2010
327 Lister, *Ice – High and Low*, p.89
328 Ken Blaiklock to the author, 14 June 2010
329 Ibid
330 Stephenson, *Crevasse Roulette*, p.48
331 Fuchs, diary, 9 March 1957
332 Ken Blaiklock to the author, 14 June 2010
333 Ibid
334 Stephenson, *Crevasse Roulette*, p.49
335 Fuchs, diary, 11 March 1957
336 Ibid
337 Ken Blaiklock to the author, 14 June 2010
338 George Lowe, diary, 16 March 1957. Courtesy of George and Mary Lowe
339 Stephenson, *Crevasse Roulette*, p.49
340 Ken Blaiklock to the author, 14 June 2010
341 Stephenson, *Crevasse Roulette*, p.49
342 Fuchs, diary, 15 March 1957
343 Ibid
344 George Lowe, diary, 16 March 1957. Courtesy of George and Mary Lowe
345 Ken Blaiklock to the author, 14 June 2010
346 Gerard, *Old Antarctic Days*, 24 December 2008 (unpaginated)
347 Author's interview with Richard Brooke, 8 August 2009
348 Gunn, *Land of the Long Day*, Chapter 8 (unpaginated)
349 Auckland Museum, MS 2010-1, Hillary, diary, 8 January 1957

350 Alexander Turnbull Library, MS90-304-2, J.H. Miller, diary, 11 January 1957

351 Gerard, *Old Antarctic Days*, Chapter 5 (unpaginated)

352 Gunn, *Land of the Long Day*, Chapter 10 (unpaginated)

353 Alexander Turnbull Library, MS90-304-2, J.H. Miller, diary, 13 January 1957

354 Gerard, *Old Antarctic Days*, Chapter 5 (unpaginated)

355 Alexander Turnbull Library, MS90-304-2, J.H. Miller, diary, 22 January 1957

356 Hillary to Helm, 29 March 1956; quoted in Helm & Miller, *Antarctica*, p.131

357 Hillary, *No Latitude for Error*, p.52

358 Alexander Turnbull Library, MS90-304-2, J.H. Miller, diary, 10 January 1957

359 Ibid, 14 January 1957

360 John Claydon, Report by Officer Commanding RNZAF Antarctic Flight 1955–58, p.42

361 Author's interview with Richard Brooke, 8 August 2009

362 Gunn, *Land of the Long Day*, Chapter 5 (unpaginated)

363 Hillary, *No Latitude for Error*, pp.79–80

364 Author's interview with Richard Brooke, 8 August 2009

365 John Claydon, Report by Officer Commanding

RNZAF Antarctic Flight 1955–58, p.42

366 Gunn, *Land of the Long Day*, Chapter 10 (unpaginated)

367 Alexander Turnbull Library, MS90-304-2, J.H. Miller, diary, 18 January 1957

368 Auckland Museum, MS 2010-1, Hillary, diary, 18 January 1957

369 Gunn, *Land of the Long Day*, Chapter 10

370 Auckland Museum, MS 2010-1, Hillary, diary, 18 January 1957

371 Alexander Turnbull Library, MS90-304-2, J.H. Miller, diary, 19 January 1957

372 Ibid, 23 January 1957 [sic]

373 Ibid, 31 January 1957

374 Hillary, *No Latitude for Error*, p.82

375 Ibid, p.83

376 Author's interview with Richard Brooke, 8 August 2009

377 Hillary, *No Latitude for Error*, p.83

378 Gunn, *Land of the Long Day*, Chapter 10 (unpaginated)

379 Author's interview with Rainer Goldsmith, 3 May 2009

380 Author's interview with Richard Brooke, 8 August 2009

381 Hillary, *No Latitude for Error*, p.86

382 John Claydon, Report by Officer Commanding

RNZAF Antarctic Flight
1955–58, p.48

383   Ibid

384   Alexander Turnbull Library,
MS90-304-2, J.H. Miller,
diary, 29 January 1957

385   Author's interview
with Richard Brooke,
8 August 2009

386   Gerard, *Old Antarctic
Days*, 24 December 2008
(unpaginated)

387   Gerard, *Old Antarctic
Days*, 24 December 2008
(unpaginated)

388   Auckland Museum, MS
2010-1, Hillary, diary,
1 February 1957

389   Alexander Turnbull Library,
MS90-304-2, J.H. Miller,
diary, 5 February 1957

390   Ibid, 8 February 1957

391   Ibid, 12 February 1957

392   Ibid, 12 February 1957

393   Ibid, 13 February 1957

394   Ibid, 17 February 1957

395   Gunn, *Land of the Long Day*,
Chapter 11 (unpaginated)

396   Ibid, Chapter 12
(unpaginated)

397   Ibid

398   Alexander Turnbull Library,
MS90-304-2, J.H. Miller,
diary, 19 February 1957

399   Ibid, 21 February 1957

400   Ibid, 22 February 1957

401   Ibid

402   Alexander Turnbull Library,
MS90-304-2, J.H. Miller,
diary, 23 February 1957

403   Ibid, 26 February 1957

404   John Claydon, Report
by Officer Commanding
RNZAF Antarctic Flight
1955–58, pp.49–50

405   Helm & Miller, *Antarctica*,
p.180

406   Hillary, *No Latitude for Error*,
pp.87–88

407   Fuchs, diary,
11 February 1957

408   Ibid, 18 February 1957

409   Ibid, 18 February 1957

410   Ibid, 22 February 1957

411   A.F. Rogers and R.J.
Sutherland, *Antarctic Climate,
Clothing and Acclimatization*,
Section IV, p.6

412   Author's interview with Ken
Blaiklock, 1 June 2009

413   Fuchs, diary, 1 March 1957

414   Lowe, diary, 21 March 1957

415   A.F. Rogers and R.J.
Sutherland, *Antarctic Climate,
Clothing and Acclimatization*,
Section IV, p.6

416   Ibid, p.7

417   Ibid

418   Fuchs, diary,
15 February 1957

419   Homard, 'The British
Trans-Antarctic Expedition,
1956–58', *British Army
Review*, No. 7 (1958), p.40

420   Fuchs to Eleanor Honnywill,
10–11 February 1957

421   Geoffrey Pratt, report
'On being IMPed',
29 August 1957. Courtesy of
Peter Fuchs

422   Fuchs, diary,
29 August 1957

423   A.F. Rogers and R.J. Sutherland, *Antarctic Climate, Clothing and Acclimatization*, Section IV, p.7

424   Lowe, diary, 8 March 1957

425   Fuchs, diary, 24 March 1957

426   Ibid, 9 March 1957

427   A.F. Rogers and R.J. Sutherland, *Antarctic Climate, Clothing and Acclimatization*, Section IV, p.7

428   Lowe, diary, 9 March 1957

429   Stratton, telegram to TAE offices, 3 May 1957

430   Fuchs, diary, 3 March 1957

431   Ibid, 30 March 1957

432   Lowe, diary, 4 April 1957

433   Ibid

434   Ibid, 14 April 1957

435   Ibid

436   Ibid

437   Ibid, 21 March 1957

438   Ibid, 7 June 1957

439   Fuchs, *The Crossing of Antarctica*, p.119

440   Lister, South Ice diary, 24 August 1957

441   Lowe, diary, 3 July 1957

442   Auckland Museum, MS 2010-1, Hillary, diary, 11 June 1957

443   Fuchs, telegram to TAE offices, 16 May 1957

444   Quoted in Lister, South Ice diary, 9 October 1957

445   Fuchs, *The Crossing of Antarctica*, p.126

446   Stratton, telegram to TAE offices, 15 July 1957

447   Ibid

448   Fuchs, diary, 24 June 1957

449   Stratton, telegram to TAE offices, 15 July 1957

450   Lowe, diary, 28 June 1957 [sic]

451   Ibid

452   Ibid, 20 August 1957

453   Fuchs, diary, 9 September 1957

454   Lister, personal diary, 22 November 1957

455   Ibid

456   Lowe, diary, 4 September 1957

457   Fuchs, diary 11 September 1957

458   Lowe, diary, 23 September 1957

459   Ibid

460   Fuchs, *The Crossing of Antarctica*, p.153

461   Fuchs, telegram to TAE offices, 12 September 1957

462   Lister, personal diary, 1 May 1957

463   Ibid

464   Lister to Fuchs, no date. Courtesy of Peter Fuchs

465   Fuchs, diary, 24 March 1957

466   Stephenson, *Crevasse Roulette*, p.70

467   Blaiklock to the author, 27 May 2010

468   Ibid

469   Lister, South Ice diary, 28 March 1957

470   Ibid, 30 March 1957

471   Ibid, 2 April 1957

472   Lister, personal diary, no date

473   Lister, South Ice diary, 30 May 1957

474   Lister, *Ice: High and Low*, p.99

475 Lister, South Ice diary,
     10 July 1957
476 Ibid, 9 May 1957
477 Ibid, 17 August 1957
478 Stephenson, *Crevasse
     Roulette*, p.71
479 Lister, South Ice diary,
     9 July 1957
480 Ibid, 2 September 1957
481 Ibid, 12 September 1957
482 Ibid, 13 September 1957
483 Ibid, 22–25 September 1957
484 Lister, personal diary,
     22 November 1957
485 Lister, South Ice diary,
     7 October 1957
486 Lister, personal diary,
     22 November 1957
487 Alexander Turnbull Library,
     MS90-304-2, J.H. Miller,
     diary, 1 March 1957
488 Gunn, *Land of the Long Day*,
     Chapter 10 (unpaginated)
489 Author's interview
     with Richard Brooke,
     8 August 2009
490 Gunn, *Land of the Long Day*,
     Chapter 12 (unpaginated)
491 Hillary, *No Latitude for Error*,
     p.89
492 Ibid, p.92
493 Ibid
494 Ibid, pp.92–93
495 Ibid, p.93
496 Auckland Museum, MS
     2010-1, Hillary, diary,
     21 March 1957
497 Cherry-Garrard, *The
     Worst Journey in the World*,
     p.267
498 Hillary, *No Latitude for Error*,
     pp.94–95

499 Helm & Miller, *Antarctica*,
     p.187
500 Cherry-Garrard, *The Worst
     Journey in the World*, p.273
501 Ibid, p.274
502 Hillary, *No Latitude for Error*,
     p.95
503 Auckland Museum, MS
     2010-1, Hillary, diary,
     24 March 1957
504 Ibid, 31 March 1957
505 McKenzie, *Opposite Poles*,
     p.45
506 Author's interview
     with Richard Brooke,
     8 August 2009
507 Gerard, *Old Antarctic
     Days*, 10 March 2008
     (unpaginated)
508 Author's interview
     with Richard Brooke,
     8 August 2009
509 Quoted by Gunn, *Land of
     the Long Day*, Chapter 13
     (unpaginated)
510 Auckland Museum, MS
     2010-1, Hillary, diary,
     21 February 1957
511 Ibid
512 Gerard, *Old Antarctic
     Days*, 24 December 2008
     (unpaginated)
513 Gunn, *Land of the Long Day*,
     Chapter 12 (unpaginated)
514 Gerard, *Old Antarctic
     Days*, 24 December 2008
     (unpaginated)
515 Gunn, *Land of the Long Day*,
     Chapter 12 (unpaginated)
516 Author's interview
     with Richard Brooke,
     8 August 2009

517 Gunn, *Land of the Long Day*, Chapter 12 (unpaginated)

518 Claydon, Report by Officer Commanding RNZAF Antarctic Flight 1955–58, p.65

519 Gerard, *Old Antarctic Days*, 24 December 2008 (unpaginated)

520 Ibid, 22 June 2008 (unpaginated)

521 Ibid, 5 February 2008 (unpaginated)

522 Gunn, *Land of the Long Day*, Chapter 13 (unpaginated)

523 Gerard, *Old Antarctic Days*, 10 March 2008 (unpaginated)

524 Marsh, *Report on Dog Sledging of the New Zealand Party of the TAE*, p.5

525 Ibid

526 Ibid, p.11

527 Ibid

528 Alexander Turnbull Library, MS90-304-2, J.H. Miller, diary, 17 July 1957

529 Claydon, Report by Officer Commanding RNZAF Antarctic Flight 1955–58, p.55

530 Hillary, *No Latitude for Error*, p.110

531 Ibid, p.97

532 Ibid, p.110

533 Alexander Turnbull Library, MS90-304-2, J.H. Miller, diary, 10 May 1957

534 Ibid, 20 August 1957

535 Gerard, *Old Antarctic Days*, 22 June 2008 (unpaginated)

536 Author's interview with Richard Brooke, 8 August 2009

537 Auckland Museum, MS 2010-1, Hillary, diary, 21 April 1957

538 Author's interview with Richard Brooke, 8 August 2009

539 Alexander Turnbull Library, MS90-304-2, J.H. Miller, diary, 13 March 1957

540 Auckland Museum, MS 2010-1, Hillary, diary, 6 March 1957

541 Hillary to Helm, 13 July 1955; quoted in Helm & Miller, *Antarctica*, p.327

542 On 5 March 1957, Hillary asked Miller to lead the dog-sledging expedition to the Pole; see Alexander Turnbull Library, MS90-304-2, J.H. Miller, diary, 5 March 1957

543 Auckland Museum, MS 2010-1, Hillary, diary, 8 April 1957

544 Hillary, *No Latitude for Error*, p.101

545 Auckland Museum, MS 2010-1, Hillary, diary, 10 April 1957

546 Hillary, Confidential Report to the Ross Sea Committee on Tentative Summer Plans; quoted in Hillary, *No Latitude for Error*, p.101

547 Auckland Museum, MS 2010-1, Hillary, diary, 16 April 1957

548 Fuchs, diary, 15 April 1957

549 Fuchs to Hillary,
29 April 1957. Courtesy of
Peter Fuchs

550 Gunn, *Land of the Long Day*,
chapter 15 (unpaginated)

551 Hillary, Confidential Report
to the Ross Sea Committee
on Tentative Summer
Plans; quoted in Hillary, *No
Latitude for Error*, p.102

552 Bowden to Hillary,
9 May 1957; quoted in
Helm & Miller, *Antarctica*,
pp.327–328

553 Gunn, *Land of the Long Day*,
chapter 15 (unpaginated)

554 Auckland Museum, MS
2010-1, Hillary, diary,
9 May 1957

555 Alexander Turnbull Library,
MS90-304-2, J.H. Miller,
diary, 9 May 1957

556 Hillary, *No Latitude for Error*,
p.104

557 Hillary to Bowden,
10 May 1957, quoted in
Helm & Miller, *Antarctica*,
pp.328

558 Gunn, *Land of the Long Day*,
chapter 15 (unpaginated)

559 Bowden to Hillary,
22 May 1957; quoted in
Helm & Miller, *Antarctica*,
p.329

560 Ibid

561 Alexander Turnbull Library,
MS90-304-2, J.H. Miller,
diary, 14 May 1957

562 Auckland Museum, MS
2010-1, Hillary, diary,
14 May 1957

563 Claydon, Report by Officer
Commanding RNZAF
Antarctic Flight 1955–58,
p.66

564 Miller, telegram to
TAE headquarters,
16 September 1957

565 Claydon, Report by Officer
Commanding RNZAF
Antarctic Flight 1955–58,
p.66

566 Ibid, p.67

567 Miller, telegram to TAE
headquarters, 5 July 1957

568 Ibid

569 Ibid

570 Claydon, Report by Officer
Commanding RNZAF
Antarctic Flight 1955–58,
p.69

571 Marsh, *Report on Dog
Sledging of the New Zealand
Party of the TAE*, p.14

572 Miller, telegram to
TAE headquarters,
6 September 1957

573 Fuchs, diary, 2 October 1957

574 Ibid, 10 October 1957

575 D.E.L. Homard, 'The
REME Contribution to
Polar Exploration', Journal
of the Royal Electrical &
Mechanical Engineers', 5,
No.1 (1959), p.9

576 Fuchs, diary,
10 October 1957

577 Ibid

578 Ibid, 11 October 1957

579 Ibid, 12 October 1957

580 Ibid

581 Ibid

582 Ibid, 13 October 1957

583 Ibid

584 Ibid, 14 October 1957

585 D.E.L. Homard, 'The REME Contribution to Polar Exploration', Journal of the Royal Electrical & Mechanical Engineers', 5, No.1 (1959), p.11

586 Fuchs, diary, 14 October 1957

587 Ibid, 18 October 1957

588 Ibid

589 Ibid

590 Ibid

591 Ibid, 19 October 1957

592 Ibid

593 Ibid, 21 October 1957

594 Ibid

595 Ibid

596 Ibid, 22 October 1957

597 Ibid

598 Ibid

599 Ibid, 23 October 1957

600 Ibid

601 Ibid, 27 October 1957

602 Ibid

603 Lowe, diary, 24 October 1957

604 Fuchs, diary, 27 October 1957

605 D.E.L. Homard, 'The REME Contribution to Polar Exploration', *Journal of the Royal Electrical & Mechanical Engineers*, 5, No.1 (1959), p.3

606 Fuchs, diary, 27 October 1957

607 Lowe, diary, 25 October 1957

608 Quoted by Lister, personal diary, 22 November 1957

609 Lister, personal diary, 22 November 1957

610 Fuchs, diary, 28 October 1957

611 Ibid

612 Ibid, 29 October 1957

613 D.E.L. Homard, 'The British Trans-Antarctic Expedition, 1955–58', *British Army Review*, No.7 (1958), p.41

614 Fuchs, diary, 30 October 1957

615 Ibid

616 Ibid

617 Ibid, 31 October 1957

618 Ibid, 4 November 1957

619 Lowe, diary, 2 November 1957

620 Ibid

621 Fuchs, diary, 4 November 1957

622 Ibid, 5 November 1957

623 Ibid, 7 November 1957

624 Ibid, 5 November 1957

625 Ibid

626 Ibid, 8 November 1957

627 Ibid, 9 November 1957

628 Ibid

629 Ibid, 10 November 1957

630 Ibid, 12 November 1957

631 Ibid

632 Ibid

633 Ibid

634 Quoted in Fuchs, diary, 12 November 1957

635 Fuchs, diary, 13 November 1957

636 Ibid

637 Fuchs, *The Crossing of Antarctica*, p.167

638 Auckland Museum, MS 2010-1, Hillary, diary, 21 September 1957

639 Ibid, 10 September 1957
640 Ibid, 13 September 1957
641 Ibid, 23 September 1957
642 Ibid, 24 September 1957
643 Alexander Turnbull Library, MS90-304-2, J.H. Miller, diary, 29 September 1957
644 Author's interview with Richard Brooke, 8 August 2009
645 Ibid
646 Gunn, *Land of the Long Day*, Chapter 17 (unpaginated)
647 Alexander Turnbull Library, MS90-304-2, J.H. Miller, diary, 7 October 1957
648 Hillary, *No Latitude for Error*, p.113
649 Auckland Museum, MS 2010-1, Hillary, diary, 27 September 1957
650 Ibid, 8 October 1957
651 Ibid, 13 October 1957
652 Alexander Turnbull Library, MS90-304-2, J.H. Miller, diary, 14 October 1957
653 Auckland Museum, MS 2010-1, Hillary, diary, 14 October 1957
654 Ibid
655 Ibid
656 Ibid, 15 October 1957
657 Ibid
658 Hillary, *No Latitude for Error*, p.118
659 Ibid, p.121
660 Auckland Museum, MS 2010-1, Hillary, diary, 19 October 1957
661 Hillary, *No Latitude for Error*, p.122

662 Auckland Museum, MS 2010-1, Hillary, diary, 19 October 1957
663 Alexander Turnbull Library, MS90-304-2, J.H. Miller, diary, 21 October 1957
664 Hillary, *No Latitude for Error*, p.124
665 Marsh, diary, 20 October 1957
666 Alexander Turnbull Library, MS90-304-2, J.H. Miller, diary, 22 October 1957
667 Ibid
668 Ibid
669 Marsh, diary, 24 October 1957
670 Ibid
671 Auckland Museum, MS 2010-1, Hillary, diary, 24 October 1957
672 Ibid
673 Hillary, *No Latitude for Error*, p.127
674 Ibid, p.125
675 Auckland Museum, MS 2010-1, Hillary, diary, 25 October 1957
676 Ibid
677 Alexander Turnbull Library, MS90-304-2, J.H. Miller, diary, 26 October 1957
678 Ibid, 28 October 1957
679 Marsh, diary, 28 October 1957
680 Auckland Museum, MS 2010-1, Hillary, diary, 28 October 1957
681 Hillary, *No Latitude for Error*, p.132
682 Alexander Turnbull Library, MS90-304-2, J.H. Miller, diary, 28 October 1957

683 Auckland Museum, MS 2010-1, Hillary, diary, 28 October 1957

684 Alexander Turnbull Library, MS90-304-2, J.H. Miller, diary, 31 October 1957

685 Hillary, *No Latitude for Error*, p.138

686 Auckland Museum, MS 2010-1, Hillary, diary, 31 October 1957

687 Ibid

688 Ibid

689 Marsh, diary, 3 November 1957

690 Auckland Museum, MS 2010-1, Hillary, diary, 3 November 1957

691 Ibid

692 Ibid, 5 November 1957

693 Ibid, 6 November 1957

694 Ibid

695 Ibid

696 Hillary, *No Latitude for Error*, p.143

697 Auckland Museum, MS 2010-1, Hillary, diary, 5 November 1957

698 Hillary, *No Latitude for Error*, p.143

699 Alexander Turnbull Library, MS90-304-2, J.H. Miller, diary, 7 November 1957

700 Ibid

701 Ibid

702 Hillary, *No Latitude for Error*, p.144

703 Marsh, diary, 8 November 1957

704 Auckland Museum, MS 2010-1, Hillary, diary, 9 November 1957

705 Ibid, 10 November 1957

706 Hillary, *No Latitude for Error*, pp.144–145

707 John Claydon, Report by Officer Commanding RNZAF Antarctic Flight 1955–58, p.79

708 Auckland Museum, MS 2010-1, Hillary, diary, 10 November 1957

709 Hillary, *No Latitude for Error*, p.145

710 Ibid, p.146

711 Ibid

712 Ibid, pp.146–147

713 Auckland Museum, MS 2010-1, Hillary, diary, 15 November 1957

714 Hillary, *No Latitude for Error*, p.149

715 Auckland Museum, MS 2010-1, Hillary, diary, 18 November 1957

716 Hillary, *No Latitude for Error*, p.154

717 Ibid, p.155

718 Auckland Museum, MS 2010-1, Hillary, diary, 21 November 1957

719 Quoted in Hillary, *No Latitude for Error*, pp.155–156

720 Auckland Museum, MS 2010-1, Hillary, diary, 21 November 1957

721 Hillary, *No Latitude for Error*, p.156

722 Ibid

723 Quoted in Hillary, *No Latitude for Error*, p.156

724 Auckland Museum, MS 2010-1, Hillary, diary, 21 November 1957

725 Hillary, *No Latitude for Error*, p.157

726 John Claydon, Report by Officer Commanding RNZAF Antarctic Flight 1955–58, pp.84–85

727 Auckland Museum, MS 2010-1, Hillary, diary, 21 November 1957

728 Lowe, diary, 7 November 1957

729 Fuchs, diary, 12 November 1957

730 Ibid

731 Ibid

732 Lister, personal diary, 9 December 1957

733 Lowe, diary, 18 November [?] 1957

734 Fuchs, diary, 26 November 1957

735 Ibid

736 Lowe, diary, 16 November 1957

737 Lister, personal diary, 9 December 1957

738 D.E.L. Homard, 'The British Trans-Antarctic Expedition, 1955–58', *British Army Review*, No.7 (1958), p.41

739 George Lowe to Anne Debenham, 17 December 1957. Courtesy of Mary Lowe

740 Fuchs, diary, 26 November 1957

741 Lowe to Anne Debenham, 17 December 1957

742 Ibid

743 Fuchs, diary, 26 November 1957

744 Lowe to Anne Debenham, 17 December 1957

745 Ibid

746 Fuchs, diary, 29 November 1957

747 Ibid, 30 November 1957

748 Lowe to Anne Debenham, 17 December 1957

749 Ibid

750 Fuchs, diary, 4 December 1957

751 Lowe to Anne Debenham, 17 December 1957

752 Ibid

753 Author's interview with Ken Blaiklock, 1 June 2009

754 Fuchs, *The Crossing of Antarctica*, p.232

755 Fuchs, diary, 10 December 1957

756 Lister, personal diary, 13 December 1957

757 Ibid, 22 November 1957

758 E.W. Kevin Walton, *Two Years in the Antarctic*, p.62

759 La Grange, 'Across Antarctica – A South African at the South Pole', *The Journal of the Mountain Club of South Africa*, No. 61, 1958 (published April 1959), p.7

760 Fuchs, diary, 15 December 1957

761 Ibid, 16 December 1957

762 Lister, personal diary, 18 December 1957

763 Hillary, *No Latitude for Error*, p.161

764 Marsh, diary, 28 November 1957

765 John Claydon, Report by Officer Commanding

RNZAF Antarctic Flight
1955–58, p.84
766 Marsh, diary,
30 November 1957
767 Alexander Turnbull Library,
MS90-304-2, J.H. Miller,
diary, 30 November 1957
768 Marsh, diary,
1 December 1957
769 Quoted in Helm and Miller,
Antarctica, pp.329–330
770 McKenzie, *Opposite Poles*, p.46
771 Hillary, *No Latitude for Error*,
p.170
772 Ibid, p.171
773 Ibid
774 Quoted in Helm and Miller,
Antarctica, p.330
775 Auckland Museum, MS
2010-1, Hillary, diary,
7 December 1957
776 Marsh, diary,
7 December 1957
777 Alexander Turnbull Library,
MS90-304-2, J.H. Miller,
diary, 7 December 1957
778 McKenzie, *Opposite Poles*, p.56
779 Alexander Turnbull Library,
MS90-304-2, J.H. Miller,
diary, 7 December 1957
780 Ibid, 8 December 1957
781 Gunn, *Land of the Long Day*,
Chapter 5 (unpaginated)
782 Alexander Turnbull Library,
MS90-304-2, J.H. Miller,
diary, 10 December 1957
783 Ibid
784 McKenzie, *Opposite Poles*,
p.54
785 Alexander Turnbull Library,
MS90-304-2, J.H. Miller,
diary, 10 December 1957
786 Auckland Museum, MS
2010-1, Hillary, diary,
10 December 1957
787 Ibid
788 Hillary, *No Latitude for Error*,
p.177
789 Ibid, p.178
790 Ibid
791 Ibid, p.179
792 McKenzie, *Opposite Poles*, p.54
793 Auckland Museum, MS
2010-1, Hillary, diary,
12 December 1957
794 Alexander Turnbull Library,
MS90-304-2, J.H. Miller,
diary, 11 December 1957
795 Hillary, *No Latitude for Error*,
p.182
796 Auckland Museum, MS
2010-1, Hillary, diary,
13 December 1957
797 Hillary, *No Latitude for Error*,
p.184
798 Auckland Museum, MS
2010-1, Hillary, diary,
14 December 1957
799 Hillary, *No Latitude for Error*,
p.186
800 Ibid, p.187
801 Alexander Turnbull Library,
MS90-304-2, J.H. Miller,
diary, 15 December 1957
802 Ibid, 16 December 1957
803 Ibid, 19 December 1957
804 Hillary, *No Latitude for Error*,
p.191
805 Ibid
806 Auckland Museum, MS
2010-1, Hillary, diary,
17 December 1957
807 Hillary, *No Latitude for Error*,
p.191

808 Quoted in Helm and Miller, *Antarctica*, p.298

809 Auckland Museum, MS 2010-1, Hillary, diary, 18 December 1957

810 Ibid, 19 December 1957

811 Fuchs, diary, 19 December 1957

812 Ibid

813 Ibid

814 Ibid, 24 December 1957

815 Ibid, 20 December 1957

816 Ibid, 21 December 1957

817 Lister, personal diary, 20 December 1957

818 Author's interview with Ken Blaiklock, 1 June 2009

819 D.E.L. Homard, 'The British Trans-Antarctic Expedition, 1955–58', *British Army Review*, No.7 (1958), p.42

820 Lister, personal diary, 23 December 1957

821 Fuchs, diary, 22 December 1957

822 Hillary, *No Latitude for Error*, p.191

823 Ibid, p.195

824 Fuchs, diary, 24 December 1957

825 Auckland Museum, MS 2010-1, Hillary, diary, 21 December 1957

826 Bowden to Hillary, 20 December 1957. Quoted in Helm & Miller, *Antarctica*, p.331

827 Auckland Museum, MS 2010-1, Hillary, diary, 21 December 1957

828 Ibid, 24 December 1957

829 Bowden to Hillary, 24 December 1957. Quoted in Helm & Miller, *Antarctica*, pp.331–332

830 Hillary, *No Latitude for Error*, p.202

831 Auckland Museum, MS 2010-1, Hillary, diary, 24 December 1957

832 D.E.L. Homard, 'The British Trans-Antarctic Expedition, 1955–58', *British Army Review*, No.7 (1958), p.42

833 Fuchs, diary, 25 December 1957

834 Ibid, 26 December 1957

835 Fuchs to Hillary, 24 December 1957. Quoted in Hillary, *No Latitude for Error*, p.205

836 Auckland Museum, MS 2010-1, Hillary, diary, 28 December 1957

837 Hillary to Fuchs, 28 December 1957. Quoted in Hillary, *No Latitude for Error*, p.206

838 Peter Mulgrew to Paul Dalrymple, 9 July 1979. Courtesy of Paul Dalrymple

839 Hillary, *No Latitude for Error*, p.206

840 Alexander Turnbull Library, MS90-304-2, J.H. Miller, diary, 31 December 1957

841 Lister, personal diary, 29 December 1957 [*sic*]

842 Fuchs, diary, 28 December 1957

843 Fuchs, diary, 29 December 1957

844   A.F. Rogers and R.J.
      Sutherland, *Antarctic Climate,
      Clothing and Acclimatization*,
      Section IV, p.10
845   Ibid p.9
846   Ibid, p.11
847   Author's interview with Ken
      Blaiklock, 1 June 2009
848   Fuchs, diary,
      31 December 1957
849   Lister, personal diary,
      31 December 1957
850   Fuchs, diary, 1 January 1958
851   Ibid, 2 January 1958
852   Lowe to Anne Debenham,
      17 December 1957
853   Fuchs, diary, 3 January 1958
854   Hillary to Fuchs,
      3 January 1958. Quoted in
      Hillary, *No Latitude for Error*,
      p.218
855   Auckland Museum, MS
      2010-1, Hillary, diary,
      29 December 1957
856   Hillary, *No Latitude for Error*,
      p.208
857   Auckland Museum, MS
      2010-1, Hillary, diary,
      31 December 1957
858   Ibid, 1 January 1958
859   Ibid, 2 January 1958
860   Ibid, 28 December 1957
861   Ibid, 3 January 1958
862   Ibid
863   Hillary, *No Latitude for Error*,
      p.215
864   Barber, *The White Desert*,
      p.129
865   Ibid
866   Auckland Museum, MS
      2010-1, Hillary, diary,
      4 January 1958

867   Hillary, *No Latitude for Error*,
      p.216
868   Fuchs, diary, 3 January 1958
869   Fuchs to Hillary,
      4 January 1958. Quoted in
      Fuchs, diary, 11 January 1958
870   Fuchs to TAE Management
      Committee, 4 January 1958.
      Quoted in Fuchs, diary,
      11 January 1958
871   Fuchs, diary, 6 January 1958
872   Author's interview with
      Roy Homard, 3 July 2009
873   Blaiklock to the author,
      5 December 2010
874   Lister, personal diary,
      5 January 1958
875   Hillary to Fuchs,
      5 January 1958. Quoted
      in Fuchs, diary,
      11 January 1958
876   Hillary to the TAE
      Management Committee,
      4 January 1958. Quoted in
      Thomson, *Climbing the Pole*,
      pp.112–113
877   Eleanor Honnywill to
      Fuchs, 21 January 1958.
      Courtesy of Peter Fuchs
878   Ibid
879   Sir Edwin Herbert; quoted
      in Honnywill to Fuchs,
      21 January 1958
880   TAE Management
      Committee to Fuchs,
      6 January 1958. Quoted in
      Thomson, *Climbing the Pole*,
      p.114
881   Hillary, *No Latitude for Error*,
      p.220
882   *The Times*, 7 January 1957
883   *Economist*, 11 January 1958

884 Honnywill to Fuchs,
     21 January 1958
885 *Illustrated London News*,
     18 January 1958
886 Honnywill to Fuchs,
     21 January 1958
887 *The Times*, 7 January 1958
888 *The Times*, 8 January 1958
889 *The Times*, 15 January 1958
890 *Daily Telegraph*,
     21 January 1958
891 Fuchs, diary, 7 January 1958
892 Lister, personal diary, 5
     [?] January 1958
893 BBC 'Men of Antarctica',
     No. 9, 'The Heart of the
     Snows', Recording TLO
     47422, 16 January 1958
894 Fuchs, *The Crossing of
     Antarctica*, p.250
895 Author's interview with Ken
     Blaiklock, 1 June 2009
896 Fuchs, diary, 8 January 1958
897 Lister, personal diary,
     15 January 1958
898 Ibid, 7 January 1958
899 Fuchs, diary, 19 January 1958
900 Fuchs, *The Crossing of
     Antarctica*, p.253
901 Fuchs, diary, 19 January 1958
902 McKenzie, *Opposite Poles*,
     p.133
903 Barber, *The White Desert*,
     p.144
904 McKenzie, *Opposite Poles*,
     p.134
905 *The Journal of the Mountain
     Club of South Africa* (No. 61,
     1958, published April 1959),
     'Across Antarctica: A South
     African at the South Pole',
     p.7

906 McKenzie, *Opposite Poles*,
     p.134
907 Ibid
908 R.F. Scott, *Scott's Last
     Expedition*, p.292
909 Stephenson, *Crevasse
     Roulette*, p.112
910 D.E.L. Homard, 'The British
     Trans-Antarctic Expedition,
     1955–58', The British Army
     Review, No.7 (1958), p.44
911 Ibid
912 McKenzie, *Opposite Poles*,
     p.136
913 Ibid, p.135
914 Barber, *The White Desert*,
     p.146
915 Quoted by Bertram
     Jones, *Daily Express*,
     21 January 1958
916 *Daily Express*,
     21 January 1958
917 Ibid
918 Slessor to Bowden,
     6 January 1958. Quoted in
     The Times, 7 January 1958
919 *The Times*, 8 January 1958
920 Auckland Museum, MS
     2010-1, Hillary, diary,
     7 January 1958
921 Alexander Turnbull Library,
     MS90-304-2, J.H. Miller,
     diary, 7 January 1958
922 Auckland Museum, MS
     2010-1, Hillary, diary,
     17 January 1958
923 Ibid, 20 January 1958
924 Hillary, *No Latitude for Error*,
     p.224
925 Auckland Museum, MS
     2010-1, Hillary, diary,
     20 January 1958

926   Ibid
927   McKenzie, *Opposite Poles*,
        p.137
928   Fuchs, diary, 19 January 1958
929   Lister, personal diary,
        20 January 1958
930   *The Journal of the Mountain
        Club of South Africa* (No. 61,
        1958, published April 1959),
        'Across Antarctica: A South
        African at the South Pole',
        p.8
931   Stephenson, *Crevasse
        Roulette*, p.114
932   Fuchs, diary, 24 January 1958
933   Ibid, 29 January 1958
934   Lister, personal diary,
        31 January 1958
935   Fuchs, diary, 31 January 1958
936   D.E.L. Homard, 'The British
        Trans-Antarctic Expedition,
        1955–58', *The British
        Army Review*, No.7 (1958),
        p.45
937   Fuchs, *The Crossing of
        Antarctica*, p.274
938   Ibid, p.275
939   Author's interview with Ken
        Blaiklock, 1 June 2009
940   Fuchs, diary, 4 February 1958
941   Lister, personal diary,
        5 February 1958
942   Fuchs, diary, 5 February 1958
943   Fuchs, *The Crossing of
        Antarctica*, p.277
944   Fuchs, diary, 7 February 1958
945   Auckland Museum, MS
        2010-1, Hillary, diary,
        31 January 1958
946   Ibid, 2 February 1958
947   Ibid, 25 January 1958
948   Alexander Turnbull Library,
        MS90-304-2, J.H. Miller,
        diary, 18 January 1958
949   Quoted in *Cambridge Daily
        News*, 21 January 1958
950   Auckland Museum, MS
        2010-1, Hillary, diary,
        22 January 1958
951   Gunn, *Land of the Long Day*,
        Chapter 20 (unpaginated)
952   Author's interview
        with Richard Brooke,
        8 August 2009
953   Ibid
954   Gunn, *Land of the Long Day*,
        Chapter 20 (unpaginated)
955   John Claydon, Report
        by Officer Commanding
        RNZAF Antarctic Flight
        1955–58, p.102
956   Fuchs, diary, 9 February 1958
957   Hillary, *No Latitude for Error*,
        p.231
958   John Claydon, Report
        by Officer Commanding
        RNZAF Antarctic Flight
        1955–58, p.103
959   Auckland Museum, MS
        2010-1, Hillary, diary,
        10 February 1958
960   Hillary, *No Latitude for Error*,
        p.231
961   Ibid
962   Auckland Museum, MS
        2010-1, Hillary, diary,
        11 February 1958
963   Lister, personal diary,
        11 February 1958
964   Ibid, 13 February 1958
965   Fuchs, diary,
        15 February 1958

966 Homard, 'The REME Contribution to Polar Exploration', *Journal of the Royal Electrical & Mechanical Engineers*, 5, No.1 (1959), p.5

967 Fuchs, diary, 16 February 1958

968 Fuchs, *The Crossing of Antarctica*, p.285

969 Auckland Museum, MS 2010-1, Hillary, diary, 14 February 1958

970 Ibid, 18 February 1958

971 Fuchs, diary, 19 February 1958

972 Fuchs, *The Crossing of Antarctica*, p.286

973 Lister, personal diary, 11 February 1958

974 D.E.L. Homard, 'The British Trans-Antarctic Expedition, 1955–58', *British Army Review*, No.7 (1958), p.47

975 Auckland Museum, MS 2010-1, Hillary, diary, 22 February 1958

976 Stephenson, *Crevasse Roulette*, pp.114–115

977 Fuchs, *The Crossing of Antarctica*, p.289

978 Lister, personal diary, 24 February 1958

979 Hillary, *No Latitude for Error*, p.243

980 Auckland Museum, MS 2010-1, Hillary, diary, 22 February 1958

981 Author's interview with Ken Blaiklock, 1 June 2009

982 Fuchs, *The Crossing of Antarctica*, p.290

983 Lister, personal diary, 26 February 1958

984 D.E.L. Homard, 'The British Trans-Antarctic Expedition, 1955–58', *British Army Review*, No.7 (1958), p.47

985 Lister, personal diary, 26 February 1958

986 Hillary, *No Latitude for Error*, p.247

987 Fuchs, *The Crossing of Antarctica*, p.291

988 Ibid

989 Lister, personal diary, 1 March 1958

990 Ibid

991 Hillary, *No Latitude for Error*, p.247

992 Lister, personal diary, 1 March 1958

993 Fuchs, *The Crossing of Antarctica*, p.293

994 *The Times*, 3 March 1958

995 Ibid

996 Ibid

997 *The Journal of the Mountain Club of South Africa* (No. 61, 1958, published April 1959), 'Across Antarctica: A South African at the South Pole', p.9

998 Helm & Miller, *Antarctica*, p.406

999 Hal Lister, *Ice: High & Low*, p.118

1000 Fuchs, *A Time to Speak*, p.259

1001 Stephenson, *Crevasse Roulette*, p.122

1002 Author's interview with Ken Blaiklock, 1 June 2009

1003 Hal Lister, *Ice: High & Low*, p.118

1004 Fuchs, *A Time to Speak*, p.263

1005 Stephenson, *Crevasse Roulette*, p.123

1006 Author's interview with Richard Brooke, 8 August 2009

1007 *Transactions of the Royal Society of New Zealand*, Vol. 87, 1959, 'Report of Representative on the Ross Dependency Research Committee', pp.31–32

1008 McKenzie, *Opposite Poles*, p.176

1009 Fuchs, TAE, Scientific Reports No. 1, Synopsis of Results, p.8

1010 Ibid

1011 Stephenson, *Crevasse Roulette*, p.122

1012 Hal Lister & Geoffrey Pratt, 'Geophysical Investigations of the Commonwealth TAE', Geographical Journal, Vol. CXXV, 1959, p.350

1013 Hal Lister, *Ice: High & Low*, p.118

1014 A.F. Rogers and R.J. Sutherland, *Antarctic Climate, Clothing and Acclimatization*, Section II, p.4

1015 *The Scotsman*, 13 May 1958

1016 *The Times*, 12 May 1958

1017 Ibid, 20 May 1958

1018 Fuchs, *The Crossing of Antarctica*, p.294

1019 Author's interview with Ken Blaiklock, 1 June 2009

1020 Author's interview with Derek Williams, 5 July 2009

1021 Hillary, *No Latitude for Error*, p.14

1022 La Grange to Hal Lister, 6 February 1991. Courtesy of Mrs Margaret Lister

1023 Phillip Law, *Interdisciplinary Science Reviews*, 2000, vol. 25, No. 3, 'Sir Vivian Fuchs – in appreciation'

1024 New Zealand *Weekly News*, 18 December 1957

1025 George Lowe, 'The Commonwealth Trans-Antarctic Expedition 1955–58', *The Mountain World 1960–61* (Ed. Malcolm Barnes), p.243

1026 Author's interview with Rainer Goldsmith, 3 May 2009

Bibliography

Arnold, Anthea, *Eight Men in a Crate: The Ordeal of the Advance Party of the Trans-Antarctic Expedition 1955–57* (Norwich: Erskine Press, 2007)

Barber, Noel, *The White Desert: His Personal Story of the Trans-Antarctic Expedition* (London: Hodder & Stoughton, 1958)

Chapman, Freddie Spencer, *Watkins' Last Expedition* (London: Chatto & Windus, 1934)

Cherry-Garrard, Apsley, *The Worst Journey in the World* (London: Pimlico, 2003)

Crane, David, *Scott of the Antarctic* (London: HarperCollins, 2005)

Filchner, Wilhelm, *To the Sixth Continent* (Banham: The Erskine Press, 1994)

Fisher, Margery and James, *Shackleton* (London: Barrie Books, 1957)

Fuchs, Sir Vivian, *A Time to Speak* (Oswestry: Anthony Nelson, 1990)

Fuchs, Sir Vivian and Sir Edmund Hillary, *The Crossing of Antarctica* (London: Cassell, 1958)

Gerard, Vernon B., *Old Antarctic Days: Vernon Gerard's Antarctic Blog* (http://www.oldantarcticdays.com/)

Giaever, John, *The White Desert* (London: Chatto & Windus, 1954)

Gunn, Bernard M., *Land of the Long Day* (http://www.geokem.com/Antarctic)

Haddelsey, Stephen, *Born Adventurer: The Life of Frank Bickerton* (Stroud: Sutton Publishing, 2005)

——————, *Ice Captain: The Life of J.R. Stenhouse* (Stroud: The History Press, 2008)

Hardy, Sir Alister, *Great Waters* (London: Collins, 1967)

Helm, A.S. and J.H. Miller, *Antarctica: The Story of the New Zealand Party of the Trans-Antarctic Expedition* (Wellington: R.E. Owen, 1964)

Hillary, Sir Edmund, *No Latitude for Error* (London: Hodder & Stoughton, 1961)

_____, *Nothing Venture, Nothing Win* (London: Hodder & Stoughton, 1975)

_____, *View from the Summit* (London: Corgi Books, 2000)

Huntford, Roland, *Shackleton* (London: Abacus, 2011)

Lister, Hal, *Ice: High & Low* (Milnthorpe: privately printed, 2005)

Liversidge, Douglas, *White Horizon* (London: Odhams Press, 1951)

McKenzie, Douglas, *Opposite Poles* (London: Robert Hale, 1963)

Riffenburgh, Beau, *Nimrod: Ernest Shackleton and the Extraordinary Story of the 1907–09 British Antarctic Expedition* (London: Bloomsbury, 2004)

Ronne, Finn, *Antarctic Command* (Indianapolis: Bobbs-Merrill Co., 1961)

Scott, J.M., *Gino Watkins* (London: Hodder & Stoughton, 1946)

Scott, Robert Falcon, *Scott's Last Expedition* (London: Folio Society, 1964)

Shackleton, Ernest, *South: A Memoir of the Endurance Voyage* (London: Robinson Publishing, 1999)

Speak, Peter, *William Speirs Bruce, Polar Explorer & Scottish Nationalist* (Edinburgh: National Museums of Scotland, 2003)

Stephenson, Jon, *Crevasse Roulette: The First Trans-Antarctic Crossing 1957–58* (New South Wales: Rosenberg Publishing, 2009)

Sullivan, Walter, *Assault on the Unknown* (New York: McGraw-Hill Book Co., 1961)

Thomson, John, *Climbing the Pole: Edmund Hillary and the Trans-Antarctic Expedition 1955–58* (Norwich: Erskine Press, 2010)

Trendall, Alec, *Putting South Georgia on the Map* (Albany: privately printed, 2011)

Walton, E.W. Kevin, *Two Years in the Antarctic* (London: Lutterworth Press, 1955)

About the Author

STEPHEN HADDELSEY is the author of seven books, including five on the history of Antarctic exploration. He has also edited for their first publication three contemporary expedition accounts. He holds a PhD from the University of East Anglia, of which he is an Honorary Research Fellow, and has been elected to Fellowship of both the Royal Geographical and Royal Historical societies.

Index

passim; on sledging 349;
on splitting the journey 357;
362, 379; plans to survey Horlick
Mountains 392; on Hillary's
survey skills 394–395; 403; career
after TAE 405, 407; 409
Blue Glacier, 280, 302
Bowden, the Honourable Charles,
243, 245, 246, 248, 324, 335, 340,
359, 369
Bowers Piedmont Glacier, 143
Bowers, Henry (Birdie), 228, 231
Britannia, 134, 136
British Arctic Air Route Expedition
(BAARE), 20
British Australian New Zealand
Antarctic Research Expedition
(BANZARE), 72
British Broadcasting Corporation
(BBC), 34, 118, 124, 207, 309,
320, 339, 350, 354, 361
British Commonwealth of Nations,
38, 40, 46, 95, 324, 363, 365, 375,
403, 411
British Graham Land Expedition
(BGLE), 23, 24, 27, 34, 35, 37,
44, 413
British North Greenland
Expedition (BNGE), 48, 101,
125, 150, 161
British Petroleum (BP), 47, 59, 405
British Schools Exploring Society,
101
British Services Expedition to the
Himalayas, 405
Brooke, Lieutenant Richard,
pre-TAE career 125; 130; on
Miller 135; 135–140 *passim*; on
Kirkwood 136–138; on US base
171, 241; reputation 178, 385;
178–182 *passim*; leads Skelton
reconnaissance 183–195; 197;
on tractors 227; on facilities

at Pram Point 232, 236; 238,
241, 243, 249, 250, 280; on
Hillary 281, 406; 294, 304; on
Antarctic mountaineering 384;
on Northern Party 282, 385;
Himalayan expedition 404
Bruce, William Speirs, 16, 19, 43,
46, 70
Bucknell, Selwyn, 132, 236, 250, 384
Butter Point, 141–144 *passim*, 170–
174 *passim*, 177, 195, 280, 284
Byrd, Admiral Richard E., 21, 238
Cambridge University East
Greenland Expedition (1929), 25
Canada, 40, 44, 50
Cape Verde Islands, 58, 62
Carlyon, Roy, 143, 189–195 *passim*,
244, 249, 280, 283, 290, 296,
298, 321–326 *passim*, 384, 397
Carse, Duncan, 24, 34, 36, 38, 39,
43, 44, 49, 410
Cherry-Garrard, Apsley, 228, 230,
231
Chile, 24, 39
Christchurch, 126, 134, 171, 233,
323, 359, 383
Christensen Canadian Enterprises,
55
Claydon, Squadron Leader John
R., on the *Theron* 58, 63, 67,
73–76 *passim*; aerial reconnaissance 75, 81, 177–179, 239; 81,
84, 92, 126; crash-landing on
the Tasman Glacier 129–132;
133, 170; desire for year-round
flights 172, 177, 183 *passim*;
establishment of Skelton Depot
181–183, 186, 194, 236, 248,
250, 281, 286, 289, 296, 301,
302; conveys RSC instructions
308, 321–324 *passim*; stocks
D700 335, 343, 345, 386, 387,
392

Fleming, Bishop Launcelot, 24, 27, 33, 36
Fossil Bluff, 28
French Greenland Expedition, 48
Fry Glacier, 243, 282
Fuchs, Vivian Ernest, background and education 24–25; and James Wordie 24, 32; and 1929 Cambridge University East Greenland Expedition 25; African expeditions 25; military service 26; early service with FIDS 27–29; directorship of FIDS Scientific Bureau 27–29; first considers trans-Antarctic journey 30; and Miles Clifford 31–33; plans for TAE 38–54; approach to fundraising 46–47; approach to recruitment 46–49, 61; leadership style 61, 84–5, 88, 98, 150, 213, 309–310, 319; conflict with Hillary 78, 80–81, 368–369; selects base site 83; discovery of Theron Mountains 95–96; views on vehicle use in Ross Sea area 127; undertakes inland surveys 151–157; plans trial journey 197–198; cancels trial journey 200; discusses location of depots with Hillary 244; South Ice reconnaissance journey 254–278 *passim*; reaction to Hillary's pole journey 320, 337, 339; requests extra depot 342–345; reaction to Hillary's recommendation to abort journey 351–352, 355, 357; reaches South Pole 363; reaches Depot 700 382; reception in New Zealand 401–403; knighthood and honours 403; writes official account 404; directorship of FIDS 404; on scientific reports

407; reputation 412–413; death 414, 417
Gawn, Ted, 130, 132, 235, 240, 302, 306, 323, 384
General Post Office (GPO), 55, 206
Gerard, Vern, 170, 173, 188, 233, 235, 237, 238
Gneiss Point, 280, 284
Goldsmith, Rainer, on Fuchs 48, 85, 94; background 55–56, 100; 122–124 *passim*; on TAE members 61, 66, 68, 76, 102, 110, 112, 119; on Hillary 62; on main hut 103; on Advance Party conditions 103–108, 113; on Mid-Winter's Day 114; journey to the Therons 120–121; 127, 150, 152, 154; on TAE clothing 184; 211, 241, 255, 258, 319; career after TAE 405–408; 413
Graham Land, 21, 23, 30, 32, 74
Gravesend, 56, 84
Great Barrier *see* Ross Ice Shelf
Greenland, 20, 21, 23, 25, 48, 184, 233, 236, 250, 280, 282, 318, 319, 405
Grytviken, 66
Guarain, 415
Gunn, Bernie, 125, 130–133 *passim*; on *Endeavour* 132–135; on storm at sea 138; Ferrar Glacier reconnaissance 142, 177; Butter Point reconnaissance 143–145; 172, 174, 177, 180, 183; Skelton geological expedition 191; 192–5 *passim*, 227–228; on Hillary 234–236, 237, 245–247; on Marsh 234, 235, 326; 245, 246, 280, 282, 299, 326, 338; on Brooke 385
Halfway Depot *see* Midway Depot
Halley Bay, 79, 80, 150, 151, 207, 214, 215, 216, 219, 253, 311, 342
Hardy, Sir Alister, 65

Shackleton's Dream